VOLUME 5

THE
WORK
AND THE
GLORY

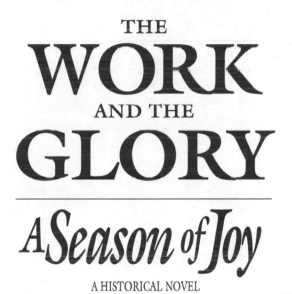

A Season of Joy

A HISTORICAL NOVEL

Gerald N. Lund

BOOKCRAFT
Salt Lake City, Utah

THE WORK AND THE GLORY

Volume 1: Pillar of Light
Volume 2: Like a Fire Is Burning
Volume 3: Truth Will Prevail
Volume 4: Thy Gold to Refine
Volume 5: A Season of Joy

Library of Congress Catalog Card Number: 94-79650
ISBN 0-88494-960-5

First Printing, 1994

Printed in the United States of America

For behold, this is my work and my glory—to bring to pass the immortality and eternal life of man.

—Moses 1:39

Preface

A year or so ago, my wife and I had the privilege to fly from Salt Lake City to Washington, D.C., then to travel by bus some two thousand miles back across much of the continent. How profoundly different are the perspectives one gets from crossing the country in those two ways, by air or on the ground!

From the ground, the cataracts of Niagara are thunderous and awesome and command a person's total attention. From the air, they are barely discernible; but then also from the air, the Great Lakes come into view, and they create an awe of a different sort. From the ground, Boston seems not to be a great city at all, but appears to be little more than a collection of seemingly independent hamlets, hidden in thick forests, connected to one another only by a web of freeways. But take to the air and that impression is instantly dispelled as one sees the sprawl of the metropolitan area which is home to millions. A drive through Iowa and Kansas is little more than daylong cornfields whipping past the window, broken only by the occasional grain elevator thrusting into the sky. But from thirty-five thousand feet, the Great Plains are so vast, stretching from horizon to horizon and beyond, that a person begins to grasp, if only dimly, that this is very likely one of the reasons the Lord called North America "a land which is choice above all other lands" (1 Nephi 2:20).

So it is with the countryside that we call mortality. By divine design, we are put on foot and must walk through that experience day by day. And most of us would not have it any other way, for mortality's day-to-day perspective brings a richness and variety and wealth of detail that would otherwise be lost. But from time to time there is wisdom in rising above those daily paths; there is value in trying to take the wider view and see what patterns stretch out around us.

In the preface to *Thy Gold to Refine,* volume 4 of this series, I commented on the starkness of the "landscape" through which the Saints were forced to walk during those terrible days in northern Missouri. Mobbings, persecutions, rape, burning, pillaging, ridicule, murder, treachery, betrayal, exile—it was one long roadway of tragedy, one ongoing disaster after another. And for the Saints there was no alternative but to plod through it step by trudging step, heads up and shoulders back. Their response to it was heroic and inspiring; they were triumphant even in the midst of the tragic. But only a fool would suggest that the trip itself was anything but incredibly grim.

As is shown in this volume, it was with great relief that the Saints turned their backs on Missouri, that they crossed the Mississippi and entered the welcome haven of Illinois. How right that after the horrors of Crooked River and Far West and Haun's Mill there should be Nauvoo, whose name means "beautiful" and whose title carries with it a sense of peace and rest!

But it was only as I neared the completion of the writing of this volume that I began to sense a pattern in all of this, a pattern which not only was true in the life of those early Saints but is true in our own personal lives as well. To that point, I had not titled this volume. But once I saw the pattern, I had the title: *A Season of Joy.*

Of all the titles in the series, perhaps this one is the most apropos, the most accurately descriptive of the contents. After the horrors of Missouri, after the terrible cost exacted by ugly, violent men, a season of joy was most desperately needed, and a season of joy was what was given. The time was not without its trials and tragedies, and, as future volumes will show, the joy was indeed only for a "season." Nevertheless, for a few short years, it was a time of recuperation and rest, of recovery and rejuvenation. But it was more than that too. It wasn't just that the Saints were allowed to sit back and catch their breath.

The Prophet Joseph, refined by the purifying fires of Liberty Jail, led his people in the building of a temple, the creation of a city, and the broadening of their perspectives of eternity. And his people, refined in the furnaces of their own afflictions, were prepared now to receive blessings heretofore withheld. In a matter of a few short years they would:

—Enjoy a time of peace and prosperity unequalled since the organization of the Church.
—Experience a day of healing, the likes of which had not been seen since the Savior walked among men.
—Reap a harvest of conversions so rich that one has to turn to Book of Mormon times to find adequate comparison.
—Receive doctrinal declarations that would open the op-portunity for salvation to the endless numbers of people in the world of spirits.
—Begin to be sealed together as husbands and wives for time and all eternity.

With my usual limited view, I thought that in writing vol-ume 5 I could press on through this season quickly. Times of peace and prosperity and security are wonderful for the people involved, but they usually make for far less compelling story-telling than conflict and adversity. I originally planned to con-clude this volume with the martyrdom of the Prophet Joseph in Carthage Jail. But this earlier season of joy was so much a part of the Lord's plan that it could not be brushed over lightly any more than the tragic days of Missouri could be hurriedly told.

And after the writing of it, I think I better understand why this is so. Just as the Lord seems to take each of us, at some time or another, through our own personal purging and purifying ex-periences, even so he also tempers those times with seasons of joy. As we approach the time when Christ shall come again to reign as King of kings and Lord of lords, there will be an increas-ing need for what some describe as a "millennial sprint." Judg-ments will close in, and we will come to realize with terrible clarity why the Lord chooses to call that time a "dreadful day."

But there will also be, I strongly believe, seasons of joy, seasons when we are allowed to catch our breath, when our vision is lifted and our understanding broadened. We will be allowed a chance to heal and be strengthened, to reflect and grow, to listen and learn and progress.

Writing of this "season of joy" that took place during the early days of Nauvoo reminded me once again of the value of stepping back, of trying to rise above the trees and rocks and bushes that line the pathways of mortality and thus to catch a glimpse of the greater views, the wider vistas that God has planned for us. And when we do begin to see that broader perspective, we see God's hand intimately involved in the history of his people. The Lord is not a Being who winds the world up and then lets it run out to its conclusion. He is intimately and intricately involved in bringing about his "work and glory," which is to bring to pass the immortality and eternal life of man. He understands perfectly what needs to happen, both in the life of the Church and in the lives of its individual members. When the fires of adversity burn fiercely around us, it is only because they are part of the learning experience of mortality. And when we are given respite and rest for a time, it is because a loving Father understands so well, and so mercifully, our inability to run without pause and to endure without relief. That is my firm belief, and the history that forms the basis for the story of A *Season of Joy* is, in my mind, a clear validation of that testimony. And for that, I am grateful.

This book is the fifth volume in a series that was first conceptualized in the summer of 1988. It was at that time that Kenneth I. Moe ("Kim") called me from North Carolina and asked if I would be interested in telling the story of the Restoration in the form of a historical novel. After several months of discussion and exploration, we formed a partnership and pressed forward with the project. It was Kim, driven by some very compelling promptings, who had the original vision of what this series could be. I will be forever grateful to him and to his wife, Jane, for their persistence in helping me to catch that same vision. They have been major contributors to the project, and though their names are not on the covers, their influence permeates the five volumes completed thus far.

I again express thanks to my wife, Lynn, for her unflagging support in this effort. Besides myself, she alone can estimate the number of hours spent in front of a computer, hours not spent with her and the family. She has been my most ardent and complete supporter. She is always my first reader and provides the most-valued critique. She is my partner, my confidant, my friend, my joy. And words cannot express the fulness of my appreciation to her.

The Work and the Glory has proven to be a gratifying success, and many people have gone out of their way to talk to me or write to me about the impact the series has had on them personally. Unfortunately, I cannot, at those times, bring forward all the others who rightfully deserve the accolades as well. So once again I take this opportunity to call the attention of the reader to the team that makes the whole project possible.

I express deep appreciation to Russell Orton, president of Bookcraft, and to all of the competent and dedicated staff that he has around him. Russell and Cory Maxwell saw the promise of the series from the very beginning, probably more clearly even than I did. They have believed in the project and its value as keenly as Kim and Jane and I have. That says a lot.

The rest of the staff at Bookcraft are professionals and their product shows it. Garry Garff is as fine an editor as I have ever personally worked with, and I have worked with many. He is a consummate historian in his own right, and in a field where there are literally hundreds of sources, many of which do not always agree on the details of history, Garry's contribution in checking the historical accuracy of the series has been prodigious. Jana Erickson, the designer at Bookcraft, is responsible for producing a highly attractive package. It has been interesting to learn that the two most common questions asked of Bookcraft are "When will the next volume be ready?" and "What color will the cover be?" To Cinda Morgan and all the rest, from the secretaries to the warehouse staff, goes a wonderful and heartfelt "Thank you."

Most novels do not contain illustrations. Here again, it was Kim who saw the value of adding visual enrichment to the story, and it was Bookcraft who suggested maps for the end sheets. These have proven to be rich additions to the series which are not of my own doing. So an important acknowledgment goes to Robert Barrett, who has produced all of the illustrations found inside the various novels (some twenty-eight of them with this volume), and to Lester Lee, who has done all of the watercolors for the cover illustrations and all of the maps.

There are others as well. Deena Nay has been my secretary on the project from the beginning, finding the time to do what was necessary in addition to her full-time occupation. Frederick Huchel has provided me with impeccable research that I have turned to again and again. Calvin Stephens, currently a mission president in California, and, in my mind, one of the finest historians in the Church, served as a technical reader and made numerous corrections and suggestions. Shawn Stringham, a longtime friend, serves as an initial reader of the manuscript and is most valuable to me because she is honest enough to tell me what works and what does not.

One additional expression of thanks belongs to the numerous authors and researchers who have put together the sources on which I so heavily rely. Many readers have expressed appreciation for the fact that the history of the Church is portrayed as accurately as possible in the novels. Most of the credit for that belongs to the men and women who authored the numerous books listed in the chapter notes. One of the most gratifying responses I hear from readers is when they tell me they are now going to those original sources because they want to know more about the history of our church.

Finally, in the preface to volume 1, we included the following statement. It seems appropriate once again to include it here as well:

"While we recognize that the Lord needs no recognition, both Kim and I have felt his continuing presence and help in this project. If there be any praise or honor due, let it be to the Father and the Son, for when all is said and done, it is their work and their glory that is described herein. Our hope is that they find it an acceptable offering of thanks to them."

GERALD N. LUND

Bountiful, Utah
September 1994

Characters of Note in This Book

The Steed Family

Benjamin, the father and grandfather; almost fifty-four as the book begins.

Mary Ann Morgan, the mother and grandmother; fifty-two.

Joshua, the oldest son; almost thirty-two as the book begins.

Caroline Mendenhall Steed, Joshua's wife; thirty-two as the story opens.

William ("Will") Donovan Mendenhall, Caroline's son; fifteen.

Olivia Mendenhall, Caroline's daughter; about three and a half years younger than Will.

Savannah Steed, daughter of Joshua and Caroline; just turned two years old as the story opens.

Jessica Roundy Griffith, ex-wife of Joshua and widow of John Griffith; not quite thirty-five as the book begins.

Rachel, daughter of Joshua and Jessica; seven years old as the story opens.

Luke and Mark Griffith, sons of John from his first marriage; six and four years old, respectively, as the book begins.

John Benjamin Griffith, son of John and Jessica; one year old.

Nathan, the second son of Benjamin and Mary Ann; not quite thirty as this volume begins.

Lydia McBride, Nathan's wife; about three and a half months younger than Nathan.

Joshua Benjamin, older son of Nathan and Lydia; not quite eight years old.

Emily, older daughter of Nathan and Lydia; thirteen and a half months younger than Joshua.

Nathan Joseph, younger son of Nathan and Lydia; about three and a half years old.

Elizabeth Mary, younger daughter of Nathan and Lydia; almost one year old.

Melissa Steed Rogers, older daughter of Benjamin and Mary Ann; twenty-eight.

Carlton ("Carl") Rogers, Melissa's husband.

Rebecca Steed Ingalls, younger daughter of Benjamin and Mary Ann; age twenty-one.

Derek Ingalls, Rebecca's husband from England; about five months older than Rebecca.

Matthew, the youngest son of Benjamin and Mary Ann; two years younger than Rebecca.

Note: Melissa and Carl Rogers have children, but they do not figure prominently in this volume.

The Smiths

* Joseph, Sr., the father.
* Lucy Mack, the mother.
* Hyrum, Joseph's elder brother; almost six years older than Joseph.
* Mary Fielding, Hyrum's second wife.
* Joseph, Jr., age thirty-three as the story opens.
* Emma Hale, Joseph's wife; a year and a half older than Joseph.
* Joseph and Emma's children: Julia Murdock, Joseph III, Frederick Granger Williams, and Alexander Hale.
* Don Carlos, Joseph's youngest brother; ten years younger than Joseph.

Note: There are sisters and other brothers to Joseph, but they do not play major roles in the novel.

*Designates actual people from Church history.

Others

Peter Ingalls, Derek's younger brother; almost fifteen.

* Heber C. Kimball, friend of Brigham Young's and a member of the Quorum of the Twelve Apostles.

Josiah McBride, Lydia's father.

Hannah Lovina Hurlburt McBride, Lydia's mother.

Nancy McIntire, a convert from Missouri.

Jennifer Jo McIntire, older daughter of Nancy; seventeen years old.

Kathryn Marie McIntire, Jennifer's sister; four years younger than Jennifer.

Abigail Pottsworth, a convert to the Church during Heber C. Kimball's first mission to England in 1837.

Jenny Pottsworth, Abigail's daughter; almost fourteen as the story begins.

* Parley P. Pratt, an early convert and a member of the Quorum of the Twelve Apostles.

* Willard Richards, called to the apostleship in July 1838 but not ordained until the Twelve reach England.

* George A. Smith, ordained to the apostleship 26 April 1839.

* John Taylor, an early convert from Canada; ordained an Apostle 19 December 1838.

* Wilford Woodruff, ordained to the apostleship 26 April 1839.

* Brigham Young, an early convert and a member of the Quorum of the Twelve Apostles.

Though too numerous to list here, there are many other actual people from the pages of history who are mentioned by name in the novel. Sidney Rigdon, Theodore Turley, Joseph Fielding, John Benbow, and many others mentioned in the book were real people who lived and participated in the events described in this work.

*Designates actual people from Church history.

The Benjamin Steed Family[†]

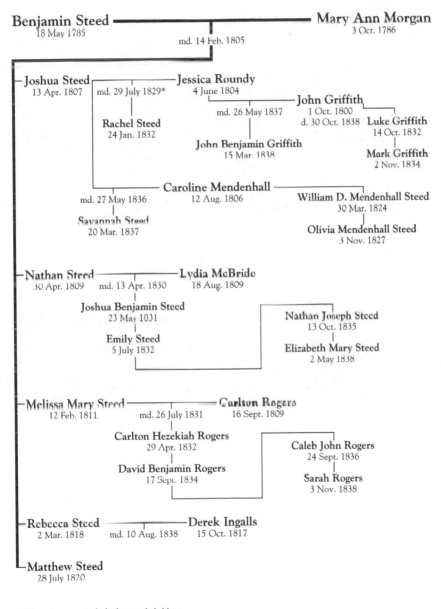

Benjamin Steed
18 May 1785

Mary Ann Morgan
3 Oct. 1786

md. 14 Feb. 1805

Joshua Steed
13 Apr. 1807

md. 29 July 1829*

Jessica Roundy
4 June 1804

Rachel Steed
24 Jan. 1832

md. 26 May 1837

John Griffith
1 Oct. 1800
d. 30 Oct. 1838

Luke Griffith
14 Oct. 1832

John Benjamin Griffith
15 Mar. 1838

Mark Griffith
2 Nov. 1834

Caroline Mendenhall
12 Aug. 1806

William D. Mendenhall Steed
30 Mar. 1824

md. 27 May 1836

Savannah Steed
20 Mar. 1837

Olivia Mendenhall Steed
3 Nov. 1827

Nathan Steed
30 Apr. 1809

md. 13 Apr. 1830

Lydia McBride
18 Aug. 1809

Joshua Benjamin Steed
23 May 1831

Nathan Joseph Steed
13 Oct. 1835

Emily Steed
5 July 1832

Elizabeth Mary Steed
2 May 1838

Melissa Mary Steed
12 Feb. 1811

md. 26 July 1831

Carlton Rogers
16 Sept. 1809

Carlton Hezekiah Rogers
29 Apr. 1832

Caleb John Rogers
24 Sept. 1836

David Benjamin Rogers
17 Sept. 1834

Sarah Rogers
3 Nov. 1838

Rebecca Steed
2 Mar. 1818

md. 10 Aug. 1838

Derek Ingalls
15 Oct. 1817

Matthew Steed
28 July 1820

†Chart does not include deceased children
*Divorced Jan. 1833

Key to Abbreviations Used in Chapter Notes

Throughout the chapter notes, abbreviated references are given. The following key gives the full bibliographic data for those references.

American Moses	Leonard J. Arrington, *Brigham Young: American Moses* (New York: Alfred A. Knopf, 1985.)
CHFT	*Church History in the Fulness of Times* (Salt Lake City: The Church of Jesus Christ of Latter-day Saints, 1989.)
HC	Joseph Smith, *History of The Church of Jesus Christ of Latter-day Saints*, ed. B. H. Roberts, 7 vols. (Salt Lake City: The Church of Jesus Christ of Latter-day Saints, 1932–51.)
JD	*Journal of Discourses*, 26 vols. (London: Latter-day Saints' Book Depot, 1854–86.)
Leaves	Wilford Woodruff, *Leaves from My Journal*, in *Three Mormon Classics*, comp. Preston Nibley, Collector's Edition (Salt Lake City: Bookcraft, 1988.)
LHCK	Orson F. Whitney, *Life of Heber C. Kimball*, Collector's Edition (Salt Lake City: Bookcraft, 1992.)

Mack Hist.   Lucy Mack Smith, *History of Joseph Smith by His Mother*, ed. Preston Nibley (Salt Lake City: Bookcraft, 1954.)

MWM   James B. Allen, Ronald K. Esplin, and David J. Whittaker, *Men with a Mission, 1837–1841: The Quorum of the Twelve Apostles in the British Isles* (Salt Lake City: Deseret Book Co., 1992.)

Nauvoo   David E. Miller and Della S. Miller, *Nauvoo: The City of Joseph* (Santa Barbara and Salt Lake City: Peregrine Smith, 1974.)

PPP Auto.   Parley P. Pratt, *Autobiography of Parley P. Pratt*, ed. Parley P. Pratt, Jr., Classics in Mormon Literature (Salt Lake City: Deseret Book Co., 1985.)

Restoration   Ivan J. Barrett, *Joseph Smith and the Restoration: A History of the Church to 1846* (Provo, Utah: Brigham Young University Press, 1973.)

Revelations   Lyndon W. Cook, *The Revelations of the Prophet Joseph Smith: A Historical and Biographical Commentary of the Doctrine and Covenants* (Salt Lake City: Deseret Book Co., 1985.)

Women   Richard Neitzel Holzapfel and Jeni Broberg Holzapfel, *Women of Nauvoo* (Salt Lake City: Bookcraft, 1992.)

A Season of Joy

It was a season of joy to those present, and afforded a glimpse of the future, which time will yet unfold to the satisfaction of the faithful.

—Joseph Smith, history, entry for
2 August 1831

Will Steed was staring at the low marshlands that formed Georgia's coastline at this point along the Atlantic seaboard. The land—if you could call it that—was about a mile off the port side of the ship. He felt a little rush of excitement, noting that the packet ship had already begun its slow turn, nosing toward the spot where the coastline fell sharply back to mark the mouth of the Savannah River. About twenty miles up that river was the city of Savannah. A few miles beyond that was the Abner Montague cotton plantation. Longtime friends of his mother, Abner and Julia Montague had taken Caroline Steed and her children in after Joshua had been killed and the family had to flee from the vengeance of the Mormon Danites.

The excitement was suddenly mingled with bitter shame. Almost four months before, Will had sneaked away from the Montague plantation, stealing a hundred dollars from his mother and another fifty from Abner Montague, and set off for St. Louis to find his father's killers. How naive he had been.

How utterly stupid. He had found them, all right, and narrowly escaped being killed himself. His mother had tried to convince him of the folly of a fourteen-year-old's trying to right things. Well, that folly had landed him here, a virtual slave as a crew member of the packet ship.

But it was almost over. Twenty miles upriver was Savannah. Twenty miles upriver was freedom. Will had lived in Savannah for a good share of his life. Once they were docked, it would take only moments for him to slip away and escape detection from even the most vigorous search. And then he would make his way back to the Montague plantation for a sweet reunion. He would fall to his knees before his mother and beg for her forgiveness, and then everything would be all right again.

"You ever been to Savannah, Steed?"

Will jumped. He hadn't heard the bosun and the other two men come up behind him. He turned back, forcing an incredulous look. "Don't you remember? I'm from Missouri."

Jiggers nodded. "Oh, yeah. That's right."

"Missouri's a long way from Georgia."

"You'll like it. It's a great port. Beautiful city."

"That's what I hear." Will felt his pulse start to slow a little. The last thing he wanted anyone to know was that Savannah was as familiar to him as the deck of this ship. Everything depended on their not suspecting anything. It was his only chance.

Jiggers seemed to have lost interest. He motioned to the men with him, pointing toward a large coil of rope stacked in the little hollow formed by the ship's bow. "That's the one," he said. "Take if aft with the other rigging."

As they stepped forward, Jiggers turned to Will. "Can you give us a hand, Steed? This is a heavy one."

Will nodded. The coil was almost two feet high, and the hemp, wet with salt spray, would be heavy. He was off duty at the moment, but he didn't mind. "Sure," he said, shrugging.

As Will leaned over and started to get his hands under the rope, suddenly the two men stepped around behind him. Surprised, he started to turn, but before he could do so, the nearest man grabbed him from behind, throwing his arms around him in a crushing grip. The other man tore the rope from Will's grasp and reached for his legs. Will kicked out. He was bare-foot—boots made for slippery walking on a wet deck—but he caught the man full in the chest and sent him sprawling.

"Get his legs! Get his legs!" Jiggers was shouting.

The man jumped up, swearing viciously, then dove for Will's legs. In a moment, it was over. They had him off the deck, and now they easily controlled his writhing body. "Let me go!" Will yelled. "What are you doing?"

Without a word Jiggers turned and headed amidships. The others followed, panting heavily under Will's weight. Halfway back, there was a small storage locker built into the bulkhead of the ship. It had a rusted padlock, which now hung open. Jiggers removed it quickly, opened the hasp, then pulled the door open. "In there," he said, jerking his head.

"What about the brig?" one of the men called.

Jiggers shook his head. "The brig's no place for a lad. Get 'im in there." They cracked Will's knee, then his elbow, getting him through the narrow door. The locker was small, about six by six, and Will noted in surprise that it had been mostly emptied. Along one end there were two filthy blankets and a burlap bag for a pillow. They lowered him over the makeshift bed, then dropped him the last two feet. He crashed to the deck, momen-tarily stunned. They backed out quickly. As Will scrambled to his feet, Jiggers started to close the door. "Sorry, Steed!" he snapped. "Cap'n's orders."

The door slammed closed and Will heard the padlock clank as it was put back into the hasp and clicked shut. He leaped to the door and hammered at it with his fists. "Let me out of here!" The only answer he got was the sound of their footsteps moving away. He pounded again, screaming, raging, cursing them.

Then suddenly he understood. Somehow they knew about Savannah. He fell back, cracking his head on a bucket that hung from one of the overhead beams. The pain didn't register at all, so bitter and deep was the disappointment sweeping over him. They knew!

He sank down on the blankets, feeling sick. Twenty miles away! It may as well have been a thousand. And then, like a flash of lightning in the blackness of a thundercloud, another thought stabbed in. Today was the first day of April. Earlier he had thought it was the perfect omen. The first day of the month would be his first day of freedom. Two days ago he had passed his fifteenth birthday. Freedom was to be his present to himself.

He dropped his head into his hands. The disappointment was like raw bile in his mouth. Once again all of his planning, all of his careful preparations were for nothing. That pattern had started in St. Louis. Everything had gone wrong so swiftly there. Finding the two men he was looking for had been relatively easy for Will. Charlie Patterson, a petty criminal who haunted the waterfront bars, had sought him out and told him he could lead him to the men he was after. The only problem was that Charlie Patterson betrayed him. He was actually in partnership with the very men Will was looking for. At the warehouse, things fell apart. Thankfully, Charlie Patterson drew the line at murder. Charlie's two partners were drunk, and one of them, provoked when Will struck him, wanted to shoot Will. When Charlie balked at that, a battle ensued. In moments, the two men were dead and Charlie Patterson was dragging Will in a blind panic down to the river. There he sold him off to a riverboat captain, who would take him downriver to New Orleans and sell him as a crew member to one of the sailing ship captains there.

When the riverboat captain sent a doctor to the coal bin, where Will was confined all the way to New Orleans, to splint Will's broken wrist, Will thought it was an act of kindness on the captain's part. One more proof of his considerable naivety, he thought bitterly. When they reached New Orleans, Will learned that the captain's "mercy" came from other motives. Will was merely moved from the coal bin on the riverboat to a filthy back room in a seedy riverfront hotel. For another week he was kept there while his arm slowly healed. Then, threatening to whip Will within an inch of his life if he favored the arm in any way, the riverboat captain took the splint off and dragged Will down to the dark, musty-smelling tavern where sea captains furtively bought kidnapped boys from the unscrupulous river runners.

Once out to sea, the captain of the *Bostonia* was livid when he learned he had bought a partial cripple. Will's arm had to be resplinted. But he was young and healthy, and by the time they had sailed to Mexico, then on to Cuba, the arm was fully healed.

From the first day the packet ship had set sail from New Orleans, Will had begun planning his escape. He knew he had to be patient. The captain had paid for two years of impressed service, and the man knew that that service was not given willingly; he expected from Will nothing less than an escape try, and when they docked in the various ports, he always assigned two crew members to escort—*shepherd* was a better term—Will until they were out to sea again. What galled Will the most now, the thing for which he berated himself most bitterly, was the fact that he had been given an opportunity to jump ship in Kingston, Jamaica, where they stopped for a cargo of rum. Once again he had his shore escort, but the two men stopped at a tavern, got themselves blind drunk, then staggered upstairs with two frightening-looking women.

The half hour Will had waited for them was one of the longest of his life. He nearly bolted three or four times, but the thought of being alone in a foreign country, with no guarantee that he could find passage home, was too daunting. And by then he knew their next stop was to be Savannah. So he had decided to wait, and he began formulating his plan.

From that moment on, he worked diligently to assuage any suspicions the captain and crew might have about his intentions. He said nothing about having been raised in Savannah. He worked cheerfully and without complaint—no small task when one remembered that the newest and youngest member of the crew was assigned the most unpleasant and unsavory of tasks. To his surprise, he found himself liking the sea and sail-ing. So it was not too hard to convince everyone that he had accepted his lot and was content to stay with them until his two years were up.

He blew out his breath in disgust. So much for his great de-ception. Now his only hope lay in the letter. The letter was his backup plan. Should he not be able to get free, he had written a letter to his mother. Using every last bit of the small cash al-lowance he was given—and the promise of more to come—he had convinced his closest friend in the crew to take the letter off the ship once they got to Savannah and find someone who would take it to the Montague plantation. The critical question was, would it reach the plantation before the ship sailed again? He wasn't sure. It might take his friend a day or two to get clear of the ship and see that the letter got into someone's hand who could deliver it. It could easily be four or five days by the time it actually reached the plantation, and by then they would be gone again.

No, he thought. It wouldn't take that long. The plantation was only five or six miles upriver from Savannah. Everyone in Savannah knew Abner Montague. Someone would take it to him. Abner Montague was a powerful man in these parts. If he knew Caroline's son was being held captive aboard a ship in Sa-vannah, the very devil himself wouldn't be able to keep him away.

Suddenly, Will had a thought. Today was April first. April Fools' Day! He shook his head slowly. How appropriate. Here sat one of the greatest fools of all.

———◆———

Some two thousand miles away, in the kitchen of their home in St. Louis, Missouri, Caroline Steed sat at her kitchen table. A letter lay before her, but she couldn't read it any longer. Tears had filled her eyes, and the lines penned by Julia Mon-tague swam before her in a meaningless blur. The Montagues had heard nothing from Will Steed. That was the essence of the brief note. There had been no letters, no messages, not even a shred of rumor about the whereabouts of Caroline's son. After four months without a word, Caroline's main hopes now centered on Savannah and the Montagues. Will had fled from there. He had no way of knowing she was gone, returned to St. Louis with Joshua. If he wrote at all, it would be to Savannah. If he returned from wherever the pain had driven him, it would be to Savannah. So when Olivia had come running home with a letter from the Montagues, her hopes had momentarily soared.

Will Steed and his adoptive father were as close as any father and son could be, so Will had been almost as devastated as Caroline when word had come that Joshua had been shot and killed by the Mormons. Most of that was untrue, as it turned out. Joshua *had* been shot, but not by the Mormons, and he was alive. He and Nathan had come to Savannah and found her and given her life again. But by then Will was gone. He would still be carrying the burden of his loss. That thought caused her as much hurt as his absence—knowing that she could not share with him the joyous news that their tragedy had turned to triumph.

Brushing at her cheeks with the back of her hand, she reached down and took the letter. Slowly, methodically, she tore it into small pieces. "Oh, Will!" she whispered. "Will! Will! Will!"

In Quincy, Illinois, about a hundred and thirty miles up the great Mississippi, and directly across the river from the state of Missouri, the sun was gone and it had been full dark now for more than an hour.

In the small house that Benjamin Steed had been able to lease from one of the residents, the Steeds were in bed. They had, as they did every night, stacked the furniture in one corner to make room, then filled the floor with beds. It was a medium-size cabin, but it had only one large room and not even an attic above. And it was now home to seventeen people.

The cabin was divided by a canvas taken from one of Joshua's wagons. It hung from a rope and divided the room into two sleeping areas. The adults—with the exception of Matthew and Peter—slept on the floor in one long row in the larger section. Peter and Matthew slept outside—rain or shine—under a makeshift stick shelter attached to the back of the cabin. Inside, Benjamin and Mary Ann were nearest the east wall and lay on straw mattresses. Lydia and Nathan also slept on a straw mattress next to them. Rebecca, now heavily pregnant with her first child, and Derek had the only mattress filled with feathers. Jessica Griffith, widowed since the horror of Haun's Mill, took a smaller straw mattress beside the opposite wall. On the other side of the canvas, blankets—no mattresses—filled the floor as well. Here the six older children shared one large bed. The two babies—Lydia's and Jessica's—slept in cribs against the far wall.

Sleeping was not the only challenge in such an arrangement. Each night a small blanket was hung across one corner to provide a bit of privacy. There they took turns changing into their nightclothes. There would be a dash out to the privy behind the cabin in the cold night air, then a grateful tunneling under the shared covers to get warm again.

"Grandma?"

Mary Ann lifted her head. The call had come from behind the canvas. She sighed and looked at Benjamin. "Which one?" she whispered.

"Sounds like Emily to me."

In the bed next to them, Lydia, having reached the same conclusion, came up on one elbow. "Emily," she said in a loud whisper, "be quiet or you'll wake the others."

"Grandma!" It was more urgent.

Lydia started to get up, but Mary Ann beat her to it. "I'll see," she said.

Beside Lydia, Nathan just shook his head. This was becoming a habit with his daughter.

Mary Ann stepped through the opening in the canvas. They kept one candle burning on the table. That was a luxury, but since Missouri, the children became frightened or had terrible nightmares if the house was totally dark. Emily, Nathan and Lydia's second child and first daughter, was six. She was sitting cross-legged, her dark eyes wide and troubled in the flickering light. Mary Ann smiled. Even with her hair ruffled, she had Lydia's natural beauty. "Yes, Emily?"

"Will we ever get a bed of our own again, Grandma?" Her eyes were so filled with pleading, and her voice so plaintive, that Mary Ann had to suppress a chuckle in spite of herself. Before Mary Ann could answer, Lydia came through the canvas. She had a finger to her lips. "Emily! You have to be quiet. Please go to sleep."

"But Mama," Emily wailed, "Luke keeps poking me with his elbow."

Luke Griffith, the same age as Emily, lifted his head. "I do not," he said indignantly. "You keep poking me."

Lydia spoke softly but sternly. "Emily, I mean it."

Emily looked around in surprise. "Nobody's asleep, Mama. Except for the babies and Nathan." She looked at her younger brother in disgust. Nathan was three and a half, and did this every night. He lay down, closed his eyes, and was gone in a matter of moments, and nothing seemed to bother him after that. Several other heads came up now, as though to prove the accuracy of Emily's statement. Young Joshua pushed himself up in a sitting position. He would be eight in May and, as the oldest of the grandchildren here in Quincy, felt some responsibility to keep things in order. "Emily, you've just got to hold still. That's all."

She swung on him. "I can't hold still," she whispered fiercely, "not when everybody keeps bumping me."

Rachel sat up now. Like her mother, Jessica, Rachel's temperament was that of a peacemaker. But she felt that she needed to stand up for her stepbrother. "Luke didn't mean to bump you, Emily." She was only six months older than her cousin but seemed considerably more mature than Emily.

"The floor is so hard," Luke retorted, "I can't help it if I just have to wiggle sometimes."

That brought Mark Griffith up to his knees beside his brother. His four-year-old face was twisted with boyish resentment. "Yeah," he said to Emily. "This floor is real hard. We can't sleep good."

The canvas moved and now the rest of the adults joined Mary Ann and Lydia. Jessica stepped across the blankets. "Children, children," she soothed, "it's all right. Don't wake up the babies. Mark, Luke, you lie down now."

"Emily," Lydia said, "lie down, and stop being difficult."

That was the ultimate betrayal in Emily's mind. Her eyes went wide and instantly filled with tears. "Mama, it's not me." She started to cry.

It had been a difficult two weeks since the family had come as refugees across the Mississippi to Quincy, and nights were the most challenging. But Mary Ann was not of a mind to complain. Most of the Saints had been driven from Missouri with little or nothing. Their family was no different in that respect. Where they differed was in the help they got from Joshua, their son, and Carl Rogers, their son-in-law. Joshua paid the rent on the house, and both he and Carl had brought food and other supplies. Many in Quincy still slept in wagons and tents, and dozens of families had nothing but blankets and bedrolls and empty sky overhead.

Mary Ann moved to a stool and sat down, holding up her hands for quiet. Emily cut off her tears, though she continued to sniff as a sign to her mother that her pride had been severely damaged. Young Joshua put an arm around his sister's shoulder as Rachel shushed her two stepbrothers into silence.

"Did you children know," Mary Ann said solemnly, "that when I was a girl your age, I had to sleep on the floor too? Only I had to do it for almost three years."

"Really?" Emily and Rachel exclaimed together. "How come?"

Mary Ann looked thoughtful, but was only trying to hide the fact that she was pleased that her ruse had worked. All thoughts of who was bumping whom were gone. "Well, when I was about Mark's age, my father decided he was going to make his living building turnpikes."

"What's a turnpike, Grandma?" Luke asked.

"A road," Mark replied sagely, pleased with himself that he would know.

"That's right, Mark. We lived in a small village in western Massachusetts. We lived in a cabin smaller than this one. But it had an attic in it, and my older sister and I slept up there. We had only blankets. And besides that, my bed was where the roof and the walls came together. So I always had to sleep on my tummy, because if I slept on my back, my toes would rub against the ceiling."

Mary Ann felt a hand on her shoulder. Benjamin had moved over to stand beside her. He was smiling down at his grandchildren. "And do you know what?" he asked soberly. "Even to this day your grandmother still sleeps on her tummy."

"She does?" Rebecca seemed surprised. That was something about her own mother she had not known.

"Yep," Benjamin said. "Actually, she starts on her back. Then after a while she rolls onto her side. But eventually she always ends up on her stomach." He squeezed Mary Ann's shoulder gently, his eyes teasing her. "It's kind of like an old hound dog. She always has to turn around three or four times before she settles down and goes to sleep."

"I do not!" Mary Ann said, poking at him.

That got even the adults, and everyone laughed. In one crib, Elizabeth Mary, Lydia's baby, stirred and whimpered softly. Lydia put a finger to her lips and pointed at the babies. "Shhh!"

Benjamin raised one arm, as if taking an oath. "It's true," he whispered. "I swear it."

"Did you have to sleep on the floor, Grandpa?" Rachel asked.

Benjamin was still weak from his bout with the illness he had contracted while imprisoned in Richmond, Missouri, with Joseph Smith, but he had not lost his sense of humor. He frowned in mock concentration. "Floor?" he harrumphed. "Who had a floor! We had to sleep on the ground outside."

The children's mouths circled into large O's, but Nathan clearly choked and Rebecca started to giggle.

"Grandpa!" Mary Ann scolded. "You stop fooling the children and tell them the truth."

He looked hurt. "We did sleep outside."

"Only when the weather was good and because you and your brothers wanted to. You had a bed."

"Yes," he mourned, "but I don't remember sleeping in it much."

She poked at him again and he stepped back quickly, chuckling. Sensing that he was playing to an audience, he went on in complete seriousness. "Actually, your grandmother and I both started out in life tied to a board, like an Indian papoose."

Nathan was surprised. "Are you serious, Pa?"

Mary Ann was nodding. "Yes, that is the truth. When we were born, children were always swaddled, as it was called."

"Swaddled?" young Joshua echoed.

"Yes. The mother would get a flat board, and then she would take long strips of cloth and wrap them around and around the baby, tying them firmly to the board."

"They didn't let you crawl around or anything?" Lydia asked, as fully interested as the children now.

"No," Benjamin answered. "People believed that if they kept the neck and back of the child straight, not only was it more healthy, but they thought it made for strong moral character. It made the child a better person."

Mary Ann smiled down at the upturned faces. "Then once the children got old enough to learn how to walk, at about a year old, they were taken out of their swaddling clothes and put in dresses. Boys and girls. It didn't matter—all children of that age wore dresses."

"Dresses?" Emily cried in amazement. "Even you, Grandpa?"

He laughed. "Even me. For Sundays my mother said I had a beautiful lace dress just like my sister."

Jessica chuckled softly. "What's the matter, Emily? Can't you picture Grandpa wearing a dress?"

"No!" Emily said in a drawn-out sound of astonishment. The others were also shaking their heads, not able to picture their grandfather in those terms.

"How long did that go on, then, Father Steed?" Lydia asked.

"Till we were about four or five. Then the boys were 'breeched,' as it was called. They got to wear trousers like grown-up men. That was a big day, I'll tell you. I can still remember my breeching day. I was prouder than a mare with a new foal. I strutted around the house and the neighborhood all afternoon in my new pants. I was big stuff."

"It was a big day for the girls too," Mary Ann came in. "Instead of the simple dress that was the same for both boys and girls, we got to wear hooped petticoats and corsets, just like our mothers and sisters."

Nathan chuckled. "And that was something to look forward to! I'd just as soon be tied behind a horse and dragged as wear a corset."

Mark Griffith yawned mightily and rubbed at his eyes with the back of his fists. Jessica, now sitting beside the two boys, pushed him gently down to the blankets. He didn't protest. Luke, watching, immediately curled up beside his brother. "I think it's time you go to sleep," Jessica said.

Rachel looked at her mother. "We wanna hear Grandma talk more about when she was a little girl," she implored.

Mary Ann nodded sagely. "All right, but why don't you all lie down. Then you can hear Grandma better."

Even Emily accepted that as a good idea. In moments they looked like spokes on a wagon wheel—heads nearly touching as they faced Mary Ann, bodies and feet pointing away from her.

"Tell them about the Sabbath and Sunday toys," Benjamin suggested, once they were all settled.

"Oh yes, Sunday toys. I had almost forgotten about those." She spoke softly now, soothing them with her voice. "We all had what we called Sunday toys back then."

Nathan and Lydia sat down beside Emily and young Joshua. Lydia began gently rubbing Emily's back. Rebecca and Derek also found a place and made themselves comfortable. The adults were as interested in this as the children.

"You see," Benjamin explained, "you have to remember that back then, in some parts of New England, the Sabbath day was observed very strictly."

"In our town," Mary Ann broke in, "it was against the law to even laugh on Sunday."

"Oh!" young Joshua breathed.

"Really?" Emily and Rachel were likewise suitably impressed.

Mary Ann nodded and went on. "As children we weren't allowed to whistle, to go outside and play, to have friends over, or anything like that on the Sabbath. So even the best of children got pretty hard to handle on Sunday afternoons." She chuckled. "I'm sure now that it was out of parental desperation that Sunday toys were born."

"So that's why they called them Sunday toys?" Lydia asked. "Could you use them only on Sundays?"

Mary Ann nodded. "Yes, but it was more than that. They were toys that always had a religious theme. They were designed to teach something about religion or the Bible."

"Like what?" Nathan asked.

"There were music boxes that played hymns, blocks for building toy churches. My parents gave us a game, kind of like checkers, only it was called the Game of Christian Endeavor. As we moved our pieces, it would teach us the rewards of virtue or the punishments for sins."

She paused, her eyes softening with the memories. "But the favorite of all the Sunday toys was the Noah's ark set."

"Like Noah's ark in the Bible?" Rachel asked.

"Yes, exactly," Benjamin answered. "I can still remember. My father came back from a trip once. He had stopped at a wood-carver's shop somewhere and bought us a Noah's ark. Oh, it was wonderful. The ark had windows in it and a ramp you could move." His eyes were soft with remembrance. "And Noah!"

Mary Ann laughed, looking at the adults. "I guess the carver was from England. In my set, Noah had on a black suit and string tie and a bowler hat. Derek would have loved it. I can still picture him, all formal and proper-looking. And his wife looked like an English mistress."

"Did it have animals, Grandma?" Rachel asked, her eyes wide as she tried to imagine what it must have been like.

"Oh yes," Mary Ann breathed, "hundreds of them. All of them in pairs. There were cows and horses . . ."

Mary Ann talked more slowly now, and let her voice drop even lower. She began to describe the animals in detail. Emily didn't make it past the pigs and chickens. Rachel hung on through the lions and tigers and other jungle animals. Young Joshua, stubborn and fierce-willed as always, nearly made it through the mythical animals that were purely the creation of the wood-carver's imagination. But eventually even he gave up. Mary Ann let her voice trail off to silence. She stood, and one by one the adults tiptoed through the curtain and back to their beds.

As they quietly found their places and settled in, Nathan reached across to Mary Ann's bed and touched his mother's arm. "That was wonderful, Mama, and not just because it got the children to sleep. I didn't know any of that about you and Pa."

"Yes," Lydia agreed instantly, "it was fascinating."

Rebecca grunted a little as she shifted the awkwardness of her weight so she could look at her parents. "I want you to do that again sometime, Mama."

Mary Ann was surprised by the reaction of her children. "All we were doing was reminiscing a little."

Rebecca shook her head. "Didn't you see their eyes as you talked to them? They were seeing their grandma and grandpa in a whole new light." She touched the bulging roundness of her stomach. "And I want our child to have that experience too."

"Amen," Derek said solemnly.

Mary Ann was pleased. They were crowded here in this cabin, and even in the day they were in one another's way. But a large part of the family was together and that meant a great deal. "Thank you, children," she said. "If that's what you'd like, we'll do it again sometime."

◆━━◆━━◆

Will Steed looked up. Though he was in near-total darkness inside the storage locker, he could tell the ship had begun to move, slowly, almost imperceptibly. It came as no surprise. He had been listening to the cry of the deckhands and the answering shouts of the dockworkers as they cast off the lines that moored the packet ship to the wharf in Savannah, Georgia.

Stiffly, Will got to his feet. The storage locker was cramped at best, and there was very little room to move around. Seventy-two hours was a long time in such narrow quarters. He reached out in the darkness, feeling for the bucket that was used for swabbing the deck and that hung from one beam. Having cracked his head on the bucket several times during his confinement, he didn't move about until he had it located.

As he stretched, working the kinks out of his legs, he felt the current catch the bow and begin to turn the ship around. Above him, he could hear the creak of winches and the hum of rope whipping through the pulleys. They were hoisting the sails. He nodded, again not surprised. Each day about this time there was always a seaward breeze. The captain would be a fool not to capitalize on it in getting back downriver.

Will felt that last shred of hope blowing away, like sand sifting between his fingers. For a moment he was tempted to press his eye to one of the cracks of light around the door, but he knew it was futile. He had tried it numerous times. The largest crack was big enough to let him know whether it was night or day outside, but that was all. He could see nothing. Besides, he didn't need to. He could picture the scenes outside his cell as clearly as though seeing them. Closest to the ship would be River Street, with its warehouses and shouting stevedores, with its cotton wagons rattling on cobblestones and slaves sweating in the heat and humidity until their faces glistened like the polished ebony of his mother's piano. And directly behind the warehouses would be Factors' Walk, where the men who bought and sold the cotton crops would come out of their offices, stand on the iron bridges that spanned the street below in a dozen places, and buy a ten- or twenty-thousand-dollar crop with the flick of a finger or the raise of an eyebrow. Factors' Walk—where he had stood with the stranger from Missouri named Joshua Steed and introduced him to Savannah.

He swung away from the door, the utter sense of loss suddenly too intense to bear any longer. They weren't coming. He had to face that. His mother had not gotten his letter. At least not in time. Will turned and slammed his clenched fist down against the wooden door, exulting in the stab of pain that shot through his wrist where he had broken it. It was the only real evidence he had left of his vast stupidity. He smashed it against the wood again, wincing sharply, wanting to punish himself.

Finally, reaching out to ward off the bucket, he moved back to the corner and the pile of musty blankets. He sat down heavily, cradling his throbbing arm against his chest. For almost two months now, ever since he had learned that the ship would be stopping in Savannah, thoughts of that city had sustained him, had kept him going. For almost two months now he had planned and schemed and waited for this time. Now those hopes were cruelly dashed.

He cocked his head, no longer able to hear the sounds of the waterfront. They had left Savannah. Soon they would slip past Salter's Island and the silent walls and cannon of Fort Jackson. From there, it was only fifteen miles or so to the open sea and fully beyond any final chance of deliverance.

Feeling sick to his stomach, Will Steed dropped his head between his knees. A great and desolate sense of loneliness roared in his ears now, drowning out any last sounds that might have come had he been listening.

C aroline closed the door to Olivia's bedroom softly, then tiptoed down the hall past Savannah's room. The door there was still open about a foot or so. Caroline glanced at it as she went by, but was not tempted to pull it shut.

As she came down the stairs, Joshua looked up from where he was reading a newspaper. His cane lay on the floor beside him. "They asleep?"

"Not Livvy. But she's about there. She's daydreaming about Matthew again."

Joshua sighed. "She's not twelve yet. When is she going to get over this silly crush?"

Caroline shrugged. "When Matthew announces he's going to marry Jenny, I guess. That will hit her hard, but it will also be the cure."

"You think he will?" Joshua asked.

Caroline nodded emphatically. "Haven't you watched them together? They'll marry. And soon, I think."

"Well," he said, tossing the paper aside, "if they do, they have my blessing." He sobered noticeably. "If Jenny's mother hadn't hid me while I was recovering . . ." He brushed it aside, not wanting to think about the consequences. He owed a lot to the McIntires. Then Joshua remembered something. "You didn't shut Savannah's door, did you?"

She smiled as she shook her head. Caroline knew better than that. For being only two years old, Savannah had an incredible ability to sense, even in her sleep, when anyone violated the solemn covenant she had extracted from them never to shut her door. Caroline and Joshua had learned that no matter how quietly they managed to do it, invariably the little red head would shoot up off the pillow, there would be an angry cry of betrayal, and it would take an hour or more to settle her down again. So even after they went to bed and turned out the lamp in the hallway, they always left her door open. It wasn't the dark that bothered her. She just did not like the thought of being shut up inside the room.

Caroline's smile broadened. Savannah didn't like the thought of being shut up anywhere. To even hold her in your arms was a major accomplishment. This one was like a colt, too full of life to be fettered by bonds of any kind.

Joshua was watching her. "What?" he asked.

She went to stand behind him, laying a hand on his shoulder. Her eyes softened. "I was just thinking about Savannah."

"What about her?"

"Is she yours or mine?"

He laughed. "There's no red hair in my line."

That was true enough. Caroline's hair wasn't the fiery red that Savannah's was, but it was a deep auburn. Caroline had inherited that from her mother and had also passed it on to Olivia. "Maybe not, but she's got your mother's eyes."

Now it was Joshua who nodded. His eyes were dark brown. Caroline's were a startling green, a gift which she had also bequeathed to Olivia. But Savannah's were of that same clear blue purity as Mary Ann's. He chuckled softly. "She may have gotten her grandmother's eyes," he agreed, "but I think she got her grandfather's stubbornness."

"Ha!" Caroline cried, slapping him on the shoulder. "I think you skipped a generation there, sir."

He looked offended. "Me? Stubborn?" He pushed back his chair, grabbed her and pulled her down into his lap, then kissed her soundly. "You better watch your tongue, woman."

"You don't think you're stubborn?"

"I bristle at the very suggestion."

"Then let's talk about moving upriver so we can be close to your family."

The humor died in him instantly and his mouth pulled down. "Caroline, I . . . we've already been over that again and . . ."

His words died as she began to laugh merrily. She had trapped him neatly. She touched his nose and pushed away from him. "I rest my case, your honor." She jumped off his lap before he could reply. "How much longer are you going to be? I'm going to write to Lydia."

"Oh, I need to check some correspondence Samuelson sent over. Maybe half an hour."

"All right. I'll be upstairs."

———◆———

Caroline stared up into the darkness. Beside her, Joshua was breathing evenly, but she knew he wasn't asleep yet. She could feel the warmth of the tears as they squeezed out from the corners of her eyes and ran down the sides of her face. After a moment, she reached out and found his hand. She held it tightly, and he, guessing at her thoughts, held her hand just as tightly.

"Why haven't we heard from him, Joshua?"

They had gone over this again and again too. "I don't know, Caroline." In the past three months since they had returned to St. Louis, they had exhausted every possibility. They had scoured St. Louis and the small towns round about. Letters had been sent to Savannah and to Independence. Joshua offered a small fortune for any information about the whereabouts of his son, or the wharf rat named Charlie Patterson. It had all proved fruitless. Though he never expressed his thoughts to Caroline, he was realist enough to know that it was like looking for one pebble in a hundred miles of creek bed. His only hope was that Will would either show up in Savannah or write to his mother there. And there had been nothing. Absolutely nothing. In the last week or so, he found himself losing hope. Three months was a long time. Maybe something dreadful had happened.

"He's not dead, Joshua."

He turned, half-startled. "I never said he was."

She didn't respond to that. Couldn't respond to that. But she had known his thoughts. "I know he's alive," she whispered fiercely. "I can feel it!"

"Of course he's alive," he said, pulling her into his arms and letting her bury her head against his shoulder. She began to weep openly now. "Will is a very resourceful young man," he said, stroking her hair. "At fourteen, he was already half running the freight yard for me. He'll be all right."

"Then why haven't we heard from him?" she cried. "Why haven't we gotten even one letter?"

Joshua just held her tight against him. "I don't know," he finally whispered. "I don't know."

They were a full two hours out into the open sea before the door to the storage locker opened. Will sat up, putting up his arm to shield his eyes from the bright light. Jiggers stepped back. "You got one hour to get something to eat from the mess. Then you're on duty again."

Will nodded, still squinting. It was a beautiful clear day, and the sunlight off the water was blinding. "All right," he said. He was grateful to be out, and he was grateful for the chance to eat. The food they had brought him during his confinement was cold and greasy.

He saw that several of the crew were watching him, but as he glared at them they looked away guiltily. Will walked slowly, letting the stiffness in his legs work itself out. Out of the corner of his eye, he saw Jiggers turn around and head aft. As soon as he was out of sight, Will immediately changed his direction slightly and crossed over to the port side of the ship, where Petey was splicing a line.

The young man, only two or three years older than Will, saw him coming and busied himself intently with his work. Will slowed his step. "Did you do it?" he hissed.

Petey glanced up at him in panic. "Blast it, Will!" he said in a low voice. "You're going to get us both thrown in the brig."

"Did you deliver it?" Will demanded, stopping a foot or two farther on, as though he saw something out over the water. "Did you deliver the letter?"

Petey still would not look at him, but after a moment, there was a soft reply. "Yes," he said. "I delivered it."

Will's shoulders lifted as he walked away. So it was done. The letter hadn't reached anyone in time to get him off the ship in Savannah, as he so desperately hoped, but it was done. Now at least his mother would know what had happened to her son.

As he started down the ladder to the mess kitchen, he felt buoyed up. There would be other chances. Maybe his mother and Abner would have someone waiting in New York. The ship still had to stop there before turning east and sailing for England. There would be other chances.

———◆———

Heber C. Kimball raised his head, and his plodding footsteps slowed. They were just entering the outskirts of what remained of Far West, Missouri. Though he was accustomed now to the scenes they were entering, it was still depressing. Far West was but a shell of its former glory. There were only about forty families left now, less than two hundred people out of some five thousand. The city still bore the grim evidence of that day in November when the legions of hell had been turned loose in its streets. Many of the cabins had no roofs. Others still had the rafters, but they were open to the afternoon sky, like the gaunt ribs of long-dead buffalo one saw from time to time on the prairie. Sod huts lay in heaps. Here and there a blackened mound bore silent witness to the torching of a haystack or the burning of a barn. Bleak, barren, almost totally deserted, it was a mournful and depressing sight.

The mental and spiritual weariness added to his physical exhaustion. In February, word had come from the south that the Missourians had released Sidney Rigdon from the Liberty jail. He had made his way east and was now in Illinois. Rigdon had been ill, and the brethren surmised that his release was a thinly disguised way for the Missourians to make sure they didn't end up with a dead man on their hands. But it had still nevertheless raised the Saints' hopes that something might be done for Joseph and Hyrum and the others who were still incarcerated. The Prophet and others had written petitions to the state supreme court judges, and so the Committee on Removal decided to appoint Theodore Turley to accompany Heber C. Kimball to the state capital to present the petitions and see if something could be done for the prisoners.

The two brethren had mostly walked on their journey, spending a little time in Ray County in order to obtain important papers related to their fellow brethren's imprisonment, papers they also wanted to show to the supreme court judges. From there they went on, stopping only occasionally to curl up on the ground, cloaks clutched tightly around them, snatching a few minutes of sleep before the cold drove them up and on again. They arrived in Jefferson City and met with judges of the state supreme court as well as with the secretary of state—the latter because Lilburn W. Boggs, the "honorable" governor of the state of Missouri, was out of town. These visits, as well as one to Judge King, who had presided at the Richmond hearing back in November, proved to be fruitless efforts. Now they were about to end their journey back in Far West, a total trip of nearly three hundred miles.

Heber turned his head and saw that his companion was looking at the ruins around them. Heber smiled, a humorless, ironic smile. "Do you know what day it is today, Brother Theodore?"

Turley was surprised. "It's Friday."

"Yes, the fifth of April." There was a long pause, then, "Nine years ago tomorrow the Church was organized."

Turley nodded soberly. He had completely forgotten about that.

Heber slowed his step for a moment. They were passing the house of Hyrum and Mary Fielding Smith. The windows were smashed out. The door was completely gone. Someone had tied a rope to one of the logs on the southeast corner and yanked it loose, collapsing the front wall. There was a crumpled chair visible in the darkened interior. A remnant of a blanket was a sodden spot in the trampled mud.

Heber raised a hand in a forlorn salute. "Happy anniversary," he murmured softly.

"You didn't even get to see the governor?"

Heber's head moved back and forth slowly.

"He was out of the city on business somewhere," Turley supplied, wanting to lessen the disappointment on the faces of the four men who sat in a half circle around the table. "But we did get to see the secretary of state."

"So it was all for nothing!" Stephen Markham said bitterly. Stephen Markham was the man Joseph had entrusted with the task of taking Emma and her family east. It was he who had seen her and the children safely across the ice of the Mississippi River and into Quincy. Though it would have been easy to just stay in Illinois and rest for a time, he had come back to help with getting the last of the Saints from Missouri. He, of all the Committee on Removal, had felt the most strongly that Heber and Turley would be bringing back good news.

Alanson Ripley leaned forward eagerly, ignoring Markham's

moroseness. "How are Joseph and Hyrum and the others? Brother Markham tried to visit them yesterday but was turned away, and it's been three weeks since I visited them."

Heber's answer showed his weariness and dejection. "Not good. We weren't allowed in to see them either. We could only talk to them through the window grate. As you know, that hole they call a jail is unbearable. There's no heat. The conditions are filthy. They can't even stand up straight, the ceiling is so low." He couldn't keep the discouragement out of his voice. "They've lost a lot of weight. You can see it in their faces." Then, suddenly remembering something, he brightened. "However, as Brother Joseph bid us farewell, he made a most peculiar statement."

"Like what?" Markham asked.

"He said, 'Be of good cheer, brethren, for we shall be delivered.'"

"He did?" Ripley blurted eagerly. "He said that?"

Markham's countenance brightened only momentarily, then fell again. "That's just Joseph," he muttered. "Always trying to be hopeful. Not wanting anyone to worry."

"No," Heber retorted, his spirits lifting. In his weariness he had almost forgotten this. "It was more than that. We told him the news about our failure in Jefferson City, of course. He didn't seem too surprised, or discouraged either. 'We shall be delivered,' he said, 'but only the arm of God can deliver us now.'"

Turley was nodding thoughtfully. "That's right. That's exactly what he said. 'Only the arm of God can deliver us now.'"

Heber stood up, all business now. "He also said that we are to get the rest of the Saints away as fast as possible."

———— ◆ ————

Back in January, when a council of the brethren had taken a solemn covenant that they would not leave anyone behind who wished to leave Far West, Theodore Turley had been one of the seven men appointed to serve on the Committee on Removal. A quiet man, a British immigrant of some years before, he was known by all as a man of complete integrity and full dependability. He was widely respected by neighbors and friends—member and nonmember alike.

Turley was physically exhausted, emotionally spent, and spiritually drained, but he stayed behind in the office of the committee after the others had left. There were a few things that needed to be done, and in keeping with his nature, he determined he would do them before he went home to greet his family.

It was nearing six o'clock as he prepared to finish up and go home. Suddenly his head came up. There was the sound of horses outside, several horses. He felt a cold chill. Horses were a scarce commodity among the Saints now. That meant only one thing: these weren't Latter-day Saints. Heart pounding, he quickly swept the papers into the drawer and started toward the back door, but then as he heard footsteps on the porch, he knew he was too late. Calmly, he sat back down and took the papers out again, pretending to be busily engaged in reading them.

When the door opened, he looked up. He didn't have to feign surprise. There were eight of them. He knew about half. Captain Bogart was a county judge and a man who hated the Mormons with total dedication. He had been one of the most deadly of the mob during the Mormon War. Doctor Laffity was a prominent resident of the county and also an avowed Mormon-hater. And finally there was John Whitmer.

That struck Turley the hardest. He had been close to the Whitmer family after they had moved to Missouri from Kirtland. He had always viewed them with a sense of awe he could never quite shake. David Whitmer had actually seen Moroni. John, Peter, Jr., Christian, and Jacob had all been privileged to handle the golden plates and see the writings that were engraved on them. Seven or eight revelations in the Doctrine and Covenants had been given directly to members of the Whitmer family. John Whitmer had been called as a historian to the Church. So when he and David had turned against Joseph and left the Church, it had hit Turley hard. Very hard! To have John

Whitmer standing shoulder to shoulder with Bogart? It was a bitter jolt.

Theodore Turley kept his hands on the table to keep them from trembling. "Good evening, gentlemen. What can I do for you?"

John Whitmer seemed to sense Turley's keen disapproval, for he quickly averted his eyes when Turley looked at him.

"Ah, Turley," Bogart said, his eyes narrow and glittering with animosity. "So you've returned."

Theodore Turley let his eyes move slowly from face to face. He kept his expression impassive, even though he felt his pulse quicken sharply. It shouldn't have surprised him that they knew of his arrival. They seemed to know everything anymore. "Yes," he admitted, "I returned just an hour ago."

Laffity leaned forward. "We heard that you were trying to get the prisoners released." There was a quick, triumphant smile. "We also heard you had no success."

Turley chose not to reply. One of the men pushed his way forward. "Is it true?" he demanded. "Is Joe Smith still going to be brought up to Daviess County for trial?"

There was little point in denying it. Turley nodded.

The man glanced at Bogart. "That's wonderful!" he exclaimed. He turned back to Turley. "Be a real shame if me and my men couldn't keep that vow we made." There was a burst of obscene laughter.

"Vow?" Turley whispered. He knew the man was baiting him, but the menace in his eyes sent a shiver up Turley's spine.

"That's right. Fifty of us in Daviess County have vowed to each other that once we've seen Joe Smith, we will not eat or drink again until we have shed his blood with our own hands." He leaned forward, his eyes narrowing down to tiny points, black, hard, glittering with ugliness and hate. "We're looking forward to your prophet's imminent arrival in our county."

Though it took every effort of will he could muster, Turley did not flinch. He smiled slightly and said, "I should very much like to be there to see you eat your first meal and break that vow."

The man's eyes widened in disbelief for one quick second; then he lunged forward. "You dare to mock me?" he cried hoarsely, slamming his fist against the table.

Bogart stepped quickly between the enraged Missourian and Turley, shoving the man back. "You'll have your day," he snapped. He fumbled in his pocket and brought out a single sheet of paper folded in thirds. He slapped it down on the table. "Are you familiar with this?"

Curious, Turley picked it up and unfolded it. He recognized it immediately, though the handwriting was not familiar to him. Some unknown person had made a copy of the revelation given to Joseph Smith in July of the previous year. It was a revelation giving instructions for the Twelve Apostles. One paragraph had been circled boldly with pen and ink. Turley looked up again. "Yes, I am."

"Read it," Bogart snarled. "The part that's marked."

Turley did so in a firm voice. "'And next spring let them—'" He stopped, and looked at the men circling him. "By 'them' it means the Twelve. 'Let them depart to go over the great waters, and there promulgate my gospel, the fulness thereof, and bear record of my name. Let them take leave of my saints in the city of Far West, on the twenty-sixth day of April next, on the building-spot of my house, saith the Lord.'"

Turley folded the paper slowly and shoved it back toward Bogart.

Bogart let the paper lie, as though it would serve as evidence if he left it there before them. "Then surely you will now give up the idea of Joe Smith being a prophet. As a rational man, you have no other choice."

Turley gave him a look of amazement, but Bogart rushed on. "Joe Smith is in prison. The Twelve are scattered all over creation. April twenty-sixth is now only three weeks away. They will not come. They cannot come."

Dr. Laffity jumped in, eager to drive the point home. "Let them come, if they dare. If they try it, they shall all be murdered."

John Whitmer stepped forward, his face grim and lined with concern. "They're right, Theodore. The revelation cannot be fulfilled. This proves Joseph is a fallen prophet. Now will you give up your faith?"

Turley shot to his feet, nearly knocking over the chair on which he had been sitting. "I tell you in the name of God," he thundered, "that revelation will be fulfilled!"

To his surprise, his response did not anger them. Instead, they roared with laughter, utterly scornful. The only one who did not was John Whitmer. He looked away, head down.

Turley didn't budge, nor did he back down in the face of their ridicule. His head jerked up and down in hard, emphatic motions. "It *will* be fulfilled," he said again.

One of the other men spoke up now. "Turley, you'd be wise to follow the example of John Corrill. He's decided to publish a book that will expose the Mormons for what they are."

Bogart latched on to that eagerly. "Yes, Corrill is a sensible man. Perhaps you could help him. Add your name to the work. Admit that you were wrong."

Folding his arms across his chest, Turley looked calmly at the men who faced him. John Corrill had been one of the early converts to the Church in Ohio. He had been called to Missouri and there had served as a counselor to Bishop Edward Partridge. He had remained faithful through the expulsion of the Saints from Jackson County and been one of the founders of Far West. Then things had soured. He, along with so many others, had turned against the Prophet the previous fall and left the Church. He had testified bitterly against Joseph and the other Church leaders at the hearing in Richmond. Turley had heard about the book he was writing that viciously attacked the Church and its beliefs.

Suddenly, Turley turned to Whitmer. "John, you have heard John Corrill testify in times past that he knew the Book of Mormon and Mormonism were true and that Joseph Smith was a prophet of God. Now he has changed his tune. So I call on you,

John Whitmer. You say Corrill is a good and moral man. Do you believe him when he once said the Book of Mormon was true, or do you believe him when he now says it is not true?"

Whitmer was taken aback by Turley's going on the offensive. "I . . ."

"Well?" Turley demanded. "There are many things that are published which some men say are true; then they turn around and say they are false."

"Do you hint at me?" Whitmer said hotly.

"If the cap fits, wear it!" Turley retorted with equal tartness. "All I know is that you have published to the world that you saw the plates given to Joseph Smith. What do you have to say about that now?"

The silence hung in the room like a pall. Every eye had turned to John Whitmer. His head was down, his eyes half-closed. Finally he spoke in a voice so low it was barely audible. "I did handle those plates," he mumbled. "There were fine engravings on both sides of each leaf. I touched them. I personally handled them." There was another long pause, then, "They were shown to me by a supernatural power."

"So," Turley said triumphantly, "why is it that the translation is not true now, then?"

"I . . ." The head ducked even lower.

"Well?" Turley bored in.

"I . . ." He took a quick breath, darting a glance toward Bogart, whose mouth was a hard, tight line. "I couldn't read those plates in the original," Whitmer finally said, "so I cannot say whether or not the translation is true."

Bogart seemed relieved, but he had also had enough. He snatched up the paper from the table. "Let's go," he snapped. They turned and started filing out. As Bogart reached the door, he half turned, his face a mask of hatred. "You tell 'em, Turley. You tell the Twelve that if they try to come back here and take their leave from Far West, we'll kill every last man jack one of them!"

Turley stared at the door for several seconds after it closed again; then he dropped into his chair, aware that his heart was pounding as heavily as if he had run a race. Then his eyes blazed and his jaw tightened with determination. "They will come," he murmured. "You wait and see."

They were seven days north of Savannah and still a day out of New York City when Jiggers, the bosun, found Will lying on the bunk in the sleeping quarters. Will looked up in surprise. The ship's officers never came down to the crew's quarters. He sat up quickly.

"Steed, the cap'n wants to see you," the man growled.

Will came to his feet slowly. He had stood watch through part of the night and had been dozing now to make up for it. "The captain?" he asked, his mind still not grasping fully.

"Come on, mate," Jiggers snapped impatiently. "Move sharply, now. He's in his cabin."

As Will came out into the daylight and moved toward the captain's quarters, he saw the furtive looks his fellow crew members gave him. They were mostly filled with pity. Angry now, he straightened his back and marched toward the ladder that led to the captain's quarters. He took the steps in threes, walked to the door, knocked sharply, then stood back, head up.

"Enter."

Opening the door, he stepped inside. There were only two small portholes in the cabin, and after the bright daylight, it took a minute for his eyes to adjust. The captain was seated at a small writing desk. He was facing Will, watching him with steady eyes. He said nothing. Will shut the door, standing at attention, determined not to speak first.

Jonathan Sperryman was young for a sea captain, no more than forty or forty-five. Thin—almost sparse—he had a shock of hair that probably once was brown, but now was mostly bleached blond by the sun and salt spray. He was tough and hard, and could flay a man with his eyes when he was angry. But he was also fair and didn't mind passing out praise when it was well deserved. After being in several ports of call and seeing the other captains and their crews, Will knew he could have done a lot worse.

The captain stirred and, still without speaking, opened a drawer. He took out a folded paper and laid it on the desk. A string was tied around it to hold it closed. Will glanced at it, then suddenly lurched forward. It was *his* letter, the letter he had written so laboriously to his mother, the letter he had paid Petey such a dear price to take off the ship in Savannah for him. He couldn't help it. He simply gaped at the letter, trying to comprehend all that its being there on the captain's desk implied. Petey had sworn he had delivered the letter. And he had. To the captain!

It was as though Will had been hit in the stomach by a swinging block and tackle. He wanted to reach out and grab something to steady himself. Sperryman, watching him closely, was satisfied. He swept the letter back into the drawer and pushed it shut again. "I don't make a habit of reading other people's mail, Steed. I don't know whom you were writing to, or why, though I have an idea."

Will said nothing. The disappointment was too crushing. If he had opened his mouth, all that would have come out was a strangled sob.

The captain's mouth hardened. "But whatever the reason, that doesn't change things," he said gruffly. "I paid two hundred dollars for you. When your two years of service have paid that back, you'll be free to go."

Will's lips set into a tight line.

The captain continued, more kindly now. "I'll be having to put you in the locker again while we're in New York, just to be sure. But if you behave yourself, you have my word that I'll mail the letter when we reach Liverpool."

Will finally nodded. Whether he would or wouldn't behave himself remained to be seen, but he knew that trying to beat this captain would be very difficult. "Is that all, sir?"

"Yes."

Will turned and moved to the door.

"Steed?"

He stopped, not turning around.

"If you were of a mind to accept reality, you've got the makings of a good sailor."

Will stood there, his back to the captain. Then finally he spoke. "Is that all, sir?" he asked again.

There was a long pause, then, "Yes. Dismissed."

Will opened the door and stepped out. He didn't look back as he went up the ladder and onto the main deck.

Chapter Notes

Heber C. Kimball's and Theodore Turley's trip to the state capital was not successful in the sense of their being able to get the prisoners released. However, their efforts probably facilitated a change of venue, from Daviess County to Boone County, for the prisoners' trial. The Prophet had petitioned the Missouri state legislature for a change of venue as early as January of 1839. As will be seen in subsequent chapters of this novel, the granting at last of a change of venue in the spring of 1839 would have a significant effect on future events.

On the same day that Heber C. Kimball and Theodore Turley returned home, a delegation of eight Missourians confronted Turley in the office of the Committee on Removal. The conversation—including the warning against the Twelve's trying to return to Far West, and John Whitmer's reluctant testimony—is reported in Joseph Smith's history. The vow to kill the Prophet was also apparently spoken in Turley's presence on this day, though it may have been a separate incident from the visit of the eight men. (See HC 3:306–8.) The revelation which told the Twelve to take their leave from Far West on 26 April 1839 is now section 118 in the Doctrine and Covenants.

Chapter Three

Matthew! Sister Steed!"

Mary Ann and her son were just coming out of the Quincy store. Matthew's arms were loaded with a box filled with sugar, flour, honey, and other staples. Both of them turned at the sound of the familiar voice.

"Brother Brigham," Mary Ann said warmly, shielding her eyes from the late afternoon sun. "Hello."

He strode up, sweeping off his hat and jamming it under his arm. He took both of her hands in his, his face filled with pleasure. "Good afternoon, Sister Steed. How good to see you." He half turned. "And Matthew. Hello, my young friend."

"Hello, Brother Brigham."

Brigham reached out and took the box from Matthew's hands and lowered it to the boardwalk. "Set that thing down, boy. We need to talk."

Matthew smiled, not protesting. That was Brigham Young. Cheerful, booming, and immediately taking charge of things.

But Matthew didn't mind. Brigham always did it with cordiality and warmth, so that people naturally accepted his leadership.

"I'm glad I caught you. I was just on my way out to your place."

"You were?" Mary Ann asked.

"Yes. How is Benjamin?" His eyes were filled with genuine concern.

"Still weak, but much recovered and getting stronger each day."

"He's back to being grumpy again because we won't let him do anything," Matthew added.

Brigham laughed heartily. "That *is* a good sign."

Mary Ann laughed too, watching Brigham with some admiration. Brigham was four years older than Joseph, but he was two or three inches shorter than the Prophet and of a much stockier build. This made him seem even older than his years. Like Joseph he was clean shaven. He wore his reddish brown hair to the shoulders. One lock of it now rippled slightly in the steady breeze blowing from the west. His eyes were blue-gray and often reminded Mary Ann of the morning sky just before the sunrise. They could dance with humor, sparkle with delight, or flash in anger at some idler who didn't want to make his own way in life or when someone dared to criticize his beloved Joseph.

"I've been meaning to come out and see Brother Benjamin, but . . ." He let it die and turned to survey the town quickly. Then he sighed wearily. "There is so much to do. More coming every day. And now they are some of our poorest." He shook his head, his mouth puckering down into a frown of concern. Then he seemed to come back to them. "There's been some bad news, I'm afraid."

Mary Ann tensed. "Bad news?"

"Yes. Brother Henry Sherwood arrived from Far West last night. The militia in Daviess County has given the brethren in Far West an ultimatum. Everyone has to be gone by Friday, April twelfth, or be killed. Everyone!"

"No!" Mary Ann gasped.

"The twelfth?" Matthew asked in alarm. "But that's tomorrow."

Brigham's face was grim. "Yes. Brother Sherwood rode for help immediately, but they were only given a week's notice. So the situation is urgent. Heber and the Committee on Removal will get the families out of Far West and as far as Tenny's Grove to escape the edict, but they are going to need help to come any farther." Now the blue-gray eyes were like polished steel—angry, determined, unbendable. "Well, we shall show them that we do not abandon our own."

He straightened. "We're going to organize a train, send as many wagons as we can to get them out. We must get teams started immediately. We haven't a moment to waste."

"You will use ours," Mary Ann said promptly and firmly. "The horses are in fine shape."

Brigham started to answer, but his voice failed him for a moment. He took Mary Ann's hands, swallowed hard, then cleared his throat. "God bless you, dear Mary Ann. I knew you and Benjamin would say exactly that. God bless you."

"Is that why you were coming out to see us?" Matthew asked.

Brigham nodded.

Matthew had a sudden thought. "Do you need drivers?"

Mary Ann's head snapped around, her eyes instantly bright with fear. They lifted to Brigham's face, wanting to plead for a negative answer. Brigham read her expression perfectly, but there was little choice. He looked at Matthew and slowly nodded. Matthew was not yet nineteen, but he had been doing a man's work for some time now. Besides that, Brigham had great confidence in this youngest son of the Steeds. Without taking his eyes away from Mary Ann, he answered. "Yes, Matthew, we do."

Matthew turned to face his mother. Nothing was said, but after a moment she bobbed her head ever so slightly, just once. Matthew hugged her quickly and fiercely, then spoke to Brigham. "I'll bring the team in. Where and when shall I meet you?"

"At the ferry. We're going to try and get as many wagons across the river today as we can. We're hoping to get two drivers for every wagon and some extra teams, so they can push into the night. What about Derek? How close is that baby to coming?"

Mary Ann answered for Matthew. "Not until June. Rebecca will be fine. Derek will want to go."

"And I'll bring Peter too," Matthew said eagerly. "He's still young, but he can spell us off from time to time." He looked at his mother. "What about Nathan?"

Brigham shook his head. "With Benjamin still recovering, we can't send every Steed. You tell Nathan to stay and care for the family."

Matthew nodded, then reached down and grabbed the box of food and started away.

"Matthew?"

He stopped, turning around to look at his mother.

"Put that box in the wagon," she said. "They'll need it worse than we do. We could also spare some of that flour Joshua purchased for us."

"Yes, Mama."

"May the Lord bless you both," Brigham murmured huskily. His shoulders seemed to lift perceptibly. Then he swung around to Matthew. "When this is over, Matthew, we need to talk. Are you still interested in working with a crusty old New Englander in setting up a carpentry business?"

A grin split Matthew's face and pleasure danced in his blue eyes. "I sure am!"

"Good. When you get back let's talk about it. I'm really serious about it."

"Yes, sir!" Matthew cried. He turned and strode away, hardly mindful of the weight he carried in his arms.

For a moment, they stood there, watching Matthew walk away. Then Brigham put on his hat. "Thank you, Mother Steed. I knew I could count on you."

———◆———

Hyrum Smith leaned over and whispered into his brother's ear. "Look, Joseph, it worked."

Joseph didn't turn his head, but Hyrum saw the quick nod against the firelight. The five prisoners were stretched out on the prairie sod, a few yards away from where Sheriff William Morgan and three of the four other guards were now asleep beneath their blankets. One of the sleeping men—probably Sheriff Morgan—was snoring loudly, sounding much like an old boar pig rooting through a garden patch.

In the faint light from the dying fire, Hyrum could see the whiskey jug. It was tipped over on its side now, all but empty. He smiled to himself. That had not been a bad investment. Earlier in the day, when the guards expressed a desire for a jug of corn whiskey sweetened with honey, the prisoners had chipped in some money to help pay for it. There had been broad hints from the sheriff and his men that their getting drunk might give the prisoners a good opportunity to escape.

The one guard who was still awake and who had not imbibed sat apart from the rest; he was the one who had probably been the most overt about his willingness to help the prisoners escape.

It was a strange set of events that had brought them to this place. At the conclusion of the Richmond hearing back in November, Joseph and the four men now with him—his brother Hyrum, Lyman Wight, Alexander McRae, and Caleb Baldwin—had been charged with treason committed in Daviess County, and Judge King had ordered that they be confined until they could be tried at the Daviess County court in the spring. Since there was no jail in Daviess County, however, Liberty Jail in Clay County had been chosen for their prison. After their having spent over four months in that miserable jail, about ten days ago Judge King had hurried the prisoners off to their trial before a grand jury in Daviess County. No doubt the bitter anti-Mormon judge was fearful that the prisoners might receive a change of venue, which the prisoners themselves anticipated would be granted them. A hotbed of anti-Mormon sentiment, Daviess County was hardly the place for a fair trial, and King knew it.

At the Daviess County trial, the grand jury had brought an indictment against Joseph and the others for "murder, treason, burglary, arson, larceny, theft, and stealing." Joseph had dryly commented that only the Missourians didn't know that larceny, theft, and stealing were all the same things. At last, however, the prisoners received a change of venue to Boone County, which was southeast of Daviess County some distance. The Daviess County sheriff, William Morgan, was put in charge of transferring Joseph and his companions to the new location. And then the rumors started. En route, the sheriff began to drop hints that he had been counseled to let the prisoners escape, since there was no chance they could be successfully prosecuted. The continuing imprisonment of Joseph Smith and the other Church leaders on such flimsy evidence was an embarrassment to the state.

Hopeful but cautious, the prisoners waited patiently for events to unfold. During the journey, with clothing and a promissory note they had bought two horses from the guards. Then, today, they had donated money for the purchase of the whiskey and after dinner had quietly watched the Missourians empty the jug. Sheriff Morgan openly told them that he was going to "take a good drink of grog and go to bed" and that he didn't care what the prisoners did after that. No one said anything more, but both the guards and the guarded knew what was happening.

"What do you think, Joseph?" It was Alexander McRae, who was on the other side of Hyrum.

Joseph rose up on one elbow. He listened for a moment, as the sheriff snorted in his sleep. Then he smiled grimly. "What do I think?" he whispered. "I think we would be better suited to flee this land of oppression and tyranny and once again take our stand among a people in whose bosoms dwell those feelings of freedom and a love for the republic which gave rise to our nation."

"Amen!" Lyman Wight breathed fervently.

"Do you mean—?" Caleb Baldwin started.

But Joseph cut in with a grin. "I mean that I think the Lord has provided us with a favorable opportunity, brethren. And if that is the case, well, I'm not one to displease the Lord. I suggest we take our leave of these kind gentlemen and that we do so in a manner that we do not disturb their sleep. And if I'm not mistaken, I think our wakeful friend over there might even help us get on our way."

———◆———

The rain of the previous two days had gone now, the clouds scudding on eastward, leaving the skies over Missouri and Illinois so clear and clean it almost took the breath away. The coolness of the morning was dissipating rapidly, and the sun was warm on the faces of the Steed women.

They had brought their chairs outside to sit in the sun. Like the children, the women were unable to bear the crowded cabin a moment longer. The breakfast dishes were done. The men were gone—Derek, Matthew, and Peter to Missouri, Benjamin and Nathan to a meeting called that morning by Brigham Young. The children were up on the small bluff behind the house. After two days of being confined to the house, they were frolicking like day-old lambs.

Mary Ann raised her head. "Listen!"

They turned, cocking their heads to better catch the sound of the children. They were out of sight, just over the brow of the hill, but their voices carried clearly. Lydia smiled. "It's 'London Bridge.' I wonder whose idea that was."

They all laughed at that. Emily, Lydia's little mirror image of herself, had been pushing hard for that particular game even before the children left the cabin. Her brother Joshua felt they needed something more active—"red rover" or maybe a good tug-o'-war. He had even found a stout piece of rope. But obviously, and as usual, Emily had carried the day.

"I don't know about that girl," Lydia said ruefully. No one missed the obvious touch of pride in her voice.

"Now, now," Mary Ann shushed, "I think it's delightful that she knows her mind."

"She does that," Rebecca agreed. She patted her stomach twice. "And if this one's a girl, I hope she's just like her."

"Hello!"

The call of greeting pulled all their heads around. Coming up the road from the direction of the main part of town were Jenny and Kathryn McIntire. The women's faces were immediately wreathed in welcoming smiles, and they raised their arms and waved.

"Good morning," Jessica called out, truly happy to see these two young women. The McIntire girls had become almost a part of the family after living with them in Far West for several weeks. Sister McIntire had found a place for them with a family in Quincy, but the girls were out to the Steed house frequently. Jenny was seventeen, Kathryn four years younger. She would be thirteen in less than two weeks.

There were quick hugs all around and clasped hands. "How's your mother?" Mary Ann asked Jenny.

"Fine, fine. She almost came, but Sister Poulsen, who lives with us, is feeling poorly this morning, so Mama thought it best to stay and help."

"That's just like your mother," Lydia said.

"I guess you haven't heard anything from Matthew and Derek yet?" Jenny asked Mary Ann. Her eyes had lowered and she blushed slightly.

Jessica watched her, fully understanding her anxiety. Until every Latter-day Saint was out of the state of Missouri, there was good reason for concern. If anyone understood the cost of hatred, it was Jessica.

"No," Mary Ann answered. "But it's just barely a week tomorrow since they left. I suspect it will still be another week at least, maybe ten days, before we hear anything."

Jenny looked crestfallen. "I know. I just keep hoping."

Rebecca nodded. Like the others, she had little doubt that before this year was over, Jennifer McIntire would be Jennifer Steed. They were already treating her as if she were their sister.

"I don't blame you for being worried," Rebecca said. "I've been miserable since Derek left. I miss him terribly."

Jessica's head came up slowly, and suddenly her eyes were glistening, but no one seemed to notice. They were all watching Rebecca and Jenny.

Lydia nodded somberly. "It is hard, isn't it? Whenever Nathan's gone, it's like half my life has been cut away from me. And the children, too. We're so happy when he returns again. It's like—"

Jessica was shocked to find herself on her feet, her fists clenching and unclenching. The world was swimming before her eyes and she blinked quickly, surprised at how hot the tears were. She was barely aware that the book that had been lying on her lap had now tumbled to the ground. The only thing of which she was fully conscious was the searing pain, so pointed and so intense that she felt her knees trembling.

Lydia's hand flew to her mouth. "Oh, Jessica," she gasped. "I . . . I'm sorry. I wasn't even thinking . . ."

Jessica shook her head blindly, waving a hand to try and show she wasn't blaming them.

Rebecca was stricken now too. "Oh, Jessie, I didn't mean . . ." She couldn't finish either, the enormity of their blunder hitting her fully now.

"No," Jessica stammered. "It's all right. I just . . ." There was one half-strangled cry of agony, then she turned and plunged away.

They were all on their feet now, watching Jessica's stumbling flight down the same road that Jenny and Kathryn had just come up. "Oh, Mama," Rebecca said, her own tears coming. "I wasn't even thinking about her losing John. I'm so sorry."

Lydia too was ready to weep. "How thoughtless of me. Shall I go after her?"

After a moment, Mary Ann shook her head. "No. I think it's best to give her some time alone."

Brigham Young raised his hands. "Brethren, could we settle down again now and deal with the next item of business?"

He got what he asked for almost instantly. The hush which swept across the meeting was total. Nathan turned and gave his father a questioning look, but Benjamin merely shrugged. To this point the meeting had been lively, but nothing really out of the ordinary. Several items of business had been handled, matters having to do with getting the last of the Saints out of Missouri and with meeting the needs of the thousands now gathering in Illinois. One important item had been the sustaining of George Albert Smith to fill one of the vacancies in the Quorum of Twelve. George A., as almost everyone called him, was Joseph Smith's cousin. He was not yet twenty-two years old, but he had proven himself faithful on Zion's Camp and throughout the troubles in Kirtland and Missouri. He was sustained unanimously by those present.

There were only four other members of the Twelve present. Brigham, as senior Apostle, presided. He was joined by John Taylor, Wilford Woodruff, and Orson Pratt. Others of the Twelve were not available. David W. Patten was dead, martyred at the Battle of Crooked River. Parley P. Pratt was still in jail in Richmond, Missouri. Heber C. Kimball was supervising the Church in Far West. Willard Richards, who had been named to the Quorum the previous July by the voice of the Lord, was serving as a counselor to Joseph Fielding in presiding over the mission in England and had not yet been ordained. John E. Page was somewhere between Far West and Quincy, trying to get his family out of the state of Missouri. Thomas B. Marsh and Orson Hyde had committed acts of apostasy (Marsh being excommunicated the month before as a result of his actions), and William Smith was disaffected.

Joseph Smith, Sr.—Father Smith—still looking very frail after the wagon ride from Far West, was there as Patriarch to the Church. Many other leaders were also in attendance.

Satisfied that he had their total attention, Brigham reached down to the table and picked up a piece of paper. He opened it up, studied it for a moment, then set it down again. "Brethren, I think you know what I have before me." Even if they didn't, he didn't wait for them to say so. "I have here the revelation given by the Lord on the eighth of July last, given to Brother Joseph in response to the request, 'Show us thy will, O Lord, concerning the Twelve.'"

He picked it up again. "As you know, in this revelation the Lord said that the Twelve were to set out the following spring—which would be now—on a mission to England. The Lord further directed that we take our leave from the city of Far West, from the temple site, on the twenty-sixth day of April next, which is now just nine days away."

He laid the paper down, then took the spectacles from his nose and began to rub them with the corner of his vest. A buzz of whispering and murmuring had exploded around him. Father Smith was looking at him, dumbfounded. Only the other members of the Twelve were not surprised. Brigham finally replaced the spectacles and looked up. "Brethren, we are here to determine what your feelings are concerning this revelation."

Instantly several hands shot up. Almost wearily, Brigham nodded at the nearest man. "Yes, Brother Barker."

The man, sitting two or three rows behind Nathan, rose to his feet. "Are you suggesting that the Twelve ought to consider returning to Far West?" he asked in amazement.

"I think that's what the revelation specified," Brigham responded dryly.

"But . . ."

"But what, Brother Barker?"

"That revelation was given almost a year ago now. At that time we were at peace in Far West. At that time we thought we had finally escaped from our enemies and all would be well. We had food, and a militia to protect us. We had no idea that by this April we wouldn't even still be in the state of Missouri."

Several heads were bobbing, and Nathan was a little surprised at who was in agreement with Brother Barker's sentiments. Brigham seemed faintly amused. "You're right, Brother

Karl. It would certainly have been helpful if the Lord could have seen the future when he gave that revelation to us."

That won him a ripple of laughter and two or three cries of "Hear, hear!"

Barker lowered his head and bulled on. "Surely the Lord can't expect you to return now. Surely he knows our conditions here. We can't even find beds for our families! Joseph's in prison. If you go and are . . ." He stopped, not daring to suggest it. "If we lose the Twelve, who will lead us then?"

The man beside him jumped up, not nearly so reticent. "You know what the reports are. The mob will be waiting for you if you try it. You'll be murdered if you go back. Haven't there been enough killings already?"

"Anyone else?" Brigham said, not responding to the warning.

The two men sat down, half angry that Brigham was unmoved. Joseph Smith, Sr., raised his hand.

"Father Smith," Brigham said with great respect. "Do you have some feelings on the matter?"

Joseph's father would be celebrating his sixty-eighth birthday in three months. His hair was a majestic white, and his tall frame still moved about with great dignity. But the physical and emotional demands placed upon him since the previous fall had ravaged him. His cheeks were gaunt, his eyes sunken. He moved slowly, and sometimes a shadow of pain darkened his eyes. It frightened Nathan in a way, for he saw some of the same signs in his own father. Their minds were still alert and their spirits strong, but some of the old fire had never been rekindled, and Nathan feared that it might never be again.

"Thank you," Father Smith said, standing with some effort so he could face the group. Brigham sat down. "Thank you for your presence, brethren. It is a grand sight to see this many priesthood holders gathered together again." He glanced at Brigham, then looked back at the group. "I am well acquainted with that revelation. I remember the day my son first read it to us. And I was thrilled to think that the Lord wanted the Twelve to go to England. We have already seen the fruits of the great work that Brothers Kimball and Richards and others did over there a couple years back."

Nathan saw that John Taylor was nodding and thought he understood why. John Taylor had been converted in 1836 when Nathan accompanied Parley P. Pratt on a mission to Toronto, in Upper Canada. John Taylor had introduced them to Joseph Fielding and his two sisters Mary and Mercy. They were also converted. Then Joseph Fielding and his sisters wrote to their brother, James, who was a minister in Preston, England, and to other relatives also living in England. Letters coming back to Canada from the island nation expressed desires to learn more about the new religion. So when Heber C. Kimball, Willard Richards, Joseph Fielding, and others arrived in England in 1837—the first missionaries to cross the ocean in the new dispensation—seeds had already been sown for the harvest of converts that took place there over the next several months. Included in that harvest were two English boys, Derek and Peter Ingalls, whose conversion had proved to have such a profound effect upon the lives of the Steed family back in America.

"However," Father Smith was continuing, "I think these brethren raise important questions. Conditions have changed. Obviously the Lord knew they would, but when conditions change, then the Lord's requirements change too. I don't think the Lord expects you brethren"—he had turned now and was looking at the Twelve—"to risk your lives simply so you can say you left from Far West. You can go to England from here. I think the Lord will accept your good will in place of the actual deed."

"Amen!" someone murmured with great fervency.

Nathan leaned over to his father. "Do you agree with that, Pa?"

Benjamin was chewing on his lower lip. "I'm not sure."

Nathan nodded. Neither was he. The fact that Brigham and his fellow Apostles were even considering returning to Missouri spoke volumes about their courage. On the other hand, the Church was in desperate need of their leadership.

Father Smith sat down again. The room quieted, everyone waiting to see how Brigham would respond to this old man who was so deeply revered. For several moments, Brigham just looked at him; then he stood again. "What you say has much wisdom, Father Smith." Again there was a long pause. "However, I feel differently about the matter, as do the others of the Twelve. I should like them to speak now."

By the time the four Apostles had finished, Nathan no longer had any doubts. Each one spoke quietly and briefly, but with solemn power. There was no boasting about what they could and would do. There was no sense of self-righteousness about them. It was obvious that they found the prospects disheartening. They had been there. They had families too. They knew what awaited them. But with that, they still bore sober testimony that they felt this was what the Lord expected of them. And if that was so, there was little else to discuss.

When the last Apostle sat down again, Brigham was up immediately. Now the group of priesthood holders was quiet. The mood was shifting, and Brigham could sense it. He glanced at Father Smith, then turned back to speak to the full group. "I still remember clearly one day back in Kirtland. I had come to the Prophet's office on a matter of business. He was weighed down with many problems and responsibilities. The Church, and Joseph personally, was under constant pressure. It seemed like the Lord was making so many demands upon him that he could not possibly bear up under the load."

There was a fleeting smile. It was just the tiniest bit rueful. "I made a comment to Joseph along those very lines. He looked up in surprise, then chided me a little. 'Brother Brigham,' he said, 'I have learned something in the years since the Lord first called me to be his servant. I want you to remember it.'

"'What?' I asked him. 'What lesson have you learned?'" Brigham's voice had gone soft and thoughtful now. "I'll never forget this. He leaned back in his chair and smiled up at me. 'I have made this simple rule for myself: When the Lord commands, do it!'"

Brigham's shoulders pulled back. "Brethren, I know not what awaits us in Missouri. But my brethren of the Twelve and I are inclined to follow Brother Joseph's counsel. The Lord God has spoken. It is our business to obey, and if we do, the Lord will take care of us." He let his eyes jump from face to face. "All those who feel they can sustain the Twelve in this decision, would you now indicate that by the voice of common consent."

Nathan felt a thrill as every hand in the room came up along with his own. Some came up a trifle slower than others, but every hand was up.

Brigham was obviously pleased. "Thank you, brethren. We shall take our leave first thing in the morning in order to reach Far West in time for the appointed day."

"Brother Brigham?"

The senior Apostle was standing by John Taylor. Both were listening to a conversation Wilford Woodruff was having with two of the brethren. Brigham turned, as did Brother Taylor. "Yes, Nathan?"

Nathan took a quick breath. He wished there were time to talk to Lydia about this. But there wasn't. "I'd like to accompany you, if I could."

One eyebrow rose.

Nathan rushed on. "I know I'm not one of the Twelve, and I know what you told Matthew about me staying with the family. But you'll need some help on the trail. And besides, Matthew, Derek, and Peter are out there. Mother is very concerned. We'll surely find them along the way somewhere, then I can help them on the return trip."

Brigham gave Brother Taylor a quizzical look. "John, what do you think?"

Brother Taylor pursed his lips. "It would be well to have Nathan along with us, but this trip could be very dangerous."

Brigham only nodded.

"I—" Nathan took a quick breath. "As you were speaking, I had a strong impression that I should accompany you."

Brigham considered that, still not speaking. "You're sure?" he finally asked.

"Only in my heart." Nathan replied, forcing a weak grin. "It may take a day or two for my head to agree."

Brigham reached out and clasped Nathan's hand. "We leave at dawn."

Jessica sat on the shore of the river, watching the muddy current move slowly by her. Spring runoff had started, and the mighty Mississippi had already risen a couple of feet higher than what it had been when they ferried across a month earlier. The water was dotted with flotsam. Tree limbs, weeds, pieces of wood, and now and then full tree trunks floated slowly by. She stared at them, half-mesmerized, glad for the chance to concentrate on something.

The tears were gone now, though her eyes felt red and swollen. The pain was subsiding too. But the hollowness, the emptiness, the complete desolation had not abated in the slightest. By the world's standards, John Griffith had not been a particularly notable man. When he had first sent Newel Knight to propose marriage to her, she had been shocked deeply. She knew him slightly—he had stayed for about a month in Haun's Mill before moving to Far West—but she had given little thought to the fact that he was a widower with two children. And certainly she had not thought about him as a marriage prospect. Jessica was a divorcée, having first been married to Joshua Steed in Independence, Missouri. In America, and especially out in the West, that carried considerable stigma for most women. It didn't matter that the dissolution of the marriage was neither her fault nor her choice. The stigma remained, and Jessica had resigned herself to the fact that she would likely not marry again.

So John's shy proposal of marriage had caught her completely by surprise. She had finally agreed for mostly practical reasons. He was a good man, a hard worker, an honest, decent person. Rachel needed a father. John's two boys needed a mother. It would mean she wouldn't be totally dependent on her own resources any longer.

So when love came, it was almost a shock. She thought she had loved Joshua when they were first married. But what developed between her and John was so much richer, so much deeper, so much finer. It had left her filled with wonder. And now all that was gone. John was gone.

The last two weeks had been the worst. In the wild flight from Haun's Mill and the deadening months of the desperate struggle for survival that followed, there hadn't been much time for grieving. There had been the recurring nightmares—her on tiptoes, her mouth open in a silent scream; John walking into the blacksmith shop with Amanda Smith's husband and sons, talking amiably, not seeing the wall of horsemen thundering toward them—but there had been no time to actually sit down and consider her loss, to let the impact of that wash over her. Compelling circumstances simply pushed that luxury aside. But now they were here. There was safety. There was time to sit in the sun and remember the times with John. And it was devastating her.

She reached down and picked up a foot-long stick at her feet. It had been polished clean by the scouring action of the water and bleached almost white by the sun. Some previous flood had deposited it this high on the riverbank to sit alone, waiting its time when the currents would rise once more, snatch it up, and send it on again.

Suddenly her vision blurred anew. Angrily, she leaned back and threw the stick hard away from her. It arched up, catching the sunlight for a moment, then plummeted downward. There was a soft plop and it disappeared. After a moment it bobbed to the surface again. It spun slowly once, caught in one of the swirling eddies. Then, picking up speed as the faster current took it, it moved away from her. Through hooded vision she watched it go, almost wanting to call out to it, to wish it well as it started alone on the long journey to that vast ocean that awaited it.

———•———

It came as no surprise at all to Jessica to see Mary Ann sitting on the porch. The sun was down now, but the western sky was still light. How long she had been sitting there, waiting for Jessica to return from her blind flight from the family, Jessica could only guess. Jessica felt a great warmth come over her at the sight. She had lost her own mother when she was a young girl. But no daughter could ever have felt more love for her own mother than Jessica felt for Mary Ann, nor could any daughter and mother have been closer.

Mary Ann stood as Jessica walked slowly up. Nothing was said. She simply opened her arms and Jessica stepped into them. For almost a minute they stood there, content to feel the safety of each other's affection.

Then finally, without pulling back, Jessica spoke. "Mother Steed?"

"Yes?"

"I think it's time I occupy myself with something of importance. What would you think if I were to try to get a school started again?"

Mary Ann pulled back to look at her.

"Now that the weather's turning, we could hold it outside until we find a place to live."

Mary Ann held her at arm's length. Her eyes were moist and filled with compassion. "I think that would be a wonderful thing, Jessie. A wonderful thing."

Chapter Notes

Joseph and the other four prisoners with him were allowed to escape on April fifteenth/sixteenth as they were in the process of being transferred to Boone County, Missouri, on a change of venue. The state of Missouri was under tremendous political pressure because of its handling of the Mormon situation. Many officials also saw that the legal basis for the incarceration of the Church leaders was no more than the thinnest of veneers, and that only further embarrassment could result from pressing the matter. According to Hyrum, one of the guards actually helped them saddle the horses. Two brethren rode while the other three went on foot. And thus, wrote Hyrum, "we took our change of venue for the State of Illinois." When Sheriff Morgan and his men returned to Daviess County and reported that Joseph Smith had escaped, the citizens were furious. The sheriff was ridden on a rail. William Bowman, a previous sheriff, was also accused of complicity in the prisoners' escape and was dragged around the main square of Gallatin by the hair of his head. (See HC 3:320–22.)

Brigham's determination to return to Far West in obedience to the revelation is documented in several places (see *American Moses*, p. 71, *Restoration*, p. 434). The five Apostles and Alpheus Cutler (who, as master workman for the Far West Temple, accompanied the Apostles in order to fulfill a commandment relative to that temple) left Quincy on the morning of April eighteenth. This was two days following the escape of Joseph and the other prisoners. The two parties passed each other somewhere en route, but Joseph and his companions stayed off the main roads to escape detection and they did not meet the Apostles as the latter journeyed westward.

Joseph's "Do it" rule is recorded in his history (see HC 2:170). The conversation in which Joseph tells Brigham of that rule is the author's device.

Melissa Steed Rogers walked slowly among the headstones. The guilt was pushing at her, chiding her for not hurrying along, but she wouldn't give in to it. Not yet, anyway. She knew she would have to very soon. It was nearing four o'clock, and she had promised Carl's mother that she would be no later than half past three. Her mother-in-law tired of the children more quickly now that she was getting older. And Sarah would be getting hungry. Melissa didn't need a clock in the store window to tell her that. Her body was making it clear enough. And that meant trouble. For a five-month-old, Sarah Rogers had a lusty appetite, and a pair of lungs that soon let everyone know if she was being badly mistreated.

The sewing club had gone overtime and she had been moving swiftly toward Carl's parents' house, thinking only of Sarah. Then she came to the cemetery. Her pace slowed, then stopped altogether. To her own surprise, she turned and went in. Why, she wasn't sure. She passed this way three or four times a week.

Maybe it was having been so recently with her family in Illinois. Maybe it was seeing all those Latter-day Saints again—muddy, hungry, sick, cold. But not beaten. She had seen that in their eyes. They may have been driven out of the state of Missouri, but they were not beaten. Even Carl had commented on it. But for whatever reason, she wandered slowly around the cemetery, looking at the gravestones.

Eight years ago her family had moved to Kirtland from Palmyra. Eight years made for a lot of memories. The grave markers brought them flooding back. There were the two small slate slabs which marked the burial site of Emma Smith's twin babies, who died within hours of their birth. Melissa suddenly wondered if John Murdock's wife was also buried here. She had died giving birth to twins the day after Emma gave birth to hers, and John Murdock gave his twins to Emma. Close by, a larger marker stood over the grave of Jerusha Barden Smith, Hyrum's first wife. And there, there was the marker for Thankful Pratt, Parley's wife—miraculously healed of consumption by a blessing from Heber Kimball, then dying a year or so later within hours after giving birth to their first child, a son. Melissa had stood very near this spot and wept during the funeral.

Across the street the great temple loomed above her. She remembered weeping that day as well—that day she had so desperately wanted to go to the dedicatory services with her family. But by then Carl was getting bitter about the Mormons and she had stayed home to maintain peace.

Melissa turned slowly until she faced northward. She could see the back end of the second house north of the cemetery. She didn't know who owned it now. Didn't care. It had been the home of Joseph Smith, Sr.—Father Smith, Patriarch to the Church. It was the home where Melissa had come five years earlier to attend a "blessing meeting" and get her patriarchal blessing.

Melissa spun around and walked swiftly out of the cemetery. Carl's mother was waiting. Sarah was waiting. But she had to do something first. Down in the trunk at the foot of her bed, folded neatly in her Book of Mormon, if she remembered correctly, that blessing was waiting. She hadn't taken it out in nearly two years. Now she felt a great urgency to read it again. And Carl's mother and little Sarah would just have to wait a few minutes longer.

———•———

"Carl?"

Carlton Rogers looked up from where he was poring over a book that contained a description and line drawings of a new line of carriages being manufactured in Pittsburgh. "Yes?"

Melissa had some flax in her lap and was carding it out into long, smooth strands. Her hands stilled. "Carl, I . . ." She smiled, suddenly overwhelmed by love. "I've never really told you what it meant to me that you would take me to see my family."

He seemed a little surprised. "You told me."

"I did?" she answered, a little sheepishly.

"Yes, several times."

She laughed, then shook her head. "No," she replied. "I said thank you. I told you I appreciated your willingness to do that for me. But—" Her voice caught and she had to swallow quickly. "But I never really told you how important it was to me. I know how your parents felt about us going, especially with the baby. But I was worried sick about my family. I didn't know if they were alive or dead. I—" She took a quick breath; then more steadily, she finished. "It's the most important thing you've ever done for me, Carl. And I love you for it. More than I can say."

Completely caught off guard by that, he laid the book down and turned to face her squarely. "Well, thank you. What brought this on all of a sudden?"

Her thoughts leaped to the folded paper that now lay in the bottom of her dresser drawer. "I . . . I don't know. I've just been thinking about it all day. And I wanted to tell you."

"Oh." He was still searching her face, but finally, he turned back to his catalog.

Melissa watched him, the flax forgotten now. His face was in profile, the lamplight behind it. She thought of that summer day when she had seen him for the first time. She was down by the river behind the Newel Whitney store. He had come up on her quietly, taking her by surprise. Her first impression had not been that he was particularly handsome. He was only a few inches taller than her own five feet five inches. His hair was red, his face freckled, his skin sunburned. The grin had been almost impudent and challenging. But she had quickly forgotten that first impression, and after only about two months had passed he had come to her father and asked for her hand in marriage.

And now they had four children.

"Carl?"

"Hmm." He didn't look up this time.

"Have you ever . . . ?" She stopped. This could be dangerous ground.

"What?" He still wasn't looking at her.

"Have you ever wanted to do something different with your life?"

His head jerked up. "What?"

The look on his face completely flustered her. "Nothing," she stammered, "I was just . . . I was just talking." She picked up the flax and began stroking the comb through it vigorously.

"No," he persisted. He closed the catalog and tossed it aside, all thoughts of carriages forgotten now. "I want to know what you said."

Not quite daring to look at him, she spoke from beneath lowered lashes. "I was just thinking about how you and Joshua got to talking that one night, about some of your ideas. I thought I sensed a little wistfulness in you then, that's all." When he just continued to stare at her, she rushed on. "I mean, you're the oldest son. From the time you were small you've worked at the stable with your father. You've never known anything else, so . . . I just wondered," she finished lamely.

He pushed back his chair and turned it around so it faced her directly. "Have you been talking to Pa?"

Now it was she who was surprised. "No. About what?"

"You're sure?"

"I'm sure," she cried in exasperation. "Talking to him about what?"

"William and David."

Now she was really baffled. William and David were Carl's brothers, the two just younger than him. They worked with Carl at the livery stable. "What about them?"

He leaned back, still not sure this was all coincidental. "You know, they were glad to see me go west with you, I think. I think they wish they had more say in running the stable."

"Oh." Melissa was stunned.

"Sometimes—" He stopped, then sighed wearily. Hardly conscious of what he was doing, he reached out and took her hand. "Do you think Joshua is happy, Melissa?"

Her eyes widened perceptibly. "Joshua? Why, yes, I do."

"I do too. What he is doing is really exciting. Freighting, shipping goods by riverboat, bringing in cotton from the South, partners in a textile mill in St. Louis."

Melissa had to fight not to stare at him. Choosing her words carefully, she went on. "Yes, I think Joshua finds great satisfaction in what he is doing."

"Yes. And you can tell he's prospering very much too."

She looked at him through lowered eyelids. "I think you could be very good at doing something like that, Carl," she ventured softly.

He looked at her, but made no response. He was lost in his own thoughts. Then abruptly he said, "Well, I've got to make a decision on one of these carriages." He turned back to the table and opened the book again.

For the next two or three minutes, Melissa forced herself to concentrate on carding the flax, but she couldn't keep her eyes from constantly rising to stare at her husband. Finally she could bear it no longer. She knew that wisdom's way would be to let it rest for a time, but then, this opportunity might not come again soon. She folded her work up and set it aside, then stood and walked over to stand behind him. She put her hands on his shoulders and began to massage them. He didn't look up, but she could tell he had stopped reading.

"Carl?"

"What?"

"What if you wrote Joshua?"

Once again his head jerked up. "Write to him? What would I say?"

She shrugged, trying to keep her voice casual. "Oh, I don't know. Just write to him. Tell him how things are going here."

He shook his head with quick, abrupt jerks, and she knew instantly that he was right. What was there to say? He would never propose something like what she was thinking.

She leaned down and kissed him on the cheek. "Just a thought. Well, I'm going to get ready for bed."

"All right. I'll be just a few more minutes here, then I'll be up."

She nodded and moved away. As she reached the stairs, she stopped again. Keeping her voice in a half-musing tone, she said, "I've got to write Caroline and thank her for all she did for me and Sarah while we were out there."

He turned to look at her. She took a quick breath. "Would you mind if I just mentioned some of this to her?" She went on hastily. "I'd be very careful about what I said."

For what seemed like forever, Carl peered at her, his brow half-furrowed. Then, to her amazement and delight, he shrugged. Trying to be as nonchalant as she had been, he said, "No, I suppose that would be all right."

She could have shouted out loud, but she just nodded. "I'll do that tomorrow."

Once inside her bedroom, Melissa shut the door quietly. She went right to the dressing table, opened the drawer, and removed the patriarchal blessing. Moving slowly to the bed, she opened the paper and smoothed it against her leg. Her eyes dropped to the one paragraph she had read so many times earlier that afternoon.

Sister Rogers, one of the great blessings of your life has been the family of your birth. Like Nephi, you have truly been born of goodly parents, and they have been like a shield and a refuge for you. Draw near to them. Do not let those family bonds come undone, and they will prove to be a blessing to you and to your children and to your children's children. Your father is a noble bearer of the priesthood. Your mother is a woman of great faith. They have much to give to you and much to give to your children. Stay close to them. Learn from them. Care for them in their needs.

She folded the paper carefully, then dropped to her knees beside the bed. Listening with one ear for Carl's footsteps in the hall, for the first time in many months she began to pray.

———•———

Emma sat back, her heart pounding a little, not daring to hope or believe. "Tell me again, Don Carlos. Start right from the beginning and tell me everything again."

Joseph's youngest brother took a deep breath. He was not impatient. He fully understood what this meant to his sister-in-law.

"All right," he began, talking more slowly now, fighting the temptation to let it all come out in a great rush as he had the first time. "As you know, a while ago my father sent Brother Lamoreaux to Missouri to see if he could get any word of Joseph's and Hyrum's whereabouts. Then Mama and young Lucy got very ill."

Emma nodded. They had not known if Mother Smith was going to live through her bout with cholera. It had been a frightening time for the family.

"Then earlier today, Brother Isaac Morley and Bishop Partridge came to the house to inquire if my parents had had any word from Brother Lamoreaux. They had not, but even as they were speaking with my mother, word came to the house that Brother Lamoreaux had returned but had had no luck in getting any word of our brothers. That, of course, was a great disappointment to everyone. Bishop Partridge was in despair. He said that he would go himself and not return until the information was obtained."

"Yes," Emma prompted when he paused a little, trying to remember all that his mother had told him.

"Mother listened to him for a moment, and then surprised the bishop and Brother Morley when she said something like this to them, 'It is all right. The Spirit, which has so often comforted my heart, speaks peace to my soul now. The Spirit whispers that I shall see Joseph and Hyrum before the sun sets tomorrow.'"

Emma shot forward. That was the part that had stunned her before. "Are you sure that's exactly how she said it?"

Don Carlos nodded emphatically. "I asked Mama specifically. She said, 'I shall see them before the sun sets tomorrow.'"

Emma sat back, feeling her pulse racing again.

"Brother Partridge was visibly upset, according to Mama. 'No, Mother Smith,' he said, 'I am perfectly discouraged. I fear we shall never again see your sons in this life. I have always believed you before, but I cannot see any way this prophecy could be fulfilled.'"

"And what did Mother Smith say to that?"

"She told me she just smiled. Bishop Partridge was ready to leave and go find out for himself, but Mother made him promise he would at least wait until tomorrow to see if her words were true or false. And he did agree to do that. It was just a while later that I arrived. Mother told me all about it and asked me to come and tell you."

Emma nodded, her hands clasped together, her eyes glowing. "Before the sun sets tomorrow. Oh, Don Carlos, could it possibly be true?"

Don Carlos was twenty-three and had two children of his own. He understood her longings. "One part of me wants to respond like Bishop Partridge, Emma. I think, could this possibly be true? Is it just a mother's yearnings for her missing sons? And then, I think of my mother. She is a woman of great faith. We have all seen that faith exercised again and again. And when I think of that, then I say, how can it possibly not be true?"

Emma was nodding slowly. He had captured her own tumult of feelings perfectly. It was too wonderful to be true. They had not the slightest shred of evidence that it could be true. But if Mother Smith said it . . . From the day of Joseph's betrayal and imprisonment, rumors had jerked Emma's emotions back and forth like a wild horse dragging a sack of straw. She had received letters from Joseph since he had been taken to Liberty Jail, and those had cheered her immensely, but the rumors still persisted. Joseph was dead. Joseph was free. Joseph had been shot. Joseph was deathly ill. The governor had given him a pardon. The governor had sentenced him to death. Emma knew full well the bitter disappointment that followed when, after reports of good news, she let her hopes rise and then learned that the reports were false.

But this. This was something more than rumor. She stood and held out her hands to her brother-in-law. "Thank you, Don Carlos. And thank Mother Smith for being kind enough to send me word of her feelings."

<hr />

Dimick B. Huntington was at the Quincy ferry by seven o'clock in the morning. Just three years younger than the Prophet, Dimick was a trusted friend to Joseph and Emma Smith. About seven months before when the troubles in northern Missouri were just beginning, at a time when testifying for the Mormon leaders was a deadly risk, Dimick had gone to Daviess County, Missouri, and served as a witness for the defense of Joseph Smith and Lyman Wight. And just two months earlier when Emma had come across the ice with her four children, Dimick had learned of her arrival and was instrumental in helping her find a room at Judge Cleveland's house a few miles east of town. So it had come as no surprise when Emma sent for him the previous afternoon and asked if he would come down to the Quincy ferry and spend the day. There was perhaps news coming out of Missouri, and she was anxious to learn of it and if it was true.

Dimick sat on the grass a few yards from the riverbank, chewing on a blade of grass. To the casual observer, it might have looked like he was dozing. But from beneath the hooded eyes, he watched the first ferryload from Missouri approaching. It came slowly, the ferryman and his son pulling steadily on the rope. On board there was only one wagon and team, but there was a small crowd of people and two horses at the back. Dimick sat up straighter and squinted his eyes. One or two of the people might be Quincy folk, gone across the river for trading purposes, but some were unmistakably Mormons. A father shepherded four children while a mother held a baby to her breast. Their clothes were caked with mud and torn in two or three places. And they had that haunted look that Dimick knew so well.

He stood up and sauntered toward the ferry as it came in close to the shore. But even before he reached it, he saw that there were no familiar faces, no eyes suddenly widening in recognition. He hung back, disappointed a little, even though he wasn't exactly sure what he was supposed to be waiting for. As the team drove off and the people disembarked, they were barely aware of him. The Quincyites simply moved off the ferry and up the street, eager to get home. The others were too excited and filled with enthusiasm to pay him any more than a quick, sidelong glance. They had left Missouri. They were safe at last.

Dimick was about to go back to his place and wait for the next ferry when he abruptly stopped. The last three getting off the ferry were men. They were leading the two horses. All bearded, with clothes even more filthy and tattered than those of the rest, they moved slowly, as though they were infinitely tired; nevertheless their eyes were filled with a quiet joy.

The first was dressed in an old pair of boots, scuffed and with several holes in the toes and along the sole. The pants, tucked into the boots, were torn in several places, one hole large enough to show bare leg. The man himself wore a dark blue

cloak with the collar turned up around his neck. A wide-
brimmed black hat was jammed upon his head, the sagging brim
putting his face in shadow. He had a growth of light beard, the
same color as the hair beneath the hat. He wasn't looking at
Dimick. He was staring up to where the city of Quincy filled the
the bluffs behind him. His eyes were a startling blue against the
full beard and the haggard face.

Dimick stepped forward slightly, staring keenly at the man.
It was the eyes that drew his gaze.

The second man was a step or two behind his companion,
coaxing one of the horses off the boat. He turned and saw Dimick gazing at them. With a slight smile, he reached out and
touched the first man's arm. The first man turned and looked at
his companion; then, following the slight inclination of the second man's head, he turned and looked at Dimick. Slowly a
weary smile broke through the growth of beard. "Dimick? Dimick Huntington?"

Dimick was barely breathing, his eyes gaping at what his
mind refused to accept. *"Brother Joseph?"*

The morning had surely been the longest of Emma's life.
She stood at the window of the Cleveland home, peering down
the road that led to the city. For the hundredth time, there was
nothing, and the disappointment pierced her through again.

Before the sun sets tomorrow.

She hadn't had the heart to tell the children, for if it proved
not to be true, it would be devastating. So she had thrown herself into a frenzy of activity to help pass the time.

With desultory strokes, she began sweeping the floor for the
fourth time in an hour. But in a few moments, as inexorably as
if pulled by a rope, she moved back to the window.

Emma started slightly, then leaned forward to peer through
the thin curtain. There were two men approaching, one on
horseback, the other walking beside him. She couldn't see the
one on foot, because he was half-hidden behind the horse. The

man on the horse was shabbily dressed, wore a beard, and slouched down as though he had had too much to drink. She felt a quick stab of discouragement and started to turn away. But at that moment the horse lowered its head, reaching out for a spear of grass along the roadside, and Emma saw that the man walking beside the horse was Dimick Huntington.

With a quick intake of breath, she leaned forward, staring now at the man on the horse. Her hand flew to her mouth and instantly there were tears in her eyes. She dropped the curtain and turned and yelled. "Julia! Joseph! Come quickly. Bring the boys."

And then she was out the door and running down the walk, her hair flying, her arms outstretched. "Joseph! Joseph! Joseph!"

Joseph was dismounting the horse and reaching for the gate when Emma came exploding out of the house. He looked up in surprise, then dropped the horse's reins. In two great strides he met her halfway, catching her up, whirling her around, then crushing her to him. There was a great sob of joy, a sound wrenched from the depths of his being. "Oh, Emma!" he cried. "My beloved Emma!"

Without a word, Dimick Huntington took the reins, turned, and moved quietly away.

"Papa?"

Emma pulled free and turned. Julia would turn eight years of age in a week. She was one of the twins (her twin brother having died seven years back) whom Joseph and Emma had adopted when Emma's twins died at birth. She was holding baby Alexander, born the previous summer in Far West. Julia was staring at her father, not quite sure who this tattered-looking stranger was who was hugging and kissing her mother.

Emma laughed through her tears. "Julia, it's your father."

Young Joseph came out the door, holding Frederick's hand. He too stopped to stare. Young Joseph was six now; Freddy, as his siblings called him, would be three in June. Young Joseph recognized his father instantly. There was a cry of joy. Joseph dropped to one knee and held out his arms. His namesake left his brother standing in the doorway and ran pell-mell to leap into them.

Now Julia believed. She came as quickly as she could, handing the baby to her mother, then fell on top of her father and brother, laughing and squealing as Joseph lost his balance and they all went tumbling.

"Come, Frederick," Emma said, beckoning with an encouraging smile. "It's Papa."

Gingerly, very tentatively, he moved toward her. Joseph sat up, sobering. He reached up and stroked the beard. "Don't let this fool you, son," he said. "It really is Papa. Come on."

With a gentle shove from his mother, Frederick finally gave in. Emma watched through her tears as father and children were reunited. He laughed and tickled and hugged and kissed, stood them back away from him to marvel at their growth. They were jumping up and down, all speaking at once, trying to tell him of all that happened since they had last seen him.

Finally Joseph stood, looking at the baby. He came forward slowly, young Joseph holding on to his coat, Julia on the other side, Frederick's hand in his. Alexander saw him coming and turned to bury his face against his mother's shoulder. "I can't believe it," Joseph said softly to Emma. "Can this really be my little Alex?" Alexander had been five months old when Joseph was arrested and taken prisoner. Now he was a husky toddler. "Is he walking yet?"

Emma smiled. "Not yet, Joseph. He's only ten months old. But watch." She stepped back and lowered the baby to the ground, holding on to one hand to steady him. "Show Papa how strong you are, Alex."

His fear forgotten, the baby began moving forward, tugging against his mother's hold. Joseph watched for a minute, tears streaming unashamedly down his cheeks. Then he reached out and swept the baby up in his arms. Alexander gave a startled howl, then began wailing, hands outstretched toward his mother in desperation. Joseph just spun him around, laughing and crying all together. "I'm back, Alex. Papa is back."

Except for a brief visit to see their parents—a visit, incidentally, which took place in the afternoon, thus fulfilling Mother Smith's prophecy that she would see her sons before the sun set—Joseph and Hyrum spent the first night of their return with their own families in a sweet and joyous reunion. The next day, while word of their return spread like a fall prairie fire, the entire Smith family—Mother and Father Smith, young Lucy, Sophronia and her family, Catherine and her family, Don Carlos and his family, William and Samuel and their families, and, of course, Joseph and Hyrum and their families—gathered at the home of Father and Mother Smith. More than thirty people were there. Children were everywhere. There were four under a year. Several were still toddling. Hyrum had both the oldest in Lovina (now almost twelve and born of his first wife, Jerusha) and the youngest in Joseph Fielding (born to him and Mary the previous November while Hyrum was in jail). To an outsider, the gathering at the Smiths' might have seemed like a cross between chaos and pandemonium, but to the family it was a time of rejoicing, the likes of which they had not seen in a long time.

Joseph's time alone with his family didn't last long. By afternoon a long line of well-wishers snaked its way from the house out through the front gate and half a block down the street. Still pale and visibly weak, Joseph greeted them all. It was as though their presence rejuvenated him, and rather than tiring, he drew strength from each one. Soon he was laughing and joking with them, sweeping younger children into his arms, dropping to one knee to solemnly shake hands with some of the older ones, slapping a brother on the shoulder, taking a sister's hands in his and sharing a joyful tear or two together. Joseph was back, and it was as if a great pall had been blown away in an instant. The Steeds were there by midafternoon, waiting their turn to greet their prophet.

"Brother Benjamin," Joseph said, reaching out to take Benjamin's hand in a firm grip, "how wonderful to see you again."

"How wonderful to see you!"

"How are you, old friend?" Joseph said, concern filling his eyes.

"Good, good!" Benjamin replied. He tried to answer in a booming voice, but it came out considerably less than that. "I'm getting stronger all the time."

Joseph looked over Benjamin's shoulder at Mary Ann. She nodded tentatively, but no one had to tell Joseph that it was not the old Benjamin Steed standing before him.

Joseph's voice was suddenly husky. "We nearly lost you in that jail down in Richmond."

"If it hadn't been for that blessing you gave me," Benjamin said gravely, "I wouldn't be here today."

"I was only the Lord's mouthpiece," Joseph smiled. "It was the Lord's blessing." He let go of Benjamin's hand and moved to Mary Ann. "Dear Mary Ann, how good to see your face again."

Tears instantly sprang to her eyes as she took his hand. "Oh, Joseph, we can't believe you're finally free. We've prayed for so long . . ." She couldn't finish.

He gathered her into his arms. "I felt those prayers. I felt all of the prayers of the Saints for us. Well, obviously, the Lord heard those prayers. Without him, we would not have made it."

Now he turned to the others. "Lydia, how are you? Where is Nathan?"

She took his proffered hand. "He went with Brother Brigham and the Twelve back to Far West."

"Of course," he exclaimed. "How like Nathan." He saw the quick shadow of fear in her eyes. "Do not despair," he said. "They will be all right. The Lord is pleased with what Brigham is doing, and he will watch over them."

The relief washed across her face. "Thank you, Joseph."

The Prophet turned slowly to face Jessica. He stepped forward, putting his arm around her shoulder. "I heard about Brother John, Sister Griffith. What a loss for you, and what a loss for us. He was a good man."

Jessica could only nod.

"I saw Amanda Smith earlier and learned of the marvelous things that you and she went through together. How is your hand?"

She held it up. On the palm was a near-perfect circle of purple scar tissue. "It's fine now, thank you. The ball went through cleanly and didn't do too much damage."

His head bobbed slowly, acknowledging all that her simple statement entailed. "The Lord has not forgotten you, Sister Jessica." She looked up at him, in surprise. "The Lord is well aware of your sacrifice and your faithfulness. And he has not forgotten you."

He greeted Rebecca and inquired about the coming birth. He asked about Derek and Peter. He turned back to Mary Ann when he learned that Matthew had gone west to help bring the rest of the Saints out of Missouri and gave her calm reassurances about her son's safety. He greeted the children one by one, calling each by name and inquiring after their welfare. He asked about Joshua and Caroline. Benjamin watched it all and marveled. It was as though there weren't another person around or another demand on his time. This was Joseph. No wonder they loved him. Not only was he the Lord's anointed, but this was a man of tremendous personal warmth and great charm. And the power of it lay in the fact that he cared. There was never any question about that. Joseph cared.

"I'd say it's gusting to seven or eight, Cap'n." The first mate of the *Bostonia* was yelling into his captain's ear to make himself heard.

The captain of the packet ship looked upward, hunching his back against the droplets of salt water whipping in almost horizontally against his oilers. Had it been in their faces, it would have stung like pebble-size hail. The sails were as taut as the skin on a pig and strained to their limits. The wind sounded like a woman in travail as it howled across the spars and through the rigging. "Maybe even a nine or ten," he grunted.

"Shall we prepare to strike the sails?"

"Not yet. Let her run, as long as it doesn't get any worse."

The mate gripped the huge spoked wheel that controlled the rudder of the ship. The ship was just cresting a wave. It poised there for a moment, the bow pointing upward, ten feet of keel exposed to the open air. Then it plunged precipitously downward. It shuddered from stem to stern as the prow caught the next wave and dug in deep enough that for a moment it looked as though the whole ship would be buried in the boiling seas. But then the nose lifted, water cascaded across the decks, and she was running up the next massive swell.

In 1805, Sir Francis Beaufort, rear admiral in the British navy, had developed the "Beaufort scale." Ranging from zero to seventeen, the numbers were used to define the effects of various winds on a sailing vessel. Zero meant a perfect calm. The smoke from cooking fires rose vertically in that condition. Two indicated a wind defined as "that in which a well-conditioned man-of-war, with all sail set, and clean full, would go in smooth water from one to two knots." Wind labeled with the number twelve meant a gale "which no canvas can withstand." Twelve to seventeen were all hurricane-force winds.

Captain Jonathan Sperryman wasn't worried about the wind going much higher. This was not hurricane season in the Atlantic. They were in the middle of a very intense spring storm, as intense as he'd seen in several crossings, but this was a solid ship and the canvas was strong. And with the wind coming almost straight out of the west, they were making good time. They could cut several hours—or more if it continued long enough—off their time. Some of the crew would be sick—were already sick—but they'd come out of that soon enough.

Suddenly he leaned forward, peering intently up the mainmast. It was seven o'clock in the evening, and with the heavy storm clouds, it was fast approaching full dark. But he could see two figures up on the second spar, working together to lash down some loose rigging.

"Who's that up there with Jiggers?" he shouted.

The first mate didn't even look up. He had watched the two go up earlier. "Steed," he called back.

The captain's eyebrows lifted. "Steed? I thought he was off watch."

"He is. He was up on deck watching the storm. Saw Jiggers going up. Said he wanted to learn more about fixin' the riggin'."

"Watching the storm?" Sperryman said in surprise.

The first mate, whose name was O'Malley, grinned. "Yeah. He was leaning into the wind like a hound sniffing out a fox. Said he loved the feel of the ship doing battle with the sea."

The captain stood there for a moment, staring up at the two shapes that were nearly lost in the rain and darkness. Fixing the rigging on a spar in the midst of a force-ten wind was not a task for the weak of heart.

"He's a natural sailor, that one," the officer said with undisguised admiration. "Fifteen years or not. I wish we had a dozen more like him."

The captain nodded absently, remembering that he had said something similar to the boy as they were approaching the port of New York. "You want some coffee?"

"Aye, sir. Thank you, sir."

"I'll bring it out." Pulling the collar of his oilskin raincoat up around his face, Sperryman turned and started away. Just as he reached the door that led to the galley, he stopped again and turned. For several moments he stood there, looking up at the mainmast; then, with a shrug, he stepped through the door and out of the storm.

Chapter Notes

Joseph and Hyrum and the other prisoners arrived in Quincy on Monday, 22 April, the day following Lucy Mack Smith's remarkable prophecy. The night after Mother Smith told Edward Partridge her sons would be returning, she had a dream in which she saw them out on the prairie. They were so weak they could hardly stand, and she awoke, grieving that she could not help them. Father Smith tried to calm her and tell her it was just from being overwrought, but she found it impossible to rest; her sons were still before her eyes, and she saw them sleep for a time and then struggle forward on their journey. She rose from her bed and remained awake throughout the rest of the night, determined that she had been shown a vision of her sons. In the morning she again told people that Joseph and Hyrum would arrive that day before the sun set. After their return and the family was gathered together, Mother Smith described to Joseph and Hyrum what she had seen, and they confirmed in every particular that that was exactly what they had been going through that night at the time of the dream. (See *Mack Hist.*, pp. 300–302.)

The depiction of Joseph and Hyrum's arrival in Quincy is based on the account given by Dimick B. Huntington, who was the first to see the Prophet at the ferry landing (see *CHFT*, p. 215; *Nauvoo*, p. 26).

While Joseph and Hyrum were happily being re-united with their families and friends in Quincy, about two hundred miles west of Quincy a reunion of a different sort was taking place. Just after sunset, Brigham Young and those travel-ing with him approached Tenny's Grove, a stand of trees about twenty-five miles southeast of Far West. Immediately they saw the train of wagons scattered among the trees. It was what they had been watching and waiting for for several days—the rescue party from Quincy had found the group that comprised nearly all of the remaining Saints from Far West.

At a run, Nathan started toward the camp, shouting out Matthew's name. He found him and the Ingalls brothers about ten wagons back, and in moments there was enough back slap-ping among Derek, Peter, Nathan, and Matthew to send clouds of dust puffing out from trail-weary clothing.

It was a substantial group that camped that night. There

were fourteen wagons and about thirty-six families from Far West. They had come southeast to Tenny's Grove, far enough to be safe from their enemies in Daviess County, then stopped to wait for the rescue party to reach them. Adding Brigham's party to that group made well over a hundred and fifty people in the camp. The arrival of Brigham and five other members of the Quorum of the Twelve from out of nowhere was a wonderful surprise to the gathering of Saints and a tremendous boost to the spirits of the camp. The euphoria was heightened by Brigham's announcement that the Twelve, after their brief stop at Far West, would return to Tenny's Grove and accompany the families to Quincy.

Only five members of the Quorum of the Twelve had left Quincy, but a couple days before, they had come across John F. Page on the trail and Brigham had convinced him to accompany them back to Far West. That made six. But Nathan had expected there would be seven.

"Where's Heber?" he asked Derek the first chance he got.

Derek looked surprised. "Didn't you know? He'll be at Far West, waiting for Brigham to come."

"What?"

"That's right. He said the Twelve would be coming, and despite the danger and the threats from the mob, he'll be at Far West to meet the brethren when they arrive."

Nathan exhaled slowly. So with Heber there would be seven of the Twelve. More than a majority. It didn't surprise him. Heber C. Kimball had the same rock-hard determination to do what the Lord asked that Brigham did. But it did sober Nathan greatly. If Brigham hadn't been absolutely insistent that they come, it would have been just one member of the Twelve standing in the main square of Far West on the twenty-sixth. He put an arm around Matthew. "Come on. Let's get your families settled for the night, and then we need to talk."

"You're absolutely positive that Rebecca is all right?"

Nathan smiled, pleased to see the anxiety in his brother-in-law's eyes. "Rebecca is fine. The last thing she said to me as I left was to tell you not to worry. This baby is going to wait until his father is home before he makes his debut into the world."

"*His* father!" Matthew smiled. "That's what Derek keeps telling us, that it's going to be a boy, but I'm betting on a girl."

"Me too," Peter said.

"I don't care what it is, as long as Rebecca and the baby are all right," said Derek.

They all nodded at that. Death of the mother or the child— or both!—was far too common an occurrence in nineteenth-century America. To have both come through in good condition was always a blessing to be accepted with great humility.

As they fell silent again, Matthew looked around. Brigham Young and the other members of the Twelve were a few yards off, huddled around a fire together in council with members of the Committee on Removal, getting a full report. Brigham had announced that the Twelve would be leaving at first light.

Matthew turned back to Nathan, who was staring into their fire. "You're not one of the Twelve, Nathan."

Surprised that Matthew had sensed his thoughts, he nodded. "I know."

Derek was watching Nathan closely now too. "We could use some help here, looking after these families' needs."

"I know that too." Nathan picked up a buffalo chip from the stack behind him and tossed it onto the fire. The embers flared and sent a spiral of sparks up into the night. "Look," he said, facing them both. "I don't know why, but at the meeting where Brigham first discussed this, I felt quite strongly that I should go. That hasn't changed."

"Then I think you need to go," Peter said simply.

Nathan was touched by Peter's firmness. Peter had been there in Far West. He had faced the lust-filled mobbers and stood between them and the Steed women. He had been shot at, hit with a rifle butt, nearly killed. And still he did not flinch.

Derek finally saw it too. "It will be very dangerous. They're waiting for you. Be careful."

Nathan pulled a face. "Thankfully, Brigham isn't out to prove anything with the mob. He says we're going in after midnight, getting the business done, and getting out again as quickly as possible. And we'll all be glad for that."

He took a deep breath. "There's something else," he said slowly. "When we're done in Far West, I may join you and the others for part of the trip east, but I won't be going straight back to Quincy with you."

As he expected, that really caught them by surprise. "What?" Derek blurted. "Why not?" Matthew asked. "How come?" Peter asked.

"I'm going to St. Louis." Nathan smiled at them in the firelight. Their expressions said it all.

"St. Louis?" Peter echoed.

"To see Joshua and Caroline?" Matthew cried.

"Shhh!" Nathan soothed, afraid they would awaken some of the children sleeping in the wagons and tents around them. "Yes, to see Joshua and Caroline."

"But why?"

Nathan hesitated for a moment. This had not come quickly. Nor easily. He had thought about it constantly for the past three days. He knew it would be a bitter disappointment to Lydia when he did not return with the others. But after turning it over and over, looking at it from every possible angle, he knew what needed to happen. So he began to speak slowly and with determination. "First of all, I want to know if they have found Will."

"Oh yes," Matthew breathed. "We have all wondered about that."

"But it's more too. We're out of Missouri now. Or nearly so. Once this business in Far West is done, it's over. This part of our lives is over."

"So?" Matthew broke in, not helped by that answer at all.

"For these past eight months, about all we've had time to think about was surviving. Well, now it's time to consider getting on with our lives." Nathan paused for a moment before going on. "Do you remember last fall when Lydia and I suggested we have a family council?"

"Yes, I remember," Matthew said. "We talked about sticking together as a family."

"More than just sticking together, Matthew," Nathan said. "We're talking about working together, planning together, putting our resources together so we can become stronger."

Derek's voice was sober. "And you think it's time for that?"

"I do," Nathan said firmly. "And when I told Brigham what I was thinking, he agreed. If I make my way down to the Missouri River and catch a riverboat, I can save several days over what it would take if I went back to Quincy and then down to St. Louis."

Derek leaned forward, staring into the fire. "Do you think Joshua would be willing to come in with us?"

Nathan thought about that. "I didn't used to, but now, I'm not so sure. If he doesn't, we can do it ourselves."

Peter grinned. "But not nearly so easily, right?"

They all laughed at that. "Yes," Nathan chuckled, "Joshua does have a bit more capital than any of us right now. But that's not really it. It's getting him and Caroline up with our family. Having Olivia and Savannah, and Will when they find him. That's what really matters." He stood up. "And that's what I'd like to propose to Joshua."

Derek's head bobbed quickly. "Give them our love."

"I will." He frowned slightly. "And will you help Lydia understand why I'm doing all this?"

"Of course."

———◆———

The night was perfectly still except for the soft hum of the crickets and an occasional hoot from some unseen barn owl out in front of them. They moved carefully, strung out in single file, staying off the hard-packed dirt of the road so their footsteps would be muffled. Their heads moved constantly, eyes searching the moonlit landscape for any movement, ears straining to catch any sounds that might signal danger.

Nathan looked up at the moon. It was nearly full and seemed to be twice as large as normal. It felt like they were walking in broad daylight. He smiled grimly to himself, knowing it was fear that was influencing his perspective. The moon was nearly straight overhead now, which meant it was close to midnight. In a few minutes, if it wasn't so already, it would be the twenty-sixth of April, the day the Lord had appointed for the Twelve to assemble in Far West and leave for their missions.

Ahead of them, now less than a hundred yards away, Nathan could see the first of the buildings of the city. They were silvery and ghostlike in the moonlight and left one feeling slightly eerie. It would be easy to mount an ambush from those abandoned cabins and buildings. Nathan reached up and let his hand rest on the butt of the pistol stuck in his belt, feeling his heart start to pound a little faster.

As they approached within the last thirty or forty paces of the nearest building—a cabin that had been de-roofed—Brigham stopped, raising one hand high so the others could see it. The others stopped instantly as well. They stood there for several moments, frozen into immobility as they scanned the night. Then Brigham cupped his hands to his mouth and there came the soft whistling call of a meadowlark. It was not a particularly good imitation, and the meadowlark was not a nocturnal bird, but it was a far sight better than calling out in a normal voice. Brigham whistled again. After a moment, there was an answering whistle, and ahead of them a figure appeared beside the cabin and waved.

"Heber?" Brigham whispered.

"Yes, it's me. Is that you, Brigham?"

The rush of relief that swept over the party was almost as tangible as the evening breeze. Brigham walked forward swiftly, as a single figure stepped out into the road. Nathan and the others followed, feeling a great wave of triumph. They had made it! Their enemies would surely be here at daybreak, determined to prevent the Twelve—should they be daft enough to attempt a return—from fulfilling the Lord's word. But their enemies were asleep now. And seven of the Twelve were here. By first light, they would be well on their way again.

Brigham and Heber embraced in a back-slapping bear hug. Then Heber broke free and held Brigham at arm's length. "Brigham! Joseph and Hyrum are free!"

It was as though he had fired off a pistol. Everyone was stunned. "What?" Orson Pratt exclaimed.

"It's true, I tell you! They were moving them from Daviess County to Boone County to get a new trial. They let them escape. They'll be in Quincy by now."

"The Lord be praised!" Brigham breathed.

Nathan closed his eyes for a moment, hardly able to believe it could be true. After all these months, Joseph freed and back among the people. Suddenly, Nathan was envious of his family. By now they would have seen Joseph and Hyrum again.

One of the men in Brigham's party caught Heber's eye. "It appears Far West has quite a hold on you, Brother Turley."

Theodore Turley smiled. "Yes. When Brother Clark and I happened upon Brigham and the rest yesterday, we decided to turn and come back with them. I wouldn't miss this for anything."

Heber nodded, turning back to Brigham and the others. "Come," he said, all business now. "We have everyone waiting."

George A. Smith jerked back a little. "Everyone?"

Heber grinned. "Of course. There are about sixteen of us. How can you have a conference without Saints?" He looked at Brigham. "I spent most of the day quietly going around to the few who are left. They're waiting for us now." He laid a hand on his fellow Apostle's shoulder. "Some weren't sure you would come, but I told them Brigham would be here or I personally would carry them out of Far West upon my back."

"Thank you, Heber," Brigham said, his voice touched with gratitude. "It is the Lord's will that we be here, so let's get on with what has to be done."

To Nathan's amazement, it wasn't just men who were wait-- ing for them at Father Clark's house. In spite of the terrible threat, three or four sisters were there, come with their hus- bands to see Brother Brigham and the other Apostles and to be present for this prophetic conference of the Church. They all crowded into the main room of the Clark home, then carefully covered the windows before lighting a single candle at each end of the table.

Even more surprising than the presence of the women was the presence of Orson Hyde. Hyde had been called as one of the first Apostles in the new dispensation, but in the final days of Far West, he wavered. He had been deeply influenced by Thomas B. Marsh's apostasy, and had gone to Richmond when Marsh turned against the Prophet. Nathan's surprise deepened even more when he saw that Brigham was not startled by the presence of his former companion in the Quorum. Heber saw it too and spoke up quickly. "Brigham, I want to speak in behalf of Brother Hyde."

Brigham stepped forward and stuck out his hand. "I received your letter, Orson," he said slowly. "But I'd be pleased to hear Heber's plea in your behalf as well." He turned to Heber. "Speak on."

"A short time ago, Brother Hyde returned to Far West," Heber began. "He came to me penitent and filled with sorrow."

Orson Hyde was watching Brigham's face intently, but was content to let Heber tell his story.

"He said that he had been very ill during those weeks when Brother Marsh set his face against Joseph. He was not in his best state of mind. He realizes it was folly for him to follow after Thomas and has come back to ask what he should do in order to make amends for his error."

Brigham nodded. That had been the thrust of Orson Hyde's letter that Brigham had received just days before they had left Quincy. "I understand."

"He has been running a school down south in order to provide for his family. I told him to close the school, return with his family, and prepare to gather with the rest of the Church to Illinois." Now Heber let his eyes move to the face of each of his fellow Apostles. "He said he was willing to do so, even though it would be difficult for him. He then asked me if I thought that Joseph and the brethren could ever forgive him. I said, 'Yes.'"

Now Heber looked back at Brigham. "I told him I would speak in his defense," he said firmly.

Brigham was silent for several moments, and the room was filled with tension. Then his face softened and he looked at Brother Hyde. "I am pleased to find that the spirit which filled your letter to me is present here tonight as well." He held out his hand again. "Of course we can forgive you."

Hyde's eyes were shining, and he stepped forward and took the proffered hand.

"Welcome back, my brother," Brigham said softly. "When we return to Illinois, we shall put the matter in Joseph's hands as to if and when you should be restored to your place in the Quorum."

"That is all I ask," Hyde said humbly. "It is more than I hoped for."

They stayed at the Clark cabin only long enough to conduct the first order of business, which was the excommunication of thirty-one members of the Church—eighteen men and thirteen women—who had apostatized and turned against the Saints. It was a sobering thing for Nathan. He knew most of those on the list to some degree and many of them well. They were not bad people. They had simply buckled under the tremendous pressures being put on the Church. By renouncing their faith, they had instantly eliminated any threat to themselves. Nathan didn't feel inclined to overlook their loss of faith, but it certainly wasn't difficult to understand what had driven them to it.

It was clear that Brigham found the matter depressing too, for as soon as the consenting vote was taken on the excommunications, he proposed they adjourn and reconvene at the temple site on the public square.

To everyone's surprise Brigham called for the meeting to begin with a hymn. To that point, they had moved in the utmost quiet and communicated only in whispers. They sang softly, many of them looking around furtively as they did so, and then Heber gave the prayer.

"Brethren and sisters," Brigham said with great dignity, "this is an inspiring sight. We are here in direct fulfillment of the Lord's commandments. One of those commandments was that we should here assemble. Today is April twenty-sixth, and let it now be noted that we are here as directed."

There was a soft ripple of sound as several murmured their assent to that statement. There was not a person here but what was aware of what it had cost to bring this assembly to this place at this time.

Brigham waited for a moment, then went on. "The Lord also gave us another commandment, and that was that we build a temple here in Far West. As you know, the cornerstones for that temple were laid July fourth last, under the direction of our beloved prophet, Joseph Smith. We should here like to recommence laying the foundation of that house, which, in a revelation to his prophet, the Lord has commanded take place on this very day. We may never finish this work, but let it not be said that we did not at least begin it."

He turned and motioned a person forward. "We have brought Brother Alpheus Cutler, the man designated to be the builder of that temple, with us for that purpose, and that shall be the first order of business, Brother Cutler."

Alpheus Cutler came forward. He had left Father Clark's early to come ahead of the group and locate a large stone, similar to the ones placed the previous July. Now, calling on several of the brethren, Cutler had them roll the stone to the southeast corner of the temple site, where very carefully, sighting on the line of the previous stones and excavation work, he had them place it. Satisfied, he turned back to Brigham. "It is done, Brother Brigham."

Brigham nodded, then reached inside his pocket and withdrew a sheet of paper. Nathan looked closer and saw that it was the same sheet from which Brigham had read to the priesthood leaders at the conference in Quincy. It was a copy of the revelation given in July of the year before. Turning so as to catch the moonlight better, Brigham looked at the revelation in silence for a moment, then read the first paragraph. "'Verily, thus saith the Lord: Let a conference be held immediately; let the Twelve be organized; and let men be appointed to supply the place of those who are fallen.'"

Nathan looked around for Orson Hyde and saw that he was staring at the ground. Like those referred to in the revelation, he had fallen, but gratefully, he was coming back.

"As you know," Brigham continued, "in that same revelation, the Lord named four to join the Quorum—Brothers John Taylor and John Page, who were ordained last December, and Brothers Wilford Woodruff and Willard Richards. Since the revelation was given, our beloved Apostle and brother David W. Patten gave his life for the kingdom, the first apostolic martyr in this dispensation. Therefore, in addition to those mentioned here, Brother George A. Smith's name has been brought forward and approved for his ordination to the holy apostleship. We should now like to proceed with the ordination of Brother Woodruff and then Brother Smith."

There was a sudden droll smile. "Brother Willard Richards is also awaiting his ordination, but has asked that he might be excused."

That brought an appreciative chuckle. Willard Richards was in England working in the mission there. He would not be ordained until the Twelve reached their destination.

First Wilford and then George A. sat on one of the cornerstones of the temple while their fellow Apostles laid their hands on their heads and ordained them, with Brigham acting as voice for Wilford's ordination, and Heber for George A.'s. When they finished with George A., Brigham again faced the congregated Saints. "Brethren and sisters, since one of our purposes in coming here is to signal the time of departure for the Twelve on a mission across the Atlantic, I would now like to call upon the Twelve to pray with us, in order of seniority. I shall begin."

Nathan knelt down on the damp grass as everyone around him did the same. Brigham moved forward, knelt on the cornerstone, and began. He spoke in a low but firm voice. In moments, it was obvious to everyone present why the Lord had brought Brigham to the place that he now occupied. He spoke with simple humility and yet great power. He poured out his heart in gratitude to the Lord that Joseph and his fellow prisoners were free, and asked that those who were still imprisoned, such as their fellow Apostle Parley Pratt, might be liberated soon. He turned his prayer to the Twelve's upcoming mission, pleading for the Lord's Spirit to be with them as they journeyed to a far-off land to serve the Lord. He prayed for their families, that the Lord would watch over them while their husbands and fathers left to serve the Lord. He asked that each of the Twelve, and any who accompanied them, would be filled with power and humility and that they would serve honorably.

"We know that through this work, O Lord," he continued, "many people shall be brought to a knowledge of the Restoration. Their hearts shall be turned to thee, and they shall enter thy kingdom. It is a time of gathering, O Lord, and the Saints here in the land of America shall be blessed as hundreds, yes, even thousands, shall gather to Zion to join them in the work.

"We know that only with thy power and thy influence can we succeed, O Father. Help us always to keep that in our hearts, to be humble and teachable, willing to submit to whatever thou seest fit to lay upon our shoulders, for only in thy majesty, and only in thy goodness, and only in thy love can we succeed."

Heber Kimball went next, then Orson Pratt. One by one, the seven of them knelt on the cornerstone of the Lord's house and poured out their hearts to God. By the time George A. had finished, a spirit of reverence and gratitude rested upon the group in a manner that left everyone somewhat awed. To Nathan's mind came flooding back memories of the dedication of the Kirtland Temple, the last time he could remember personally witnessing such an outpouring of the Spirit. He felt chills run up and down his back. He could hear women weeping around him. He could sense that all were deeply moved.

When George A. returned to his place, Brigham nodded at his brethren. "Thank you," he said, obviously as touched as everyone else. Then he straightened. "We shall now close by singing another hymn. Hymn number twenty-three." He gave them a stern look. "And we'll have none of this singing as if you're afraid someone is going to hear you."

There were sheepish chuckles and smiles all around.

"The Lord said that his soul delighteth in the song of the heart. We are here by appointment. Let us sing to the Lord, and let us sing worthy of his praise."

Smiling, John Taylor stepped forward, hummed a pitch, then raised his hand.

> This earth was once a garden place,
>   With all her glories common;
> And men did live a holy race,
> And worship Jesus face to face,
>   In Adam-ondi-Ahman.

Any fears of who might be listening seemed to disappear. They sang full throat, but with a sweetness that was like an angel's choir. Once again shivers began coursing up and down Nathan's back. He had to stop twice during the third verse, his voice too choked up to continue.

> Her land was good and greatly blest,
>   Beyond old Israel's Canaan:
> Her fame was known from east to west;
> Her peace was great, and pure the rest
>   Of Adam-ondi-Ahman.

Rebecca and Derek and Peter had moved to Di-Ahman, their sod hut overlooking the sweep of that lovely valley. Now, like Far West, Di-Ahman lay in ruins, abandoned by the Saints and left to whatever covetous eyes should rest upon her.

Nathan swallowed hard, then lifted his head and joyously sang the final verse.

> Hosanna to such days to come—
> The Savior's second comin'—
> When all the earth in glorious bloom,
> Affords the saints a holy home
> Like Adam-ondi-Ahman.

The song finished, but the music hung on the air like the morning mist that sometimes rises from a newly plowed field. After a moment, Brigham stepped forward one last time. "Thank you, brothers and sisters." He glanced up at the moon, which was now halfway down in the sky. "We shall meet back again at Brother Clark's house, where we shall breakfast and be on our way." Once again that quiet little smile stole around the corners of his mouth. "It would probably be judicious if we were to be quit of the city before daybreak. However, there is a little time. Since this will be the last chance we may have to walk the streets of Far West, I suggest you are free to do so. Just watch the time and be back to the Clarks' in no more than half an hour."

———•———

Nathan moved slowly along what had once been one of the main streets of Far West. He reached out with the toe of his boot and kicked at a tuft of grass right in the middle of the street, amazed at what he was seeing in the moonlight. Last fall, the dirt of this street had been packed so hard from wheels and hooves and human feet, that in the late afternoon, when the traffic lessened, young children drew hopscotch courts on it with small pieces of soapstone. Boys bounced rubber balls on it as though it were a hardwood floor. And now grass and weeds were shooting up all through it. In another season or two, it would be barely discernible as a road anymore.

He lifted his eyes. Here and there, Nathan could see a wisp

of smoke coming from a chimney, and he moved very carefully past these places, but mostly, Far West lay in ruins. Though the Missourians coveted the rich farms abandoned by the Mormons, for the most part they were caring for them from their own homesteads. That was partly because the militia set loose by General Lucas had wrought so much devastation. There were few houses and barns that hadn't been unroofed, pulled apart, burned, or vandalized. He guessed that in five or six years, Far West would be like the streets—nothing more than a mound here and there to remind you of what once had been.

He passed his and Lydia's cabin, letting his step slow only a little. It was a shell. The front door was gone completely. Someone had knocked the posts out from under the roof overhang, and it leaned at a crazy angle. There was a gaping hole in the roof where someone had yanked out the cross beams and the sod covering had collapsed. Through the doorway, he could see the moonlight shining inside the house. The memories rushed in upon him. Inside that cabin, Joseph Smith had given the Steed family a sermon on forgiveness, then brought Joshua Steed—alienated for eleven years—in to them to see if they had listened to what he had taught them. There was nothing in the cabin now, except the mounds of sod from where the roof had collapsed.

He moved on, toward the cabin where his father and mother had lived. As he came up on it, he stopped completely. It was a heap now, with only the back wall partially standing. In fury, someone had either pushed the walls in or tied ropes to them and pulled them over with a horse. The recollections of better times continued in Nathan's mind. How many evenings had the family gathered here for dinner and then sat around just to talk? He and John Griffith had sat on the porch and talked about the land and farming and the future. Here Rebecca and Derek had shyly announced their engagement, and had spent the first night of their marriage. Here Nancy McIntire and her girls had announced they wanted to join the Church.

He moved slowly around to the back of the ruined cabin.

Was the reaping machine still there? It had been Joshua's present to his father, brought all the way from St. Louis. The mob had fallen on it in mindless rage. It had been a shattered wreck throughout the winter months. Now it was completely gone.

Nathan moved slowly to the window in the partial back wall and looked through it. There was no house to see into anymore, but he looked anyway. There was nothing left here either. No furniture. No handcrafted cabinet made by Matthew, with the help of Brigham Young, and given to Matthew's mother as a gift. No rugs, no crockery, no beds. Suddenly his eyes were drawn to a hole in the floor, all that was left of the root cellar his father had dug beneath the main floor of the cabin. He shook his head. That was where Peter Ingalls had taken his stand against the ugliness of evil men. That was where Joshua had come in at the last moment and shot one of those men down, winning for himself later a bullet in his back. Will Steed was still lost to the family because of what had taken place here in those few horrible minutes, so the legacy of evil lived on even now.

Nathan turned away from the window, suddenly quite depressed. He looked up at the moon. It was lower in the sky now. The half hour was nearly gone. He moved away swiftly, headed for the Clark cabin. And then, to his surprise, his spirit lifted. What he had said to Derek and Matthew and Peter a few nights back was true. Missouri was behind them now. It was over.

Greatly cheered, he broke into a light trot. They had come to Far West, the task was done, the Lord's commandment fulfilled. It was faces east now and on to a new life.

Chapter Notes

On his way to Far West, Brigham, as he later put it, "helped the Lord fulfill His prophecy." He and the others with him met John E. Page on the trail. Elder Page, who had been ordained an Apostle the previous December, had lost his wife and two children during the extreme hardships of the Missouri persecutions. He remarried shortly before leaving Far West to take his family to safety. When the Twelve found him, his wagon was overturned in a mud hole and the Apostle was up to his arms in soapsuds from a spilled barrel of powdered soap. Brigham asked him to return to Far West with them. Dumbfounded, Page replied that he didn't see that he could do that, since he needed to get his family to Illinois. But Brigham promised him that they were out of the reach of the mobs and that his family would be fine. When Page asked how long he had to get ready, Brigham's answer was simple: "Five minutes." Thus another member of the Quorum returned to Far West to fulfill the Lord's commandment. (See *American Moses*, pp. 71–72; *Revelations*, pp. 232–33.)

The details of the return to Far West and the conference held there during the early morning hours of April twenty-sixth are given in several places (see, for example, *HC* 3:335–40; *LHCK*, pp. 252–53; and *CHFT*, p. 226). The author had to add some detail to the actual conference held at one of the member's homes and at the temple site, but the general outline of events is as they happened, including the singing of "Adam-ondi-Ahman."

John Alpheus Cutler attended the conference at Far West in order to fulfill a revelation given on 26 April 1838. Among other things, this revelation designated the following 26 April—the same date designated, in another revelation, for the Twelve's departure from Far West—as the day on which the Saints were to "re-commence laying the foundation" of the Far West Temple (see D&C 115:11). The work of building the temple had begun with the laying of the cornerstones on 4 July 1838, and, presumably after a winter break, work was to resume on 26 April 1839. Thus, in obedience to this revelation, Alpheus Cutler, as master workman for the temple, recommenced laying the foundation by placing a large stone near the southeast corner of the temple site.

Whether Orson Hyde was actually present for the 26 April conference is not indicated in the histories, but his penitence and his coming to Heber for counsel and help are a matter of record (see *LHCK*, pp. 244–45). Orson Hyde had written a letter to Brigham Young dated 30 March 1839 (see *American Moses*, pp. 71, 447), so the author's assumption is that Brigham had received it before leaving for Far West. Later, Orson Hyde gathered with his family to Illinois, and there, on 27 June 1839, he made his formal confession to the Church and was restored to his office in the Quorum of the Twelve (see *HC* 3:379). He remained faithful thereafter, making his famous trip to the Holy Land in 1841 and dedicating it for the return of the Jews.

The Prophet's history tells of an interesting event that happened after the 26 April conference as Brigham and the others prepared to leave Far

West and return to Illinois. It had to do with Isaac Russell, who had apostatized and left the Church:

"As the Saints were passing away from the meeting, Brother [Theodore] Turley said to Elders Page and Woodruff, 'Stop a bit, while I bid Isaac Russell good bye;' and knocking at the door, called Brother Russell. His wife answered, 'Come in, it is Brother Turley.' Russell replied, 'It is not; he left here two weeks ago;' and appeared quite alarmed; but on finding it was Brother Turley, asked him to sit down; but the latter replied, 'I cannot, I shall lose my company.' 'Who is your company?' enquired Russell. 'The Twelve.' *The Twelve!*' 'Yes, don't you know that this is the twenty-sixth, and the day the Twelve were to take leave of their friends on the foundation of the Lord's House, to go to the islands of the sea? The revelation is now fulfilled, and I am going with them.' Russell was speechless, and Turley bid him farewell." (HC 3:339–40.)

Chapter Six

The Church of Jesus Christ of Latter-day Saints was organized on April sixth, 1830. Part of the instructions given to the Church on that day was that the Saints were to meet in conference on a regular basis. In these "general" conferences, where as many of the members were to be in attendance as possible, the business of the Church was to be conducted.

The last conference of the Church had been held in early October 1838. At that time, the situation in northern Missouri was extremely tense. Joseph Smith, away from Far West on important Church business, was not at the conference, and neither were several other leaders. By mid-October, things were in a crisis; and then, in early November, Joseph Smith and the other members of the First Presidency were arrested and incarcerated. Brigham Young and Heber C. Kimball held priesthood councils, but not regular conferences.

It was not surprising, therefore, that one of the first things Joseph did after his return was to call for a general conference of the Church, the first to be held under the First Presidency's direction since July of the year before. The dates were set for the fourth, fifth, and sixth of May. Perhaps never before had the Saints gathered in conference with greater joy. They were out of Missouri and sheltered by the kindness of the residents of western Illinois. Food, though not abundant, was at least adequate. Their leaders, save a few, had been freed and returned to them. And with all of that, spring had arrived in full blossom. The weather was warm, the air clear, and new life was in evidence everywhere. It was indeed a time for rejoicing.

Joseph Smith stood at the north end of the large field known as the Presbyterian campground, which was a short distance outside of the town of Quincy, Illinois. The field was already half full as Benjamin Steed and his family arrived, and still the Saints streamed in behind them. They came mostly on foot, but a few from the more outlying areas rode in carriages, wagons, buggies, or carts. Joseph saw the Steeds immediately and waved, though he was thronged with well-wishers and greeters. Benjamin waved back; then, turning to Mary Ann, he pointed to an open spot not far from where Joseph was standing. "Let's go up there," he said wryly. "I know your hearing isn't as good as it used to be."

Mary Ann looked startled for a minute; then as her family laughed, she chuckled too. Benjamin's ears were just beginning to lose their sharpness, and it galled him terribly. To have him admit to it, even if it was in such an offhand way, was significant progress. "All right," she teased him back. "If you're sure that's close enough for me."

There were eleven of them in all as they spread their blankets and settled in. Derek, Peter, and Matthew had returned with the Twelve and the last of the Saints from Missouri the day before, which brought the number of adults to eight. Only Nathan was not there. Jessica and Lydia had secured two girls from a neighbor to look after the smaller children, so there were only three there from the second generation—Jessica's Rachel and Lydia's Emily and young Joshua.

Mary Ann looked around. The Saints who had arrived sat on the grass, they sat on stools, they sat on nearby doorsteps and porches. Some who lived closest had brought chairs. Many more stood, leaning against the side of a wagon, or just holding the reins of their teams, shifting their weight back and forth. But whatever their position or their comfort, the Saints had come to sit at the feet of their prophet, and they were ready to be taught. Here and there a baby fussed a little, but even smaller children seemed content to play quietly around their parents' feet.

A small table with three chairs was set just behind Joseph. This would be the pulpit. At 11:14, Joseph turned to Hyrum and to Sidney Rigdon and waved them to their chairs.

"Good," Derek said to Rebecca, "he's going to start on time." Derek admired promptness, but some Church members lacked the same attitude. And it irritated him when some of the leaders would then delay the beginning of the meeting to wait for the latecomers. He had once dourly observed to Peter that some of the greatest time wasters in the world were Mormons who came to a meeting on time.

As the three members of the First Presidency took their seats and the crowd noise dropped off sharply, Benjamin was stirred deeply. The last time he had seen all three of these men together was lying on the floor, chained together, in a Richmond, Missouri, jail.

At precisely 11:15, Joseph nudged Sidney and he stood and called the meeting to order. The quiet swept across the multitude as though someone were spreading out a blanket over the sound. Sidney raised his hands. "Brethren and sisters," he cried, "how good it is to be assembled again with you in conference! I would propose that the first order of business be to appoint Joseph Smith, Junior, as the chairman of this conference. All in favor."

Thousands of hands lifted.

"Any in opposition to that proposal?" He paused and looked around. Not a single hand went up. "Thank you. We shall sing a hymn and begin the meeting with prayer. Then our beloved Brother Joseph shall address us."

When Joseph arose after the hymn and the prayer, he rose slowly. It had not been quite two weeks since his return to the Saints, but already Benjamin could see the color and strength returning to him. He was still down at least ten or fifteen pounds from his normal weight, but the deep weariness and the gauntness were almost gone.

Joseph looked out over the assembly as the quiet became even deeper. Then he smiled, a deep, broad smile of complete satisfaction. "Brothers and sisters," he said loudly, so that his voice would carry. "I cannot tell you what feelings fill my heart at this moment as I look out upon your faces on this beautiful spring morning. I have much to say to you. I have longed for the opportunity to say it for many months now. At last, through the providence of the Lord, I am able to take fellowship with you. We—and I include all of us who were in prison these last months—thank you for your prayers in our behalf. Let us not forget to continue to pray for Brother Parley Pratt and his companions who are yet locked up in that miserable dungeon in Richmond. May the Lord soften the hearts of their enemies as he did the hearts of ours."

There was that quick boyish grin that was so much a part of him. "Even Governor Boggs couldn't withstand the power of that many prayers, and we are free at last."

For a moment, Benjamin thought the congregation was going to burst into applause. One certainly felt like it, hearing Joseph again. Behind Joseph, Hyrum and Sidney were smiling at the warm spirit that permeated the crowd. Mary Ann leaned against Benjamin's arm. "Isn't it wonderful to have him back!" she murmured.

Lydia, Jessica, and Rebecca all nodded along with Benjamin. It *was* wonderful!

"I have much in my heart that I would like to say, but first an item of business." He stopped and looked around, letting his gaze sweep across the buildings of the city which were visible from here. "We are filled with gratitude to the good people of Quincy and surrounding towns here in Illinois. They have opened their arms to our people. In dramatic contrast to the actions of the Missourians, they have accepted us with kindness and charity. We shall everlastingly be in their debt, and I hereby say that the angels of heaven have recorded their deeds for all the eternities to read."

Heads all over the congregation were bobbing up and down. Because of the goodness of the people of Quincy, disaster had been averted. Lives had been spared. The Saints had respite.

"But Quincy cannot be our home," Joseph was saying now. "Our numbers are too great, our needs too numerous. We must have a place we can call our own. We must have a place where the Saints can gather." His eyes took on a certain fierceness now. "God is not through with this people yet. He has a great work for us yet to perform. Many of you still live in the most wretched of conditions. You have no homes. You have no possessions. You live out in the sun and sleep under the stars. And that is not God's will for us."

Sunburned faces and blistered lips evident throughout the congregation bore silent witness to the reality of Joseph's words. The Steeds had been richly blessed, primarily because of Joshua's prosperity and generosity, but far more typical were those who dwelt in ragged tents or slept out in the open fields.

"In the nearly ten years since this church was organized," Joseph cried, "we have seen it swell in numbers. There are now thousands of the Latter-day Saints. But this is only a beginning of our destiny. As Daniel foresaw almost twenty-five centuries ago, this church is the stone which is cut out of the mountain without hands, and"—he punched each word now with great emphasis—"*it will roll forth until it fills the whole earth!* Write it down, brothers and sisters! This work is just beginning, and we must carry it forward. We must continue to send our missionaries throughout the world, even in our poverty and want, to proclaim

Conference near Quincy

the gospel to all that will hear. And we must have a place where we can build a temple—"

He stopped, and let the ripples of shock spread across the group. "That's right," he smiled. "God has great things to give us, and only in his house can those things come. It will take great sacrifice and great effort on our part, just as it did in Kirtland, but *we shall have a house of the Lord!* And we must gather together so we can build that house. We must bring scattered Israel from the four corners of the earth so that we can the better accomplish the work and will of God."

Benjamin was watching Sidney Rigdon closely now. His head was down and he was staring at the ground. *Good!* Sidney had come home from his imprisonment several weeks earlier. Immediately he began preaching *against* gathering. It was collecting into large groups that brought down the wrath of the non-Mormons upon them, he said. They must scatter to be safe. It had irritated Benjamin considerably because he was almost certain Sidney did not speak for Joseph on this matter. Nor for the Lord.

"As you know," Joseph went on, "three days after Hyrum and I returned to you, some of the brethren and I went north looking for a place of our own. And we have found one."

Now there was an open buzz of excitement and Joseph had to stop. He waited for it to quiet again, then went on. "We have found a little settlement forty or fifty miles to the north of here called Commerce. Isaac Galland, whom many of you know, has been most valuable in helping us locate land for sale at Commerce and across the river in Iowa Territory. We think the site in the Commerce area, with the blessing of heaven to the Saints, has much promise. It nestles in an elbow of the Mississippi, where the river makes a wide, sweeping bend to the west. This means that our site is bounded by the river on three sides. It is a most beautiful setting."

Matthew was nodding. The day before, he had seen Brother Hyrum at the blacksmith's shop, and Hyrum told him about the sites that Joseph and the others had visited. But Matthew was also a little surprised at the announcement, for Hyrum said there was only one stone house and a few log cabins at Commerce and that much of the site was impassable swampland.

"Brothers and sisters," Joseph said, raising his voice even higher, "I tell you here and now that it is the will of the Lord that we gather to our new home. We are to build a city there. We are to show the world that we have not been beaten down, that we still hold up the banner of liberty to all comers, and that we still worship our God in accordance with his command."

Emma Smith sat on the front row with her two oldest children. Joseph looked down at her and smiled. "Sister Emma and I will be moving to Commerce immediately after the close of this conference. We hope all others will follow our example as soon as they are able."

He stopped for a moment, and his countenance gradually became more somber, though it was not in any way sad. "And now, my dear friends, I feel to address you on some other matters, matters pertaining to our recent imprisonment and other events that have befallen our people." There was a quick, rueful expression. "I have had much time to rehearse what I would like to say to you this morning. The bedbugs and the cockroaches and the mice who inhabit Liberty Jail are perhaps the most preached to creatures on earth right now."

He let the laughter roll, his eyes moving slowly across the faces of the people he loved and who loved him. He turned to Hyrum. "There is no finer people on earth," he said in a voice loud enough for those nearest him to hear. "No finer." Hyrum nodded vigorously in agreement.

As it quieted again, Joseph turned back. "The reports of your sufferings were almost more than we could bear. Oh, how we longed to stand with you in those trying circumstances! But it was not the Lord's will that it should be so. We were in the hands of a hardened people in whom there was to be found very little justice or mercy."

Now there was a quick flash of anger in his eyes. "All the threats, murders, and robberies which the officers of the state of

Missouri have been guilty of are entirely overlooked by the executive of the state, who, to hide his own iniquity, must of course shield and protect those whom he employed to carry into effect his murderous purposes. But notwithstanding their determination to destroy me and those imprisoned with me, and although at three different times we were sentenced to be shot and had the time and place appointed for that purpose, yet through the mercy of God, in answer to the prayers of the Saints, we have been preserved and delivered out of their hands. Once again we enjoy the society of our friends and brethren, whom we love, and to whom we feel united in bonds that are stronger than death. And the Saints now reside in a state where I believe the laws are respected, and whose citizens are humane and charitable.

"During the time I was in the hands of my enemies, I felt great anxiety respecting my family and friends, who were so inhumanly treated and abused, and who had to mourn the loss of their husbands and children who had been slain—"

His voice cut off abruptly and he let his eyes sweep across the congregation, singling out specific individuals. Here was Jessica Griffith, sitting with the Steeds, now a widow because of the events at Haun's Mill. A few feet away was Amanda Smith—a husband and one son dead, another boy with a hip blown away by a mobber's rifle. Further on was Sister Patten, wife of David W. Patten, the President of the Quorum of the Twelve who had been shot at Crooked River and died a short time later. There was John Page, another Apostle. He had buried a wife and two children in Far West, martyrs of a different kind as they succumbed to bitter cold and starvation conditions. There wasn't a soul in the whole congregation who didn't know firsthand the things about which Joseph was speaking.

Joseph went on more slowly now, his voice heavy with emotion. "I have felt great anxiety for those who, after having been robbed of nearly all that they possessed, were driven from their homes, and forced to wander as strangers in a strange country. Yet, despite these anxieties, with regard to the situation that my fellow prisoners and I were in I felt calm, resigned to the will of our Heavenly Father. He has saved us frequently from the gates of death and given us deliverance. And notwithstanding that every avenue of escape seemed to be entirely closed, and death stared us in the face, and that our destruction was determined upon—as far as man was concerned—yet, from our first entrance into the enemy's camp, I felt an assurance that I, with my brethren and our families, should be delivered.

"Yes, that still small voice, which has so often whispered consolation to our souls, in the depths of sorrow and distress, bade us be of good cheer, and promised deliverance. As you can imagine, this gave us great comfort. And although the heathen raged, and the people imagined vain things, yet the Lord of Hosts, the God of Jacob, was our refuge; and when we cried unto him in the day of trouble, he delivered us. For this, I call upon my soul, and all that is within me, to bless and praise his holy name."

"Amen!" someone cried.

"Amen!" responded Joseph heartily.

"Amen!" the congregation roared as one voice.

Rebecca shifted her weight, feeling the hardness of the ground beneath her. "Can I lay my head on your lap?" she asked Derek in a tiny whisper.

"Of course." He helped her stretch out, getting her awkward bigness comfortable again. When she was settled she looked up into his eyes and smiled at him. How glad she was to have him back again. Now the baby could come anytime. She was no longer concerned.

"The conduct of the Saints," Joseph continued, "under their accumulated wrongs and sufferings, has been most praiseworthy. Your courage in defending your brethren from the ravages of the mobs; your attachment to the cause of truth under circumstances that were the most trying and distressing which humanity can possibly endure; your love for each other; your readiness to afford assistance to me and my brethren who were confined in a dungeon; your sacrifices in leaving Missouri, and assisting the poor widows and orphans, and securing them houses in a more hospitable land—all of these conspire to raise you in the estimation of all good and virtuous men. And all of these have secured for you the favor and approbation of Jehovah, and a name as imperishable as eternity. Your virtuous deeds and heroic actions while in defense of truth and your brethren will be fresh and blooming when the names of your oppressors shall be either entirely forgotten or only remembered for their barbarity and cruelty."

Lydia looked down at her children. Emily was playing with the grass at the edge of the quilt, her attention waning, but young Joshua was sitting with his legs crossed, leaning forward, watching Joseph with complete concentration. She reached out and touched his hair. He glanced at her, smiled, then immediately turned back to follow Joseph's words. Lydia watched him proudly. He was so like Nathan, this son of hers. Serious, reflective, and so committed to doing whatever the Lord asked of him. She felt a wave of gratitude and wished Nathan were here so she could tell him that.

Joseph turned now, coughing and holding his chest. Hyrum stood quickly and retrieved a pitcher and a glass from beneath his chair. He poured Joseph some water and handed him the glass. Mary Ann watched in concern as Joseph took three deep swallows, then smiled at his brother and handed the glass back to him. That alone attested to the cost Liberty Jail had wrought upon the Prophet's strength and health. Joseph rarely had to pause while giving a sermon. She had seen him speak for up to two hours without any signs of tiring.

Joseph's face softened. "Thank God we have been delivered. And as for some of our beloved brethren and sisters who have sealed their testimony with their blood, and have died martyrs to the cause of truth—" He stopped and quoted softly from the lines of a hymn. " 'Short though bitter was their pain, Everlasting is their joy.'

"Let us not sorrow as 'those without hope.' " Tears had welled up and now began to trickle down his cheeks. This time he made no effort to stop them. All across the congregation men and women were weeping now too. The words he spoke brought the memories back, keenly, poignantly, powerfully. "The time is coming when the hearts of the widows and fatherless shall be comforted, and every tear shall be wiped from their faces. The trials they have had to pass through shall work together for their good. These trials shall prepare them for the society of those who have come up out of great tribulation and have washed their robes and made them white in the blood of the Lamb."

Benjamin suddenly started. He could hear the weeping all around him. His own wife and children had tear-stained cheeks. But in a flash of insight, he understood something. This was not the weeping of the desolate. There was sorrow for the loss, sorrow for the emptiness, but they were equally tears of joy. Joseph was reminding them of their faith—a faith purged in the fire, a faith which, like steel, came only by way of the forge and the hammer and anvil.

Joseph paused now for a long time, almost a full minute. He seemed not to want the tenderness of the moment to pass too quickly. Weary, he finally went on. "Marvel not, then, that we are persecuted. Remember the words of the Savior: 'The servant is not above his Lord. If they have persecuted me, they will persecute you also.' All the afflictions through which the Saints have to pass are fulfillment of the words of the prophets spoken since the world began." Now his shoulders lifted and his head came up. "My dear brothers and sisters, we have been through much. We have lost much. We have suffered much. But let us never forget that it is the Savior, Jesus Christ, whom we serve. And there is nothing that has come upon us which he himself does not personally know, that he himself has not personally endured. This is why he alone can ask us to forgive our enemies. The Lord does not expect us to completely ignore what happened to us in Missouri. He has commanded us to seek redress from the government. But let not hate fill your hearts for those who have treated us thus. We have been commanded to forgive and leave vengeance in the hands of God. Let us pray for them who despitefully use us, as he said while he was among the children of men. And if we endure our trials well, as he did in every way, he shall lift us up and exalt us on high. And that, my dear friends, is worth the riches of the earth and whatever ridicule the world may heap upon us."

And then in one single burst of clarity, Benjamin Steed saw it. He took a deep breath, and felt the fire down deep in his lungs. He was getting better—slowly—but the pain, the shortness of breath, the maddening lack of strength and energy were still part of his legacy from a sixty-mile forced march in a blizzard and nights without heat in the Richmond jail. Now he and his family were here in Quincy, living in a borrowed house paid for by money borrowed from one of his children. In Kirtland, Benjamin Steed had been comfortably wealthy. He lost it all. Turned his back on it and walked away. In Far West, he and Mary Ann started out with virtually nothing, but within a year, through diligence and hard work, they had a farm and a small but comfortable house. They lost it all! But there was no sadness, no regrets. Instead, he found his spirit soaring with the realization of what it all meant. When his life was over he would be called to stand and be judged before the Master. Is this what it took to keep company with the likes of Abraham and Peter and Lehi and John the Beloved? Then so be it! The Saints of ancient times faced no less—ridicule, mockery, oppression, exile. Martyrdom! It was worthy company to seek.

Without thinking, Benjamin began to nod. It was a terrible cost, but if one could stand before the Master when it was all over, if one could stand tall and erect and without shame and hear those wonderful words, "Well done, thou good and faithful servant; you have been faithful in a few things, now I make you ruler over many things; enter thou into the joy of thy Lord"—if one could do that, Joseph was right: the cost was worth it.

Now Joseph's face was positively radiant. "The Lord God has seen fit to deliver us and bring us safely out of the hand of the oppressor. We shall make our petitions for redress as commanded, but shall we not then go on with the work we have to do?"

Young Joshua, so caught up in what Joseph was saying, not remembering that Joseph was not speaking to him personally, responded instantly. "Yes!" he called out. Lydia, Mary Ann, and the rest of the family looked at him in surprise. Emily giggled. Several people around them turned, smiling. The boy's face flamed instantly red.

Joseph swung around too, but he was not amused. He was deeply touched. His eyes caught Joshua's and held them. "That's right, young Joshua Steed," he cried proudly. "That is the answer the Lord wants to hear." He turned back to the congregation, his eyes blazing with determination. Now his voice was like the roar of a lion. "What say ye, my brothers and sisters? You have heard it from the mouth of a child. Is not this what the Lord expects of us?"

"Yes!" several called out.

"Then shall we not do it?"

Benjamin reached across and laid a hand on young Joshua's shoulder. "Yes!" he cried. "Yes!"

Now it rolled across the congregation. Heads were up, eyes were on fire with determination, hearts were aflame with faith. "Yes! Yes! Yes!"

Chapter Notes

As is recorded in Joseph's history, on 24 April, two days following his return to Quincy, he "met the Church in council" (HC 3:335), but it was not until the first week of May that a formal conference was held. The minutes indicate that land purchases recently made to the north were sanctioned by the conference and that the next conference was to be held in Commerce in October. As for Joseph's speech on the first day of the conference, the minutes record only this: "A hymn was then sung, when President Smith made a few observations on the state of his peculiar feelings, after having been separated from the brethren so long, etc." (See *HC* 3:345.) However, under date of 22 April, the day of his return from imprisonment, the Prophet's history contains his thoughts about what had happened in Missouri, and in the novel many of those thoughts are presented as part of his conference address. Thus, while the author has taken some liberties to create the introductory and concluding portions of Joseph's speech to the Saints, the great majority of the speech as given here is based on Joseph's words as recorded in the 22 April journal entry. (See *HC* 3:327–32.)

An interesting postscript to the Missouri persecutions is a 1976 executive order issued by Christopher Bond, then governor of the state of Missouri. The statement officially rescinds the extermination order issued by Governor Lilburn W. Boggs 138 years earlier. The 1976 order reads:

"WHEREAS, on October 27, 1838, the Governor of the State of Missouri, Lilburn W. Boggs, signed an order calling for the extermination or expulsion of Mormons from the State of Missouri; and

"WHEREAS, Governor Boggs' order clearly contravened the rights to life, liberty, property and religious freedom as guaranteed by the Constitution of the United States, as well as the Constitution of the State of Missouri; and

"WHEREAS, in this bicentennial year as we reflect on our nation's heritage, the exercise of religious freedom is without question one of the basic tenets of our free democratic republic;

"Now, THEREFORE, I, CHRISTOPHER S. BOND, Governor of the State of Missouri, by virtue of the authority vested in me by the Constitution and the laws of the State of Missouri, do hereby order as follows:

"Expressing on behalf of all Missourians our deep regret for the injustice and undue suffering which was caused by the 1838 order, I hereby rescind Executive Order Number 44 dated October 27, 1838, issued by Governor W. Boggs.

"In witness I have hereunto set my hand and caused to be affixed the great seal of the State of Missouri, in the city of Jefferson, on this 25 day of June, 1976. (Signed) Christopher S. Bond, Governor." (Quoted in Richard Neitzel Holzapfel and T. Jeffery Cottle, *Old Mormon Kirtland and Missouri: Historic Photographs and Guide* [Santa Ana, Calif.: Fieldbrook Productions, 1991], p. 285.)

Joshua Steed slowed his step as he approached the hardware store. He leaned heavily on his cane, limping with exaggerated care. His leg—paralyzed when the bullet entered his back and passed through his body—was definitely improving. He had started with nothing, no feeling, no ability to make it respond, total dependence on a crutch. Then gradually it began to improve. Now around the house sometimes he even set his cane aside and still managed.

But he didn't want the man behind him to know that. Stopping completely, Joshua turned his head, as though his attention was caught by the tools in the window. He stepped over to examine them more closely, but in actuality, only did that so he could see down the boardwalk behind him in the reflection of the store's glass front.

He stiffened a little. The man was still there, coming very slowly now, obviously surprised by Joshua's sudden change of pace. Swearing softly under his breath, Joshua turned and moved away in long, awkward strides. He had first spotted the man as he came out of his office at the textile warehouse. The man had been some distance away and Joshua couldn't get a good look at him, but he fell in behind Joshua, moving more quickly when Joshua sped up, slowing when he lagged a little. If Joshua turned away, he would spin around, hiding his face. Joshua didn't like it in the least.

He walked steadily but not hurriedly up the street, then turned a corner into a narrow alley. The moment he was out of sight, he broke into a hobbling run. The alley went through, then opened onto the next street, but about halfway down there was a small open area behind one of the buildings. He ducked into that and flattened himself against the wall.

There was a startled cry as the man turned the corner and saw that Joshua was gone, and Joshua heard him break into a jogging run. As the figure flashed by him, Joshua launched himself, dropping the cane to free his hands. He hit him hard, driving him to the ground. In an instant, he had a hammerlock on the man and pressed his face into the dirt.

"Who are you!" Joshua hissed into his ear. "Why are you following me?"

To Joshua's amazement, the man began to laugh. He turned his head as far as possible and looked up at Joshua.

Joshua rolled off him and came up to his knees, stunned. *"Nathan?"*

Nathan sat up, brushing the dirt off his face. He grinned. "I expected you to be glad to see me, but I must say, this is really more than was necessary."

Nathan was shaking his head by the time Caroline finished talking. "I'm very sorry," he said. "I was sure that you would have at least heard from Will by now."

She looked away, fighting to keep her composure. "The only thing I can figure is that he thinks I'm going to be angry with him for stealing that money and running off. But if we only knew where he was . . ." She looked away, biting her lip. "He still thinks Joshua is dead."

Joshua, sitting next to his wife on the sofa, took her hand. "Caroline, he'll come to his senses. We've just got to give it some time."

"He's not dead," she said fiercely, looking at Nathan. "I know that he's not dead."

Nathan nodded soberly. The thought had crossed his mind and it must have shown on his face. "Maybe he did write and it's just gotten lost. You know how mail service can be."

She nodded wearily. "I know. I've tried to think of every possible reason."

Savannah was sitting on Nathan's lap. Now she had had enough of this adult conversation. She reached up and tugged on her uncle's jacket. "Where's Gampa?"

Nathan laughed, looking down into those large, deep blue eyes which were now very grave. "Grandpa is in a place called Illinois, Savannah."

"Where's Gamma?"

"Grandma is there too. They miss you."

"Wanna see Gampa."

Hugging her to him, Nathan looked at Joshua. "Sounds like a good idea to me."

"Me too," Caroline said. She was not smiling as she looked at Joshua.

"Me too," Olivia blurted. "Can we go see them, Papa? Can we? Please?"

"Whoa!" Joshua cried, holding up his hands. "Uncle Nathan just got here. Let's get him settled in his room first, and get him fed. He looks pretty hungry to me."

———

"What are you thinking?" Joshua finally asked. "When you talk about a family enterprise, what have you got in mind?"

Nathan leaned back in his chair, lifting one knee and holding it with his hands. "A store."

"A store?"

"Like a dry goods store?" Caroline asked, also clearly surprised. Dinner was over now. Savannah was in bed, and they were talking in the parlor. Olivia sat quietly, knowing that if she wanted to be part of this, she had better act like an adult and not interrupt.

"Yes," Nathan answered. "Only a dry goods store with a full line of products. Cookery, fabrics, spices, tools, sewing things for women, maybe even hats and a basic line of ready-made clothing for men and women. Dresses, shawls, boots, pants, jackets."

Joshua's one eyebrow had risen slightly, so Nathan hurried on. "You've got to remember that there are almost twelve thousand Latter-day Saints in Illinois right now, and more coming. They need a lot of goods."

"Doesn't Quincy have stores?" Joshua asked.

"We're not staying in Quincy. We've got to have a place of our own."

Joshua started a retort, then closed his mouth again, remembering his amazement the first time he went to Far West. What had been open prairie just months before was a full city humming with activity. Telling the Mormons that such things were impossible was a little fruitless. "A store," he said instead. "It is an interesting idea."

"A store is just the beginning," Nathan said eagerly. "That will be good for Lydia and me." He looked at Caroline. "You know that Lydia's parents had a store in Palmyra. She grew up with it."

"No, I didn't know that."

"She was good at it, too," Joshua supplied.

"We plan to have Mama and Papa help," Nathan said. "Pa can't farm anymore. It would kill him."

"So he's not getting any better?" Joshua asked with concern.

Nathan frowned. "Oh, yes, he's improving still, but . . ." He shook his head, rushing on now as the ideas came tumbling out. "Anyway, there's the others to consider. Matthew and Brigham Young are talking about getting a cabinet shop going again. We could sell through the store the furniture and other products they make. Take special orders. Jessica will probably want to go back to teaching school again. I've been thinking that once we find a place, we are all going to have to have houses. Maybe we could add an extra room to hers that she could use for a school."

"That's a good idea," Caroline said. "Lydia told me she is a wonderful teacher."

"Yes. And that's the point," Nathan went on eagerly. "We go with our strengths. Each person doing what they do best. Derek wants to farm. He loves that. Maybe we could decide what crop is best, then market that too."

"You really have been thinking about this, haven't you?" Joshua said with a laugh, but also with admiration.

Nathan leaned forward. "Yes, I have. For many nights now. It makes good sense economically, but it brings the family together too. That's what I like best about the idea."

"That's what I like best about the idea too," Caroline said softly, looking directly at Joshua.

The room went quiet. Joshua was frowning deeply. Then he laughed, brushing it aside. "You know there's thinking, and then there's dreaming. Wild dreaming."

Caroline was not about to be put off. "Is it dreaming to want to be close to your family, Joshua? And . . ." Now her voice became filled with concern. "And it would also be out of the state of Missouri."

He threw up his hands. "Let's not start on that again, Caroline. We're fine here. No one from Jackson County is going to learn that I'm still alive. And if they do, who cares anymore?"

"Right," she shot right back at him. "That's why you attacked a complete stranger when he tried to follow you home."

"Now, it wasn't like that, and you know it," Joshua said testily.

Nathan grunted. "It wasn't? That's exactly how I recall it."

Joshua swung on his brother. "Well, what were you doing sneaking around following me anyway? Why didn't you just come right up and say hello?"

"I was going to your office when I saw you come out. Then I thought it might be fun to follow you home and surprise you and Caroline at the same time."

Caroline bored in now, with a quiet anger of her own. "Joshua, you've always been honest. That's one of the things I love about you. So you look me in the eye and you tell me you have not been worried about us being here in St. Louis. You tell me that the reason you now call your business Samuelson and Associates rather than Samuelson and Steed has nothing to do with your concerns about being found."

"It's not that. I just . . ." But she had him, and he knew it.

Her eyes were suddenly shining. "You thought Nathan was someone from Jackson County, didn't you?"

He looked away.

"Didn't you?"

"All right, but I was just being cautious."

"Well, if *you* are worried about that, how do you think *I* feel?" His mouth opened, but she went on quickly, fiercely now. "You forget. I saw those men who shot you! They sat across the table from me with their leering grins and their terrible breath and told me in detail how you died. They sat across the table and looked at me in a way that made me feel like I needed to bathe. Then they burned our house down around us. They followed us all the way to St. Louis." She looked away suddenly. "They drove our son away from us."

"Those men are dead, Caroline," he said. "We're safe now."

She just looked at him and shook her head in disbelief.

Nathan knew it was not directly his affair, but he couldn't help siding with Caroline on this. "What would the people in Jackson County do if they did know you were still alive? After all, you did kill a man, a member of the militia. Isn't that worthy of a court-martial?"

Joshua turned on Nathan, angry, but before he could speak, Olivia leaned forward. "Papa?"

He barely glanced at her. "What?"

"I still have nightmares about somebody finding us."

It was as if she had punched him. He turned to gape at her. "You do?"

She nodded slowly. "I didn't want to tell you."

For several moments they all sat there. Caroline had dropped her head and was staring at her hands, which were clasped in her lap. Nathan was studying the pattern that had been painted on the wall so as to resemble wallpaper. Olivia was watching her father with imploring eyes.

Finally Caroline looked up at Nathan. "We got a letter from Melissa a few days ago."

"You did? How are they?"

She glanced quickly at her husband, then away again. "Fine." There was a moment's hesitation. "She hinted that Carl might consider coming out west and going into some kind of business partnership with Joshua."

Nathan's jaw dropped. "Really?"

She nodded, but Joshua jumped in on that. "Don't make more of that than what it is. That could just be Melissa talking."

She started to answer that, but he went on quickly. "But even *if* Carl were willing—a very big *if*, I think—the best place for us to set up would be right here in St. Louis. So let's stop talking about moving. I'm not about to move up in the middle of twelve thousand Mormons. We're happy here."

"No!" she said wearily. "*You're* happy here. That's all."

Nathan decided a little lightness was in order. "So that's it. You're worried that you might come up there with all those Mormons and get converted."

Joshua snorted in disgust.

"Look," Nathan said, serious now. "Why don't you just come back to Quincy with me for a visit. Mother would be so pleased to see you again. Then you can look the situation over. Maybe you could operate out of Quincy. That would still take you out of the state of Missouri."

Joshua's look was still hard, but finally he turned to Caroline. "You never told me you were unhappy here," he finally said.

She sighed. "Joshua, how many times have you and I talked about the possibility of moving north to be closer to your family? Doesn't that tell you something?"

He sat back. He looked at Nathan. Then he looked back at his wife again. Finally, he shook his head and turned to Nathan once more. "You know, brother, every time you come it seems like all you do is cause me grief."

Nathan looked at him steadily, then slowly smiled. "I can't think of a more deserving man."

Again the room fell silent as Joshua looked at his wife. Then after several moments had passed, he turned to Olivia. "Did I ever tell you about your Uncle Nathan, Livvy?"

"No, what?"

"He's got a lousy sense of direction. Gets lost at the drop of a hat. I was always having to find him when we were kids."

"I beg your pardon," Nathan said, surprised at this sudden attack. "I don't ever recall your having to find me."

Joshua went right on as if Nathan hadn't spoken. "If we send him up north by himself, he'll probably miss Quincy by a hundred miles if he misses it by a yard."

Nathan was staring. Caroline's head had come up and her face registered shock.

Now at last, Joshua turned to Nathan. "If the Mormons are moving out of Quincy, I suppose you're going to need more wagons, aren't you? The Steed clan is getting to be pretty substantial."

Nathan nodded gravely. "Couldn't possibly do without them."

Caroline reached out and grabbed her husband's hand. "Do you mean it, Joshua? Can we go back with Nathan?"

He nodded. "But don't be getting your hopes up about moving there permanently." Then, in spite of himself, his face grew thoughtful. "But it is an interesting business opportunity. It might not hurt to look around a little."

She threw her arms around him and kissed him soundly. "Thank you, Joshua."

Olivia went to them, trying to get her arms around her mother and father. "Oh, thank you, Papa. Thank you."

Joshua pulled a face. "It's really not fair, you know."

"What?" Caroline asked.

"Nathan I can handle. Knock him around a bit if he gets too pushy. But when my three girls all gang up on me . . . You telling me you're not happy. Livvy and her bad dreams." His eyes registered disbelief. "Even Savannah, asking to see her grandpa." He shook his head helplessly. "Trying to stand up against the three of you—I might as well try to spit on a prairie fire."

<hr />

Will stopped for a moment outside the captain's cabin. He tugged at his shirt, stuffing it down inside the rope belt that held his pants up, keenly aware that the pants—the only pair he owned—were nearly worn through at the knees. They were bleached out to a pale gray by the combination of sunshine, wind, and salt spray that had also bronzed his face and arms to the color of dark honey. His shoes were scuffed and the little toe on his right foot poked through the thin leather.

He spit on his hands, rubbed them together quickly, and then smoothed down his hair as best he could. The last time he had cut his hair was while he was on the Montague plantation back in December, five months before. It was long and shaggy and grew as thick as the mane of one of his father's Conestoga horses. He had no mirror to look at. It would have surprised him to find that if he passed by any but his closest friends or family, they probably wouldn't recognize him.

Finally, as ready as he could be, he lifted a hand and knocked firmly.

"Enter."

Opening the door, Will stepped inside. "Mr. O'Malley said you wanted to see me, sir."

The captain was sitting in the big chair next to his bunk reading a large, old-looking book. He stood, moved over to the desk, and set the book down. "Yes, Steed, I did. Come in. Have a seat."

Will looked around, then took a small four-legged stool beside the table. There was a padded chair in the corner, but somehow it didn't seem appropriate to assume too much and sit in that. He pulled the stool out and sat down across from the captain.

"Coffee?"

"No, thank you, sir. I just had breakfast in the galley."

"Oh. Fog lifting at all?"

Will glanced out the small porthole in the bulkhead. Outside, it was a uniform gray. "No, sir."

"Ever have fog like this back in Missouri?"

Will looked up, a little startled. The captain had never made any reference to Will's home. For that matter, he had never made reference to anything about Will's former life. Will shook his head. "No, sir, not like this."

"In England they call it pea soup. Nothing quite like it anywhere else in the world."

"We'll have to wait for it to lift, then?"

"Yes, but it's still early. It'll burn off in the next hour or two so the steamer can come out and take us into Liverpool. It's up a river, you know, and we have to have an escort."

"That's what Jiggers said." Will kept his face expressionless, still puzzled by the chitchat. He kept stealing glances at the captain, who was absently pushing a paperweight around with the tip of his thumb. He did not see any anger in the captain's eyes, which made him all the more curious. Normally, only serious infractions of the ship's rules brought a man to the captain's cabin. Will thought he was clean, but he was still nervous. One could never be sure.

The captain stopped playing with the paperweight. He folded his hands across his stomach and leaned back, studying the boy before him. "How old are you, Steed?"

"Sixteen."

One eyebrow came up.

"Well, I will be on my next birthday."

"Which is?"

Will looked away. "Next March." That was still ten months away.

There was a hint of amusement in Sperryman's eyes. Then he opened a drawer and pulled out a piece of paper, folded in thirds. Will recognized it instantly. It was the letter he had written to his mother several weeks before. Then his eyes widened. The last time the captain showed that letter to him, it had been tied with a string. Now the string was gone.

Captain Sperryman was looking at Will steadily. "I told you before, I don't read other people's mail. I think that's a man's own affair."

Will looked at him sharply. But the string was gone. The letter had been opened.

"Until this morning," the Captain added, seeing the disbelief on Will's face, "I was going to mail it from Liverpool today, like I promised. But then"—he shrugged—"I thought it best to know more about you."

Will's lips set in a hard line. He had poured out a good deal of his heart and emotions in that letter to his mother. "You could have asked," he said tightly.

Sperryman seemed unperturbed. "I'm sorry about your father."

Will was staring at his hands, which were in his lap. He was both embarrassed and angry to be uncovered like this.

"Who killed him?"

Will hesitated; then, strangely, he wanted the captain to know. He had held it in for months now. He looked up. "The Mormons." There was an instant tinge of guilt for that. Hugh Watson and Riley Overson were Missourians, not Mormons, and it was they who had killed his father. He had learned that in a warehouse in St. Louis. But going into all that required such a convoluted explanation, it was easier to just say it was the Mormons. Besides, if it hadn't been for the Mormons and the problems they created in northern Missouri, his father would never have been up there in the first place. So in a way . . .

"Mormons?" the captain said, pronouncing the word tentatively.

"A group of religious fanatics," Will said shortly, not wanting to explain further.

"Oh. Well, I'm sorry."

There was another pause, this time longer, but the captain's eyes never left Will's face. "How'd you come to get sold down the river?"

"I was stupid," Will said without hesitation. He would not be soft on himself. "I trusted a man that I should have known wasn't trustworthy."

"And your mother has no idea what has happened to you?"

"You took my letter, remember?" Will retorted, not trying to hide the bitterness in his voice.

"That I did." It was said without either rancor or regret. He reached in the drawer again and pulled out a pipe. The bowl was carved in the shape of a dragon. It was very Oriental-looking, and Will wondered if it had come from China. He stared at it as Sperryman pulled over a tin of tobacco, stuffed the pipe, then put it in his mouth without lighting it.

Shoving the pipe to one corner of his mouth, Sperryman began talking as though Will weren't there. "I wasn't shanghaied and sold off to a ship's crew. I ran away and became a stowaway on a warship. The War of 1812 had just begun. I wanted to be in it. I was just barely thirteen."

Thirteen? Will leaned forward, surprised by this sudden turn in the conversation.

"It took me fifteen years to make first mate. Another seven to make captain." Finally, he looked directly at Will. "But I loved it from the first. I was born for the sea."

Will nodded slowly, his mind calculating quickly. If Sperryman was thirteen at the beginning of the War of 1812, that meant he was forty now. Will had not thought much about his age before. He seemed timeless. His face was like untanned leather and the blue eyes perpetually squinted. But he was right. It showed in every part of him. He was born for the sea.

"So were you, Steed."

Will jumped a little.

"You were. You've taken to sailing like you've been walking the deck of a ship since you were a toddler."

That was an exaggeration, Will thought. For the first three days out of New Orleans the weather had been rough, and he had been as sick as he could ever remember being. But that had passed, and he had found himself exulting in the freedom of the ocean's vastness. He was fascinated by the intricacies of the rigging and determined he would quickly master how it all worked. And though he missed his family fiercely, being on the rolling deck of a ship felt like he had returned to something that was second nature to him.

Sperryman reached in the drawer and pulled out a long self-strike match, scratched it against the side of the table, and touched it to the tobacco. As he puffed the pipe into life, he watched Will steadily through the smoke. When he had it going to his satisfaction, he pulled it out of his mouth and jabbed it in Will's direction. "I can save you five or six years," he said bluntly.

"What?" Will blurted.

There was a hardness now, a challenge in the line of his jaw. "You come with me and I'll make you a ship captain by the time you're thirty."

Will rocked back, stunned.

"But if I'm going to do that, you gotta be with me, Steed."

"I—" Will clamped it off. He was too dumbfounded to know what to say.

The captain jammed the pipe back in his mouth, then picked up the letter. "I'm sorry about your family. And I don't blame you for wanting to let your mother know where you are. I'll mail this as soon as we dock." He tossed it across to Will. "Add anything you want, then get it back to me."

Will picked it up slowly.

The captain puffed twice, blew the smoke out of his nose, then moved the pipe to the corner of his mouth again. "Like it or not—legal or not—I paid good money for you, Steed, and I can't throw that away. You fight me, and I'll throw you in that locker every time we sail into port. You owe me two years and I'll not have a day less." Then his eyes softened a little. "If I had my way, I'd give you a couple of months leave, let you go look up your mother. But I don't have my way, so that's that."

"Are we going back to Savannah soon, sir? That's where my mother is. That would only take a day or two of shore leave for me to see her."

Sperryman shook his head. "Life doesn't always work out as neatly as we'd like."

"What are you saying, sir?" Will asked slowly.

"Haven't you heard? I told the crew they were not to say a word to you, but I never thought we'd go this far without your knowing. We're taking this load of tobacco and shoes on to China."

The breath went out of him. "China?"

"Yes. We'll stop in France and add some wine to the cargo, then it's on to Canton." Suddenly his face was infused with excitement. "Ah, you'll love China, Steed. And there's a fortune to be made there. Last ship the company sent made a profit of three hundred percent."

Will barely heard him. *China!* China was an eighteen-month round-trip voyage out of America. *Eighteen months!* No wonder the captain didn't want him to know. That would be enough to tempt a man to steal one of the lifeboats and see if he could make his own way to land.

Now there was the slightest touch of sympathy around the captain's mouth. "Look at it this way. When we're back, you're time will be up. You can go home if you choose." He was all business again. "You've got real promise as a sailor, Steed. And that's why I've called you in. Jiggers wants to make you apprentice bosun."

"Bosun?" Will pulled away from his thoughts. The bosun (shortened by generations of English sailors from *boatswain*) was the officer in charge of all the rigging, anchors, and cables on a ship. Jiggers was the bosun for the *Bostonia*. It was an important position on a sailing ship.

"Yes. And I concur." Sperryman shook his head in amazement. "But at fifteen? That's two years quicker than I made it. That ain't bad."

"But, I—"

"From your letter it sounds like your pa left your mother pretty well fixed."

Will was still dazed by it all—China, now an opportunity to be apprentice bosun. "Yes," he murmured. "I suppose she is."

"Then it's not like she needs you there to care for her."

He shook his head. Not in that way.

Then as quickly as it had come, the kindness was gone. The captain's voice became clipped and efficient. "It's not like you'll see her if you say no. But say yes, and you'll not spend your days in port rotting in that storage locker." He puffed furiously on the pipe. "Jiggers is due to become first mate on another ship when we get back. You prove yourself on the way to China and back and I'll make you full bosun in his place."

He stood up abruptly, signaling that the interview was over. "But I'd have to have your word on it, Steed. I think you're an honest man. Give me your word you won't bolt, and you'll have a chance to see Liverpool. Otherwise, it's back in the locker before we start in."

Will stood slowly. "I understand." He wanted to rub his eyes, see if he could make things come into focus a little quicker. "Can I have a little time to think about it, sir?"

"You've got until the steamer arrives."

"Thank you." He turned and started for the door.

"Will?"

He looked around in surprise. It was the first time the captain had used his given name. "Aye, Captain?"

"I'm sorry about all that's happened. I can't do anything about that now, and neither can you. But I think you can make something good out of it, if you're willing."

Will considered that, then nodded. "Aye, sir. I'll let you

know, sir." He opened the door and stepped out, closing it behind him. For a moment he stood there; then he walked slowly
down the passageway and out into the thick fog that hung over
the ship.

———•———

Will looked out of the tiny porthole, the only source of light
in the small room that served as the crew's living area. The sky
was definitely lighter. The fog was lifting. He dipped the pen in
the inkwell, and wrote even more quickly than before.

I hope you can understand, Mother. Even if I had a
choice, I would probably still choose to go with the captain.
When Pa was alive, I thought I would be happy being in the
freight business with him. But now that he's gone, I couldn't
bear to go back to it. I have wondered what to do with my
life. I know Mr. Montague has offered to bring me in with
him on the plantation, but I find the thought of that not at
all to my liking. I really do love the sea, and to be a ship's
captain by the time I am thirty. Where else could I get such
an opportunity?

He looked up sharply. The sound of a boat's whistle pierced the
air. The steamer that would tow them up the Mersey River and
into Liverpool was approaching. Writing furiously now, he finished:

Don't hate me. I still miss Father terribly, and this may
help me get it from my mind. I shall be returning in the fall
of next year. Then, even if I choose to remain a sailor, I
shall get shore leave and come and see you. I am excited
about China. I can still remember back when we were living
in Savannah. I heard sailors talk about China and dreamed
that I might go there someday. Now I shall. Kiss Olivia and
Savannah for me. I miss them terribly, as I do you. Be safe.

Your loving son,
Will

He picked up the blotter, rolled it across the page, folded the new sheet in with the other one, then stood up. The string was gone. He would have to leave that to the captain.

As he came out on deck, he saw immediately that the fog was thinned out to the point that he could see a hundred yards or more of water. Jiggers was standing right above him, beside Mr. O'Malley and Captain Sperryman at the wheel. Off the bow, the steamer from Liverpool was swinging around, coming in close enough to throw them her lines.

At the sight of Will, the bosun's head jerked forward, his jaw jutting out. "Steed," he screamed, "who told you you could spend the day getting your beauty sleep? Your ugly face is beyond help. Now, get amidships and help those men with the lines."

"Aye, sir," Will answered cheerfully. He stepped forward, reaching up toward the captain, holding out the letter with its latest additions. "Sir, could you mail this for me?"

The captain took it, his eyes narrowing. "I could."

Will kept his face expressionless. "Could you read it and check my spelling?"

There was the tiniest flicker of understanding behind the somber countenance. "I could," he said again.

"Thank you."

Jiggers watched for a moment; then, satisfied they were done, he leaned forward. "You got pilings in your ear, Steed?" he roared. "Get yourself amidships, mister, or you'll have midnight watch until the good Lord sees fit to make the sun shine in England again."

"Aye, sir!" Will shouted back at him, then turned and trotted away.

Chapter Eight

As the Saints gathered for the third day of the conference on Monday morning, Joseph Smith was watching the incoming people. When he saw the Steeds, he motioned to his daughter and whispered something to her, pointing in their direction. She nodded, then walked quickly toward them. "Good morning," she called as she came up to the family.

"Good morning, Miss Julia," Mary Ann said warmly. "And how are you this morning?"

"Very well, thank you." Julia was just barely eight. The Steeds had been part of the large assembly that gathered at the river to see her baptized by her father a few days before. She turned to Derek. "Brother Ingalls?"

"Yes?"

"Father would like to speak with you for a moment." Then she looked at Matthew. "And you too."

Derek looked at Rebecca in surprise, then shrugged. "All right." He and Matthew fell in behind Julia as she trotted back to her father.

Joseph immediately pulled away from the people with him and came over to shake their hands. "Thank you, brethren. I'd like to visit with you for a moment, if we could."

"Certainly, Brother Joseph," Matthew said. "Is there something you need?"

He smiled, the blue eyes crinkling around the corners. "Well, actually it's not me who needs it."

"Who, then?" Derek said, thinking there might be a family in difficulty.

"The Lord."

"The Lord?" Matthew blurted.

Joseph nodded soberly. He reached out and laid a hand on Derek's shoulder. "You wouldn't have to leave until after the baby is born."

Suddenly Matthew guessed what this was about. "Do you need us to go help some more people come to Quincy?" he asked.

Joseph laughed right out loud at that. "Well, in a manner of speaking." Then slowly the smile died away. He turned his head and looked to where the family was waiting. All of them were looking in their direction with open curiosity. Joseph still had his hand on Derek's shoulder. He squeezed it gently. "And dear Rebecca. Will she ever forgive me?"

"For what?" Derek asked. "Where do you need us to go?"

"Back to your native land."

Derek's jaw went slack and he gaped at the Prophet.

"*What?*" Matthew gasped. "To England?"

Joseph nodded slowly. "We're going to ask a few brethren to accompany the Twelve. And who better, Derek, than a native Englishman who is as faithful as you?"

Derek was finding it difficult to catch his breath. "England?" he said softly.

"Yes. I feel quite strongly that you should go. Wait for the baby to come, then get your affairs in order and prepare to go with the brethren."

"England!" Matthew breathed. "That's wonderful, Derek! We'll watch over Rebecca and the baby."

A tiny smile played around the corners of Joseph's mouth.

"Not *we*, Matthew, *they*. *They* will take care of Rebecca and the baby." As Matthew's eyes widened, Joseph peered at him. "Normally we do not send brethren out on foreign missions until they have had a chance to preach locally first. And you are younger than normal. But Brother Brigham is insistent. He says he wants Matthew Steed ordained an elder and sent along with the Twelve."

"I . . . I don't know what to say."

Again Joseph turned and looked toward where their family was waiting. He shook his head and frowned. "Not only am I going to have Rebecca angry with me, but now there's going to be a pretty Irish lass who may never speak to me again either."

He straightened, looking pleased. "Brethren, it's time for us to begin the meeting. If you are of a mind to accept this call from the Lord, we'll propose your names to the assembly." A wry look stole across his face as they both nodded numbly. "You may wish to break the news to your family. That might be easier than hearing your names read out from the pulpit."

They both just looked at him, their minds still sluggish with shock. He slapped them both on the shoulder and gave them a little shove. "Thank you, brethren," he laughed. "I knew I could count on you."

After supper, Jenny and Matthew excused themselves from the family and walked down along the river. At first, the conversation had steered away from the mission call, but it was inevitable that it would turn back to that. So finally Matthew looked at her. "I know it's going to be difficult for you."

She stopped, her chin coming up defiantly. "Is that what you think?" she exclaimed.

Matthew stopped now too, totally surprised. "What?"

She kicked a rock, sending it splashing into the water. "You think my testimony is that weak? I'm not one of those giddy girls that can't bear to have her beau leave her."

Matthew was amazed at her reaction. "Jenny, I . . . I was only trying to say it's going to be hard for us—"

"No, not us," she snapped. The Irish temper was getting a full head of steam now. "You said it would be hard for *me*."

He couldn't believe what he had triggered. "I'm sorry. What I meant was—" He shook his head. "Since Brother Joseph talked to us today, my head has been spinning. I'm not sure what I'm saying anymore."

She rode right over it. "You really think I would try and talk you out of going?" There was a little explosion of disgust. "Don't you know me better than that by now?"

He was in full retreat, frantically waving the white flag. "Jenny, I said I'm sorry."

"You're just saying that because I'm angry."

Matthew stared at her for a moment, then threw up his hands in exasperation. "Of course I am! If you weren't angry, there wouldn't be anything to be sorry about."

"Oh." The simplicity of the logic took the wind right out of her sails.

Tentatively, he reached out and took her hand, and though she gave it to him reluctantly, she didn't pull away. They walked on, past the ferry that was still shuttling across the river, past the last of the houses, and toward a spot where the willows and brush grew thick along the riverbank. Someone had cut a path through the tangle, and Matthew turned into it. It was narrow, and the overhanging growth was low enough that they had to bend over to pass.

About a hundred feet through the thicket, the path opened up onto a small clearing. Fifty feet across and surrounded on all but the river side with the thick undergrowth, it was as private as if they had the whole world to themselves. A huge cottonwood tree, uprooted by some long-ago flood, lay nearly parallel to the water. Matthew hopped up onto it, then reached down and pulled Jenny up beside him. He found a place where the bark had peeled off, leaving smooth, aging wood beneath it, and with a grand flourish motioned for her to sit down. "There you go, Miss McIntire. Your very own seat for what promises to be a spectacular sunset."

She looked at the sky. He was right. There were long fingers of high clouds, the kind that were tinged with orange and then red as the sun went down. She curtsied. "Why, thank you, Mr. Steed." She sat down. "What a pretty place," she said, wrapping her arms around her knees.

"Thank you, madam." He plopped down beside her and took her hand again.

Suddenly her eyes narrowed. "Is this where you bring all the girls?" She started to withdraw her hand.

He groaned inwardly. "You know better than that. You're the first one."

She jerked away. "The first? How many others will there be?"

He rolled his eyes, seeking mercy. "How come you keep setting a bear trap for me every time I say something?"

She looked at him for several moments, her eyes nearly hidden beneath the dark lashes. Then she dropped her head, her cheeks reddening. "Because I can't believe every girl in Quincy isn't chasing after Matthew Steed."

"Really?" he laughed. "Shows how little you know. If they chase, I run."

The light sprinkling of freckles darkened in contrast as her blush deepened. "You're not running now."

Are you chasing me? he nearly quipped, but his better judgment intervened in time. "No," he said instead, "I'm not running now."

She sighed and laid her head against his shoulder. "This really is a beautiful place. It reminds me of Ireland."

"You can remember Ireland?" he asked in surprise. "I thought you came to America when you were still a little girl."

"I was five. I don't remember much, but I remember how green and beautiful everything was. You know, Ireland is just across the Irish Sea from England. Mother is so excited. She's going to make a list of family members and give it to Brother

Brigham in case some of the missionaries go there. She's already written to her sister about the Church."

A breeze stirred her hair and one lock fell down across her forehead. He hesitated, then reached up and pushed it back into its place. A sudden intensity came over him. "I'm going to miss you, Jennifer McIntire."

Her eyes were suddenly glistening. "And I'll miss you, Matthew Steed." Embarrassed, she looked away. "Don't you know that's why I was angry with you?" she whispered.

"It was?"

"Of course. I have to be faithful and support you when you do what the Lord asks of you, but down deep, I already hurt so badly I want to double over and cry. So when you talked about it being difficult for me, I got angry with you."

That slow grin that was so Matthew stole across his face. "Yes, that makes sense."

She slapped playfully at him. Then they both grew serious again. Matthew reached out in wonder and laid his hand against her cheek. "Jenny, I've been thinking a lot about you."

"Yes?"

"This isn't just because of what happened today."

"What were you thinking, Matthew?"

He searched her eyes, then slowly, shyly, almost so hesitantly that for a moment Jenny thought he was going to lose his courage, he leaned over and kissed her gently on the lips. She reached up and laid her hand over his and kissed him back.

"About what, Matthew?" she asked again, a little breathlessly.

His shoulders straightened. "There's a lot of young men that might take a fancy to a beautiful Irish girl."

"Go on!" she said, truly startled by the unexpected compliment.

"Well, you *are* beautiful. And a year is a long time."

"Will it be *only* a year?" she asked plaintively.

"Brigham thinks so. But that doesn't count the time coming and going."

"I don't know if I can bear it."

"Well, I can't bear the thought of coming back and finding someone else has stolen you away from me."

She shook her head emphatically. "You can stop worrying about that right now."

"Well, what if we were . . ." He stopped, groping for the right word.

"What if we were what?" she asked, her eyes wide.

"Well, suppose we were promised. Then when I returned, well, we could . . . I mean . . . But that would only be if you wanted to be. If you'd rather be free, I'll understand. It's just that—"

She clamped her hand over his mouth. "In Scotland they have a word. We use it in Ireland too."

"What is it?"

"Jo."

"Jo?"

"Yes, jo. J-O. Jo."

"What does it mean?"

Again her cheeks flamed and she had to look away. "It is used only of a woman. Here you talk about being promised. Over there, a boy asks a girl if she would be his jo."

"So what does it mean?" he asked again.

Now she looked at him squarely. "It means sweetheart, darling, a woman who is beloved."

"Really?" he asked.

She took his hand again. "Do you remember what my full name is?"

He hadn't thought of it for some time, but he did remember. "Jennifer Jo McIntire," he said in wonder.

"Yes."

Now very sober, he took both of her hands. "So will you be my jo, Jennifer Jo?"

There was a demure lowering of her chin. "Yes, Matthew. I would like that very much."

For a long moment he just stared at her, his eyes grave.

Then to her surprise he got slowly to his feet. He turned to face the river, tipped his head way back, cupped his hands to his mouth, and hollered, "Ya-hoooo!"

From somewhere behind them a flock of birds exploded upwards, screeching angrily. When he turned back, Jennifer was laughing up at him. "You're crazy," she said.

"I am," he admitted. He reached down and pulled her up to face him. He kissed her soundly once, then again. "Come on, Jennifer Jo," he grinned. "We'd better get back."

———•———

Matthew and Derek were carrying things out to the wagon. They weren't leaving for Commerce until the next day, but the packing was under way. The older children streamed in and out of the house, bringing the lighter items. Not that moving was going to be much of a challenge. Most of their belongings had been either ruined or plundered during the fall of Far West. All but one or two pieces of the furniture they were using now came with the rented house.

"Uncle Matthew?"

He looked down. Six-year-old Emily had a pile of dish towels and was holding it up toward him. Her dark eyes were troubled. "How can you make the wagon go without horses?"

He smiled as he took the towels. "The team is still in the pasture, Emmy. We're not leaving until tomorrow."

"Oh." It was as if he had taken a great worry from her shoulders. Noticeably brighter, she turned and ran back into the house.

Her cousin Rachel watched her go and then handed up a small box filled with a few of her mother's dishes. Originally the full set of dinnerware had been purchased by John Griffith for his first wife. When she died and he remarried Jessica Roundy Steed, he had given it to her. Now John was dead, and only a few pieces had been spared by the mob at Haun's Mill. Derek took the box and stowed it carefully between a pile of bedding. Jessica had precious little. It wouldn't do to break any of it.

When he turned back, Rachel was still watching him. Though she was Jessica's daughter in temperament—quiet, thoughtful, sensitive—her ties to her natural father, Joshua Steed, were evident. Her hair was long and dark brown, almost black except in full light. It hung down in natural ringlets which only recently were gradually starting to straighten somewhat. "Derek?"

"Yes, Rachel?"

"Will we have a house up in Commerce?"

He laughed lightly. "There won't be one waiting for us, but yes, we'll build homes once we get there. We will—"

He straightened, staring down the street. Rachel turned, lifting a hand to shade her eyes. Matthew saw them and turned as well. "What?" he said. Three wagons were rumbling up the road toward them. It was the lead driver they were all looking at.

"Well, I'll be!" Derek exclaimed.

"Nathan!" Matthew exploded. "It's Nathan."

Young Joshua was just coming out of the house with some winter clothing. "Papa?" he said, squinting in the same direction. Then with a squeal he dropped his load onto the porch. "Papa! Papa!"

He darted to the door and yanked it open. "Mama! Mama! Papa's home!" And with that he was gone, racing down the road toward the approaching wagons.

Derek leaped down to stand beside Rachel. "Look, there's Uncle Joshua and Aunt Caroline too."

Rachel started jumping up and down. "And Olivia. There's Olivia."

"Yes." Derek turned as Lydia came bursting out of the house. "Nathan's home," he called, "and he's brought company."

———•———

The moment Joshua climbed into the wagon, he knew Caroline was still awake. The children were sleeping inside the house—Olivia with Rachel and Emily, Savannah with little Nathan—but there were already wall-to-wall Steeds when it came to sleeping, so Joshua and Caroline insisted on sleeping in one of the wagons they had brought up from St. Louis.

After she had gotten Savannah asleep, Caroline excused herself and came out to the wagon, claiming exhaustion from the seven-day trip. But Joshua knew better. Caroline was not exhausted. Caroline was angry—very angry—and now, as he carefully stepped through the canvas, he knew she was still awake. And still angry.

It had all started at supper. A joyous mood filled the crowded room. Olivia talked excitedly with her cousins. Savannah sat on Grandpa's lap and refused to be moved. Caroline and the women gathered in close to share all the news. The men moved off to another corner to catch Joshua up on the move to Commerce. It was then that Matthew announced the news. He and Derek had been called to England. It was like a bucket of ice water in the face and Joshua reacted instantly. He couldn't believe what he was hearing. They didn't even have homes and they were talking about leaving the family and going on missions? That was nothing short of sheer, unadulterated stupidity.

His blunt, unbending words dashed the festive mood in an instant. Caroline tried to warn him off, first with her eyes and then with the tart suggestion that this was really none of their affair. That only galled him the more. He had let Nathan persuade him to come north to discuss the possibility of a family business. And now half the family was leaving? He felt disgusted and betrayed.

Mary Ann eventually managed to change the subject, and the conversation limped on to safer things. But the moment Savannah was asleep, Caroline was gone. Joshua deliberately waited for a time, hoping that if he stalled long enough, Caroline would be asleep. It hadn't worked.

He sat down heavily on a wooden chest and started to pull off his boots. She was barely visible in the darkness. "All right, let's hear it."

For several moments it was silent, then, "I said my piece inside."

"No," he said wearily, "you only said half of what's on your mind." He could hear her breathing—shallow, rapid. Angry! He hadn't seen her this angry in a long time. "Well, it is pure folly," he snapped. "What's next? Nathan going back to Canada? Pa going off to India or some such place? Why don't they just call Peter too? Young Joshua, for that matter. They may as well take every Steed male in sight and send them away."

"And what if they do?" she flung back at him. "What business is that of yours? Your family happens to believe in their God. And their belief is strong enough that it moves them to action. That's what's bothering you. It's not that they're leaving. It's that they're being good Mormons again."

"Oh, come on, Caroline, that's got nothing to do with it, and you know it. Here they are. They don't even have a home. They're leaving tomorrow to move north. To what? To nothing! Rebecca is with child, and they want Derek to leave as soon as the baby's born? Some prophet that asks that of his people."

"Again I say, it is their life. This is not our affair and you had no right to tear into them like that. You were abominable to act that way."

He slammed a boot down. "That's right, it is their choice. And it's my choice whether or not I come up here and try to set up a business in company with my family. You think about that. All these highfalutin promises to get me up here, then bang! every one of them up and leaves."

"Oh," she said with withering scorn, "did I miss something in there? I heard about Derek and Matthew. Who else is leaving?"

"No one for now," he flung back at her. "Can you guarantee me they won't get called too? Nathan? Pa?"

She rose up on one elbow. "Look, Joshua, you have never wanted to live among the Mormons. That's the real reason behind all this. It has nothing to do with England or missionaries or anything else. You've just been looking for the right excuse and now you've found it. What you really ought to do is go back in there and thank them."

He jumped up, banging his head on one of the hoops that held the canvas in place. Swearing, he dropped down again and grabbed his boots. "I can't reason with you. I'm going for a walk." He stuffed his foot into one boot, not caring whether it was the right foot or not, and started yanking it on.

Caroline sat up. She watched him until both boots were back on and he stood. There was a sudden pleading in her voice now. "Joshua, they haven't tried to make you into a Mormon. No one in your family is waving the Book of Mormon at me. So why are you so dead set against them? Why are you trying to make them believe like you do?"

His mouth opened, then he clamped it shut again. He was fuming, too angry to speak. He climbed out onto the wagon seat and hopped down. "Don't wait up for me," he hurled back over his shoulder, then stalked away.

"Joshua?"

Stopping, he did not turn.

"I checked with the bank in St. Louis before we left. I have all that money I got from the settlement in Savannah."

He spun around in spite of himself, caught totally by surprise by this turn in her thoughts. When Caroline Mendenhall had agreed to marry him back in Savannah three years ago, in return for selling her house and a promise to leave the city she had gotten a healthy settlement from the dishonest business partners of her first husband. The total had been twenty thousand dollars. Joshua maintained that it was her money and he refused to take any part of it. He didn't want her to ever think his love for her had anything to do with her finances. He once thought of investing it for her, but even that might be seen as though he was trying to benefit from it, so he finally put it in the bank and let it sit. He hadn't thought about it for several months. Her bringing it up was like a bolt of lightning out of a clear summer sky.

"Yes?" he said cautiously.

"When we return, I'll be taking it out and investing it in that store Nathan talked about."

He nearly choked. "Are you serious?" he finally managed.

Suddenly she was standing at the opening in the canvas. "You still don't understand, do you?"

"Understand what?" He was groping, trying to see ahead to where she was going.

"This isn't about a store. And it isn't about starting a business. It's about family. Your family. Because I don't have family. Our children don't have any cousins or aunts and uncles or grandparents except yours. I thought you understood that. I thought that was why you agreed that this is what we should do. And the whole time, all you can think about is the Mormons and missionary work."

He didn't answer.

"Well, obviously, I was wrong. I didn't understand you as well as I thought I did." He could see her straighten visibly and her voice became tight and hard. "And obviously you don't understand me. So I'll say this as straight and honestly as I know how. I'll be taking that money and helping Nathan and Lydia start their store. I'll have to hold some out. The girls and I will need a home of our own. But the rest will go to Nathan and Lydia."

"You and the girls?" Her words were pummeling him now.

It was as though he hadn't spoken. "I'll go back with you to St. Louis long enough to get my money and what few things I need. Then I'll be coming up. And I'll not be staying in Quincy either. I'm going wherever the family is going."

There was a soft creak from the wagon, and he realized that she was no longer standing in the opening. "Caroline—," he started, taking a step forward. But she was back inside again. For almost a minute he stood there, staring at the closed wagon flap. Finally, he turned and walked slowly away.

———•———

It was after midnight when Joshua returned. He moved up softly and stopped, listening. There was no sound. Behind him, the house was completely dark. He sat down on the grass and pulled off his boots. He unbuttoned his shirt and removed that too. Finally, he moved to the wagon and climbed up into it as carefully as he could. He set his clothes down in one corner and, moving very slowly, climbed into bed.

The moment he lay down, he sensed she was still awake. He didn't say anything, just turned on one side, facing her. After a moment, she turned also, and slid into his arms. He held her then, neither of them speaking.

Finally, when he felt the wetness against his shoulder, he reached up and brushed at her hair. "I'm sorry, Caroline."

He felt her head nod against him. Then after another long time, she looked up at him. "You know I would never leave you, don't you?"

"Yes." Which was mostly a lie. Her words earlier had been terribly convincing.

"I couldn't bear it," she whispered, then snuggled in against him. In a few minutes, her breathing slowed, then deepened into sleep. When she stirred and half rolled away from him, murmuring softly, he slipped his arm carefully out from under her head, pulled the blanket up around her shoulders, and kissed her softly on the cheek. She didn't stir. He lay down again, turning onto his back. It was a long time before Joshua's eyes closed and he stopped staring up at the canvas that arched over the two of them.

By seven o'clock, the Steed family were up and going. The beds which filled the floors during the night were folded up and put away, and they were in the midst of preparing their last breakfast in this house. Grandpa was supervising the children in some last-minute packing.

When the door to the house opened and Caroline and Joshua stepped inside, every head came around. It was as though some unseen magician waved his wand over the room and instantly froze everyone in position. The children's eyes grew wide and the tension in the room shot up like a Chinese rocket.

Joshua and Caroline stood there for a moment, knowing the reaction their entry had caused, then Caroline smiled. "Good morning," she said cheerfully. Joshua had one hand on her shoulder and she reached up and laid her hand over it. "How is everyone this morning?"

It was as if a fresh breeze swept through the cabin. "Fine." "Good morning." "Good morning, Mama." It came out in a chorus of relief.

Mary Ann put down a fork and came over to Caroline. She gave her a quick hug. "Good morning. Did you—" She had started to say, Did you sleep well? but opted for a safer question. "Are you two hungry?"

Caroline smiled. "Starving!"

"Good. It's almost ready."

Joshua raised his hands. "I have something to say," he said solemnly. He laughed as everyone tensed again. "We may as well get this over with. Then we can get on with the day without all of you feeling like you have to walk on eggshells around me. I . . . I want to apologize for last night. I acted"—he glanced briefly at Caroline—"abominably. What I said about the missions, well—" He stopped again, looking around the room, suddenly realizing that not everyone was there. "Where's Derek and Matthew?"

"Gone to get some milk from up the road."

"Great!" he groaned. "The two who most need to hear this."

"Go on," Caroline prodded gently.

"Well, I'm sorry for what I said. It was rude and uncalled for. And basically, it's not any of my business if Derek and Matthew leave."

Jessica nodded quickly, greatly satisfied. What she had seen last night had been shades of the old Joshua Steed and it had deeply upset her. Benjamin relaxed, nodding slowly.

"You were just tired," Mary Ann said. "You had a long journey."

Joshua smiled at that, as did several others. How like their mother, always looking for the best in people. Now Joshua seemed a little less sure of himself. "Caroline and I have been talking." He looked at Nathan. "I won't be able to invest with you and Lydia in the store."

Nathan's shoulders visibly sagged. Lydia's countenance fell. "Oh."

"I really wanted to, but someone else beat me to it."

Bewildered, Lydia looked back and forth between Joshua and Caroline. Caroline was smiling broadly now too. "I don't understand," Lydia stammered. "Who beat you to it?"

In three steps, Caroline reached Lydia's side. She took both of her hands in hers. "I did. I have some money from the sale of my home in Savannah. Would you and Nathan ever consider me as your business partner?"

Lydia was dumbfounded. "You?"

"I know I don't know much about running a dry goods store," she rushed on. "But you do. You could teach me. My mother had a dress shop when I was younger, and I helped her a lot. Olivia could help too. We'd love that, working with you and Nathan every day."

"Yes," Olivia cried, as surprised as everyone else by what her parents were saying, but picking up on it quickly. "Oh, please Aunt Lydia. Let us do it. Please!"

Nathan was staring at his brother, who was grinning like a kid now. "You really mean it?" he blurted.

"*She* really means it," Joshua answered. "Caroline wants to do this. And I agree. I think it's a wonderful thing for her, if you two don't mind."

"Don't mind!" Lydia cried, throwing her arms around her sister-in-law. "This is even more wonderful than I ever dreamed."

"But . . . ," Mary Ann started, "but that means you'd have to . . ."

Joshua was nodding. He turned and looked at Caroline, appearing a little rueful as he answered his mother. "It means we would have to move up north with you."

One hand came to Mary Ann's mouth, and her eyes were instantly glowing. "Oh, Joshua."

Olivia squealed in delight. "We're moving up here!" she cried to Rachel and young Joshua. They started dancing around her, yelling and shouting.

"I had no idea how important this was to Caroline," Joshua said softly, still looking at her. "We'll probably come to Quincy first, get a base established. Then when you get established, we'll move up and help you get the store started."

Rebecca moved over to Joshua and went up on her toes and kissed him firmly on the cheek. It was such a simple and spontaneous act that he was startled. Everyone laughed at his expression.

Caroline turned to Nathan. "Did you tell Mother Steed about Carl and Melissa?"

Nathan nodded. "I did. Mama says she can't believe it could ever really happen."

"We'll write them today before we leave, tell them everything," Caroline said. "Maybe we can persuade Carl to come out and be partners with Joshua. He could handle the livestock while Joshua did the wagons and the shipping side of the business."

Mary Ann's eyes were swimming. "This is the most wonderful news."

Benjamin stood and came slowly over to face his oldest son. Joshua's smile faded, and for a moment they stood there, face-to-face, both as solemn as if they were victims of tragedy. Everyone turned to watch, half holding their breath. Then Benjamin's mouth slowly softened. "I'll say this, son. When you make up your mind to say you're sorry, you really do it right."

Chapter Nine

Nathan straightened, and wiped his forehead with the sleeve of his shirt. It came away stained and wet. He turned and eyed the progress they had made so far that morning. The four of them—Matthew, Nathan, Derek, and Peter—had taken their shoes off and left them on a dry hump of ground, had rolled their pant legs up to their knees, and now were standing in water and muck above their ankles. They were at the east end of a long ditch that ran straight as an arrow through the swampy terrain, ending where the riverbank dropped off to the water's edge. This was the third ditch they had started in the past week. Two more main channels and a couple of short laterals, and they would have pretty well covered the ten-acre plot of farmland that had been allocated to Derek by the committee Joseph had appointed to arrange for the distribution of land.

Derek saw that Nathan had stopped and he straightened too, holding his back as he arched it stiffly. "Get one of them new John Deere steel plows and a good team," he observed, "and we could dig this ditch in an hour and a half."

"If you didn't mind losing the team," Nathan said dryly. The land around them was a treacherous place for a man, let alone a team. There were swampy bogs, low hillocks of dry, matted grass, numerous ponds—large and small—of open, standing water. One could step onto what looked like solid ground and have it give way to a deep, black, grasping mud beneath. The muck was usually only a couple of feet deep, and the quip about losing the team was an obvious exaggeration, but this was no place for working horses.

Worst were the swarms of mosquitoes. The full heat of summer had brought them out in huge swarming clouds. They settled on any living thing like soot from a fire, driving livestock and man alike to near madness. The four of them wore wide-brimmed hats, and kept neckerchiefs tied around their necks. Their faces were smeared with black mud, leaving only the pink of their lips and the white circles around their eyes showing. This helped, but not totally.

A movement caught Nathan's eye. He lifted a hand and pointed. "Hey! There's Jenny."

Matthew looked up in surprise, turning in the direction Nathan was looking. Sure enough, it was Jenny, coming toward them, picking her way carefully around the bogs, trying to stay on the faint path the men had made as they came through the swampy area.

"Is it time to eat already?" Peter asked, glancing up at the sun.

Derek pulled a large rag from his back pocket and wiped his forehead. "No, it's not even eleven o'clock yet."

Jenny saw that they were looking at her and waved.

Matthew waved back. "Careful," he called. "That spot by the cattails is really soggy."

Jenny had a large rag in one hand that she constantly waved back and forth in front of her face, trying to ward off the hordes of mosquitoes. As she came up next to where their shoes were, she stopped dead and began to laugh. "I'm sorry," she started, deadpan, but then she couldn't hold it and began giggling again. "I thought you were somebody I knew." She turned away, feigning confusion.

Matthew pulled a face at her and stuck his shovel into the soft mud. "Very funny. The mud keeps the mosquitoes off," he said, climbing out of the ditch to stand beside her. Without thinking, he reached up and slapped at his cheek. When his hand came away, there was a tiny patch of blood and a squashed mosquito there.

Jenny laughed, then reached out, took his arm, lifted it to his cheek, and wiped the spot off with his sleeve. "I see," she said soberly.

"What brings you out here?"

She got instantly serious. "Joshua and Caroline are back."

Nathan, Derek, and Peter had stopped working to watch. "Already?" Nathan asked in surprise. Joshua and Caroline had helped them move up to Commerce, then returned to St. Louis to wrap up affairs there. It was only the first of July. Joshua had talked as though it would take him as long as August to get back.

"Yes. He's got two wagonloads of lumber and shingles. Father Steed says to come home. He wants to try and get cabins roofed before we get another rainstorm. He says the ditches will have to wait."

"Two loads," Derek said, sloshing down the ditch, then jumping out beside Matthew. "That's great. Joshua has a way, doesn't he?"

Nathan also climbed out of the ditch, then turned to give Peter a pull up as well. As they all came together, Matthew lifted his left leg and examined it closely, then rolled down the pant leg. He did the same with the other. He moved to Derek and then suddenly stopped, looking at the back of his legs. "Bloodsucker, Derek," he said. He stepped to him. "Hold still."

Jenny turned to look and saw the slimy green blob, about an inch and a half long, attached to Derek's flesh just below the back of the knee joint. It was a swamp leech. She shuddered as Matthew leaned over, pulled it off, and dropped it to the ground. It left a raw spot tinged with blood where it had been. Peter picked up the nearest shoe and crushed the leech beneath the heel.

Matthew wiped his feet off on the grass, then sat down and began to pull his socks on. Peter and Nathan checked each other for leeches as Derek sat beside Matthew. As they put on their shoes, Jenny surveyed their morning's labors. "Phew!" she said, wrinkling her nose. "This stinks worse than I thought."

"Yeah," Derek agreed. "It's bad enough anytime, but digging into it doesn't help."

"Is it going to work?" she asked dubiously.

Matthew's head bobbed quickly up and down and he pointed to the nearest ditch. "Look. You can see water trickling toward the river. It's not much, but it's draining, all right."

Derek turned and looked too. "Give it two weeks and this land will be ready to plow. And what land it's gonna be. Look at that soil. Look how black it is."

Matthew looked at Derek incredulously. "Two weeks? Tell you what. In two weeks, you plow, I'll watch."

Derek reconsidered. "All right, maybe two weeks isn't enough. Let's give it fourteen days."

Jenny laughed as Matthew just shook his head. Besting Derek took some doing, even from Matthew. She smiled at this black-faced Englishman. "By the way, Rebecca came down with me. She and Mother Steed are waiting for us by the big tree."

"Rebecca came?" Derek asked, surprised.

"Yes. She fed Christopher and he went right back to sleep, so she left him with Rachel."

Derek grinned proudly. "That's all that boy does is eat and sleep."

"Be grateful," Nathan laughed. "Elizabeth Mary is over a year old now, and still sleeps through the night only about half the time."

Matthew carefully wiped his hand on his pants, then took Jenny's hand. "Let's go down to the river first, and we'll wash this mud off."

When they reached the river, Jenny stood beside them and talked as they splashed water on their faces and arms. "Caroline said they've found them a house to rent in Quincy and that Joshua has already started work on a corral and stable so he can bring his teams up. They brought the girls with them."

Matthew half frowned as he stood up. "So Olivia's here too?"

Jenny laughed merrily and slipped her arm through his. "Yes. So there'll be no holding hands when she's around."

The others laughed, but Matthew didn't find it that amusing. He blew out his breath in a little expression of frustration. "Jennifer Jo, Olivia is just going to have to get used to the idea of you and me. She's not even twelve yet, for heaven's sake. Does she really think I can wait that long for her to grow up?"

She shook her head, giving him a chiding look. "Don't be too hard on her, Matthew. When you're almost twelve and deeply in love, reality seems far away."

Matthew pulled a face, but Jenny just laughed again. "Come, your mother and Rebecca are waiting for us."

Nathan and his mother walked along, arm in arm. The July sun was hot and the air heavy and still. Beads of moisture stood out on Nathan's forehead, and the back of his shirt was dark with sweat. Jenny, Matthew, and Peter—still young and full of energy—had gone on ahead and were almost to the homesite. Derek and Rebecca were a few paces behind Nathan and his mother. Christopher Joseph Ingalls had been born only three weeks before and Rebecca wasn't back up to full strength yet. Equally weighty in slowing her step was the knowledge that Derek would soon be leaving her. Joseph Smith had called a meeting for the morrow so that he could give the Apostles their instructions before they departed. Derek would leave with them, which meant Rebecca's time with him was very limited now. So she savored every opportunity to be with him alone.

The leisurely pace was fine with Mary Ann. They were moving up a slight rise, and the long, sweeping curve of the Mississippi was visible behind them. She loved the view from here. On the far side of the river—the Iowa side—she could see evidence of settlement there. Commerce had only one stone house and a scattering of cabins when the Saints began to arrive, so many of them had crossed the river to Montrose. Old Fort Des Moines was there, and they found temporary shelter in the deserted barracks. Brigham Young and Wilford Woodruff lived in Montrose, along with some of the other leaders. Joseph had purchased large tracts of land on that side of the river too and encouraged the Saints to build a settlement there as well.

She lowered her gaze again. In every direction, the landscape was verdant and lush. Willows and cottonwoods formed a darker line near the water. Elsewhere a hundred different shades of green caressed the eye. And through it, just starting to really take form, were the dark black slashes of the drainage ditches—dozens of them—that the men were digging.

Directly ahead of them was the Steed homesite. Land in Commerce had been divided into building lots large enough to have a home and an ample garden plot, perhaps even an animal or two. Each able-bodied Saint was charged five hundred dollars for a lot. Under Joseph's direction, those who had suffered the most in Missouri were given their lots free of charge. Joshua had purchased six lots for the Steeds; Caroline had acquired an additional one for the store, two blocks away from where the houses would be. Cabins, waiting now only for the roofs to be shingled, occupied four of the six lots.

The smallest would be Benjamin and Mary Ann's. It had one main room with a stone fireplace on one end; and then off the back wall there was a small room, barely big enough for two beds, where Peter and Matthew slept. It wasn't much, but it was sufficient to begin with. Next to it on the south was Nathan and Lydia's home. Since they had four children, it was almost twice as big, but still had only two rooms and an attic loft. Across the street from that one was Derek and Rebecca's. It was closer to the size of Benjamin's, but they had built it in such a way that it could be easily expanded as Christopher got additional brothers and sisters.

Jessica's cabin was the largest of the four. Like Nathan and Lydia, she too had four children, but—over her protests about getting special treatment—the family had decided to add an extra room on the back. It would be a place to hold school when fall came. At night it also served as Jenny and Kathryn's bedroom. Nancy McIntire was a proud woman, and though the Steeds begged her to come north with them, she refused to do so until she could get enough money to make her own way. She did agree to let the girls come, for they could earn their board and room by helping Jessica and Lydia care for the children, but she herself remained behind in Quincy for now.

Beside Derek's home, one of the two additional lots would be for Joshua and Caroline, and—if all went as planned—the other would be for Melissa and Carl. The lot for the store was on the corner of what promised to become a major intersection in the town. With cash at a premium, the land allocation committee had been so pleased with Joshua and Caroline's cash purchase, they had insisted on giving them that lot for the store.

As Mary Ann let her eyes come all the way around to the east where the land rose to form gentle bluffs, she was struck again with the activity that was everywhere present. There was an amazing number of structures under construction. Log cabins, sod huts, frame homes, stone houses, barns, sheds, stables—they dotted the landscape everywhere one looked.

Mary Ann marveled at how quickly things were happening. Today was the first day of July. It had not yet been a full two months since they had sat in general conference and heard Brother Joseph ask them to come north. Ever one to set the example, less than a week later Joseph, along with Emma and their children, moved into one of the few standing cabins at

Commerce, which was quickly dubbed the "Old Homestead." That settled it for most of the members. If Brother Joseph moved north, they would follow. And for the past six weeks they had streamed upriver.

It had been a busy time for the Steeds as well. In addition to clearing and draining Derek's acreage, and building four cabins, they had been blessed with the arrival of a new family member: on the tenth day of June, Rebecca Steed Ingalls had given birth to a healthy son, the first baby from a Latter-day Saint family to be born in the settlement of Commerce.

"It's really something, isn't it?" Nathan said.

Mary Ann looked up and saw that he too was looking at the frenzy of activity going on around them. "It really is," she said. That reminded her of something. "By the way, did you hear what Joseph is thinking of calling our new city?"

"No, what?"

Rebecca and Derek had closed the gap between them and were right behind them. Rebecca heard her question and was interested too. "I thought it already had a name."

Mary Ann shook her head. "Joseph says Commerce is all right for a small river settlement, but he wants a name fitting for a city of the Saints."

"So what is it?" Derek asked.

"Nauvoo."

"Nauvoo?" Rebecca echoed, repeating the name slowly.

"Yes. N-A-U-V-O-O. Nah-vuh." She exaggerated the pronunciation a little to cement it into their minds. "It's a Hebrew word, he says. He says it means 'beautiful.' It also, according to him, carries with it the idea of rest."

"Nauvoo," Rebecca mused. "Yes, I like it."

Nathan slapped at the back of his neck but missed the mosquito. "Well, it *is* beautiful except for the unclean air."

Mary Ann frowned. "Speaking of unclean air, the sickness has started."

Derek and Rebecca moved up to walk beside them. "The shakes?" Derek asked softly.

Mary Ann nodded dolefully.

"Who?" Nathan demanded, the concern clear in his voice.

"I saw Emma this morning. Father Smith has it. He was up most of the night with the chills and fever. One of the Whitney children has come down with it. Emma says there are others. It just seems to be starting."

An air of gloom settled over them with that news. The shakes—or ague, as it was more commonly named (pronounced egg-yoo by the settlers across America)—was something to be dreaded. So called because of the violent shaking that often occurred during the intermittent chills and fever, the sickness was found throughout the continent, but was especially prevalent in warmer climates and in areas which contained substantial wetlands. The fact that tiny protozoa which attacked the red blood cells and caused the debilitating infection were passed to humans from the bite of the female anopheles mosquito would not be discovered for another sixty years. People attributed the ailment to the musty, foul-smelling odor caused by the rotting vegetation so common to swamps and marshes. Thus came its formal name—malaria—from two Italian words meaning, literally, "bad air."

They walked on in silence, and Nathan brushed absently at the mud caked on his pants. The mud carried the odor of the swamp too. Was he bringing that bad air back to his own family each day? He shook his head, determined that he would be more careful about bathing in the river after each day of digging.

As they neared their homesite, Mary Ann lifted her head. Up ahead she could see her family. They were clustered in a tight circle around Joshua and Caroline and talking loudly. "What is it?" she exclaimed to Nathan, feeling her heart drop. Was it bad news?

"I don't know," Nathan said grimly. He took her elbow and they increased their step.

Matthew saw them first and spun away from the group to run to her. "Mama, come quick. There's news."

"What?"

The rest of the family instantly fell quiet, stepping back. Joshua and Caroline were in the center of the crowd. Caroline was weeping. Olivia was holding her mother with one hand and patting her back with the other.

Alarmed, Mary Ann stepped forward quickly. "Joshua? What is it?"

He looked up at the sound of her voice. Quickly he came forward, leaning heavily on his cane, and took one hand. "One of my teamsters just brought us a letter from St. Louis. My business partner sent it up to us."

"A letter?" Mary Ann said. Turning, she saw the letter in Caroline's hand. "Is it from Melissa? Are they coming?"

"No," Caroline whispered. "Our friends the Montagues forwarded it on to us from Savannah." She was smiling and crying all at once. "It's not from Melissa. It's from Will. Will is alive!"

***

Mary Ann was staring into the fire, almost mesmerized by the dancing flames. With the urgency to get the cabins shingled, there hadn't been much chance to talk about the news of Will's whereabouts. But now supper was done, and the children were bedded down. "China," she mused, almost to herself. "So there is no way to even write to him." It wasn't a question.

"No," Caroline said, jabbing at the coals with a stick. "He wrote this to Savannah. He still thinks I'm there with the Montagues." Sudden tears welled up, shining in the light of the fire. "He still thinks Joshua is dead."

Joshua reached out and put an arm around her. "But at least we know that he's all right."

"All right?" she cried. "He's fifteen years old and on a boat sailing for China. It will be next fall before we can see him."

Lydia was near tears too, but she jumped in quickly. "Joshua's right, Caroline. At least you know. And he is well. This is what we've all been praying for. That we could know where he is and that he would be all right."

Nathan nodded in surprise. He hadn't thought about the prayers that were part of the Steed family life every night and morning. Grandparents, aunts and uncles, cousins—for the past six months, everyone had been praying for Will Steed. That he would be found. That he would be safe.

"Will is going to do fine," Benjamin broke in. "It's a real loss to not be able to see him for a time, but that sea captain knows what kind of boy you've raised. I'm not surprised he wants to take him under his wing."

"But another year!" Caroline exclaimed. "It's already been so long. Now another year and more. And out there with all those men. You forget. I lived in Savannah. I know what kind of men sailors are."

Benjamin straightened. "Caroline," he said softly.

She looked over at him.

"It's not just the captain who's taken him under his wing," he said.

Her eyes widened, slightly puzzled.

"The Lord is looking out for your son," he finished. "And he'll bring him back to you in his own good time."

Chapter Notes

John Deere invented the first steel plow in 1837. Along with Cyrus Mc-Cormick's grain reaper, this was a major factor in opening the Great Plains to the sodbusting farmers who would eventually make it into one of the greatest food baskets in the entire world.

The first use of the name "Nauvoo" found in print does not occur until August 1839, more than a month later than shown in the novel. It is not known how soon before the August 1839 instance Joseph chose the name. The meaning of the word is as given here (see HC 4:268).

On the third of July, 1839, the men of the Steed family finished nailing the last of the split-cedar shingles on the back room that would become Jessica's school. It was the last of the four cabins to be done. They paused for several moments to survey with satisfaction their handiwork, then immediately set about moving their meager belongings from the tents and wagons into the four cabins. That night, for the first time in nearly ten months, they slept under their own roofs again without fear.

The next morning, they joined others living nearby for a brief celebration of their country's birthday. One year before in Far West, they had erected a liberty pole as part of their Independence Day celebration, and then saw it struck by lightning a few days later. It proved to be a grim omen of things to come. So while there was rejoicing on this day—they were out of Missouri, they had a new home, and their prophet was free—it was tempered by concern about what the future might once again hold.

Immediately after the celebration, Joshua and Caroline started back for Quincy. Olivia begged to stay behind with her cousins, but Caroline insisted that she needed Olivia to help with Savannah. They were still getting their home in Quincy established, and Joshua was working day and night to get the business started. So promises of a quick return had to do for now.

That evening a little before sundown, Benjamin and Mary Ann had the first visitors to their new home. When they saw who it was, they immediately sent out back for Matthew to join them.

There were four visitors in all, and each one of them an ordained Apostle.

Brigham Young and Heber Kimball sat side by side. This was not surprising, for they had been close friends since Brigham had moved to Mendon, New York, in 1828 and become neighbors with the Kimballs. Both were thirty-eight, their birthdays not two weeks apart, which made them both about four years older than Joseph. They were a sharp contrast, these two. Both were laborers, craftsmen—Brigham a carpenter, joiner, and glazier, Heber a potter. But beyond that, the similarities ended. Brigham was about five feet ten inches tall and stocky in his physique. But when he stood, he tended to be stoop-shouldered, which made him seem shorter than he was. Heber, only slightly taller in actual inches, stood erect, almost stately and majestic. He was powerful of frame—his torso thick and strong from early years blacksmithing with his father—and beside him, Brigham looked almost slight of build. Heber's eyes were nearly black and could pin a person with their flashing intensity. Brigham's were a blue-gray and were most often mild—except when his temper was aroused, at which time they could darken into thundering storm clouds. Brigham's hair was a reddish brown. It was full and straight, worn almost to the neck, where it turned under slightly. Heber was mostly bald. What hair he did have was black and worn thick. He let it grow down in thick sideburns that reached to the jawline. But different as they might seem, Mary Ann knew of no other two men who shared bonds as close as these two.

John Taylor and Wilford Woodruff were contrasts of a different sort, and considerably different from the two senior Apostles. They were only now becoming friends through their association in the Quorum, but before that they had barely known each other. Both were younger than Joseph Smith—Wilford by a little over a year, John Taylor by three years. They came from widely differing backgrounds. John Taylor had been born in England. He had emigrated to Canada when he was about twenty, and a few years later he married Leonora Cannon. It was there in Canada that Parley Pratt and Nathan Steed found the Taylors and brought them into the Church. John Taylor was almost regal in stature, with strong facial features, and he had a love for fine clothing. Brigham affectionately referred to him as their "dandy," or sometimes called him "Prince John," all of which Brother Taylor took in good humor. Together these qualities combined to give him an air of great dignity and respect. He spoke slowly and deliberately with a British accent that was softened little by his years in North America. Like Brigham, he was clean shaven and had a full head of hair, but his hair had a slight wave to it and was nearly silver now, even though he was barely over thirty. Basically quiet and more reserved by nature, John was a skilled wood turner and cabinetmaker, but he was also well educated and loved to read.

Wilford Woodruff was the shortest of the four, not more than five feet eight inches tall, but, like Heber, was powerful of build and a strong worker. His eyes were light blue and were the most arresting feature of the man. They were piercing, almost alive with power, and when he spoke, one could barely pull away from being drawn into their depths. His dark hair was thinning, and he was the only one of the four who wore a beard. He wore it Greek style, going around the bottom of his jaw and chin but leaving his face clean shaven. He had prominent cheekbones, and that, along with the beard, had a tendency to make his face look gaunt at times, especially when he was more somber. Mary Ann did not know him well, but in the few times she had been around him, she learned that this look was deceiving. His temperament was gentle and naturally cheerful. He easily forgave and was free of jealousy or misgivings about others. He dressed simply and lived simply. Both she and Benjamin were very impressed by the man and by his manner.

They visited briefly about the family and the new homes, then Brigham cleared his throat. He looked at Matthew. "Brother Joseph and the First Presidency came across the river the other day and had a meeting with the Twelve and some of the Seventies. Joseph is anxious that we prepare for our departure."

"How soon?"

"As soon as possible. John and Wilford may get off right away. Heber wants to finish his cabin so his family can get out of that leaky lean-to they're living in now. And I have to get my Mary Ann and the children settled as well. So he and I may be a little longer."

Heber leaned forward. "But we are hoping to get away before the month is through."

Good. Matthew understood full well what it meant for these married men to leave their families for a year or more, but he was ready, chomping at the bit, as they said.

"It was a wonderful meeting," Brigham went on. "Joseph and the First Presidency blessed the new members of the Quorum, Brother Wilford and Brother George, as well as Brother Turley and some of our wives."

The others were nodding in agreement with that. "It was indeed wonderful," Wilford spoke up. "They promised us that if we are faithful we shall return to the bosom of our families again and that they will be cared for in our absence."

Mary Ann reached out and laid a hand on Matthew's arm. "I am pleased to hear that."

"They also promised us," Wilford continued, "that we should

have great success on our missions and see many souls enter the Church as a seal on our ministry."

Brigham was excited all over again in the remembering of it. He stood and began to pace as he spoke. "Joseph spoke to us. He gave us a key. That's what he called it. A *key!* He said that no matter what befalls us—persecutions, afflictions, bonds, imprisonments, even death—we must see to it that we do not betray heaven, that we do not betray Jesus Christ, that we do not betray the brethren, that we do not betray the revelations found in the Bible, the Book of Mormon, or the Doctrine and Covenants. No matter what, we must remain faithful. That is the key."

The room fell silent as the power of Joseph's words flowed through his senior Apostle and into the room. Then suddenly Brigham straightened. "What are we doing? We should have Derek here to hear all this too. That was why we came." He looked at Matthew. "We need to plan for our departure, and we also wanted to share some of Joseph's instructions with those who are going to accompany us."

"Then let's go," Matthew said. "Derek is just across the street. He'll be pleased to see you."

Brigham reached out and shook Benjamin's hand. "It is good to visit with old friends." Then to Mary Ann, "Have Nathan bring you and Lydia across the river sometime. My Mary Ann would love to see you again."

"Phoebe as well," Wilford spoke up.

"I will."

It was several moments before the door opened to reveal Rebecca standing there. Matthew was surprised. It was barely dusk now, but Rebecca was in her nightdress, and there was no lamp or candles burning inside. With the one small window facing west, it was quite dark inside.

At the sight of the men with Matthew, Rebecca looked startled. "Oh," she blurted. She pushed quickly at a strand of hair, then tucked another one back in place. "Good evening, Brother Brigham. Brother Heber."

"Good evening, Sister Rebecca. Is your good husband at home?"

Matthew was still peering inside the cabin, puzzled at what he saw. "Is everything all right, Becca?"

There was movement in the corner and a faint moan. "Come in, brethren. It's all right. Come in."

Rebecca looked first at Matthew, then to Brigham, and finally to Heber. It was Heber who had converted and baptized Derek and Peter while he was on his first mission to England. He was almost like a father to the two boys and considered Rebecca as if she were one of his own flesh and blood too. "He's got the shakes," she whispered.

"What?" Matthew blurted. He and Derek had been digging ditches until just a few hours ago. Derek had looked a little more tired than usual, but had said nothing.

Heber nodded solemnly, then stepped forward and laid his hand on Rebecca's forehead. "You've got the fever too," he declared.

She looked away, and then in a weak, barely audible voice, she answered. "Yes, I'm afraid I do."

———◆———

On Sunday, July seventh, three days following the visit of Brigham Young and his fellow Apostles to the Steeds, a meeting was called. Joseph's charge and blessing to the Twelve five days earlier had stirred their hearts and strengthened their determination to leave as soon as possible. With Joseph's blessing, they determined they would formally bid farewell to the Saints before departing for England.

The meeting lasted until about five-thirty that afternoon, and those present went away rejoicing. When Matthew and Jenny returned and reported on the meeting to Derek, now too weak to even rise from his bed, he was terribly depressed. He

was certain the Twelve would have to leave without him. In reality, there was no need for him to worry about that, for the
ague had begun its deadly work on both sides of the river. Brigham fell sick shortly after his return to Montrose. Wilford
Woodruff returned to find his wife and baby critically ill.
Within a few days of the meeting, virtually every member of the
Twelve either was sick himself or had serious sickness rampag-
ing through the family. Any plans for an immediate departure
were forgotten.

Nor was the little Steed homesite and its four cabins spared.
Derek was too weak to raise his head off the pillow. Rebecca was
worsening and Lydia had to take baby Christopher and nurse
him for her. The day after the Sabbath, Benjamin broke out in a
cold sweat. By late afternoon he was huddled in bed, shaking violently. Then it moved to Nathan's home. Their third child,
little Nathan, was hit particularly hard and was gravely ill.
Next, their own baby, Elizabeth Mary, started in with it and so
Lydia had to pass Christopher on to Jessica. He would have to
drink milk from a bottle as best he could. So far Jessica was
spared, but Mark, her younger stepson, was in bed and barely
moving, and what was a blow to everyone, Jenny and Kathryn
McIntire came down with it next and could no longer help with
the children.

By mid-July it had become an epidemic. It was as though
the legions from some dark, foul place had been unleashed on
the community, moving from house to house, from tent to tent,
from open bedroll to open bedroll, touching old and young alike
with their accursed plague. First it was dozens, then hundreds,
then literally thousands who were stricken. The demons of the
plague selected member and nonmember alike, but the Saints
were particularly hard hit. There had been too many months of
malnourishment, too many winter nights without heat, too
many trips to polluted wells and dirty streams. Nauvoo, Montrose, Quincy—all up and down the Mississippi, the desolating
sickness swept across the land.

Lydia stopped and peered at the scene that lay before them. She brushed a hand across her eyes, thinking that her vision was betraying her.

"Oh my heavens . . . ," Jessica breathed.

They had heard that Joseph and Emma were taking some of the sickest of the Latter-day Saints into their home to care for them, but nothing had prepared them for what they were seeing now. The Old Homestead had a large yard, with grass that swept right down to the reeds along the riverbank. Now the yard had disappeared under a sea of sick humanity. This was what stopped Jessica and Lydia so abruptly. The house was surrounded by small tents, makeshift lean-tos, a few carts, and one or two wagons without covers. They took considerable space, but every inch not occupied by those temporary shelters was filled with blankets and quilts, bedrolls, sheets—anything that could provide some cover over the ground. There was hardly room to step between them. And on every bed, in every tent, stretched out in every wagon and lean-to were the sick of Nauvoo. It was like a vast, open-air hospital ward. People lay huddled together, cloths or towels pulled over their faces to ward off the sun. Some slept fitfully; others moaned softly; a few thrashed back and forth as the fever raged in their bodies. Here and there someone knelt beside the sickest ones, spooning broth into their mouths, or mopping a clammy brow with a wet cloth.

"I had no idea it was this bad," Jessica murmured, her voice filled with a horrified awe as they walked slowly toward the cabin. Lydia just shook her head. The sight of all the suffering around her made her nauseated, and she reached out for Jessica's arm.

"Are you all right?" Jessica asked anxiously, peering at the paleness of her face.

Lydia started to nod her head, but then she knew that bravery alone wasn't going to do it. "I need to sit for just a moment," she stammered.

Jessica took her by the elbow. "Let's get you into the shade there by the house," she said. Then as she started steering Lydia around and through the people, she saw Emma Smith. "Oh, there's Emma. Over by the well."

Emma was drawing up a pail from the well just east of the house. She saw them at the same moment they saw her, and one hand lifted in greeting. She immediately set the bucket down and came toward them.

"Come," Jessica said to Lydia. "A drink will do you good."

"Lydia," Emma said as she came up to them, "are you all right?"

"It's just the heat," Lydia said, forcing a wan smile. Her head turned in spite of herself, and she feebly waved one hand toward the surrounding scene. "And . . . this."

"Yes," Emma said, brushing at a trickle of sweat just below the line of her hair. "It's unbelievable, isn't it?"

"There are so many," Jessica said as they reached the step of the house and she helped Lydia sit down.

Emma walked quickly to the pail of water she had drawn. She got a dipper that was sitting on the edge of the well and filled it. When she came back, she handed it to Lydia and sunk wearily down on the step beside her.

Lydia drank deeply from the dipper, savoring every swallow. The water was cool and sweet and tasted wonderful. She felt herself begin to steady almost immediately. "Oh," she sighed luxuriously, "that is good!"

"Yes, it's a wonderful well." Emma untied her bonnet, pulled it off, and let it drop to her lap. Jessica watched her with a little anxiety. Emma normally wore her lustrous black hair in thick ringlets at the back of her head. Now they were limp and almost shapeless in the heat and humidity. Her eyes were missing that vibrancy that was part of her natural beauty, and there were large dark circles beneath them. She looked exhausted.

"Here," Emma said, taking the dipper and starting to rise, "let me get you one too, Jessica."

Jessica snatched the dipper from her hand. "You sit right there," she commanded. "I'll get a drink for myself."

A young sister whom Lydia recognized but couldn't name came up beside them. She hung back, not wanting to interrupt. "What is it, Mary Beth?" Emma asked.

"Are there any more wet cloths?" she asked. "My husband says he is burning up."

"I haven't been inside for a while," was the response. "See if there are any left in the kitchen. On the table."

"Thank you."

Jessica drained the dipper, then returned. She sat down on the grass in front of Lydia. "Where's Joseph?" she asked Emma.

A shadow crossed Emma's face and she looked away.

"Not Joseph too!" Lydia cried.

"Yes, last night. He can barely move."

"We heard that it was Father Smith that was ill," Jessica said.

Now Emma's despair was almost total. "Him too," she whispered. "We thought we had lost him yesterday."

"And now?" Jessica asked.

"A little better, but still very bad. We are praying very hard for him. Thankfully, Mother Smith is doing better." Lucy Mack Smith and her youngest daughter, also named Lucy, had come down with cholera shortly after arriving in Quincy, and both had been very seriously ill for some time.

"What about your children?" Lydia inquired.

Emma bit her lower lip. "Young Joseph is just starting in with it. Little Frederick has been quite bad for two days now." She looked out across the chaos around her, and then to no one said, "Sister Zina Huntington died last week."

"No," Jessica exclaimed. With their own illness consuming them, she had not heard that. So the deaths had begun.

"Will it never end?" Lydia burst out, feeling Emma's burden as if it were her own.

Emma reached out instantly and laid a hand over Lydia's. "It's all right, Lydia. I'm doing all right."

"Is Joseph in the house?" Jessica asked.

Emma smiled briefly, half in sadness, half in great love. "No, he's in one of the tents out back. The two boys are with him."

Jessica merely nodded. A woman had told her that Joseph had moved his family out into a tent to make room inside the house for the more desperately ill. Every bed, and most of the floor space, inside the house was quickly filled once the sickness began. Then they started putting the overflow in the yard around the house. It was not surprising to Jessica that Joseph would not reclaim his rights to his own house even though he himself was ill.

"Sister Smith! Sister Smith!"

They looked up. A man was near the corner of the house, beckoning frantically. "Come quick. It's my wife."

Emma nodded and lifted a hand. "I'll be right there, Brother Barker." She stood slowly, as if it cost her a tremendous effort of will. She looked down at Lydia. "It is so good to see you two. How are things with your families?"

Lydia looked away.

Jessica answered for her. "Nathan is down now. Little Nathan is very bad. The baby too."

"What about Father Steed? Joseph heard that he was ill now too."

"Very," Lydia managed, fighting hard not to cry now. "He's so weak. Mother Steed is down also. Even Matthew. But it's Father Steed and little Nathan we are most worried about." There was a pause and she looked away again. "We were hoping Joseph might come and give them a blessing."

"Sister Smith," the man called, his voice thin with desperation. "Please!"

"I'm coming." It came out with a touch of sharpness. Then she looked back to Lydia. "I'm sorry, Lydia. Others have asked too, but Joseph can't even rise from his bed."

Lydia finally looked up at Emma, the pain etching deep lines into her face. "Would you ask him if he could at least pray for us? Would you ask him to pray for my babies?"

Emma nodded slowly. "Yes, of course. He can do that." She looked around, gave a long sigh of total weariness, then turned and followed the man through the sea of bodies that filled the yard around them.

———•———

The fever broke shortly before eleven p.m.

It was as though he had been walking in those clouds of heavy black smoke that belch from the great cotton mills of New England. Now suddenly he was in the clear and the darkness was gone. He inhaled deeply, drawing in air slowly, savoring it as though it were the breath of life itself.

Reaching up, he laid the back of his hand against his cheek. It was cool and dry. Marveling at the change, he let his senses explore. He could feel the wetness beneath his head where his sweat had drenched his pillow. His nightshirt was equally wet, and he could feel the scars on his back pressing against it. Beside him, he could hear Lydia's soft breathing, though she was turned away from him and faced the wall.

Moving very slowly, so as not to wake his wife, Nathan slipped out of bed, and stood up. He could feel that his body was weak and in need of food and water, but there was no dizziness, no waves of nausea, no blurred vision that made him feel like he was going to pass out again. His spirit soared in exultation. This was not just another brief respite, which was so typical of the ague. It had passed! He could sense that throughout his body. The fever was passed.

He padded silently over to where a bucket of water sat beside the small cupboard that held their few dishes. Careful not to bump anything, he took the cup beside the pail, dipped it in the water, and drank from it deeply. The water was lukewarm and stale, but he didn't care. He filled the cup again and drained it. He could feel his body welcoming the liquid, as a dry patch of ground welcomes a stream turned onto it.

Satisfied, he turned and moved into the smaller room on one end of the cabin. Through the feverish haze that was his memory of the past few days, he remembered the baby's piteous crying, little Nathan's moaning, Lydia and Jessica bathing the small body, trying to stem the raging fever as little Nathan writhed back and forth in pain.

He moved to the small bed where his son lay, and listened. The breathing was labored and intermittent. Twice it stopped and Nathan held his own breath for what seemed like minutes until it started again. The boy half turned in his bed and there was a soft whimper of pain. Nathan reached out his hand and gently laid it on his son's forehead. He jerked back in shock. It was as if he had touched the bottom of a hot frying pan.

Deeply alarmed now, Nathan went back out to the pail of water. Feeling in the darkness, he found a rag, then poured a cup of water on it. As he was wringing it out, he heard Lydia stir behind him. He turned.

"Nathan?"

"Yes, it's me."

She sat up. "What are you . . . Are you all right?"

He moved toward her. "Yes. It's left me. I feel fine."

"Thank the Lord," she breathed.

She reached out for him, but he only touched her hand briefly. "Little Nathan is burning up again. I've got a wet cloth."

In an instant she was out of bed. She walked swiftly to the fireplace, took down the candle, and knelt down on the hearth. The small bed of coals they used to cook still smoldered dully. Leaning over, she blew softly on the coals as she held the wick of the candle to them. It began to smoke, then burst into flame.

When she came into the room, Nathan was kneeling beside his son's bed, gently touching the cloth to his forehead. The boy's eyes opened and for a moment he looked up into his father's face, not comprehending what he saw. Then a fleeting smile touched the corners of his mouth and one hand feebly lifted to touch his father's arm.

Lydia put the candle in a pewter holder and set it on the floor behind them. She knelt beside Nathan and reached out for her son. The eyes fluttered open again as she touched his cheek. "I hurt, Mama," he whispered. "I hurt."

Tears were trickling down her cheeks as she took his hand. "I know, darling. I know." His eyes slowly shut again, the effort of keeping them open too much for him.

She looked at Nathan, stricken. "This is the worst he's been," she said. "What are we going to do?"

Nathan shook his head. Both of their heads jerked around as little Nathan's breathing suddenly stopped. His chest was fully expanded, his back arched slightly. They stared at him in horror; then after a moment, the breath went out of him in a long sigh. There was another heart-wrenching delay; then finally, his chest lifted and he started breathing again.

"Go get your father," Lydia said, rocking back on her heels. "I want you to administer to him."

Malaria came and went in cycles varying from one to four days. It had three distinct stages in each cycle—the teeth-chattering chills which lasted from ten to thirty minutes a bout; the extremely high fevers, some as high as 105 degrees, which brought accelerated pulse, shallow breathing, and then severe headaches, vomiting, and diarrhea; and finally the drenching sweat when the fever broke.

Fortunately, Benjamin Steed had finished a cycle earlier that day. He looked terrible—his hair was disheveled, his chin was stubbled with gray whiskers, his eyes were dull, his energy was drained—but he was at least functioning again. Mary Ann had started in with the chills as she was preparing for bed a few hours before. Now she was fully into the second stage of fever. When Nathan woke them up and told them about little Nathan, Mary Ann tried to get up and come with them, but Benjamin absolutely forbade it. She sank back on the bed, too ravaged to carry through with her wish.

In the New Testament, the Apostle James instructed the early Church in this manner: "Is any sick among you? let him call for the elders of the church; and let them pray over him, anointing him with oil in the name of the Lord."

Benjamin led out, putting one drop of the olive oil from Nathan's bottle on top of little Nathan's head. He handed the bottle to Nathan, then laid his hands on his grandson. "Nathan Joseph Steed," be began softly, "as an elder in The Church of Jesus Christ of Latter-day Saints, I put this holy oil upon you, oil that has been consecrated by the power of the Melchizedek Priesthood for the purpose of healing the sick and administering to their needs. And this I do to the end that you may receive a blessing by the power of the priesthood, and in the name of our Savior and Redeemer, Jesus Christ, amen."

He lifted his hands, and Nathan leaned forward now. He placed both hands on little Nathan's head, and Benjamin then laid his hands back on top of Nathan's hands. For several moments, Nathan knelt there, looking inward, searching his soul for faith, silently pleading with the Lord that he might speak His will.

Then he began. "Nathan Joseph Steed, as your father and grandfather, we lay our hands upon your head and by the power of the priesthood which we hold, we seal upon you this anointing." He paused, taking a quick breath. "Nathan, we bless you now by the power of this priesthood. We bless your little body that is racked with sickness and pain. We pray for the Lord to look down upon you and have mercy and to heal you if it be his will. We bless you that this fever which torments you may be lifted and taken from you. You are a great treasure . . ."

He had to stop and swallow hard. "You are a great treasure," he went on more slowly now, his voice husky, "to your parents and to your grandparents. You have brought joy into our lives with your sweet and gentle spirit, and we thank our God that he has sent you to our home."

Lydia could not hold it in and began weeping.

And then suddenly, Nathan's prayer of administration became something else. "O Lord," he continued, his voice low and filled with pleading, "we know of thy great wisdom. We trust in thy great love. We know that thou hast watched over and blessed us richly with thy blessings." He had to stop again, and now tears were coursing down his cheeks as well. "We know that this precious child is a gift from thee, that he was thine before he was ours. We see so little of thy purposes and plan, but we know that all that thou doest is for our best good. We know that thy will is what will bring us the greatest joy. So if it is thy will . . ." He stopped, not wanting to say what he was feeling, but feeling it too strongly to push it aside. "If it is thy will that this son of ours should return to thee, then . . ."

Lydia started to sob beside him. She clenched her hands together and began to rock back and forth as the pain washed over her.

"Then may we accept thy will, O Father, and be strengthened in our determination to live so that we may see this precious son again with thee and thy Son in the holy resurrection." Barely above a whisper, he finished. "And this blessing we give, and this prayer we offer thee in the name of thy Beloved Son, who gave all that we might live with thee and have eternal life, amen."

Within ten minutes after Benjamin had returned to his bed, little Nathan's breathing smoothed and then deepened. The soft whimpering stopped, and he fell into an undisturbed sleep. The fever did not break, but it cooled noticeably. Lydia experienced a burst of euphoria, sure that the Lord had chosen to spare their son. Nathan wanted to believe it too, wanted so desperately to have it be so. But wanting it didn't dispel the strong feelings he experienced during the blessing of his son. His gloom quickly smothered her elation and she fell silent, moving a stool over beside little Nathan's bed.

Sometime after three a.m., little Nathan slipped into a coma. There was no distinct difference in his breathing, nor any other sign of the change, but Lydia knew it instantly. Without a word, she gathered him into her arms and carried him to the rocking chair out in the main room. She sat down and began to rock slowly, humming a children's lullaby she had sung to him when he was a baby, staring across the room, seeing nothing.

Around six-thirty, not long after the sun had risen above the eastern horizon, little Nathan opened his eyes for a moment. He looked confused and lost, but then he saw his mother. He reached up and touched her cheek with one hand, then let it fall back again. Nathan, sitting in a nearby chair, stood and moved swiftly to stand beside his wife. As he looked down, his son's eyes closed again, and after a moment, his breathing just died away.

Chapter Notes

Details of the meeting in which Joseph gives the Twelve instructions, including the key about remaining faithful, can be found in the Prophet's history (see HC 3:382–92; see also *American Moses*, p. 73, and *MWM*, pp. 59–60). The 7 July meeting in which the Twelve give their farewells to the Saints is also described in Joseph's history (see HC 4:1–3).

By mid-July 1839, malaria was a full-scale epidemic among the Saints. The scene around Joseph and Emma's cabin is accurately portrayed, as is the fact that Joseph himself became very ill but would not turn others out of his house so that he would have a place to sleep. (See *CHFT*, pp. 217–18; *Women*, pp. 41–42.)

In the revelation known as "the law of the Church" (D&C 42), Joseph Smith received instructions similar to what is given in James 5:14. The Lord declared to the Prophet Joseph, "And the elders of the church, two or more, shall be called, and shall pray for and lay their hands upon them [the sick] in my name." The modern revelation contains an important addition not found in James: "*And if they die they shall die unto me.*" (D&C 42:44, emphasis added.)

They buried little Nathan late that same afternoon. Nathan chose the upper corner of the plot that was to become Derek and Rebecca's farm. The land rose gently there and one could see the river and Iowa beyond. When he had asked Lydia about the site, she had only nodded numbly.

There was no lumber for a coffin and no lining for the grave. There were no pallbearers, for, without a coffin, there was no pall, or cloth, that usually would be draped over a coffin. They wrapped the small form in a quilt, then laid him carefully in the hole Nathan and Matthew had dug earlier.

There were only four present to witness the burial— Nathan, Matthew, Derek, and Lydia. The pestilence was everywhere now, sweeping the community like a besom of destruction. There were no others—no other family members, no neighbors, no friends, no Church leaders.

There should have been only three. The sickness was on Lydia now too, and that, coupled with the shock of losing her son, had left her in terrible shape. With every step, her legs trembled and threatened to collapse. But there was no question about whether or not she would come. So Nathan asked Matthew to carry the body, and he steadied and half carried Lydia to the site.

It was not a long service. While Lydia wept, Nathan gave a short prayer of dedication. Then he picked up a handful of dirt and let it trickle out of his hand and into the grave. For a long time he stared into it; then he turned and took Lydia by the elbow and turned her back toward the house. Matthew and Derek waited until Nathan and Lydia were several rods away, then slowly began shoveling the earth back into the hole whence it had come.

"Joshua?"

He stepped fully into the room, smiling broadly. "Hello, Mama."

"Joshua! How wonderful!"

He came across the room to where she sat in the rocking chair, huddled in a quilt. He dropped to his knees in front of her and took her in his arms. "Oh, Mama," was all he could say again, as he pulled her to him tightly.

Matthew watched for a moment, then stepped forward. "Hello, Joshua."

Joshua stood, sorrow briefly darkening his face, and then they too embraced. "How's Pa?"

Matthew shook his head. "Not good. He's sleeping right now."

"Your father is very ill," Mary Ann said in quiet resignation. "Is Caroline with you?" she asked.

Joshua turned and dropped down beside her again. "No, she couldn't come." He smiled proudly. "But we have some good news."

Mary Ann stared at him for a moment; then her face was wreathed in smiles. "She's with child?"

"Yes," he said proudly. "A month or so after Christmas."

"That's marvelous," she said, greatly cheered by that news. "Is she all right?"

"Yes. Olivia had the fever for a few days, but Caroline and Savannah have been fine, thank heavens." Now he frowned. "Quincy is hit real bad with the sickness too. There have been a number of your people who have died."

"Here too," Matthew said softly.

Mary Ann's head dropped. "We lost little Nathan."

Joshua leaped up. "No!" he cried.

She nodded, swallowing hard. "Day before yesterday."

"How awful. How's Lydia?"

Mary Ann just shook her head.

Joshua's mouth twisted even more downward as he turned to Matthew. "I'm afraid I have more bad news."

Matthew straightened slowly, his eyes wide.

"I'll go with you to see Jenny and Kathryn."

"Oh, no," Mary Ann cried, one hand coming up to her mouth.

Joshua's head went up and down slowly. "Mrs. McIntire died four days ago." He turned away. "We tried everything, but there was nothing we could do."

Only gradually was Mary Ann aware that daylight had come. Her eyes were still closed, but through her eyelids there was no longer the deep blackness. With an effort, she opened them. Without moving her head she let her eyes take in what was directly before them. She was half-turned, lying on one side, so she was facing the window. Through the curtain she saw that it was daylight, but still not very bright. It was either heavily overcast or still very early in the morning. She suspected the latter, but didn't care enough to turn over so she could see the clock. Her body was on fire again, and it burned every ounce of energy just to lie there.

Beside her, Benjamin groaned and stirred. She turned her

head toward him. His eyes were open, staring at the ceiling. His hands had the blanket up around his face and clutched it tightly. She reached out and laid a hand on his arm and felt the slight trembling of his body. Her heart dropped. This meant the beginning of another cycle of the illness. In a few minutes he would fall into that bone-rattling, teeth-chattering chill that drained every drop of strength from the body.

He turned his head slightly, and forced a crooked smile. "Mornin'," he whispered.

She squeezed his arm and forced herself to smile back. It was a feeble effort to hide her shock. Had he fallen so far since she had last been functioning enough to notice? His chin and jaw were covered with thick gray whiskers. His cheeks were sunken. His eyes were lifeless and had difficulty in focusing. His skin was pallid, with a sickly yellow cast to it. He had turned fifty-four in May, but now he looked more like eighty-four.

"How are you?" he croaked.

She nodded and lied. "Better."

"Good." his breathing was shallow and rapid, and even that much talking seemed to exhaust him.

His eyes closed again, and after a moment, she decided he had gone to sleep once more. But then he spoke. "Do you remember the dream?"

"The dream?" she asked, not sure what he meant.

"Yes. The plain." Getting full sentences out was difficult, and he had to gasp out words between breaths.

Her eyes widened in surprise. *That* dream. She hadn't thought of it for months now. "Yes," she finally said.

"Tell me."

She closed her eyes, letting the images flood over her again. It had been a wonderful thing, and it had come at the most desolate time in Far West. She could still remember the great joy she had felt both during the dream and afterwards. It was a feeling that lingered for many days and was a great comfort to her during those dark times.

The dream had begun with only her. Mary Ann found herself on a vast, open plain, walking steadily forward. There was not a tree anywhere to break the vastness of the landscape, but neither was it desolate or barren. There were flowers every-where, butterflies, birds—the beauty of it all filled her with a great sense of joy and wonder. Gradually she became aware that she was moving towards something, a glittering point in the distance, a source of light so brilliant that it seemed to be the source of the radiant daylight rather than a sun overhead.

Then to her surprise, Nathan appeared out of nowhere. He called and waved, and ran to join her, taking her hand. A moment later, Melissa did the same, then Matthew. Her family began appearing rapidly now, each one raising a hand in greeting and running to join them. There was no particular order. They just came, first one by one, then in pairs and small groups. Lydia, Derek and Rebecca, Jessica and Rachel and the two Griffith boys, young Joshua, Emily. They were laughing and singing and pointing eagerly to the great light in the distance, which they could now tell was a glorious, glowing city, lying on the horizon, beckoning them onward.

When she finally finished describing the dream again to Benjamin, he was silent for a long time. She turned and saw that his eyes were glistening. "And I wasn't there?" he finally asked.

Now Mary Ann understood. The tears spilled out of the corners of her eyes and trickled down her cheeks, feeling hot even against her burning skin. "No," she whispered. "You were in the city, waiting for us. I knew that. That was one of the reasons we were so anxious to reach it."

His hand came across the bed and found hers. "I've always loved you, Mary Ann Morgan. Did you know that? From the first day I saw you working on that turnpike with your father, I loved you."

She couldn't hold it back; the weeping overflowed. "And I've always loved you, Benjamin Steed," she said in a fierce whisper. She went up on one elbow and kissed him hard.

When she dropped back again, he smiled slowly at her. "I always heard about that, but I never believed it."

"What?"

"Love stronger than death. Now I do." He rested for a moment. "I'll be waiting for you, Mary Ann." A faint smile came and went. "Don't take forever."

"You stop talking like this," she scolded. "You're going to be all right."

"Mary Ann?"

She turned her head.

"I want to talk to Lydia."

"Lydia?"

"Yes. Today." He stopped, his chest rising and falling. "If I'm asleep when Nathan comes, tell him. Please!"

"All right," Mary Ann said, feeling a great sense of desolation come over her.

"And Joshua. I must talk to Joshua too. Tell him."

She turned her head away, the tears streaming down her face now. "I will, Benjamin."

———————•———————

Lydia came to Benjamin's bedside late that afternoon. She was still pale and moved very slowly, but for the moment, at least, the fever had left her. Over both Lydia's and Nathan's vigorous protests, Mary Ann got out of bed, dressed, and insisted that Nathan take her over to Jessica's so she could see how things were there.

As they shut the door, Lydia dragged a chair over to the bed and sat down slowly. The weariness and hopelessness in her face left her looking almost like another woman. Benjamin closed his eyes for a moment. *O Lord,* he prayed silently, *I need thy strength. Please help me.*

When he opened his eyes again, he saw that Lydia was watching him with grave concern. "Are you sure you can do this, Father Steed?"

He nodded, and reached out his hand for hers. He tried to squeeze it to reassure her, but the gesture was so feeble it had just the opposite effect. With some effort, he shifted around and pulled the pillow up under his head more so that he could face her directly. "How's the baby?"

Instantly, Lydia began to cry. After a moment she pulled her hands away from his, and buried her face in them. "Oh, Father Steed," she whispered in anguish, "what shall I do if I lose her too?"

He watched her for a moment, then gently asked, "What did your parents say?"

She looked up, surprised by the change of subject. Joshua had picked up a letter in Quincy. It was from Palmyra, New York, from Lydia's parents, written while they thought Nathan and Lydia were still living in Quincy. That was a great surprise, for she had not heard from them in over a year.

She straightened slowly, sniffing back the tears, brushing at her eyes with the back of her hand. There was a deep sigh, and her shoulders lifted and fell. "Papa is not well. Mama wants me to bring the children—" Her voice faltered; then she fell apart. Now the sobs racked her body with great shudders. "Oh, Father Steed," she finally choked out between sobs, "why has God done this to us? Haven't we suffered enough? Why did he take my son?"

He didn't answer, feeling the anguish as if it were his own. Finally, he began in a halting voice to try and answer her question. "In the Book of Mormon, it says, 'Seek not to counsel the Lord—'" He stopped as he saw her frown, but then he went on, resolutely. "'But take counsel from his hand, for he counseleth in wisdom and in mercy.'"

She looked away, her mouth tight.

"He counseleth in wisdom and mercy," he said again, falling back against his pillow. "I know that is true, Lydia."

She swung on him. "Was it merciful to take little Nathan away?"

"I—"

Her voice had gone harsh, almost brittle. "You haven't been out, Father Steed. You haven't seen the yards filled with the sick and the dying, the little children burning with fever and crying for relief." She stopped. "The graves." Suddenly her face crumpled and she had to look away. "Tell me. Where is the mercy in all of that?"

He watched her, the pain in his heart more unbearable than the fire of the fever.

"Sister Hatch came over yesterday," Lydia went on. She was looking at the floor and not at Benjamin. "I know she was trying to comfort me, but . . ." Suddenly her head came up and there was a hard challenge in her eyes. "She said it was God's will. She said that God has called little Nathan home. With all the thousands of people who are older and ready to die, does God really need one more little baby?" She was greatly agitated now. "John Griffith was gunned down at Haun's Mill. Was that God's will too? Is God's work so limited that he has to take John home and leave Jessica a widow with four little children? Doesn't Jessica need John more than God needs him right now?"

Lydia saw the weariness in Benjamin's face and was instantly repentant. She slumped in her seat and reached out to take his hand. "I'm sorry, Father Steed. You are so sick, and here I am troubling you with my problems."

Benjamin looked up at the ceiling. He had called for Lydia because he guessed she was struggling right now, but he was shocked at how deeply the tragedy had torn at her moorings. He really believed he could say things to her that might make a difference, things which even Nathan couldn't say at this point. But now, in a sudden flash of understanding, he saw that she did not need answers from him. She didn't need anyone else preaching to her. He turned and smiled, letting all the love he felt for this beautiful, brave woman show in his eyes. "Lydia?"

She looked at him, but didn't respond.

"I didn't like you at first, did you know that?"

Her eyebrows lifted in surprise. Then finally a tiny smile broke through the tears. "Yes," she said softly, "I knew that very well."

He took a breath, surprised that he was getting stronger.

"There you were, the only child of Josiah McBride, one of Palmyra's wealthiest citizens. And there I was, both of my sons, children of a dirt-poor farmer, smitten silly over the very sight of you."

Lydia wiped the last of the tears from her cheeks. She knew what he was doing, but she didn't care. She needed this. "Nathan told me what you said when he and I were going to get married."

"What?"

"About mules not running with thoroughbreds."

He frowned. "Well, it was true. You were way above what the Steeds were."

"Oh," she teased, "I thought you were suggesting I was the mule."

He started to protest, then saw her eyes and smiled with her. He lay back, gathering his strength for a moment. "After you got married, I saw how hard you worked and I started to alter my opinion. But do you know when it all really changed?"

She shook her head. "No, when?"

"That day you were helping Nathan butcher a pig."

She laughed right out loud at that, surprising even herself. "I remember that day like it was yesterday. It was awful."

He laughed now too, deep and throaty as the memories warmed him. "You were carrying young Joshua at the time, weren't you?"

"Yes. And everything smelled so awful. I could look at a piece of bread and butter and want to throw up." She cocked her head. "Say, how long had you been standing there that day watching me trying to hold that carcass steady, anyway?"

He chuckled. "Long enough to watch Nathan open it up and see you lose your breakfast." Now he squeezed her hand with real power. "At that instant, I knew my son had married a very unusual woman."

That brought the tears back to her eyes. "Thank you, Father Steed," she said very softly. "You are as dear to me as my own father." On an impulse, she left the chair and dropped to her knees beside him. She laid her head against his arm, crying openly again now. "Don't leave us, Father Steed," she whispered fiercely. "Please don't leave us. I can't bear to lose you too."

He laid a hand on the back of her head, stroking her hair slowly. "Lydia?"

She didn't lift her head. "Yes, Father?"

He started a little as he realized she had not finished his title. Suddenly there was a lump deep in his throat and he could barely get it out. "There's still more hogs to be cleaned."

She flinched a little as the impact of his words sank in. "I don't know if I can do that anymore," she cried.

"You can!" he said. "You can!"

———◆———

Five minutes later when Nathan and Mary Ann returned, they were still that way, Lydia kneeling by Benjamin's side, both of them holding hands. Benjamin waved Nathan over weakly. The Lord had heard his prayer and given him strength to speak with Lydia. Now he felt completely drained.

"Yes, Papa?"

"Where's Joshua?"

"He's with Derek and Rebecca right now. He said he'd be over to see you in a few minutes."

"All right." He breathed deeply, searching for energy. "I know you're too old, but I'm going to do it anyway."

Nathan looked puzzled. "Too old for what?"

"To tell you what to do."

"What do you want me to do, Papa?" Nathan said. "You know I'll do it."

"Promise?"

"Of course."

Benjamin nodded, satisfied. Now he looked at Lydia, though he continued to speak to Nathan. "Take her home."

"What?"

He came up partially on one elbow. "Take Lydia home. To her parents."

"But . . . ," Lydia said, as floored by his words as Nathan was. "*Promise?*" It came out with sudden ferocity.

"I . . . well, yes, I guess," Nathan stammered. "Yes."

Benjamin sank back. "As soon as you are able. With the children."

Mary Ann was staring at him too. He looked at her and smiled, very faintly. "Josiah McBride needs to see his grandchildren."

Lydia's head tipped back and she was looking up at her husband, her eyes large and liquid and pleading. "Would you, Nathan?" she whispered.

"I . . . ," he started, still a little dazed. Then he stopped and, shaking off the indecision, said firmly, "Yes, I will. Of course."

She lowered her head and closed her eyes. "Thank you," she breathed. Then to Benjamin, "Thank you, dear, dear Father Steed."

Joshua sat at his father's bedside for several minutes before Benjamin's eyes opened. His eyes widened for a moment, and then there was a quick, satisfied nod. "I'm sorry," he whispered. "I guess I'm getting old."

Joshua smiled. "You're also very sick."

Benjamin nodded again and licked his lips. They were dry and cracked.

"Can I get you a drink?"

"Yes."

Joshua left the small bedroom, and in a moment returned with a tin cup of water. He put his arm under his father's shoulders and helped him sit up. As he watched him drink, Joshua was shocked at how much weight his father had lost.

"Thank you," Benjamin said as Joshua laid him back down. He was breathing hard, challenged by even that little an effort. He lay there, his eyes closed, until he recovered a little. Then he opened them again and turned to face Joshua. "I wish Caroline had come."

"She wanted to. But she's feeling very sick with the new baby."

"That's wonderful. The baby, I mean."

Joshua grinned. "It *is* wonderful."

"I—" He took a breath and started over. "I was hoping to see her again. And Savannah."

"You will, Pa," Joshua said, struggling to keep his face expressionless. "You will. I'll bring them up in a week or two."

"Too late."

Joshua leaned over, peering into his father's eyes. "It's not too late! You stop talking like that."

Benjamin smiled faintly. "Are we going to fight over this too?" he asked.

Joshua laughed in spite of himself. "No," he agreed. "Let's not."

Suddenly, to Joshua's astonishment, Benjamin's eyes were filled with tears. "Thank you," he whispered.

"For what?" Joshua asked in surprise.

"For coming back. For all you've done for the family."

"They're family, Pa. I'm just glad I'm able to help."

"For forgiving me."

Now Joshua's vision was suddenly blurred. He swallowed hard. "No, Pa. Thank *you* for forgiving *me*. I was so blind. So stupid."

One hand came up and stabbed at the chest beneath the nightshirt. "Me," Benjamin said slowly. "That was me."

Shaking his head, Joshua just laid a hand on his father's arm. He thought of all the years of bitterness and hurt. The years of running and trying to deny how deeply he missed his family.

Benjamin's eyes closed again, and for a long time he was silent. Joshua finally decided he had slipped into sleep, and started to pull back. But Benjamin's hand shot out and grabbed his arm. His eyes opened and were perfectly lucid as he gazed up at his son. "I have nothing to leave you."

"What?"

"No will. Nothing except this cabin. Not much."

"Pa, stop it! You're going to get better."

It was as if Joshua hadn't spoken. "Nothing of the world, anyway," Benjamin said. "Nothing to put in a box."

"Pa—," Joshua started, but Benjamin gripped his arm with sudden power, cutting him off. "You're happy, aren't you, Joshua?"

Joshua rocked back slightly, completely caught off guard by the question. "I . . . well, yes."

"*Really* happy?"

"Yes, Pa. I'm happier than I have ever been."

"Good." Benjamin breathed more deeply, as though trying to gather strength. "Caroline's wonderful."

"Yes," Joshua murmured. "The best thing that ever happened to me."

"Children wonderful."

"Yes, they are. We have really been blessed."

There was a small triumphant smile. "By whom?"

Under different circumstances Joshua might have responded with another answer, but he looked down at his father and said simply, "By divine providence."

"By God."

Joshua shrugged. "Whatever you want to call him."

"By God," Benjamin repeated. His eyes slowly closed again.

"You'd better rest now, Pa. We'll talk some more in the morning."

The eyes didn't open, but a smile stole slowly across his face. There was a deep chuckle. "Don't panic, son," he said. "I'm not going to preach to you."

Joshua's eyebrows lifted, and then he saw that his father was looking at him. He chuckled now too, amazed that his father had read his discomfort so clearly. "All right, but you're not going to make me into a Mormon, Pa."

"Don't want to," came the instant reply. "Only you can do that." With an effort he turned onto his side, putting his hands under the side of his face so that he could look directly at Joshua. "I was happy too."

Joshua nodded slowly. "I know you are, Pa. I can see that."

"No, not just now. Before."

"Before what?"

"The Church."

"Oh."

"I was!" he said firmly. "Good life. Farm. Wonderful family." His voice softened. "A wife that . . ." He couldn't finish, just shook his head. "A good wife."

"Yes, Papa. Mama is a wonderful woman."

"Like you," Benjamin said. There was an urgency in him now. "It was good. No complaints."

Joshua nodded, not exactly sure what his father was trying to say.

Benjamin drew in a deep breath, staring past Joshua now. "But when the gospel came . . . So much more. Thought I had everything. But so much more."

Now Joshua saw where all this was going, and strangely he didn't resent it. He leaned forward. "I know, Pa. I can see that it has made you very happy. And I'm glad for you."

Benjamin's voice grew fainter now. "But there's more, Joshua. So much more."

Joshua didn't answer, just touched his father's arm to let him know he understood.

A great sigh went out of Benjamin, and Joshua knew this had been what he wanted to say. On an impulse, Joshua leaned over and did something he hadn't done since he was a boy. He kissed his father on the cheek. "You rest now, Papa."

Benjamin's eyes flew open in surprise, then he smiled. "Yes."

"I'll see you in the morning."

There was a bare nod and the eyes closed again.

Joshua stood and stepped back from the bed. But he didn't move beyond that. For a long time he stood there, watching this frail old man who had come to mean so much to him. Finally, when Benjamin's breathing had deepened and he was clearly asleep, Joshua turned and left the bedroom, closing the door quietly behind him.

Chapter Twelve

By the morning of July twenty-second, 1839, Nauvoo, and Montrose across the river from it, looked like one vast battle zone. In a matter of weeks, the ague and the bilious fevers had taken a greater toll than Governor Boggs's infamous extermination order, and a quiet desperation had settled over the settlements of the Saints.

———•———

"What if the Prophet is still too sick to come?" Derek said, between breaths.

Nathan shook his head, hurrying along. "I don't know."

Mary Ann had come to Nathan's cabin in a panic an hour before, totally distraught. Benjamin was in a semi-coma and slipping rapidly. Mary Ann, still very weak and only half functioning herself, had begged them to go for the Prophet. Joseph had healed Benjamin once, in the jail at Richmond. It was their only hope, she said.

"I don't know," Nathan said again grimly.

As they turned south on the road that would take them to the Old Homestead, Nathan pulled up short. Derek nearly bumped into him, then stepped around him to see what had brought him up.

A large crowd of people was coming toward them. Joseph was in the lead, but the people swarmed around him, some running out in front, some trotting backwards so they could listen to what he was saying as he strode along. Everyone was talking excitedly. Some were jumping up and down, greatly exercised. Several of the Twelve were walking alongside Joseph.

"What is this?" Derek asked, gaping at the sight. To see so many people up and walking was amazing. And Joseph. Joseph was better again.

Before Nathan could answer, the Prophet turned off and walked to a tattered tent. A woman was at the tent flap, brought out by the noise. The Prophet went right up to her and took her hands. He said something. She nodded and stepped back. Joseph followed her inside the tent. Heber Kimball and John Taylor went in after them.

Then Nathan gasped, leaning forward, gaping. "There's Parley!" he exclaimed.

"Parley Pratt?" Derek asked dubiously. "How could that be?" Back in November, Parley had been part of a group of brethren charged, unjustly, with murder in connection with the Battle of Crooked River in Ray County; and so he and four others had remained prisoners in Richmond, while the Prophet and five others, charged with treason, were taken to Liberty Jail in Clay County. In April, Joseph, Hyrum, and the others with them had escaped from Missouri. But Parley had not been so fortunate. The last Derek heard, the Apostle still had not been released. Could it be that he had somehow managed to get free and make his way to Illinois?

"It *is* him!" Nathan cried. He broke into a run, waving his hat. "Parley! Parley!"

Derek saw Parley now too. He was standing beside his

brother Orson and John E. Page, another member of the Twelve. He darted off, sprinting to catch up with Nathan.

Parley saw them coming and shouted something. Then he too was running, arms outstretched. He and Nathan collided hard, nearly knocking each other down, but Parley recovered and swept Nathan up in a huge bear hug, swinging him around and around. Derek was grinning widely as he came up to join them.

"I can't believe it," Nathan said finally. "When did you get free?"

"July fourth," Parley said, laughing merrily. "Independence Day. Best one I ever had. But I didn't arrive in Quincy until a few days ago, and I'm just now up here."

Nathan stepped back, eyeing his friend up and down. Parley Pratt was a stout man, built somewhat along the lines of Heber Kimball, but he didn't look it now. He had lost thirty or more pounds, and his clothes hung on him loosely.

Parley sobered. "It is a marvelous story. There isn't time now to tell it, but I shall come see you." He clamped a hand on Nathan's shoulder. "How are you, old friend?"

A frown darkened Nathan's brow and he shook his head. "Not well. My father is dying. We have already lost one son. Our baby is critical." Nathan turned now, looking at the crowd milling around the tent waiting for Joseph. "We came to see if Joseph might be well enough to come give my father a blessing." And then he couldn't keep the surprise out of his voice. "We were afraid that Joseph was still sick. What is going on, Parley? What is happening?"

"A miracle!" Parley burst out. "A marvelous miracle."

"What?"

He grabbed Nathan by the arm, his fingers digging into the flesh. The excitement danced in his eyes. "I've only just joined them, but Orson has told me the full story. This morning Joseph *was* ill, very ill. But as he was lying in his bed, he said the power of God came upon him. He rose from his bed and blessed Emma. She was immediately made well. He blessed his children. They were made well. Filled with the Spirit of God, he began to move about the house. As you know, he has many people there, caring for them."

"Yes, we know," Derek responded.

"He healed them, each one. Then he went out into his yard. That's where Orson was. He too was very sick. Joseph moved from tent to tent, commanding people to rise or to be healed. He then sent Orson for the Twelve so we could accompany him. That's when I joined them."

"And all these people?" Nathan began, his voice tinged with wonder.

"Most of them were too sick to walk as this day began," Parley said eagerly. "We've been moving from house to house, from tent to tent. Time after time, Joseph reaches out." He shook his head, his eyes shining. "It's a miracle!"

At that moment, the noise behind them rose again. They turned. Joseph and the others were out of the tent. The woman came out behind them. She was sobbing with joy, and threw her arms around the Prophet. "Thank you, Brother Joseph. Oh, thank you!"

He smiled, patting her on her shoulder. "Thank the Lord, Sister Bonner. I am only an instrument in his hands."

John Taylor saw Nathan and Derek talking with Parley and walked over to join them. He was smiling broadly.

"Again?" Parley said to his fellow Apostle.

Brother Taylor nodded, his eyes filled with wonder. "Yes, again and again, over and over. It's unbelievable. He reaches out and speaks a word, and they are healed."

Nathan grabbed the Apostle's arm, his voice urgent, but for the first time on this day it was filled with hope. "My father," he said. "He's dying. Do you think Joseph could come?"

The Prophet had turned from the woman and was looking in their direction. He came swiftly over. "Nathan. Derek. Good morning."

"Brother Joseph," Nathan said, taking his outstretched hand. "Father is very bad. Can you come see him?"

Pain filled Joseph's eyes. "My old friend and counselor? But of course I shall come." He looked up, his eyes measuring the number of tents and cabins that lay between where they were and the Steed homesites. "We will be stopping along the way," he said after a moment. "But you return to Mary Ann. Tell her we are coming. We shall be there soon."

Nathan nodded, the relief so powerful he didn't trust his voice to speak.

"Thank you, Brother Joseph," Derek said huskily. "We'll tell her."

"I'm coming," Joseph said calmly. "Tell her I'm coming."

—•—

"Brother Benjamin."

There was no response. Benjamin Steed lay motionless on the bed, his face as gray as the previous night's ashes in the fireplace. His chest rose and fell quickly, and there was a raspiness to the sound of his breathing.

"I think he's in a coma," Joshua volunteered.

Joseph ignored that. "Benjamin Steed," he said in a commanding voice.

There was a flutter of eyelids and the body stirred slightly.

This time the Prophet spoke even more firmly. "It's Joseph, Benjamin."

Mary Ann held her breath. Nathan leaned forward, staring. Matthew, who was sitting by the bedside, holding his father's hand, looked up in surprise. "He just squeezed my hand," he whispered.

Joseph laid a hand on Matthew's shoulder. "May I?" he said.

Matthew slipped out of the chair, passing Benjamin's hand to Joseph as the Prophet sat down in his place. The five Apostles who were accompanying Joseph had come into the cabin with him. There wasn't room in the small bedroom for everyone, so some stood at the door looking in. Heber went up on his toes so he could see over Mary Ann's head. "Brother Benjamin," he called. "It's Heber Kimball. We've come to say hello to you."

Joseph took Benjamin's hand in both of his and raised it up in front of him, as though he were going to pray. The movement was enough to break through the veil of unconsciousness. Benjamin's eyes opened slowly. For a moment, he simply stared at nothing; then finally he turned his head slightly.

"Hello, dear friend," Joseph said, smiling warmly.

The tip of Benjamin's tongue darted out, licked briefly at the cracked lips. "Hullo." It was no more than a croak.

Joseph pulled the hand closer to him, and leaned over so his face was only a few inches away from Benjamin's. "It's time for you to get up, old friend." He heard the gasps from behind him, but went on smoothly. "There's a lot of sickness across the river. Brother Brigham is sick. We're going over to see if we can help. I'd like you to come with me."

Joshua took a step forward, anger darkening his features. "Joseph, are you out of your—"

Nathan reached out and caught his arm, holding him back. Mary Ann turned and shook her head quickly at him.

Benjamin seemed unaware of any of that. But a look of amazement filled his eyes. He shook his head back and forth once. "Can't," he whispered hoarsely. "Thought you had come—" He had to stop and draw in several quick breaths. "To say goodbye."

Joseph laughed lightly. "Nonsense, old friend." The smile faded away. "Do you want to die, Benjamin?"

Again came the almost imperceptible shake of the head.

Joseph straightened. His shoulders pulled back, and his face was infused with sudden determination. It was as though a bright light had suddenly been thrown across his features. His eyes shone with fire and power. "Then in the name of Jesus Christ," he said in a voice loud enough that it startled those behind him, "I command you to rise from your bed and come with us across the river."

For several moments time hung suspended. No one moved. Not a sound came from anywhere. Every eye was locked on the figure lying motionless on the bed. Then, slowly at first, and with considerable effort, Benjamin began to draw in a breath. It was as though he hadn't breathed for several minutes and now needed to take in sufficient air to make up for the loss. Even as his chest rose, expanding outward and then outward even farther, his eyes cleared and color flowed into his cheeks. At last his lungs had reached their full capacity. For a moment, he held the air in, body frozen immobile, and then in a long, slow sigh, it all came rushing out again. It was a sound of great relief, a sound of poison being expelled from both mind and body, a sound of shucking off the clutching hands of whatever it was that had him in its grip.

And then, pulling heavily on Joseph's hand, Benjamin sat up.

Joshua was gaping, too stunned to believe what his eyes had just seen. Mary Ann gave one great sob and rushed to the bed, dropping to her knees and throwing her arms around her husband. Nathan looked at Matthew, whose eyes were like two great pewter plates. They both just shook their heads in wonder.

All business, Joseph stood up. "He's very weak," he said to Mary Ann. "Water will help. Perhaps a little food. But not too much for now." He turned back to Benjamin. "I want to see the rest of your family. We'll be back in a few minutes." There was that wonderful, flashing smile again, teasing Benjamin. "It would probably be better if you changed out of your nightshirt." He leaned over and, in a conspiratorial whisper, added, "You know how much Brother Taylor likes a well-dressed man."

Joseph touched Mary Ann's shoulder. "We'll be back. He'll be fine now."

With tears streaming down her face, she rose and faced Joseph. She reached out and took his hands. "Thank you, Joseph. Thank you."

Serious now, he shook his head. "Don't thank me, Mother Steed. You know as well as anyone where the thanks belong."

"Yes," she whispered.

Joseph swung around and started to the door. He stopped in front of Joshua, who was still staring at him with his mouth open and his eyes a little dazed. "We'd be pleased to have your company as we visit the rest of your family, Joshua."

———◆———

At Jessica's house, sickness had taken a double toll. Not only had it swept through the seven of them with varying severity, but the news of the passing of Nancy McIntire had devastated Jenny and Kathryn mentally and emotionally as well. Joseph went through the children, starting with the baby, laying his hands on them and blessing them one by one. Luke and Mark were next, followed by Rachel. When he blessed Jenny and Kathryn, there was an added measure of comfort given and promises of a future reuniting of mother and daughters.

Surprisingly, however, Joseph didn't lay his hands on Jessica, as he did the others. He simply went to her bedside and knelt down beside it. Her face was covered with a sheen of sweat, but she had the blankets pulled up around her chin and was shivering slightly. Joseph reached out and took her left hand. He turned it over. The scar from where the mobber's ball had passed through the door and then through her hand was a round circle of purple and red. He touched it with the tip of his finger. "Sister Jessica," he said quietly, "do you remember what I said to you that day you and the others came to visit, the day after I arrived in Quincy?"

She started to shake her head no, then remembrance came and she quickly nodded. "You said the Lord hasn't forgotten me."

"That's right. He is aware of your sacrifice. All will be well with you."

"Thank you."

He looked at her in amazement. "Do you believe me so easily?" he asked.

"Yes."

"Oh, that all had such faith," he murmured. "No wonder the Lord loves you!"

Derek had put the fever behind him four days before. Rebecca was nearly recovered from her bout of it as well. And baby Christopher had mercifully been spared any signs of the ague. His only discomfort came when the sickness reduced Rebecca's milk supply and they had to look elsewhere for someone to nurse him. Seeing that things were not so desperate there, Joseph stayed only for a few moments. As he prepared to leave, he turned to Rebecca. "Dear Sister Rebecca," he began, "the Lord well knows what it will mean for you when your good husband accompanies the Twelve across the sea. He is very pleased that you willingly accept this sacrifice and do not try to hold your husband to your bosom. Fear not about Brother Derek's safety. He returns to be among his people, and the work that he shall do shall be great. But when it is done, he shall return to you in safety, bearing many sheaves upon his back."

Rebecca's eyes shone with gratitude. She went up on tiptoe and kissed Joseph on the cheek. "Thank you, Brother Joseph."

To Nathan's surprise, when they reached the door of his cabin, Joseph turned, holding up one hand. "If you please, brethren, perhaps it is best if only Nathan accompanies me inside."

They nodded and stepped back. To Joshua's surprise, he felt sharply disappointed. He suddenly realized that watching Joseph minister to the needs of the Steed family had been fascinating. He caught himself. He had almost said in his mind, *inspiring*.

The two men went inside, Nathan going first. The interior was dim, the only light coming through two small curtained windows. Lydia was in the rocking chair, Elizabeth Mary in her arms. The baby was crying softly, barely whimpering, with weak, shuddering sobs that shook her body. Nathan moved swiftly over to them. "How is she?" he asked anxiously.

Lydia shook her head. Then the movement of someone by the door caught her eye and she looked up quickly. She had seen only Nathan come in.

"It's Brother Joseph," Nathan explained.

"Joseph?" she echoed numbly. One hand came up and brushed at her cheek, as though there were a spot there that needed removing.

"Hello, Lydia."

"Joseph, how good of you to come."

"Emma sends her love and inquires after your health." Then before she could answer, he stepped closer, peering at the baby. "May I?" he asked, holding out his arms.

Wearily, Lydia passed the baby up to him. Immediately the one-year-old began to cry in earnest again. Joseph cuddled her against his body and started to croon softly to her. Then, as he walked slowly back and forth across the room, he began to speak. "Elizabeth Mary Steed," he intoned, "by the power of the holy priesthood of God, I take you in my arms. In the name of our Savior and Redeemer, I rebuke the affliction that has come upon you."

The cry softened, then died to a whimper.

"You have a long life before you as a daughter of Zion. The work of the kingdom must go forward, and as part of that work, the Lord needs righteous, faithful women who will uphold his work."

Elizabeth Mary stopped crying completely now. Lydia came to her feet, her eyes wide, staring in dumbfounded amazement.

Joseph's voice lowered until they could barely hear him. "You are one of those chosen to be a mother in Zion, and you shall live to bring forth sons and daughters into the world. And that promise I make to you in the name of the Lord God of Israel, amen."

Smiling now, he stepped to Lydia and handed the baby back to her. Lydia looked down at her, still not quite believing. The baby's eyes were closed, and Lydia could feel the steadiness of her breathing.

Joseph turned to Nathan. "The other children?"

Lydia pointed. "In there, but they are all right now. They're playing."

"And what about you?" Joseph asked softly.

She tried to meet his gaze but couldn't. Her jaw started to tremble ever so slightly as she fought to keep rein on her emotions. Nathan moved to her and took the baby. "Let me put Elizabeth Mary down."

Lydia did not protest. She handed her to him, then returned to her rocking chair. She sat down and began to rock slowly back and forth, her eyes focused on a spot somewhere out in front of her.

Joseph took a stool from beneath the table and set it down in front of her. "And what about you, Lydia?" he asked again, even more gently than before.

Her head came up slowly, and now instead of tears, there was just pure anguish. "If you had come sooner, you could have saved him, couldn't you? Like you just did for Elizabeth Mary. You could have healed little Nathan too." It was a pleading cry for understanding, for some kind of solace.

Joseph shook his head wearily. "It is not me that saves a person, Lydia, it's "

"If that's true, then why didn't God save my child? Why didn't he send you here sooner?" She buried her face in her hands and began to weep silently. Nathan had come back out and now stood watching the two of them. He seemed to sense that it was better that he stay back.

"I don't know," Joseph answered in honest simplicity. "I don't know why he spares one and takes another."

"Is it because I haven't been faithful enough? Has Nathan not given enough to the Lord? What did we do wrong that this should happen to our son?"

"Tragedies aren't always caused by our sins." He leaned forward, speaking in great earnest now. "Lydia, the Lord has other purposes in life besides punishment. He takes many away in infancy, that they may escape the envy of man and the sorrows and evils of this present world. They were too pure, too lovely to live on earth."

Her chin lifted and she blinked back the tears.

"Yes," he said, glad that he had finally pierced through her sorrow. "And if that's true—and it is!—then rightly considered, instead of mourning we have reason to rejoice. First because a child like your little Nathan is delivered from evil, and second because you shall soon have him again."

His voice deepened and he spoke with great conviction. "All children are redeemed by the blood of Jesus Christ. They have no sin or uncleanness in them, and the moment they leave this world, they are taken to the bosom of Abraham. Think about that, Lydia. Your son is now in the bosom of Abraham. He's in paradise. He is assured a place in the celestial kingdom. Would you call him back from that?"

She shook her head slowly. "I keep telling myself all of that, Joseph. I'm supposed to know this is true. I used to." Now the agony made her voice heavy and twisted. "I was so sure I had a testimony. Now it seems to be slipping through my fingers like it was sand. I can't get ahold of it anymore."

He reached out and touched her arm briefly. "You only doubt what you don't know, Lydia, and that is yourself." He took a deep breath, still searching her face. "You need to find yourself. You are far stronger than you think."

She shook her head slowly, wanting to believe but not finding it within her. Joseph reached out and patted her hand. "Don't give up," he said, very softly. "Keep searching."

He stood abruptly and spoke to Nathan. "Well, Benjamin will be waiting for us. We need to cross the river."

Lydia's head came up with a snap now, and shame flooded over her. She hadn't even thought to ask Nathan how his father was. She looked to Nathan. "How is—" Then it hit her what Joseph had just said. "Benjamin is going with you?"

Nathan walked over to stand beside her now. "Yes, Joseph blessed Papa."

"But . . ."

He smiled down at her. "I know. I'll explain everything later. But Father is fine. He's going to live."

As Joseph and Nathan joined the others in the yard, Joseph turned his head and looked back at the cabin. "Nathan," he said, "I think it would be best if you stayed with your family. Your mother will need some help as well."

"Yes."

Then he stunned them all, but none more than Joshua. Joseph reached out and took him by the arm. "Joshua, I think it would be good if we had someone accompany your father as he goes with us. Would you be willing to do that?"

"I . . . well . . ." And then he found himself nodding. "Yes, of course. Let me go get my father. We'll . . . we'll be right with you."

———————

They took a ferryboat across the river, then headed straight for one of the old military barracks where Brigham Young lived with his family. Though Joseph had been on this side of the river before, visiting the members of the Twelve who lived here, he let John Taylor take the lead.

When Nathan had rushed back home, breathless with the news that Joseph was coming, he had told them what was happening. Joshua had been openly skeptical. It irritated him that his family looked to this man as though he were some kind of supernatural being with supernatural powers. And as for the report that Joseph was healing people everywhere, Joshua put that down as the hysterical reaction of people too long in the grips of the fever.

Then Joseph had come to Joshua's father. This was no secondhand report. Joshua had seen it with his own eyes. He had seen Joseph bless Jessica's two boys and seen immediate results. Nathan told him about Elizabeth Mary, and he could not disbelieve him. His skepticism was now tempered by wonder and amazement and some very deep questions. The rational part of Joshua Steed was still reeling. He followed along now, searching for some kind of logical explanation for what he was witnessing.

"Here we are," John Taylor said, and they turned in at one of the old barracks buildings.

Joshua didn't know Brigham Young. He had heard his family talk a lot about him, about his leadership when Joseph was in Liberty Jail. As a teamster who knew what it took to move freight and people, Joshua was impressed with the reports of what Brigham had done to organize the exodus from Missouri.

As they moved up to the building, Joseph knocked firmly. A moment later, a woman, heavy with child, opened the door. "Sister Mary Ann," Joseph exclaimed, "how good to see you again."

She blinked against the brightness of the sunlight. "Brother Joseph?"

"Indeed!" he boomed cheerfully. "We understand you have a sick husband."

"Why, yes, he's—"

"Joseph? Is that you?"

Brigham's wife stepped back. "Come in," she said. Then turning, she called back inside. "Brigham, it's Brother Joseph."

A man on the bed half raised himself. He was squinting at the light. "Brother Joseph," he said, weakly, but eager. "What brings you here?"

"It is a day of God's power," Joseph replied. "We are going about healing the sick, and we wish you to be with us."

Brigham fell back a little. "But I myself am sick. I have not been able to leave my bed for two days now."

"Then it is time," Joseph said cheerfully. Then instantly, in that same powerful voice he had used with Benjamin, he commanded, "Brigham Young, in the name of the Lord, I command you to leave that bed and to be healed of your illness. Come with us."

Joshua felt his pulse start to race. He stepped sideways, so he could see the man before them more clearly. Brigham lay there, momentarily stunned by the Prophet's call. Then he threw back the covers, swung his legs over the edge of the bed, and sat up. His wife gave a little cry and one hand flew to her mouth.

"Give me just a moment," Brigham said. "I shall need a shirt."

The company soon moved on to Wilford Woodruff's place. Wilford was one of the few who thus far had escaped the illness. He responded immediately to Joseph's request that he accompany them. As they strode down the walk from Wilford's place, Joseph looked at Brigham Young. "Are there any that need our help here in Montrose?"

Brigham nodded quickly. "There are many. Brother Elijah Fordham is especially ill."

Wilford Woodruff clucked his tongue sadly. "We may be too late. My wife heard not more than an hour ago that he was breathing his last."

"Take me to him," said Joseph.

As they moved off, people swarmed around them. Word that the Prophet was on this side of the river was spreading through the community of Saints with great rapidity. Those well enough to walk were flocking in now. Many came with urgent requests that he come to their homes and help their families.

The Fordham cabin was another small one, newly built. When the woman opened the door, it was clear that she was badly distraught. The sight of Joseph was surprising but seemed to bring her little comfort. Only partly coherent, she said that her husband was dying. Joshua and Benjamin stepped back as the rest of the members of the group started in the cabin. There were now seven of the Apostles with Joseph, and others started to push in behind them. In the doorway, Joseph held up his hand. "Brethren and sisters," he said kindly, "there just isn't the room. We'll be out in a minute or two."

Then once again catching Joshua totally by surprise, Joseph beckoned to Benjamin. "Brother Ben, I brought you over here because I need your faith. Would you come in with me and the Twelve? You too, Joshua."

Half-dazed, Joshua nodded and followed the others inside.

Once in, Joseph shut the door, then turned to the bed in one corner. A figure lay on it, but there was no movement. Joshua stepped back. The smell of death was in the room. The man's wife was right. This time they were too late.

Without hesitation, Joseph walked right up to the dying man and took hold of his right hand. "Elijah! This is Brother Joseph. Can you hear me?"

Fordham's eyes were open, but they could have been made of glass. He stared upwards at the ceiling, and as Joshua watched closely, he could not see him even blink. With the toe of his boot, Joseph pulled a nearby chair over, so that he did not have to let go of Fordham's hand. He sat down, and for what seemed like a full minute or more he gazed into the eyes of the man before him.

Joshua felt a jolt, as if someone had jabbed him. There was no question about it. The visage of the man was changing. The locked jaw was softening, the glaze over the eyes starting to fade a little. There was a softening of the whole body. And then he moved. There was a deep sigh, and Elijah Fordham turned and looked up into Joseph's face.

"Elijah," Joseph said again, this time in a very low whisper. "Do you know me?"

The entire group held its breath, and then came the reply, equally soft. "Yes."

There was a collective sigh, as breaths were released and several of the men began to smile.

Joseph did not turn his head a fraction of an inch. He just kept his eyes burning into those of the man before him. "Do you have the faith to be healed, Elijah?"

Again there was that interminable pause, then painfully, "I fear it is too late. If . . . if you had come sooner I think I could have been healed."

"Do you believe in Jesus Christ?"

"I do," came the feeble reply.

Joseph rose, and Joshua leaned forward, his pulse suddenly pounding, leaving a roaring sensation in his ears. Erect as a steel

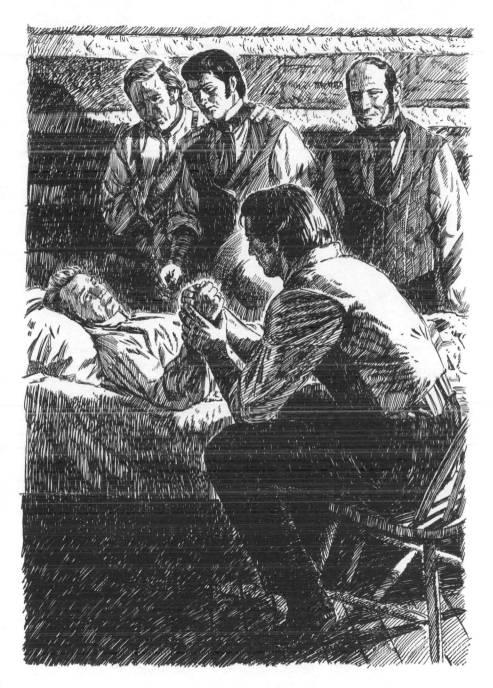

"A Day of God's Power"

rod, Joseph stood there, still holding Fordham's hand in silence. When the Prophet finally spoke, Joshua jumped noticeably, as did several others, for he thundered it out. It did not seem like Joseph's voice at all, and it was as though the very foundations of the house trembled.

"Brother Fordham, I command you, in the name of Jesus Christ, to arise from this bed and be made whole."

As calmly as though he were rising from an afternoon nap, Elijah Fordham sat up. Color rushed back to his cheeks. He swung his legs over the side of the bed and stood up. He took three steps toward his wife, who was staring in shock and disbelief and was crying uncontrollably now. He walked awkwardly, but Joshua saw that that was because his feet were bound in poultices. He kicked them off impatiently, then spoke to his wife. "Have we any bread and milk?" he asked.

———————

By the time they returned to the ferry landing later that afternoon, Joshua no longer doubted the reports Nathan had brought back that morning. He had been a living witness of exactly the same scenes. After Elijah Fordham dressed and had his bread and milk, they started around Montrose. From house to house, from tent to tent, from lean-tos to wagons to open bedrolls they moved. Old people, young children, babies, women, girls, grandmothers—it made no difference. In that calm, unruffled manner Joseph moved among them. He spoke, he counseled, he commanded. But everywhere they went, they left people dramatically better than before they had come. Joshua's mind was spinning. He didn't know what to say. He knew full well that if he were sitting in a room and heard himself describing what he had just witnessed, he would immediately scoff and brush it aside. What shook him so deeply now was that he couldn't brush it aside. He had seen it for himself.

"Brethren?"

Joshua turned. The Apostles were gathered in a half circle around their prophet. Their eyes were fixed on him. Joseph looked very tired, totally drained. "I must return to my family. We have done much good here today."

"Amen!" John Taylor said quietly. There were other murmurs and nods of assent.

"But there are still many who are in need of God's blessings." He let his eyes move from face to face. "You are the Twelve. You hold the holy apostleship. When the Savior called his original Twelve he laid his hands upon them and sent them out to preach the gospel, to heal the sick, and to cast out devils. That is the same power which you hold. Go forth. Do as you have seen me do. Bless the people."

Now the looks turned to uncertainty, but Joseph's words were so sure, so matter-of-fact, that they started to nod.

"Give my best to your families, and—"

"Mister Smith! Mister Smith!"

Joseph looked up. A man was running toward them, waving his arms frantically. They all turned now, and Wilford Woodruff squinted into the afternoon sun. "That's Amos Queensley," he said, looking back at Joseph. "He's not a member of the Church. But he's been good to us."

The man ran up and came to a stop in front of Joseph. Panting heavily, he tossed out the words between intakes of breath. "Mr. Smith. Please! I heard what you were doing."

"Yes."

"My children," he gasped. "I have twin girls. Three months old. They are dying." He clutched at Joseph's coat. "Please come! Please!"

Joseph's face was filled with compassion, but after a moment, to everyone's surprise, he shook his head. "I am totally exhausted," he said to the man. "I must get back." But then as the man's countenance fell, Joseph went on. "But I shall send someone."

He thought for a moment, then reached inside the frock coat he wore and withdrew a red silk bandanna handkerchief. He took it in both hands; then, to Joshua's utter amazement, he lowered his head and closed his eyes for a moment. Finally he straightened and handed the cloth to Wilford Woodruff. Woodruff was startled. "Take it, Wilford," Joseph said. "Go with this man. Wipe the faces of the children with this handkerchief and bless them and they will be healed."

Wilford stepped back.

"Do it," Joseph said gently.

Tentatively, Wilford reached out and took the red cloth. "I will, Joseph."

Joseph laid a hand on his arm. "Wilford Woodruff, as long as you keep this handkerchief, it will serve as a league between you and me. Now, go, and God be with you."

The man grabbed the Prophet's hand, thanking him profusely, then stumbled off after Wilford Woodruff, who had started up the riverbank. Joshua was incredulous, and it showed on his face. Benjamin nudged him. "Go with them, Joshua."

Joseph turned at that. He gave Joshua a long searching look. "Yes, Joshua," he finally said. "Go with them. See with your eyes and know with your heart."

It was almost dark when the door to the cabin opened and Joshua stepped in. Benjamin and Mary Ann were at the table, reading the Book of Mormon. Matthew wasn't there, having gone over to Jessica's to be with Jenny.

Joshua came in and shut the door. He took off his hat and dropped it on the small table there. Mary Ann stood up. "You must be starving, Joshua. Let me get you some soup and bread."

"Yes," he said heavily. "I am hungry."

As she moved to the fireplace, he came over and sat down across from his father. For several moments, they looked at each other, searching each other's faces. "Well?" Benjamin finally asked.

Joshua almost flinched, as if he had been dreading the question. "Well what?" he half growled.

"Did Brother Woodruff use the handkerchief?"

Joshua looked down, staring at his hands. "Yes."

"Well?" Benjamin persisted. Mary Ann turned now to watch her son.

"It worked. Almost immediately. The twins are going to be all right."

Benjamin leaned back, nodding very slowly. "And how do you explain that?" he asked.

Joshua didn't look up. "I don't know," he finally said. "I just don't know."

Benjamin wanted to leap up and shout, but he didn't. "Joshua?"

"Yes, Pa?"

"What you and Caroline have is good. It's very good." He finished slowly, emphasizing each word. "But there is *so much more.*"

Chapter Notes

July twenty-second, 1839, came to be known as, in Wilford Woodruff's words, "a day of God's power." The healings were so frequent that only a fraction were recorded. Some of the sources say that Joseph went to every house. The demonstration of priesthood power continued on the west side of the Mississippi, with the most dramatic healing being that of Elijah Fordham, which is told here almost word for word as recorded by Wilford Woodruff (see *Leaves*, pp. 76–77).

There is some discrepancy in the sources as to which of the Twelve accompanied Joseph on the Nauvoo side and then crossed over on the ferry to Montrose with him. The author's choice reflects statements by Heber C. Kimball, Wilford Woodruff, and Parley P. Pratt (see *LHCK*, p. 263; *Leaves*, p. 75; *PPP Auto.*, p. 254).

It is also Wilford Woodruff who tells of the handkerchief experience. He kept it as a token of the bond between him and Joseph, treasuring it throughout the remainder of his life. (See *Leaves*, pp. 78–79.)

Joseph's comments on why little children are sometimes taken are found in his recorded teachings (see *Teachings of the Prophet Joseph Smith*, sel. Joseph Fielding Smith [Salt Lake City: Deseret Book Co., 1938], pp. 196–97).

For a long time after Joshua stopped speaking, Caroline just sat there, watching him, wanting to go to him and hold him, and yet knowing that if she moved, it might drive away the mood that lay so heavily upon him. He was staring at his hands, examining them intently as he slowly turned them over and over, as if somehow the explanation for which he was so desperately searching had been there for him but now he had let it slip away.

Finally he looked up, almost surprised to see that she was still there. "I don't know," he said wearily. "Maybe they just believe in Joseph so strongly that he's like some powerful medicine to them. So when he speaks to them it . . ."

It trailed off slowly as the fallacy of his reasoning showed itself. He looked toward the window. "That man named Fordham. I saw him, Caroline! When we first went in, I was sure he was dead. Then I saw he was breathing, but that's about all there was. His eyes were wide open, like a corpse's. He didn't even know we were in the room. When Joseph first spoke to him, he didn't even blink." One hand began to rub his cheek. "*He didn't even blink!*"

She waited a moment, then asked softly, "And your father too? You saw that for yourself?"

He jumped up and began to pace, almost angrily. "Yes! I was there, not four feet away. Just hours before that, we had our last talk—he gave me his deathbed farewell." He closed his eyes for a moment. "He thought he was going to die." He turned and looked at her in wonder. "He *was* going to die, Caroline. And now, he's as strong as he's been in months. You won't believe it."

"Thanks be to the Lord for that," Caroline whispered. Even the thought of losing Benjamin filled her with a piercing ache. And with that, she decided to risk saying what had been on her mind almost from the moment her husband had started to tell her about the day of healing. "Joshua?"

His eyes finally focused on her. "Yes?"

"We told Nathan and Lydia that once everyone got their houses built and things were established up there, we'd start the store. Well, maybe it's time we move to Nauvoo."

To her complete amazement, he nodded almost immediately. "Maybe so."

She was dumbfounded. "Do you mean it?" she cried.

He nodded slowly, surprised at how easily the answer had come. He came over and sat down beside her on the sofa. He took her hands in his and peered into her eyes. "I'm not any more excited about living with ten thousand Mormons than I have ever been, but . . . It wasn't just Pa, Caroline. Mama nearly died too. When I think that we might have lost them both, well . . . I've thought about it all the way down. I can't make up for all those lost years by only seeing them for a few days every two or three months. The business here is established. I've got a good foreman. Let's move as soon as possible."

She lifted the hand that held hers and pressed it against her cheek. "Yes, of course. Immediately."

When Joshua said as soon as possible, he meant it. There was much to do—a business to leave, things to pack, letters to write to his partner in St. Louis—but he threw himself into the tasks with a frenzy. His freight company in Quincy already consisted of twelve wagons, half again that many teams, and a stable and corral. His plan was to split the assets half and half between Quincy and Nauvoo. That left six wagons available for the move up. Caroline decided that that was ample for their needs, but Joshua shocked her by saying that she had only one for their household goods. The furniture would have to wait for a return trip. The other five would be loaded with lumber and other building materials.

Nauvoo was in a building boom, and supplies, limited to begin with, would be nearly impossible to get. With his typical foresightedness, Joshua didn't want to be a burden on the family. He would bring his and Caroline's new house with them. Labor would be no problem. Between his family and their Mormon neighbors, he expected a good turnout at the house-raising. He figured three days, maybe four at the most, and they would have the walls up and roof on. They could finish the inside at their leisure then.

They left on the fourth day of August. The wagons were heavily loaded, so their progress northward was slow. Normally the fifty-mile trip took about two days. But in this case, it took almost three. They arrived in Nauvoo on the afternoon of the seventh. This proved to be fortunate timing, for if they had been even a day later, they would have missed the chance to say good-bye to Derek.

The valise was pitifully small, but even then, Derek had barely enough to fill it. At the bottom was his Book of Mormon and four copies of the tract Parley Pratt had written a couple years before. It was called *A Voice of Warning* and had proven to be an effective missionary tool. These were a gift from Parley himself. On top of that was the ragged winter coat that had gotten him across the plains of northern Missouri. There was a woolen shirt, a pair of mittens Rebecca had knitted for him. He stuffed in the one extra pair of socks he owned, then carefully wrapped the package of food Rebecca and Mary Ann had prepared for him and placed it on top of his clothes. He buckled the strap of the valise slowly, straightened, and lifted it to the floor. Only then did he turn to face his wife.

Rebecca was sitting on the bed, holding Christopher. Her chin was up but quivering. Her eyes were steady but shining. She tried to smile at him, but the trembling spread to her lips, and then her face crumpled and she had to look away. Derek stepped to her instantly.

"I know, I know," she said, angry with herself. "I promised I wouldn't cry."

Suddenly the reality of his departure hit Derek with tremendous force. He bent down and took Christopher. Rebecca had fed him while Derek packed, and now he was asleep again. He barely stirred as Derek carefully lifted him and then started to walk back and forth, cradling him against his body. He reached out and rubbed the short fuzz of hair with the side of his finger, and then in one great tide of emotions, he was battling his own tears.

Christopher would be two months old in two more days. Right now, he did little but eat and sleep. He seemed to visibly grow with every passing day. How big would he be when Derek finally returned? Now he did nothing more than goo at his mother and smile when he had a little gas. By the time Derek returned, his son would be eating solid food, and chattering like a squirrel.

Ever since Joseph had called him in May to go to England, Derek had known this was going to be a sacrifice of sorts. But he mostly thought in terms of leaving Rebecca alone to care for a house and a newborn child. He thought of ten acres of ground that would have to wait for the plow before it could produce.

He thought of being separated from Rebecca and Christopher and the rest of the family. But he had not, until this very moment, thought about it in terms of sacrificing the other things— the changing of the blue-gray infant eyes to a permanent color, the hair coming out in its fulness, kissing a scraped knee, bouncing him until he giggled and Rebecca had to ask him to stop because he would start spitting up. It was as if he were given a perfect glimpse of all that he was going to miss. And it hit him hard. It felt like someone had grabbed his soul and was determined to wring it absolutely dry.

Vision blurring, he walked slowly to the small cradle and laid his son down. He put the blanket around him and tucked it in. Then turned back to Rebecca. She was up and into his arms in a second. Her shoulders began to shake convulsively against him. He pulled her to him and buried his face against her hair. "Oh, Becca," he cried hoarsely, "how shall I ever do without you?"

He kissed Rebecca good-bye at the door, sending her back in to be alone with Christopher and her tears. As Derek came out of the house, only Mary Ann and Benjamin and Matthew and Peter were waiting. Wisely, Mary Ann had told the family that the farewell dinner the night before was the time for saying good-bye. That was good. He couldn't bear much more. These were not his blood relatives, these Steeds, but he had never had family except for Peter, and the Steeds had filled that place about as well as any man could ask.

Nothing much new was said as he hugged Mary Ann and shook Benjamin's hand one last time. When he and Peter embraced, though, he couldn't have spoken if he wanted to. Peter was crying softly, and without shame. They had not been apart since Peter was born, these two brothers. This was another cost Derek hadn't counted on.

Finally he straightened and stuck out his hand to Matthew.

Matthew gripped it hard. "I wish I was going with you," he exclaimed.

"Aye. But you'll not be far behind us. If nothing else, we shall meet in New York."

"Yes." Brigham Young and Heber C. Kimball were both deathly ill. So were their families, and Heber was determined to complete a home for Vilate and his children before leaving. So Matthew would not be leaving for a few weeks yet, and he was keenly envious of Derek.

Derek looked around. There was no sign of his two companions. He pulled out the watch Joshua and Caroline had brought as a going-away gift. It was ten minutes past eight o'clock. "You haven't seen Elder Taylor or Elder Woodruff?"

Benjamin shook his head. "We haven't seen anyone. Are you sure you were supposed to meet them here?"

A shadow of concern crossed Derek's face. Reports had come across the river in the past few days that both Wilford Woodruff and John Taylor had illness in their families as well. Wilford was reported to be very sick. Derek had started worrying that they too might have to call for another postponement. But then late yesterday afternoon a note had been delivered. It was terse but to the point. "Derek. Leaving tomorrow sure. Meet you at your cabin, 8:00 a.m. sharp. JT."

He peered up the street. Nothing. He looked towards the river to see if there were any boats coming across. Both Wilford and John lived in Montrose. But there was nothing on the river either. His heart fell. He couldn't face another delay, another departure, another time of saying good-bye. He turned with sudden determination. "I'll bet they meant the boat landing." He reached down and got his valise, then lifted his hand. "Good-bye." He turned quickly—to say or do more would have been beyond him—and strode away.

No one was at the boat landing, but as Derek looked out across the river, he saw a flat-bottomed rowboat just setting out from Montrose. With no other options in sight, he sat down to wait. Ten minutes later, he was gratified to watch John Taylor step out of the boat, reach for a small suitcase, then thank the man who had brought him across. As he came up the riverbank, he frowned, looking around. "Where's Wilford?"

Derek shrugged. "I haven't seen him."

"But he left an hour or more before I did. Brother Brigham rowed him across in a canoe."

"Was he coming to my house?"

John shook his head. "No, I told him I'd get you. I thought he was going to wait for me here, though." He looked up toward town, openly worried. "He was feeling very poorly."

"We talked about saying good-bye to Brother Joseph," Derek suggested. "Maybe he went there."

To their surprise, they saw Joseph coming swiftly toward them as they turned the corner onto Water Street. He saw them and waved, and increased his stride even more. "Derek, John." As he reached them he looked at the cases in their hands. "Good. So you've started, then."

"Sort of," John answered. "But we've not been able to find Brother Woodruff. We were thinking that he might be at your house."

There was a brief frown. "No, I haven't seen him, but someone told me that you two were down at the river and that Wilford is at the post office. I was just coming down to find you." He took Derek's arm. "Let's go to the post office and see what we can find."

The report was correct. Wilford was at the post office, but he wasn't there to transact any postal business. They found him out back of the building, lying on a side of sole leather. Though the temperature was in the eighties and climbing rapidly, Wilford lay huddled in a ball, shivering violently, hugging himself in an effort to keep it under control. His face was pale, his cheeks hollow, his eyes dull and lifeless.

As Joseph's shadow fell across his face, Wilford opened his eyes. "Good morning," he said, barely making a feeble croak.

"Well, Brother Woodruff," Joseph boomed, "I see you have started on your mission."

There was a barely perceptible nod. "I came across the river this morning, but this is as far as I got."

"Well, a start is a start."

Wilford lifted his head, licking his lips. "If you ask me, I feel and look more like a subject for the dissecting room than a missionary."

Joseph laughed. "What did you say that for? Get up, and go along. All will be right with you."

Slowly Wilford uncoiled. Trembling and weak, he got to his knees. John Taylor reached out and helped him to his feet. Wilford steadied himself against his fellow Apostle.

"Good, Brother Wilford. Good. You're on your way now." Joseph shook their hands in turn. "Godspeed, my brothers. You are embarking on a great work." The Prophet walked away. They watched him go for a moment, then Derek took Wilford's other arm and they started off in the opposite direction.

Half an hour later, as they passed by the last home and started along the road that led south to Warsaw, then on to Quincy, Derek noted that John Taylor kept turning his gaze westward across the river. Montrose was hard to see from this point because the island in midriver mostly blocked their view. But Derek thought he knew what John was looking for. He had to fight his own urge to keep looking back over his shoulder to see if he could identify which rooftop belonged to his cabin. Wilford didn't look anywhere but down. He was too occupied with keeping one foot moving in front of the other to even lift his head.

Derek turned. "You know," he said, thoughtfully, "it is a good thing we all have a strong witness that this call is from the Lord."

"Why is that?" Wilford asked feebly.

Derek's shoulders lifted and fell. "Otherwise, one could find some pretty good reasons for just staying home."

───────◆───────

Lydia sat quietly, watching Nathan methodically packing the last of the children's clothing into the small trunk Joshua had lent them. As Nathan folded Joshua's and Emily's winter coats, the guilt surged upward again and she had to look away. It was only August fifteenth. Was she really going to keep them in Palmyra until winter set in? She knew the question lay heavily on Nathan's mind too, but he didn't dare ask it of her.

Oh, my darling, patient Nathan. Forgive me. Please forgive me.

He put the last piece of clothing in, looked around, then straightened and turned. "Is that everything, then?"

She smiled wanly and nodded. "Yes, thank you." She wasn't even aware that tears had welled up and were trickling down her cheeks.

Shutting the trunk and lifting it to the floor, Nathan came to her. He took her hands and lifted her up. Without speaking he took her in his arms and held her tightly.

"I'm sorry, Nathan. I'm so sorry."

"Don't," he said gently. "It's all right."

She pulled away, whirling around so her back was to him. "It's not all right!" she said fiercely. "This is ridiculous. You need to be here. *I* need to be here now." She realized the words were tumbling out of her and that she was nearing hysteria, but she couldn't stop it. "The store was our idea, remember? And now we're leaving, just when Caroline is ready to start on it."

She spun back around, seeing a solution now, grasping at it. "Maybe you ought to stay, Nathan. Young Joshua's eight now. He'll be a big help with the baby, and Emily and—" She saw instantly how foolish she sounded and she bit down on her lip to cut it off.

Nathan pulled her to him with great gentleness. "Lydia, I'm not sending you to Palmyra alone. That's settled."

"Tell me how much our passage is going to cost."

He sighed. She had asked before, and he had always managed to parry the question or tease her out of it. This time he sensed there was no doing that. The plan was to go by wagon down to Warsaw, about twelve miles south, and there catch a steamboat going downriver. They would book passage to Cairo, Illinois, where the mighty Ohio emptied into the Mississippi. The Ohio was navigable almost right to its source, north of Pittsburgh, so they would take a steamboat as far east and north as possible. From there, they would take a stage to Buffalo, then finish the final leg on the Erie Canal. It was a longer route this way, but much easier. But it wasn't going to be cheap. "Joshua estimates it will be between twenty-five and thirty dollars each," he said.

As her eyes widened, he rushed on. "That's for you and me. The children should be only half fare, and he thinks they won't charge us anything for the baby."

So nearly a hundred dollars! She felt sick. In Nauvoo right now, that represented a small fortune.

"I'll pay Joshua back out of our share of the profits from the store. It's all right."

She just shook her head, stunned by the magnitude of what her weakness was costing them.

Again he lifted her head, only now he looked deep into her eyes. "Lydia, we *are* doing this. I made a promise to Pa, and I made a promise to you."

"But I feel so guilty!"

"I understand," he said, "and I wish I could make that go away, but either way, we're going. No matter what." A smile began to play around the corners of his mouth. "If you wake up in the morning and say, 'I've changed my mind,' I'll just have to throw a rope around you and drag you along behind the wagon."

She smiled in spite of herself. "Would you really do that?"

"I would," he said sternly. "You're not going to deprive me of a chance to see your parents again."

At that she laughed right out loud, and it startled her that she still had a laugh in her. "Since you and my father get along so well, right?"

Now he was serious again. "Your parents need to see their grandchildren again, Lydia. Pa's right. We need to do this. And it's not just for you."

She laid her head against his shoulder. "Don't give up on me, Nathan. I'm trying to hang on."

"Give up on you?" he asked with mock incredulity. "After making you into the wonderful woman that you are?"

"You have!" she retorted, finally coming totally out of her tears. She knew he was doing this for this very purpose and loved him all the more for it. She went up on her toes and kissed him long and hard. "You are the rock in my life, Nathan Steed. Don't you know that?"

He took her face in both hands. "And you *are* my life, Lydia McBride," he whispered back at her. "Don't you know *that?*"

"Yes," she said happily. "I do. If it weren't for that . . ." She couldn't finish. The thought was too awful to even contemplate.

He decided to change the subject. "Maybe we can come home by way of Fairport Harbor and Kirtland. See Melissa and Carl."

"Oh," she cried, "I hadn't thought of that. Would it be too far out of the way?"

"Not much. It's out of the way going out, but a natural way to come back."

"That would be wonderful." She grew more thoughtful. "You're not as optimistic about Carl and Melissa moving out here as Joshua is, are you?"

He shook his head.

"Why not? You said yourself Melissa's letter was quite hopeful. Joshua is convinced they're coming."

"I know. But there's something I know about Carl that Joshua doesn't."

"What?"

"I know his father. I know Hezekiah Rogers and Joshua doesn't."

———•———

Hezekiah Rogers was in a towering rage. Carl hadn't seen him this angry in years. "Pa—," he started, trying to get a word in.

Hezekiah swung on him, eyes flashing with bitterness. "It's Melissa who's put you up to this, isn't it?"

"Melissa? No, I—"

"Her and her Mormon family. That's what's behind you wanting to leave. I knew I shouldn't have let you go out west to see her family."

"Oh, Pa, come on!" Carl's own anger was starting to rise now. "You're the one who said that I haven't let William and David take a big enough part in the livery business."

Hezekiah's eyebrows shot up, signaling his fury. "And that means you just walk away? I want you to give them more say, not give them the business."

Marian Rogers looked back and forth between her husband and son with open anxiety. "Hezekiah," she said, trying to soothe.

She might as well have been speaking to the hitching post. He turned away, throwing up his hands. "So this is what I get? I give you my whole life's work, teach you the business from the very first, and this is all the thanks I get. I can't believe what I'm hearing. This from a son of mine?"

"Pa"—Carl was pleading now—"Joshua Steed is a very successful businessman. He's got one of the largest freighting businesses in St. Louis. He's a partner in a cotton mill. This isn't some wild-eyed dream I have. This is an opportunity for us to expand our family business. Do something that could really be exciting. I'm not abandoning what you've done. I'm just saying, let's expand it. Let's open another livery stable out there. Or, you and William and David could purchase goods in Cleveland and ship them on out west. We are in a strategic position for getting badly needed goods out there. There is a lot of money to be made."

"But it's six hundred miles away," his mother broke in. "Couldn't you stay here and let this Joshua do the work out there?"

Carl blew out his breath in frustration.

His father pounced on that. "Oh, no," he snapped to his wife. "That's just it. It's not just going into business with this man. That's not enough. It's leaving here. Turning his back on us. Becoming a Mormon. And after everything we've done for him."

"I'm not becoming a Mormon!"

"Don't you shout at your father!" his mother cried.

Carl surrendered. He could see that he wasn't going to win. Not tonight. Not ever. "I'm sorry, Pa," he muttered. "I'm sorry I ever brought it up. I just thought it sounded like a good idea."

Long after Carl was asleep, Melissa lay awake, staring up at the ceiling. There were no tears. The disappointment was too total, too shattering for that. They would come later. Maybe when Carl had left in the morning. For now there was just this tremendous sense of loss and an overwhelming feeling of desolation.

"Hello, pumpkin head," Joshua said, sweeping Savannah up in his arms as she darted across the room at the sight of him.

"Joshua," Caroline said in exasperation, "don't call her that."

"Well, look at that hair. I swear it gets redder every day."

"I punkin head," Savannah said to her mother.

"See?" Caroline laughed. "Now you've got her saying it."

Joshua reached up and ruffled Savannah's hair. "Well, I think it's beautiful. Don't you, punkin head?"

"Yes, Papa. I pretty."

Joshua chuckled deeply. "Heaven help the man who gets in her way when she turns sixteen." He turned, looking around.

"And speaking of turning sixteen, or hoping that they were turning sixteen, where's Livvy?"

"Upstairs in her room."

"Still mourning because she found out that Matthew and Jenny are promised?"

Caroline smiled somewhat sadly. "Exactly. Lost love comes hard to one who is not yet twelve."

"Well," he said, letting Savannah slide to the floor again, "I have just come from the freight yard. One of our wagons came in from Quincy. I have something that just might cheer her up."

"What?"

He looked somber. "Just might add a little excitement to your life too." Without waiting for her response, he lifted his head. "Livvy! Come down, please."

———————

"What is it, Pa?" Livvy asked, walking quickly around the wagon and trying to see through the gap in the back.

"You have to guess."

"Oh, no," she groaned, "I hate guessing."

"You too, Mother."

Joshua had the canvas laced down tight so there was no way to get even a clue. "Give us a hint," Caroline said.

"Yes, Papa, give us a hint."

"All right. It was something that we used to have."

"In St. Louis?" Caroline asked, almost as curious and excited as Livvy.

"No."

"In Independence?" Livvy asked, catching on to the game now.

"Yes."

Caroline pursed her lips, thinking.

"I don't know, Papa. Tell me. Please!"

"It was something that always told me whether you were happy or sad."

Caroline swung around, mouth opening in surprise.

He shook his head, warning her off.

Livvy's face screwed up in concentration.

"It's very big, Livvy," Caroline said, now that she thought she knew what it was.

Joshua chuckled. "Very big. And heavy."

"Oh, please, Papa. Please."

Joshua surrendered. "All right. I'll give you one peek. Then you must guess."

They moved to the back of the wagon, and Joshua loosened the ropes which closed the canvas. He lifted one corner and Livvy leaned forward. There was a sharp gasp, then she started jumping up and down. "A piano! A piano!"

"Oh, Joshua," Caroline cried, "how wonderful. I've missed it terribly."

Putting one hand on the bouncing shoulder, Joshua steadied his adopted daughter. "As soon as we get it inside, I want you to promise me you'll play me something happy."

"Oh, yes, Papa. Yes! I promise!"

———◆———

Nathan laid a hand on Lydia's shoulder. "We'd better go down and pack our things," he said gently.

She nodded absently, not looking at him. For the last two hours, she had been up on top of the canal boat, feasting her eyes on the sights around her, drinking in the familiarity as if it were clear, pure water. Now they were the only ones on top. All of the passengers—who together made up only about half a load this late in the season—were down inside making last-minute preparations for disembarking. But Lydia couldn't stand to miss this. It was Saturday, September fourteenth. What with waiting for riverboats two days in Warsaw and five in Cairo, it had taken them one month to make it this far. She had waited one full month to see these sights.

What amazed her most were the trees. She had forgotten how many there were. Thick stands of virgin forest, acre woodlots behind every farmhouse, trees lining up along the creeks and rivers like protecting armies. The prairie had nothing like this, and she had forgotten how much she loved it. "Where are the children?" she asked, still looking out over the landscape.

"The baby's asleep. Joshua and Emily are packing their things." He smiled. "They are so excited."

Now she turned fully to him. "So am I, Nathan." One hand came out in a sweeping gesture, taking it all in—the farmhouses, the wheat fields, the canal snaking its way from Buffalo all the way to Albany. "This is home." Her voice caught. "I . . . I've really missed it."

He put an arm around her waist. "I know."

"Thank you," she whispered.

He leaned down and kissed the top of her head. "You're welcome."

"Low bridge," bawled the young man who led the mules which towed the canal boat eastward at a steady four miles per hour.

Nathan and Lydia crouched down as the boat passed under a footbridge. Two young boys were above them, calling down at them, trying to get them to wave back. Lydia did so, smiling happily. As they came out from under the bridge and straightened again, Nathan lifted his eyes. The canal ran in a straight line now for some distance out ahead of them. About a mile away, he could see the faint outline of buildings. "Look, Lydia. There's Palmyra."

She went up on her toes, peering eagerly. At first she didn't see them, but then she let her eyes follow the canal and there they were—the first of the warehouses that lined Canal Street. "Oh, yes, Nathan. There it is!" She grabbed his arm. "Come on, we have to pack our things."

———————

"Are you sure you don't mind?" Lydia asked guiltily.

They were on the dock, waiting for the canawlers to get

their luggage from one of the cargo compartments. Nathan shook his head. "No, you go. Young Joshua and I will be there as quickly as we can get our stuff together."

"All right." She turned, searching. Emily was about fifty feet away, following closely behind Elizabeth Mary, who was moving as quickly as her little feet could carry her from this place to that. For a sixteen-month-old, steamboats and stagecoaches and canal boats were far too confining, and after a month of it, she was like a young calf let out in the pasture for the first time.

Lydia went up on her toes and kissed Nathan hurriedly, then moved across the dock area to her two daughters. "Emily, come. Let's go. Papa and Joshua will be along in a minute. Come on, Elizabeth Mary. Let's go surprise your grandmother."

"How far is it, Mama?" Emily asked.

"Not far. Just a block or two."

As they moved away from Canal Street and turned onto Main Street, Lydia and the girls drew curious stares from the local residents. Normally, canal passengers got off the canal boats to stretch but stayed near the dock area until the boats were under way again. One couple, whom Lydia recognized as members of her parent's Presbyterian congregation, stared at her openly as they passed. It was obvious she looked familiar to them too, but they weren't sure why.

Have I changed that much? Do the years rob me of my identity so completely? She shook it off. With a little effort she could have come up with their names, but she didn't want to. She merely nodded at them as they passed. Until she was really home again, she didn't want to speak to anyone.

Her step slowed and then stopped. There was a new sign over the store's entrance. The lettering was exactly the same— "General Dry Goods Store—Josiah McBride, Proprietor"—but it was a definite cut above the one she had known. The letters were carved into the wood and painted a bright gold. It was much more bold and striking, but to her surprise, it left her faintly sad. Without consciously thinking about it, she had wanted everything to be exactly the same as when she had last been here.

"Do you remember it, Emmy? This is Grandpa's store."

They had last come here in the spring of 1834, five years ago now. Emily had turned two during that visit. She looked up, her eyes squinting. "Kind of," she said dubiously.

"Well, it doesn't matter." Lydia reached down and picked up Elizabeth Mary. "Come, let's go in."

As she opened the door, a bell tinkled, and she smiled. That hadn't changed. She pushed it further open and looked down. Yes, it was the same tiny brass bell that had hung on that door for as long as she could remember. It cheered her immensely to see it there.

They stopped for a moment just inside, letting their eyes adjust to the interior gloom. She breathed deeply, instantly recognizing the wonderful combination of smells that assaulted her— ginger, cloves, cinnamon, leather, molasses, tobacco, sawdust, dried fish, onions, gun oil. She closed her eyes. It was like the Balm of Gilead to her, and she savored it warmly.

"Good afternoon. May I help you?"

Lydia opened her eyes and turned half around. It was a young girl, eighteen or nineteen. *Like I was when Joshua and Nathan first started coming here.* She was behind the counter and watching Lydia expectantly.

"Is Mr. McBride in?"

Before the girl could answer, there was a noise from behind a stack of barrels. A head poked around. A hand reached up and pulled the spectacles lower on the nose. Dark eyes peered over them at the new customers. "Yes?"

Lydia was instantly overcome and could not speak. She just reached out and took Emily's hand and moved forward two steps.

Josiah McBride came out fully from behind the barrels. He had a large book and a pen. He was taking inventory. It was so utterly familiar, so perfectly like she remembered it, that tears sprang to her eyes.

Suddenly the curious look turned to shock. The book lowered slowly, the jaw dropped. "Lydia?" It came out in hoarse amazement. "Is that you?"

"Hello, Papa."

He came forward slowly, not able to believe what he saw. "It *is* you!"

"Yes, Papa. It's me."

He tossed the book aside, not caring where it landed. He looked over his shoulder. "Hannah!" he bellowed. "Hannah, come quick." He swung back around to the girl. "Go get Mrs. McBride," he barked. "Hurry!"

The girl darted off, and then Josiah McBride did something that would forever live in Lydia's mind, and which made all of the effort, all of the sacrifice, all of the cost of getting here worth every penny it took. He stepped forward and put his arm around Lydia and the baby, pulling them close. "Lord in heaven," he cried, "it's my Lydia."

———•———

"But didn't you get my letter?"

Hannah McBride shook her head. "No. We haven't heard a word since we wrote you almost three months ago. We decided you weren't going to answer."

"But I wrote to you and said we would be coming. That was around the first of August."

"It never came," her father said. "But it doesn't matter. Not now. This is better than a hundred letters." He was sitting down in the chair that customers could use while waiting for orders to be filled. Emily stood beside him, one arm resting on his shoulder. Elizabeth Mary, always shy, still clung to her mother, her head buried against her shoulder.

I can't believe it," Hannah was saying, smiling at Emily. "Look at her. She's not a little girl anymore. She's a beautiful young lady."

Josiah reached up and patted the hand on his shoulder.

"And so much—" He had to stop. He pulled out a handkerchief, removed his glasses, and wiped at his eyes. "Do you know
how much you look like your mother did when she was your
age?" he half whispered.

"Everybody says that," Emily replied, ever the pragmatist.

He laughed, hugging her tightly. "I'll bet they do."

Lydia had to force herself not to stare at her father. Her
mother had aged, but she still looked much the same. But her
father was shockingly different. He had lost twenty or thirty
pounds. His shoulders were stooped, his cheekbones protruded
sharply, his hair was almost totally white. He looked fifteen or
twenty years older than when they had last seen him. She had
to fight back the tears every time she looked at him.

"And this one," Hannah said, moving over to put a hand on
Elizabeth Mary's head. "We've been so anxious to see this one."

"Can't you even say hello to your grandmother?" Lydia said,
reaching up to lift her daughter's chin. Elizabeth Mary shook
her head and ducked down again.

"You said young Joshua is with Nathan," her mother said.
"What about little Nathan?"

Lydia jerked as though she had been struck. She hadn't
made that connection. They hadn't gotten her letter. They
didn't know. In a low voice, she quickly told them. Thankfully,
just as she finished, and before they could begin asking questions, the bell tinkled again and they all turned. Nathan and
young Joshua stepped inside, looking around.

"We're back here, Nathan," Lydia called.

Josiah McBride pushed to his feet and Hannah turned expectantly. As they came forward, Nathan reached out and laid his
hand on young Joshua's shoulder. They must have talked about
what to do on the way over, for he gave him a gentle shove, and
Joshua's face broke into smiles. "Grandma. Grandpa." He ran
forward and threw his arms around his grandmother.

Nathan came forward, hand outstretched. "Hello, Father
McBride."

Then came the second stunning surprise of the day. Josiah McBride ignored the outstretched hand and in one long step had his son-in-law in a bear hug, pounding him on the back. "Welcome, Nathan. Welcome home."

Chapter Notes

Wilford Woodruff and John Taylor were the first of the Twelve to leave for England, departing from Nauvoo on 8 August 1839. Wilford was not the only one desperately ill. He left his wife pregnant and so sick they had to leave their first child, a daughter, with another family. John Taylor left his family ill and housed in a single room in Montrose. Wilford's comment about being more a candidate for dissection than a missionary and Joseph's reply to him are reported by Wilford himself. (See *Leaves*, pp. 83–84; *MWM*, pp. 67–68, 284–85.)

$\mathbb{A}$ very ill Brigham Young left Montrose, Iowa, and crossed the Mississippi River to Nauvoo on September fourteenth. Mary Ann Young, also sick, was left with a ten-day-old daughter and with the rest of their children so ill that none of the family could even go to the well for a pail of water. Brigham had lost nearly everything in Missouri and was so destitute that each member of his family had only one set of clothes. One of the brethren helped Brigham make it the thirty or so rods to the riverbank and rowed the Apostle across in a boat. By the time they reached the other side, Brigham could barely move. Another Church member, Israel Barlow, put him on a horse and carried him to Heber Kimball's house, where he totally collapsed again.

The Kimball family were in about the same straits as the Youngs. Heber was violently ill. On August twenty-third, Vilate Kimball gave birth to David Patten Kimball. Still weak from childbirth, she was no better than her husband. The only one well enough to help fetch food and drink for the rest of his family was little four-year-old Heber Parley Kimball.

Learning that Brigham had not made it any farther than across the river to Nauvoo, Mary Ann Young, leaving all but the baby in the care of friends, crossed the river on the seventeenth of September and persuaded a boy to take her to the Kimballs'. Her intent was to come over and help nurse Brigham, but just as it had done to him, the effort of getting that far exhausted her, and she simply joined her husband and the Kimballs in their sickbeds.

It had been almost six months since Brigham had led his fellow Apostles to the square at Far West, Missouri, and there, shortly after midnight, fulfilled the commandment of the Lord. Six months! It had been over a month since Wilford Woodruff and John Taylor had left. And he and Heber, the two senior Apostles, still lay languishing in Nauvoo. In Brigham's mind, it was long enough. Sickbed or not, it was time to leave. That night, he sent a girl to the Steeds with a message for Matthew. It was time to pack. They would leave in the morning.

———•———

Matthew slowed his step, looking around. The yard was filled with evidence that Heber had just recently completed this log cabin—wood chips, tree limbs, logs that had split in the wrong place. The door to the cabin was shut, and no one was in sight. A wagon and a team of mules were standing in the yard. A boy, about fifteen, stood beside the wagon, holding the reins. "Mornin'," Matthew said.

"Mornin'," the boy replied cheerfully.

"Where's Brother Brigham?"

"Inside. Said they'll be out in a minute."

Matthew felt his hopes rise. The girl who brought the note had said the two Apostles were too sick to even get out of bed. So along with packing, Matthew spent a good part of the night worrying about how they were going to make a journey of a thousand miles or more when they couldn't even walk. Matthew himself was still a little wobbly in the knees from his own illness, so the sight of the wagon was a welcome one indeed.

"You gonna fetch us on down the road?" he asked.

"Yep. Pa says I'm to take the brethren as far south as Brother Duel's house." The boy's eyes dropped to see Matthew's suitcase. When he looked up, there was new respect in them. "You goin' with them?"

"Yep," Matthew said, trying not to look too proud.

Behind them the door opened. They turned and saw Brigham standing there, leaning heavily on the door frame. He raised one hand and waved feebly. "We're coming, brethren. Hold on."

Matthew walked quickly toward the door as Brigham gave one last wave to someone inside and shuffled out. In two steps Matthew reached him and was giving him his arm. From inside, he could hear children crying and the weeping of women. Brigham stopped, turning his head. Matthew looked back too. In the light from the doorway, he could see partly inside the cabin. Vilate Kimball was lying on a bed, her newborn at her side. Heber was kneeling beside her, gripping her hand, and weeping along with her.

Matthew looked away, feeling again the pain of his final farewell with Jenny this morning. And they weren't married yet. He could only imagine what it must be costing these brethren to leave wives and children in such desperate circumstances.

"You'll have to help me up," Brigham said as they came around to the back of the wagon. "I can't do it."

The boy had the tailgate of the wagon down, and together he and Matthew helped Brigham up onto the wagon bed. The boy's mother or father had laid out some blankets, and Brigham collapsed gratefully upon them, breathing heavily, his face grimacing with the pain. "Help Heber," he gasped.

Heber was down on his knees on the front step, his arms around his four-year-old son. "Young Heber," he said, stroking the boy's cheek with the back of his hand, "be my brave little man and care for your mommy and your brothers and your sister."

The boy was stoic, his eyes large and round but not filled with tears. "I will, Papa."

"God bless you," Heber said. He tried to stand, but couldn't. Matthew jumped to his side and put a hand around his waist. The boy took his other arm, and they helped him hobble to the wagon, then climb up to lie beside Brigham. Matthew closed the tailgate carefully, watching anxiously as the two of them lay there, totally drained even by what it had taken to get into the wagon. He shook his head. *A thousand miles? This is insane.*

He climbed up onto the wagon seat alongside the driver and nodded grimly to him. The boy, greatly sobered by the condition of his passengers, flipped the reins lightly. "Hee yaw!" he called softly. "Giddyap there, mules." The team lunged forward and the wagon began to roll.

They had gone no more than ten rods when there was a croak from the wagon box behind them. "Stop!" It was Heber who had called out.

As the boy reined up, Matthew looked back in alarm. Heber's face was twisted in agony. He looked as though death itself had come to ride with them. Had they discovered so quickly that they couldn't bear the journey?

But Heber wasn't looking at Matthew. He wasn't looking for help. He was looking at Brigham. And when he spoke, Matthew realized it was a different kind of agony he was feeling.

"What is it, Heber?" Brigham managed. "What's the matter?"

"This is pretty tough, isn't it? I feel as though my very heart is going to melt within me."

Brigham's head had been turned away from his companion. Now he turned to face him. His eyes were filled with tears and his cheeks were wet. He had turned away to hide his weeping. "I don't know if I can endure it," he whispered.

Heber nodded; then his shoulders lifted and fell and a certain determination touched his mouth. "This is no way to leave our families, us stretched out in a wagon bed, them too sick to even bid us farewell. Let us rise up and give them a cheer."

"Of course," Brigham said instantly. "Yes, let's do it."

He came up on one elbow, then reached out and grabbed the side of the wagon to steady himself. He grunted, panting heavily with the effort. Matthew was on his feet and starting to lean over to help, but Brigham waved him off with a shake of his head. He staggered upwards, teeth clenched together, until he was standing. Heber got to his knees, then had to stop. His head dropped and he gasped for air. But like Brigham he refused any help, and finally lurched to his feet.

Heber's cabin was on a small hillock, and the wagon had just reached the bottom. Its back end faced the cabin. Clutching each other to steady themselves, the two Apostles swept off their hats. Waving them in great circles over their heads, they shouted as loudly as they could, which wasn't much more than a hoarse croak. "Hurrah! Hurrah for Israel! Hurrah! Hurrah for Israel!"

After a moment, the door of the cabin opened and Vilate Kimball was standing there in her nightdress, blinking at the bright sunlight. In another moment, Mary Ann Young stood beside her. Like their husbands, they clung to each other in a desperate attempt to steady themselves.

"Hurrah!" the men shouted one last time. "Hurrah for Israel!" The hats made one last circle.

Matthew was staring, hardly believing what he was seeing. The women were likewise stunned. But then Vilate's arm came up and a broad smile broke out across her face. Mary Ann began to wave, at first slowly, then enthusiastically. "Good-bye!" they cried. "God bless you."

"And God bless you!" Brigham said. His arm fell, all strength to keep it up completely gone. "God be with you."

The two men sank back down heavily, first to their knees, then rolling over onto their backs, drawing breath like men saved from the depths of the sea. "All right," Brigham said haltingly to Matthew and the boy. "You may drive on."

With the departure of the Twelve for England and the coming of fall, things in Nauvoo began to settle down. The cooler weather brought a respite from the ague, as it usually did, and life returned somewhat back to normal. Building continued at a rapid pace as the Saints continued to pour into Hancock County, Illinois, and its surrounding areas.

Things settled in for the Steed family as well. Melissa wrote and told the family of the reaction of Carl's father to the suggestion that Carl and Melissa and their children move west. That came as a major disappointment, especially to Mary Ann. But other than that, the plan devised by Nathan and Lydia for a family cooperative moved ahead steadily.

The Monday after Matthew left with Brigham and Heber, Jessica began the first day of classes in her new school. There were twelve students. When young Joshua and Emily returned from Palmyra— whenever that would be—she would have fourteen. But even twelve left the small room quite full. They ranged in age from just under seven to seventeen years. Three were family—Jessica's own Rachel, turning eight in January; Luke Griffith, her older stepson, who would turn seven in mid-October; and Caroline's Olivia, who would be twelve in November. Three were adopted family—Peter Ingalls, now fifteen, helped Jessica with the teaching; and the two McIntire sisters, Kathryn, now thirteen, and Jenny, almost eighteen, lived with Jessica to help with the children as their pay for the schooling. The other six students were neighbor children, their families paying Jessica in meager services or future promises.

There were no chairs, only two long benches. The benches were made from split logs, and though Matthew and Peter had spent days smoothing them with a drawknife, a person could still pick up a sliver or two in the backside if he or she became too restless. Jessica had only enough slate boards for eight and had to rotate them around for writing and arithmetic lessons. Her most treasured items were the five sets of McGuffey readers Joshua and Caroline had brought as a present from St. Louis.

While teaching in Missouri, she had managed to find several copies of *The New England Primer* and had used that as her reading textbook. But she had never really liked them. First printed over a hundred years earlier, the *Primer* had been a staple of American education ever since. It contained a hefty dose of prayers and pieties along with basic reading material, which was fine. But many of the lessons, couched in verse to make them easier to memorize, were dour in their content and illustrated with pictures to match. It was the pictures that Jessica loathed. For example, the letter F was taught with the rhyme, "The idle Fool is whipt at school," and a wicked-looking schoolmaster with a long switch proved the point. The Y entry suggested, "While Youth do chear, death may be near," a Puritan reminder that one ought to take one's happiness with a dose of gloom. Here a skeleton was shown arriving at a party of children.

But the new readers were sweeping the country now. A schoolteacher named William H. McGuffey had written new reading textbooks for the Ohio public schools. Volumes one and two of the *Eclectic Readers*, as they were titled—or the "McGuffey readers," as they were more commonly called—were published in 1836 and became an instant success. Three more volumes came out the next year. McGuffey infused the books with a high moral tone. One might read stories like "True Manliness," or "Perseverance," but there was none of the grimness of *The New England Primer*. Children loved to study from them, and parents were pleased with the fact that their children were being taught important values. The five sets were a gift of inestimable worth to Jessica, and word that Jessica Griffith had the latest in educational materials was already spreading through Nauvoo.

The Steed store opened for business on the first day of October. It was not the only store in Nauvoo, but there was no question that it was the most spacious and had the broadest selection. They opened their doors to a brisk business that steadily increased almost daily. With Nathan and Lydia in New York, Caroline—now midway through her pregnancy—took the lead in running the store, but got consistent help from the women and older children of the family.

Joshua shuttled back and forth between Nauvoo, Quincy, and St. Louis on a regular basis, maintaining freight offices in each place. With the influx of population, the need for goods in Nauvoo outpaced the ability of the haulers to bring them in. By October, Joshua had doubled the number of wagons and teams he owned and still could not keep up with the demand. He and Benjamin worked with Joseph and the city leaders to get a steamboat landing built so Nauvoo could become a stop for the riverboats. Bringing in freight by boat was considerably less expensive than bringing it in by wagon.

Mary Ann was being matriarch and grandma to a growing clan, but with the store done, the school up and running, and Joshua's business burgeoning, Benjamin found himself with little to do. Now fully recovered from any effects of the summer's illness and his imprisonment the previous fall, the drop in activity left him increasingly restless. So on the tenth day of October, without saying anything to Mary Ann, he left their cabin and moved south, toward the Old Homestead.

Benjamin heard the noise of the children while he was still several rods away from the cabin where Joseph and Emma lived. Moving more slowly, not wanting to disturb whatever was happening, he came around the corner of the building and stopped. Instantly he started to chuckle.

The Old Homestead property was on the corner of Water Street and Main Street fronting the river. The cabin faced south, providing a wonderful view of the Mississippi as it straightened out again and headed for St. Louis and New Orleans. But that was not what made Benjamin stop. Joseph Smith was out in front of his house, where the grass sloped down to the water's edge. A blindfold was tied around his eyes, and he was down on all fours. Julia, young Joseph, Frederick, and Alexander were dancing around him, taunting and yelling at him.

With a roar he came up on his knees, his hands clawing at the air, striking out blindly in the direction of their voices. They screamed and scattered, darting away from the "bear's" deadly claws. Little Alex, not yet eighteen months old, was the slowest, his fat little legs pumping hard but not moving him nearly fast enough. Growling, and obviously peeking out from beneath the blindfold, Joseph grabbed Alex and went down, rolling over and over, "biting" Alex's arms and stomach and neck. Laughing, screeching, hollering for help, Alexander struggled to get free. Instantly his siblings responded and swarmed Joseph to the ground.

"Good morning, Father Steed."

Turning in surprise, Benjamin saw that Emma was standing at the door. She had seen him pass her window and stepped out to say hello. "Good morning, Emma."

"Bang! Bang!" Young Joseph was pointing his finger at his father and fired off two "rounds." With a great yelp of pain, Joseph stiffened, threw his hands in the air, then rolled over and went limp. Alex scampered free.

"Yea! Yea!" the children cried, dancing around the fallen monster.

Emma just shook her head. "I'm glad it's you, Benjamin."

"Why's that?" he said, still smiling as he watched them poke at the bear and make sure he was truly dead.

"Some of our newer converts would find it hard to believe that this is the prophet of the Lord."

Benjamin was nodding. He knew exactly what she meant. "Well, I think it's wonderful."

"It's wonderful to have him home again," she said, her voice soft as she looked in Joseph's direction. "Really wonderful."

Joseph heard their voices and sat up, pulling off the blindfold. "Good morning, Brother Benjamin," he called out. Scooping up Alexander, he stood and started toward the house. Frederick gave a whoop and dove, throwing his arms around his father's leg.

"Oh, no!" Joseph cried in horror. "The alligator's got me." He started forward, dragging Frederick with him. That was too much for the others. Young Joseph grabbed the other leg and hung on. Julia collared him around the waist and dug in her feet. "The alligators have got me! The alligators have got me! I have to get out of the river." He came forward, lurching and moaning, dragging the giggling reptiles along behind him.

When he reached the step where Benjamin and Emma were waiting, he collapsed. "I made it!" he breathed in relief. "I'm safe."

✦

"Is there anything I can do to be of help, Joseph? I . . . I guess I'm feeling kind of useless at the moment."

They were walking west along Water Street toward the river. Joseph stopped and looked at his old friend in surprise. "Emma said something to you, didn't she?"

Benjamin shook his head. "No. About what?"

"About me coming to see you."

Now Benjamin was genuinely puzzled. "No, she didn't say anything."

"Well," Joseph said, laying his arm across Benjamin's shoulder and moving forward again, "I have been thinking about you ever since conference."

"Oh?" The second general conference since Joseph's release from prison had been held just a few days before.

"Yes, as you remember, I preached a great deal on the importance of missionary work and having the Spirit with us as we teach the gospel."

"Yes, I remember it well."

"Well, at first I thought maybe it was time to call you on a mission."

Benjamin started just a little, and Joseph immediately laughed. "You would be a good one, Benjamin. You have much wisdom and maturity that some of our younger brethren could profit from. But no, that's not what the Lord has in mind."

"*Does* he have something in mind for me?"

"I think so."

That was encouraging. Benjamin felt an immediate lift. "What?"

"Well, I've been thinking about it a lot. You've been a great help to me over the years, Brother Benjamin, and you and your family have always stood by me. And you worked so profitably for us on the building committee for the Kirtland Temple. You have been a great strength to the Church."

"Thank you. I find great joy in being of service."

"I know. And so . . ." His eyes grew thoughtful. Benjamin waited. "There is much to do here," Joseph began, speaking slowly, as if he were still working it out in his mind even as he spoke. "You had a lot of experience in developing land back in Kirtland, didn't you?"

"Yes. I worked with Martin Harris and others. We developed some twenty or thirty building lots in the city."

"I'd not thought of that for a time. That's it, then."

"What?"

"I'd like you to be on the committee for allocation of land and for planning our growing city."

Now it was Benjamin who stopped. That was one area that hadn't even crossed his mind as a possibility. "I would like that, Joseph."

"Then it's done! I'll talk to Hyrum and the others this very morning."

"I would be honored."

"And Benjamin?"

"Yes?"

"It's not time yet, because our people need to get homes built and occupations started, but we *are* going to build a temple to our God in this place. It is the Lord's will. Maybe soon we can make an announcement."

"That would be wonderful!"

"And when we do, I want Benjamin Steed on the building committee again." He slapped him on the back. "Fair enough?"

Benjamin looked at Joseph and started to speak, but his voice betrayed him. He swallowed hard, then tried again. "If it weren't for the Lord, I wouldn't be here having this conversation with you, Joseph. You ask what you will, and I shall give you the best that I have."

———•———

Caroline looked up as the door opened and a rush of cold air blew in. A man stepped inside, turning his back as he shook off the water from his umbrella onto the porch. Outside, the rain still came down in sheets, and she could see he had not remained completely dry. His boots were muddy and his pant legs wet to the knees.

He shut the door, stood the umbrella in the corner, then turned around. It was Joseph Smith. "Good afternoon," he said cheerfully.

Jenny McIntire was standing next to Caroline. It was late afternoon and school was over, so Jenny was helping Caroline in the store. Not that she needed much help. With the storm, there were very few people out and about.

Jenny smiled brightly at their visitor. "Good afternoon, Brother Joseph."

"Afternoon, Jenny."

"Good afternoon, Brother Jos—" Caroline caught herself, coloring slightly. "Good afternoon, Joseph," she amended. Being around Mormons all the time, one easily fell into the "brother and sister" habit.

Joseph laughed softly, but said nothing. He walked across the room to face them. He wore no hat, and his hair was damp against his forehead. "Oh! What a storm! There's enough mud out there to rebuild the Tower of Babel."

Caroline and Jenny both nodded. Nauvoo's mud—black, thick, clutching—was worthy of world fame.

Now that twinkle, which was so characteristic of him, began to dance in his eyes, but his face was completely sober. "I had to stop and help Sister Emmaline Barney on my way over. She had started across the street and got both feet stuck down good and firm. Lost both of her button shoes. Don't think we'll ever see them again in this life."

Caroline started to giggle. Jenny laughed right out loud.

"Pretty near lost her completely," he went on, still as sober as a hanging judge. "If I hadn't come along, I think she'd have gone straight through and been speaking Chinese before morning."

Caroline lost control at that. She rocked back, holding her stomach. Jenny lost it too, doubling over as the laughter bubbled out of her.

Now a tiny smile began to play around his eyes. "Finally hooked up a span of oxen, threw a rope around one of them hoops under her skirt, and got her out of there in the nick of time."

"Oh, stop!" Caroline cried. "The baby." Tears were coming to her eyes.

Chuckling now, Joseph waited until their laughter subsided. Then he watched as Caroline straightened. "How *are* you doing, Caroline?"

She laid one hand on her stomach. "Quite good, really. I think it's going to be a healthy one, the way it keeps kicking me."

"That's good. Emma asked me to be sure and inquire."

"Tell her thank you for me."

"I thought you were leaving for Washington today," Jenny spoke up.

"Tomorrow. We're off tomorrow."

With nothing happening in Missouri to give the Saints redress, Joseph had decided to lead a delegation to the nation's capital. Petitions were drawn up, depositions taken, losses cataloged. Now they would ask the federal government for justice. No one had much hope for it, but as Mary Ann had explained to Caroline, God had asked it of them to make sure their skirts were clean.

Noting that Joseph's eyes had lifted and he was scanning the shelves, Caroline got down to business. "What can we do for you today?"

He looked around. "I'd like to get a Christmas present for Emma. I know it's still almost two months away, but I doubt we'll be back before then. I would like to buy something now and have you deliver it to her if we haven't returned."

"We'd be pleased to do that for you."

Now he looked a little sheepish. "And I could use some advice. I was hoping that you'd be here. I'm not very good at these things."

They walked around the store together, Joseph peering at this thing or that, Caroline and Jenny suggesting and pointing out various items. Finally he settled on a brooch, a rose carved from a piece of whale bone. It would set off her fair skin and dark hair wonderfully. As Caroline began to wrap it up, she looked up at him. "I enjoyed your sermon on Sunday."

"Thank you. I am pleased that you have started to come to worship services with your girls." A bit of a teasing smile played around his mouth. "Any suggestions for the preacher on how to improve?"

"No, but . . . well, I did have a question about what you said."

Joseph swung around and pointed to the corner of the room. "Let's sit down. I've got a few minutes. I thought finding something for Emma would take longer than this."

They moved toward where the stove stood in an open area. Around it were two chairs, a small table for playing checkers, and a couple of stools. A really successful store always had a place for folks to visit or sit for a spell, especially in poor weather.

He waited until they were settled, then leaned forward, his face serious again, his eyes earnest. "All right, what bothered you?"

Caroline glanced at Jenny, hoping for help, but Jenny just shook her head. "I'm here to listen."

So Caroline took a quick breath, then plunged. She had been thinking about this ever since Sunday. "You talked about forgiveness," she began tentatively.

"Yes."

"You said that even though you are trying to seek redress from Congress for the wrongs done in Missouri, the Saints shouldn't be harboring any feelings of hatred or bitterness against those people in Missouri. You said that it was time to forgive and move on, leaving judgment in the hand of the Lord."

"The Lord has been very clear in this matter."

She bit her lower lip. "I know. I know the New Testament says that we must forgive too. But you said more than that. You said something about it being a sin if we don't forgive others."

He smiled gently. "I was just quoting the Lord, Caroline."

"I know. Jenny showed me where it was in the Doctrine and Covenants. And that's what's bothering me. It says that if I don't forgive, I have the greater sin."

"Yes, that's how the Lord says it."

Now her mouth was set and her eyes touched with bitterness. "All right, here's my question. Last fall, three men—all Missourians—came to the house of Father and Mother Steed in Far West. They found Mother Steed, Rebecca, Lydia, and Jessica in a root cellar and started to do unspeakable things to them. Joshua came just then and stopped them. One man was killed. Later the other two men shot Joshua in the back because he stopped them. The only reason they didn't kill him is because they were poor shots."

"Yes, Benjamin told me all about this."

Her head bobbed curtly, acknowledging his comment. "Those same two men then came to Independence and burned down our house. We were lucky to get out alive. And those same two men—" She looked away, coming close to the edge of control now. "And those same two men are the reason why my son is on some ship on its way to China now. And why I won't see him for another year."

She took a breath. "And you're telling me that my sin is greater than theirs if I don't forgive them? I'm sorry, but I have trouble understanding that."

"That's not surprising. This is one of the most difficult principles of the gospel to really live properly."

"Why?" she burst out angrily. "I remember that day in Far West—that day when Nathan brought Joshua home to see his family again for the first time in eleven years. I'll always remember how you came and taught us about forgiveness and what it did for our family. But Joshua had changed. Joshua was trying to be a better person. I can see why we have to forgive someone like that. But these men didn't change. Why must I forgive *them*? Why doesn't the Lord talk about *their* responsibility to me? I hate those men! I hate what they did! I rejoice that they are dead because I know they cannot harm us any further."

She straightened slowly, a little shamed by the intensity of her emotions. "I'm sorry. As you can see, I have some very strong feelings about this."

"Understandably." Joseph leaned back, his eyes never leaving her face. Jenny did not move, but just watched the two of them. Finally, he leaned forward again. "Let me teach you just one principle that might help answer your question."

"I'm listening."

"Let me ask you one question, and I'd like you to think about it carefully. Why do you suppose God requires that we forgive if we are the innocent party? Like you say, it doesn't seem fair."

The question caught her off guard. "Well—"

"Think about it for a minute."

She did, and found that it put a whole new twist on things. She had always wrestled with the principle from her own point of view. But trying to see it from God's point of view was different. "I guess," she finally ventured, "because he forgives us."

"Yes, and why would you want to do it just because he does it?"

Her mind was working hard now. "I suppose because I want to be more like him."

He nodded, pleasure showing in his eyes. "Yes, exactly." He sat back, as though she had her answer.

"But I don't understand. What are you suggesting?"

"Don't you see, Caroline? What those two men did was a terrible sin. No one is arguing that point. They have probably lost any chance for salvation. But the principle of forgiveness isn't for them. It's for you!"

"For me? What do you mean?"

"God gives us the gospel so that we can be happy. The Book of Mormon says that man is that he might have joy. That's what we're after, joy."

"Yes, I agree with that."

"So these rules, these principles God gives us—such as, 'you are required to forgive all men or there remaineth in you the greater sin'—these aren't just something God thinks up to keep us busy. They are the principles which make us happy. And why do they make us happy?"

It was a rhetorical question and he didn't wait for her to answer. "Because they make us more like him. They help us put on the divine nature, as the Apostle Peter called it. Forgiveness is one of the attributes of God. If you can't forgive, then you are not like the Savior and our Heavenly Father. And if you're not like our God and like his Son, then you cannot find a fulness of joy. That's what it's all about."

Caroline was following his words very closely, marveling. They were so clear, so pure, so simple. "I see," she said slowly.

Now he was very serious. "I want you to think about the Savior for a moment. This is the Master, the one who suffered for the sins of all mankind. He took upon himself sins of every hue, thousands of them—millions, even! He trembled in agony and bled at every pore so that he could pay the price for those sins—yours, mine, Joshua's, everyone's. Now, can you picture yourself standing before this perfect, holy Man at the Judgment and saying, 'I'm sorry but I cannot forgive those two men who shot my husband'?"

She couldn't meet that penetrating gaze. It seemed to strip her defenses completely away. Her eyes dropped to look at her hands. "No," she whispered.

"Nor can I."

———•———

For several minutes after he left, Caroline stood at the window, watching the tall figure slowly disappear into the thick curtain of rain. Jenny stood beside her. "He makes it so clear," Caroline finally said. "It is so logical. Why haven't I ever thought of it in that way before?"

Jenny looked at her, debating about whether to speak her mind. But she decided it needed to be said. "Caroline, what you've got to remember is this—Joseph is a remarkable man. Even his enemies admit that. But he's more than that. He's a prophet of God. And God has endowed him with his power and his Spirit. That's what you're feeling right now. You have just been taught by a prophet."

Chapter Notes

Details of Brigham Young and Heber Kimball's poignant departure from their families, including their final "Hurrahs," are recorded in Heber's journal (see *LHCK*, pp. 265–66; see also *American Moses*, pp. 74–75, and *MWM*, pp. 70–71).

Though the specifics are furnished by the author, the scene in which Joseph is playing with his children is typical of him, particularly during this time in Nauvoo. He loved young people in general and was always a caring and loving father to his own children. In numerous entries in his journal history his feelings for his family are evident (see, for example, *HC* 2:45, 297–98, 307, 405; 5:182, 265, 369, 500, 515).

The substance of the interchange between Joseph and Caroline on forgiveness is not drawn from any particular speech or sermon that he gave. But it is known from his history that Joseph spoke on forgiveness on more than one occasion during this period (see, for example, *HC* 3:383; 4:110, 162, 425). The Saints were still healing from the wounds of Missouri and from betrayals by some of their own leaders, and this may have been the reason he so often took up the subject.

Joseph was one to practice what he preached. Orson Hyde, a member of the Twelve, left the Church with Thomas B. Marsh in October of 1838. They both made outrageous accusations about Joseph and swore to them. When he came back and asked for mercy, Orson not only was forgiven but was eventually restored to the apostleship as well (see *HC* 3:379; 4:2, 12). W. W. Phelps, another prominent leader, also fell away and during the Richmond hearing testified against the Prophet and the other Church leaders. But when he wrote in 1840 and asked Joseph for forgiveness, Joseph's response was, in part: "You may in some measure realize what my feelings, as well as Elder Rigdon's and Brother Hyrum's were, when we read your letter—truly our hearts were melted into tenderness and compassion. . . . I can assure you I feel a disposition to act on your case in a manner that will meet the approbation of Jehovah, (whose servant I am). . . . I shall be happy once again to give you the right hand of fellowship, and rejoice over the returning prodigal." (See HC 4:141–42, 162–64.)

Joseph left for Washington, D.C., on 29 October 1839 to petition the federal government for redress for the wrongs committed against the Saints while in Missouri. After receiving no satisfaction, he left the capital in February of 1840 and returned to Nauvoo in March. It was during the Prophet's visit to Washington, D.C., that President Martin Van Buren made the famous statement, "Your cause is just, but I can do nothing for you." (See HC 4:80; 5:393; CHFT, pp. 220–21.)

Brigham Young, Heber Kimball, and Matthew Steed moved slowly eastward. The boy took them in the wagon fourteen miles south of Nauvoo and dropped them off at a member's house. That man took them in his wagon twelve miles more and gave them each a dollar. When they got as far as Quincy they had to stop for five days while the two Apostles tried to regain a little strength. While they were there, George A. Smith, along with two companions, caught up with them, stayed with Brigham and Heber briefly, then went on ahead of them.

George A. was the youngest of the Twelve and the last to leave Nauvoo. Like the two senior Apostles, he was in terrible shape. The fever had affected his eyesight, leaving him almost totally blind and completely dependent on his two companions. He had been in such terrible shape when he left Nauvoo that his uncle Joseph Smith, Sr., accused someone of robbing the burying yard.

After their brief respite in Quincy, Brigham's party started out again, turning east now, leapfrogging across the prairie by horseback, wagon, buggy, or stagecoach, or on foot, traveling without purse or scrip, depending on the goodness of a few family members who lived on the route, other members of the Church, or complete strangers. They would push on as long as the health of the two Apostles let them, then stop to rest when they could go no farther.

On the night of October fifth, seventeen days out, they arrived in Springfield, the capital of Illinois. Much to their surprise and joy, they found George A. and the others there waiting for them. They stayed in Springfield for almost a week, preaching to the small group of Saints while they rested and recuperated. Still so sick that the Saints had to rig a bed for him in a wagon, Brigham Young decreed that the three Apostles and their companions move on.

Though they had no way of knowing it, they had begun to gain ground on another of their fellow Apostles. Wilford Woodruff, John Taylor, and Derek Ingalls started from Nauvoo nearly six weeks earlier than Brigham's party, but John Taylor had become so ill in Germantown, Indiana, that he was confined to his bed for nearly a month. Derek had suffered a relapse as well, though not nearly as severe as Taylor's. Finally, at Taylor's urging, Wilford Woodruff went on without them. After a long and slow recovery, Derek and Brother Taylor finally started east again.

Then came another setback to Brigham's group. In Terre Haute, Indiana, Heber—once again too sick to travel—was taken to a local doctor who was supposed to be a faithful member of the Church. The doctor, so drunk he was barely coherent, mistakenly gave Heber a large dose of morphine. Within minutes Heber was writhing on the floor. As the night wore on, they nearly lost him. Brigham sat by his bedside as he retched over and over. The vomiting saved his life but left him terribly weak. The next morning, after much discussion, George A. and his companions went on without Brigham and Matthew and Heber, with the promise they would wait in Kirtland. Heber, barely able to speak, bravely predicted that he would reach Kirtland before them.

Two other Apostles were moving east independently of the others. Parley and Orson Pratt, in better financial and physical condition than any of the others, left Nauvoo on August twenty-ninth, traveling in a carriage with Parley's wife and three children. Parley had been a missionary in New York City and had several friends there. He felt his family might fare better with them than if they were left in the barely developing settlement of Nauvoo. Orson and Parley decided to go by way of Detroit to visit their parents.

So by late October, there were five missionary parties moving toward New York City in some kind of rough tandem with each other—the Pratt brothers, in the most northerly route; Wilford Woodruff, out ahead of everyone and traveling by himself; John Taylor, recovered enough to be moving again with Derek; George A. and his companions; and Brigham's group.

In Dayton, Ohio, when George A. and his party arrived they were joyfully surprised to find John Taylor and Derek staying with some of the members there. After a short rest, together they pushed on to Cleveland, their last stop before Kirtland. If they were surprised in Dayton, they were dumbfounded in Cleveland, for Brigham Young, Heber Kimball, and Matthew Steed were already there. Without knowing it, Brigham's group had passed the others the night before while they were stopped at a tavern for lodging. Only when John Taylor's party arrived in Cleveland the next day at the hotel where Brigham and the others were staying were the two groups happily reunited.

———◆———

Derek and Matthew sat on the boardwalk across from the hotel, with their heads close together. The stage for Kirtland was not due to leave for another ten minutes, and they eagerly took the opportunity to catch each other up on the news.

At first, Derek peppered Matthew with questions about how things were at home. Though Matthew's reports were now almost two months old, they were six weeks fresher than what Derek had. He reported on the store and the school (both nearly ready to open when he left Nauvoo) and on each of the family members, giving particularly detailed reports on Rebecca and baby Christopher. He told him of a second letter from Will, posted from France on the night before he set sail for the long run to China.

After a few minutes of that, Matthew changed the subject. "By the way," he said, "Caroline and the girls started going to worship services with us the last two weeks before I left."

Derek's eyebrows rose. "She did? That's wonderful."

"Yes. We were all surprised."

"And Joshua didn't mind?"

Matthew shook his head. "Well, Caroline said that he didn't particularly like the idea, but being with Joseph on that day of healing really affected him. He says he'll let it be her decision."

"But he wouldn't go with her?"

This time Matthew's head shook back and forth even more emphatically. "Not on your life. He won't even come over to our cabin for family prayer. That bothers Caroline a lot. She doesn't expect him to come for the scripture reading—"

"Does Caroline come to that?"

"Every night. Even when we're reading the Book of Mormon. But anyway, she says that since the prayers are mostly for the family anyway—especially for Will—Joshua could at least come and listen. But he's always got some excuse or another."

Derek sat back. He, of all the family, still believed that Joshua would someday have a change of heart and accept the gospel. Joshua's reaction to watching Joseph use the power of the priesthood to heal had been very encouraging to Derek. After all, Nancy McIntire had joined the Church and she had been staunch Irish Roman Catholic. Who would have predicted that?

"What about Carl?" Matthew asked. "Do you think he's another Joshua?"

Derek shrugged. "I don't know, but I don't think his feelings against the Church run nearly as deep."

"I wish they could come out to Nauvoo."

"I know," Derek sighed. In addition to the bitterness of Carl's father, there was another obstacle, as Derek saw it. Brigham had determined that on their way east they should stop at Kirtland to visit the small group of Saints who had stayed when the rest fled to Missouri. But Brigham had also said that most of the Saints who stayed in Kirtland were either too poor to move or too weak in the faith to follow the Prophet. Those, combined with the apostates who, a couple of years back, had turned against Joseph, didn't make for a lot of wonderful examples left in Kirtland that would change Carl's feelings about the Mormons.

Matthew grinned broadly. "I can't wait to see the look on their faces when we knock on their door this afternoon."

"Yeah!" Derek answered, with a smile. "Knowing Melissa, I don't think we'll be getting to bed very early tonight."

———— • ————

Melissa sat across the table from Matthew and Derek. "There's plenty more," she said, watching Matthew mop up the last of the gravy with a thick hunk of bread.

He looked a little sheepish. "Are you sure?"

She laughed merrily. "Yes. Now I know why Papa said he'd rather have four horses in the barn than you at the supper table."

He looked hurt. "You've got to remember that we haven't been eating real good since we left Nauvoo."

"I'm just teasing you. I think it's wonderful. How about you, Derek?"

He held up his hands to shield off any such suggestion. "No, I'm already hurting. But thank you, Melissa. It was wonderful. It is the best we've eaten in some time."

"I'll say," Matthew said, spearing the last piece of steak on his fork.

Melissa took the plate and went to the stove, filling it half up again. When she sat down, she was shaking her head. "I still can't believe it. Matthew and Derek right here in Kirtland, sitting in my kitchen."

Matthew flashed her a grin. "We thought you might be a little surprised."

"Surprised? I thought I was going to fall off the porch when I opened the door yesterday afternoon and saw you two standing there. And it is so good to have some of the Twelve with us in Kirtland again. I didn't know Brother Young or Brother Smith as well, but to see Brother Kimball and Brother Taylor again—it was just like old times."

Derek leaned forward slightly. "Are you sure it's all right with Carl if Brigham and Heber stay here with us? We can find other members of the Church who would take them in."

Melissa shook her head quickly. "You were there last night. It wasn't me pushing the idea."

Carl had surprised her no less than he had surprised Matthew and Derek the previous evening when he insisted that two other missionaries besides their own family members stay with them. Brigham and Heber, who were Matthew's companions, determined they would be the two. Then this afternoon Carl astounded her even further. When Hezekiah Rogers learned that Mormon missionaries had come to town and that some of them would be staying with his son, he railed bitterly against their return to Kirtland, vowing to go to the town council and drive them on. Carl responded testily. Since when did common citizens of the United States of America have to account to local residents in order to enter a city and take lodging there? The Kirtland residents had driven them out once; wasn't that enough, for heaven's sake? It was another sign of the growing tension between Carl and his father.

"I've written a letter to Mama and Papa," Matthew said. There was a shy smile. "And to Jennifer Jo. Could you help me post them tomorrow, Melissa?"

"And I plan to write to Rebecca tonight," Derek added.

"Yes, yes," Melissa said. "I want to write Mama a long letter too."

Derek gave her a sidelong glance. "There's no way, then, that Carl would ever come west?"

The corners of her mouth pulled down. "No. At first, I was surprised at how willing he was to consider the whole idea. Going into partnership with Joshua really appealed to him. I really got my hopes up. But his father is so absolutely against it. He's threatened to totally cut Carl off from everything if he leaves. And Carl has worked hard to make the business what it is now."

"That's too bad—," Derek started, but then a knock at the door cut him off.

Young Carl, Melissa's oldest, was playing in the parlor with his two brothers. "I'll get it, Mama," he called, jumping up and running to the door. Melissa arose and stepped to the kitchen door. There was the sound of booming voices and she looked back at Derek and Matthew. "It's Brother Brigham and Brother Heber," she explained. Then to them she called, "We're in here, brethren. Come in."

As they came in, hats under their arms and cheeks rosy from the cold, Brigham smiled at Matthew. "Are you *still* eating?"

Matthew's mouth was full, and he began to chew more rapidly so he could answer, but Melissa answered for him. "As far as I'm concerned, he can eat all night long if he likes. And how about you? Would you brethren like some supper?"

"We ate with the Thompsons. Thank you anyway."

"Well, you know where your room is," Melissa said. "You must be very tired."

"Indeed," Heber said. "Thank you again—and your husband—for such warm hospitality."

"It is our pleasure. Carl had to do some work at the livery stable. He'll be back in a half hour or so, but he said not to have you wait up."

"You have a fine husband, Sister Rogers," Brigham said. "A fine man."

"Thank you." She started toward the door that led down the hall to the bedrooms, then stopped. "Do you know how long you will be staying in Kirtland?" she asked, not wanting to appear too forward, but eager to know. Now that they had visited with some of the Saints, they might have a better idea.

Brigham saw through it immediately and was happy to answer her concerns. "In some ways, this is like returning to our spiritual home, Sister Melissa. I wept as I passed the temple today."

"Amen," Heber said quietly.

"And there are still quite a few members here. We'll stay for a time. At least a week, maybe more."

She clapped her hands together. "A week! That's wonderful!"

Brigham looked over at the table at Derek and Matthew. "We talked to some of the brethren—Martin Harris, the Johnsons. I think they'll agree to let us have a meeting in the temple sometime."

"Really?" Derek exclaimed. That was more than they had hoped for.

"Good," Matthew grunted. He lifted another slice of bread, heavy with butter. "Give me a week or ten days, and maybe I can stock up enough on Melissa's cooking to carry me on to New York City."

Brigham pulled a face, then looked soberly at Heber. "Then you and I had better tighten our belts, because when this lad is through, the whole of the state of Ohio will be in famine."

———————

Carl Rogers turned his head. Through the doorway of his bedroom he could hear the soft murmur of voices. Frowning, he pulled the covers back and sat up. Beside him, Melissa was breathing deeply and did not stir. With business prospering, Carl had recently added a wing to their house and they now had four bedrooms. To accommodate their new houseguests, they moved their three sons together into the end bedroom and took baby Sarah—just now a year old—in with them. This left a bedroom for Matthew and Derek, and another for Brigham Young and Heber Kimball. But putting three boys—a seven-year-old, a five-year-old, and a three-year-old—into one room, with the two younger ones sharing the same bed, had proven to have its challenges. Last night it had taken them almost a full hour to finally settle down and get to sleep. Evidently, tonight was going to be a repeat.

Reaching for his robe, Carl quietly opened the door and went out, readying a stern lecture for his sons. The hallway was dark except for a crack of light coming from the second doorway, the bedroom where Young and Kimball were sleeping. There was no sound from the end bedroom. Thinking that his sons had heard him, he padded quietly down the hall, but as he passed the second door, he realized what the problem was. Brigham Young and Heber Kimball were still awake and talking. He turned to start back to his own room, but their voices came clearly through the thin partition of the door and he stopped for a moment to listen.

"Are you sure?"

It was Brigham's voice.

"I'm positive," Heber's voice replied.

"All along I assumed it was you." Carl heard a soft noise and realized someone was turning the pages of a book or sheets of paper. "All right, let's start over." Brigham was clearly perplexed. "When we left Pleasant Garden, how much did we have?"

"Thirteen dollars and fifty cents."

"Right. That's what I have marked. And we have come four hundred miles since then by stagecoach, paying eight to ten cents per mile."

"That is correct."

"And the three of us have eaten three meals a day during that journey, and for each of those we have been charged fifty cents."

"Again correct."

"And we paid fifty cents apiece for each night's lodging?"

There was some amusement in Heber's voice. "Yes, that is what I recorded."

The silence stretched on for some time, and Carl felt a little guilty for eavesdropping. But he was curious about what all of this meant.

Then Brigham spoke again. "But that's not possible. We started with thirteen-fifty and now have only one York shilling left. And yet we have paid out a total of eighty-seven dollars!"

There was a soft laugh. "Yes, Brigham, we have."

"Did anyone give you money during that time?"

"Not one soul."

Carl heard a deep sigh, more of bewilderment than resignation. "All along, I thought you had some secret purse about which you had not told me. I kept thinking that you were slipping money into my pockets or into my trunk each day so that I would not be embarrassed. I was amazed that you had those kinds of resources and had not told me about them."

"I had not told you about them because I had no such resources."

"But then . . ."

Now Heber's voice carried as much sobriety as Brigham's. "Do you remember the prophet Elijah and the widow of Zarephath? There was only enough flour and oil for one more small meal, yet they ate from it for many days."

"Yes," Brigham answered. Now there was wonder in his voice.

"Someone put that money in your trunk or in your clothing," Heber concluded. "But it wasn't me. And it certainly wasn't Matthew."

———◆———

For a long time after he climbed back into bed, Carl Rogers lay awake, staring up at the ceiling. The day after the missionaries' arrival, when his father had jumped on him about taking the Mormons in, Carl had bristled and lashed back at him, defending their right to be here. Not only had he stunned Melissa with that, he had completely surprised himself. Now he was trying to sort out in his own mind why he had defended them so vigorously.

He knew that part of it was that he still rankled over his father's stubborn refusal to let him go west to work with Joshua. Carl resented it. He was ready for a change. He was ready for a challenge. Kirtland really offered neither anymore. So his father's rebuff was like a rock in the soft part of a horse's hoof. The longer it stayed, the more it bothered. The relationship between him and his father had definitely soured.

But it was more than that too. Carl had been one of those longtime Kirtland residents who had gladly sent the Mormons packing two years before. He found them and their religion highly distasteful. But his trip out to Missouri and Illinois to help Melissa's family had softened those feelings greatly. Not only was he touched by the plight of the exiles, but he was shocked and infuriated that such a thing could happen to people in America, a republic where considerable blood had been shed so that people could worship as they chose. Surprisingly, he had also been impressed with how the Mormons were reacting to their experience in Missouri. There was no wringing of their hands, no bitter denunciation of their enemies, no turning from their God. It was how he had always pictured the Christians taking their licks from the Romans. He and Joshua had even talked about it. They didn't give much credence to the Mormons' faith, but one surely had to admire their courage.

There had been another row with his father earlier today. Brigham Young volunteered to build some shelving and cabinets in the livery stable office as partial payment for Carl's hospitality. Carl had gladly accepted, pleased that they had the integrity to want to repay him in some way. But Hezekiah Rogers was livid to think that he had a Mormon right there at the business for everyone to see. When he demanded that Carl send him away, Carl really got angry with his father and refused to back down.

Later Carl realized it was more than the tensions between them. It was more than standing up for the rights of a downtrodden group. What it came down to was that he liked these men. It was that simple. He just liked them. They were not sophisticated men of the world. They were working men—craftsmen, laborers, men with calluses on their hands and sweat in their eyes. As for religion, instead of trying to poison his mind as his father said they would, they barely mentioned the subject. Twice Melissa asked this question or that about the Church, which they answered, but then they moved right on to other topics.

But now there was this thing about their funds. If it was true, it was a miracle. Like in the Bible, just as Heber had suggested. Like it or not, religion had intruded itself now, without the missionaries ever having brought it up. And the way it came about made it all the more bothersome. If they had told him about the money at the table or while they were working together at the stable, Carl could have handled it more comfortably. It was easy to embellish a story, especially if you were trying to impress someone with your faith and piety. But they hadn't even known he was there in the hallway. He was positive about that. And there was no sham in Brigham's amazement. The man had been genuinely shocked to learn what had happened.

Carl, unlike Joshua Steed, was a religious man. He took Melissa and the children to church each Sunday. He tried to let the Christian ideals guide his business and personal dealings. He believed in the Bible and that the miracles described therein were true. His only problem was that he didn't believe they happened anymore. God had done his work. He had spoken to men and worked with his children and left a record of that for future generations. Miracles were Bible stuff. Angels and visions and revelations were for those long-ago days, not the nineteenth century. Those days were over now.

Beside him, Melissa murmured softly, then rolled over onto her side, facing him. He turned his head just as she opened her eyes and saw that he was awake. Her eyebrows lifted in surprise. "Are you all right?"

"Yes."

"How long have you been awake?"

"I just . . ." He turned over onto his side. "I thought I heard the boys talking, so I got up to see if they were all right."

"And?" she said, lifting her head now to see him better.

He shook his head. "I was wrong. They're fine. Go back to sleep now."

She lay back down, and in a moment her eyes closed again. Carl's did not. He continued staring upwards, his mind far too occupied for sleep.

Chapter Notes

Information about the movement eastward of the England-bound missionaries, with their various hardships and delays, is found in several sources but summarized nicely in MWM (see pp. 67–73). There were others who were called to go to England or who joined the missionaries for part of their travels, but it seemed burdensome in this work to try and keep track of every missionary traveling with the various groups.

In the novel, Brigham and Heber are welcomed into the home of Carl and Melissa Rogers. In reality, while some received them warmly, the brethren recorded that for the most part, the help given by the Saints in Kirtland was less than it had been in other towns. Heber, who was a potter by trade, says he ruffled the feathers of some of the brethren there by comparing them "to a parcel of old earthen pots that were cracked in burning." Before the missionaries finally left Kirtland, in order to get sufficient money to move onward they had to sell the horse and wagon given to them by other members. (See MWM, p. 73.)

The miracle of the replenishing money supply was recorded by Heber C. Kimball (see LHCK, p. 273). The details of the amounts spent and totals accumulated, as well as Brigham's assumption that Heber was secretly furnishing the money, are taken directly from that account, although the inclusion of Matthew in their calculations is obviously fictional.

Young Joshua Steed climbed down from the ladder and moved it a few feet farther along the wall. Then he went up again and continued dusting the glass chimneys for the hurricane lanterns. Below him, Josiah McBride sat in a chair, sipping a cup of tea. He watched his grandson with open affection. "You're a good worker, Joshua."

"Thank you, Grandpa."

"Your mama taught you that, didn't she?"

"Yes. Papa too. We all have chores. Papa says it builds character."

Josiah laughed. "Your father is exactly right. And you do have character. It shows."

Young Joshua stopped, the feather duster poised in midair. "Papa says part of living the gospel is being a good person, and a man can't be a good person if he doesn't care for his family. And to do that you have to learn to work."

The older man peered more closely at his grandson. That was pretty deep wisdom for an eight-year-old. "When does your pa teach you all those things?"

"Mostly when we read the scriptures. Sometimes when we're working together."

"You read the Bible?" Josiah asked.

"Yes. And the Book of Mormon and the Doctrine and Covenants." If he saw his grandfather's frown, he gave no sign. "We read the scriptures every night together before we have family prayer."

"Reading the Bible is good," Josiah grunted.

"I especially love the Book of Mormon."

Josiah straightened, then motioned with his hand. "Come down here, son. I want to talk with you."

The boy made two last passes with the duster, then came down the ladder. Josiah patted the chair next to him. "Sit down, Joshua."

As the boy did so, Lydia's father set his cup aside and leaned forward. "Joshua, I want to talk with you about the Book of Mormon."

"All right."

Josiah took a quick breath and looked around. Nathan and Lydia were out visiting some of Lydia's friends, but he wanted to be sure. Then he lowered his voice. "I know what your mother and father believe about that book, Joshua, but there's something you need to know."

"What?"

"Joseph Smith didn't really write it."

Young Joshua blinked in surprise. "He didn't?"

"No. There was a man by the name of Solomon Spalding who wrote a book called *Manuscript Found*. It was a story about finding a record in a cave which tells about the Indians and where they came from."

Young Joshua's face wrinkled, concentrating, a little puzzled by what he was hearing. Josiah hurried on. "This book by Spalding was written long before Joe Smith came along."

Joshua broke in. "Grandpa, Brother Joseph doesn't like to be called Joe. He says his name is the same as Joseph in the Bible. So he likes to be called Joseph."

"Joseph Smith is a pompous fool!" Josiah snapped. Then, seeing the shock on his grandson's face, he immediately dropped his voice again. "Joseph, Joe—that doesn't matter. What I want you to know, Joshua, is this. The Book of Mormon is really nothing more than Joe's—Joseph's—taking the story of Solomon Spalding and making it his own, then telling people he got it from God."

Now Joshua was clearly perplexed, and Josiah felt a little burst of exultation. "That's right. His partner actually wrote it for him. Rigdon . . . what's his name?"

"Sidney Rigdon."

"Yes, that's the one. Believe me, I knew Joe Smith from the time he was a young boy. He had no school learning. He could barely write his name or speak an intelligent sentence. He couldn't have written that book."

"But Grandpa, he didn't write it. Mormon wrote it. And other prophets. Brother Joseph only translated it."

"A pack of lies to hide the real truth." He leaned forward and grabbed Joshua by the shoulder. The boy winced a little. "I'm telling you, Joshua, Joe Smith made the whole thing up. And he's hoodwinked all those people by telling them a pack of lies."

Young Joshua was looking at the floor now, and it was obvious he was troubled. Finally he looked up. "Have you read the Book of Mormon, Grandpa?"

Josiah rocked back, his mouth twisting. "Certainly not."

"If it's not true, Grandpa, why does it make me feel so good when Papa reads it to us?" He ventured a tentative smile. "I'm starting to read it on my own now, but some of it is pretty hard."

"Your parents are very good people, Joshua, but they have been blinded by Joseph Smith. You need to hear the other side. Remember, there's more to all that stuff about angels and golden plates than they've told you."

The oldest son of Nathan and Lydia stood and faced his grandfather, and now his mouth was set. "I know you don't like Joseph Smith, Grandpa, but I do. I like to hear him teach us the gospel. I like it when he tells us what the Lord wants us to do."

Josiah came right up out of his chair, openly angry now, but young Joshua went on quickly. "I'm sorry you don't like him or the Book of Mormon, Grandpa. But I know Joseph is a prophet of God. I was baptized this year. Papa laid his hands on my head and gave me the gift of the Holy Ghost, and the Holy Ghost tells me the Book of Mormon is true."

Then before the sputtering Josiah could respond to that, young Joshua spun around. "I'd better go find Emily and Elizabeth Mary. Good-bye, Grandpa."

"And what did you say?" Nathan asked, looking at Lydia over his son's shoulder and warning her off with his eyes.

Joshua told them, simply and without any sense of pride.

When he finished, Nathan just shook his head, his eyes suddenly moist. He took his son by both shoulders. "You answered him exactly right, son. I'm very proud of you."

"Thank you, Pa. Can I go play now?"

Nathan stood, again shooting Lydia a look that said, *Not now*, and gave his son a playful shove toward the door. "Yes."

Once the door closed, Lydia shot to her feet, eyes seething. "That makes me furious!"

Nathan was still watching the door where Joshua had just been. "That's just your father."

"Just my father!" she cried, shocked that he was so calm.

"Honey, your father is old and tired and sick. He's mellowed a great deal in a lot of ways. But expecting him to change what he believes about Joseph Smith and the Mormons at this late date in his life is not being very realistic."

"He can believe whatever he wants," she snapped, "but I won't be having him trying to poison our children. Has he taken Emily aside too? Are we going to have to make sure they're never alone with him?"

Nathan let it all come out, watching her with some amazement. This was his old Lydia back. He hadn't seen this much fire in her for some time.

She stopped her pacing and spun around. "We're going home, Nathan."

He rocked back. That was a little more fire than he had expected.

"We are. I'm going to start packing right now. We'll leave in the morning."

He walked over to her, but she suspected what he was about to do and whirled away from him. "I am. I mean it. I won't have him doing this."

"We're not going home, Lydia."

She swung around, staring at him in disbelief.

"We're not. Not yet."

"You don't care about what he's doing?"

"Of course I care."

"Then why won't you do something?"

He ignored that question. He reached out again and pulled her to him. She didn't fight him this time. "Can I tell you why we're not going home yet?"

"Why?"

"Because we're not done yet with why we came."

"We came because I ran away," she burst out. "We came because I couldn't face life anymore. We came—" She took a deep breath. "We came because I lost my son and when I did I was afraid I was also losing my faith."

He was nodding solemnly. "Actually, we came for two other reasons. First, our children needed to see their grandparents. That would have been reason enough. The second reason, and far more important, was that you needed to take a step back, let yourself recover a little from the past year and a half."

"What's that supposed to mean?" she asked, suddenly defensive.

"It means that when you and me got sick this summer, we lost our ability to function in a normal way. We had to go to bed so we could recover. Well, sometimes our minds or our spirits get sick too. That's all that's happened to you. You haven't lost your faith at all. You're just tired and weary and sick at heart."

"And you really think that's all it is?" she asked, hope finally touching her voice.

"Yes!" He wanted to shake her and make her believe him. "Think about what you have gone through in the past fifteen to eighteen months." He started ticking them off on his fingers. "An eight-hundred-mile move from Kirtland to Missouri while heavy with Elizabeth Mary; persecution, mobbings, and imprisonment of loved ones while you were in Far West; being dragged out of a root cellar by some filthy Missourians and being saved at the last second; watching one of those men shot and killed before your eyes; going through a winter with your children, not knowing if they'd have enough food to survive, and facing that alone because I was off helping Joshua find Caroline."

He stopped and took a quick breath. "And that only gets us to January. Add in another two-hundred-mile exodus with four children; living in a one-room cabin with seventeen or eighteen people for weeks at a time; getting—"

She was shaking her head and he stopped. "Other people have faced worse than I have. It's true, we were crowded in that cabin, but we *had* a cabin, thanks to Joshua. I lost a son, but Jessica lost her husband. Amanda Smith lost a husband and a son. Emma? I could name more. They went through worse than I did, and you don't see them falling apart like some child who doesn't get his way on the school playground."

"You lost your son, Lydia. That alone is enough to put many women over the edge, but add that to everything else and it's an incredible load. It's like you were put in a barrel and then rolled off a mountain. You bounce and you crash, you bruise your ribs and your arms and your legs. And all it does is roll faster and hit harder and crash louder than before. No wonder you're feeling a little battered. No wonder you feel like you've lost your bearings. But your heart is all right. Your faith is there, as strong as it ever was. All you need to do is what you do when your body is sick. You need rest. You need a chance to recover. And this is why we came—and why we aren't going to pack and leave in the morning."

He stopped, letting out his breath. He hadn't planned on quite so passionate a speech.

After several moments of searching his face, she finally spoke. "And you really think that's all it is?" she asked again, finally starting to accept his words.

"I know that's all it is." There was a fleeting smile. "In fact, I can prove to you that you haven't lost your faith."

"How?"

"Why were you so angry just now about your father and young Joshua?"

"Because he's trying to convince Joshua not to believe in . . ." She saw the trap he had sprung on her, and stopped.

"If you really had lost your testimony, you wouldn't care what your father believes or what Joshua believes."

"I hadn't thought of it that way."

He kissed her tenderly. "Well, while you're thinking about that, let me say something else. The next time you start whipping yourself because you're not all that you'd like to be, you just walk into your son's bedroom and take a long look."

"You mean at young Joshua?"

He nodded. "There he is, not yet nine years old. His grandfather—a man in his sixties, wise, sophisticated, good with words, whom this boy admires and loves very much—challenges the very fundamentals of his faith. Does he falter? No. Does he doubt? No! Does he run away in fear? No! He bears his testimony to the man." His eyes were misty with pride now. "And he does it more simply and more profoundly than many men—including his own father—could ever do."

"Yes." It was only one word but it said it all. Yes, I know that what young Joshua did is all you say. Yes, I know that what you say about my anger toward Papa is true. Yes, I know that what you are saying about faith and testimony and healing are true.

"That boy would not be what he is if you were not what you are, Lydia. You think about that, because you know it is true.

And that should give you a joy and satisfaction that runs more deeply than all the mobs, all the persecutions, and all the losses that this life can hold for us."

———•———

Melissa was sitting in front of the mirror, brushing her hair with long, even strokes. She watched as Carl polished his boots, brushing them to a high gleam with the same methodical rhythm she was using. Finished finally, he held them up, peering at the shining surface. He gave them one last rub on the sleeve of his robe, then set them down beneath the chair where he already had tomorrow's clothes laid out.

He looked around for a moment, as if he had misplaced something, and caught her looking at him in the mirror. He smiled briefly, then went to the wardrobe and began rummaging through it.

"Carl?"

He poked his head around the door.

She took a quick breath. "The brethren are having worship services tomorrow. This will be their last before they leave."

He nodded perfunctorily. "I know."

Her one eyebrow arched a little. "You do?"

"Yes. Derek told me about it this morning."

He was so matter-of-fact about it, she was taken aback.

Shutting the wardrobe door, he came over and stood behind her. He took the hairbrush from her and began brushing her hair for her. "You want to go?" he finally asked.

She stopped herself from jerking around to stare at him, but her eyes were staring at him in the mirror. "Yes. Yes, I would. Would you mind?"

He had a sardonic expression as he met her eyes in the mirror. "No. I was hoping we could go to the evening meeting Brigham was telling us about as well as the ones during the day. It will be held in the temple too, but he said that it was only for a few of the elders."

Now she did spin around to look at him directly. "'We'?" she echoed.

He tossed the hairbrush onto the night table and leaned down, putting his face into her hair. He always loved to smell it after she had just washed it. He breathed deeply. Only then did he straighten and find her eyes in the mirror again. When he spoke, it was with studied nonchalance. "After having those brethren living with us for two weeks now, I think it would be a nice thing if we went to hear them preach their last Sunday. Don't you?"

Her expression made him laugh. "Now, don't be jumping to conclusions here," he warned. "I'm just curious, that's all. I've been impressed with these two Apostles of yours. They're good men. I'd like to see what kind of preachers they make."

She stood up slowly, moving close to him. "You're not teasing me?" she asked softly. "You really would go?"

He kissed her on the nose. "Yes, I really would."

"That's wonderful!" Then she immediately frowned. "What will your father say?"

"Well," he said slowly, not seeming too concerned, "my father has never been a profaning man. That could very possibly change after tomorrow."

By spring of 1836, when the Kirtland Temple was dedicated, Carl and Melissa Rogers had been married almost five years and had their first two sons. By that time, Carl's initial indifference toward the Church had, with persistent encouragement from his father, turned into open antagonism. At first as a concession, Melissa started going to his Methodist church services on one Sunday, then to her own on another Sunday. But each new request on her part to attend this meeting or that triggered additional conflict. None of it was terribly ugly or uncontrollably bitter, but it could often get heated and left a residue of tension in the home that lasted sometimes for days. So gradually concession turned to compromise and then to surrender. By nature Melissa was more of a peacemaker than a confronter, and contention bothered her deeply. Eventually, not only did her attendance at church stop, but even her personal forms of worship died away, and she and Carl slipped into a mutual understanding to leave discussions of Mormonism alone.

Her keenest regret over her willingness to settle for peace over principle was that she had not attended the dedicatory services of the Kirtland Temple with her family. She had gone to her father's home that evening and listened to them all as they described the almost unbelievable outpourings of the Spirit they had experienced. Even now, three years after the fact, almost any time she walked past the great building with its beautiful Gothic windows, the regrets for giving in on that particular point came flooding back.

But on the afternoon of this day, as she and Carl walked slowly homeward from the temple, those feelings did not surface. She didn't even think of them. She was still in a near-euphoric state of mind to think that Carl—and at his request—had gone with her to two meetings of the Saints. The group was nothing like the crowds that had once filled the temple, but the smallness of the congregation made for a more intimate service. And it gave Brigham, who spoke in the morning meeting, considerable time to develop his message on how The Church of Jesus Christ of Latter-day Saints was like the church that Christ established while he was on the earth. She was particularly grateful that Brigham had quoted almost exclusively from the Bible. Melissa suspected that that was partially for Carl's benefit. She couldn't be sure, because during the hour-long sermon Brigham hadn't seemed to look directly at Carl more than a time or two.

This afternoon John Taylor had also preached a fine sermon and acted as though there was nothing at all unusual about having Carl present.

"Do you know what Derek told me?" Carl asked.

"What?" she said, coming out of her thoughts.

"He said that Brigham considers himself to be a very poor preacher. Says that it is sheer pain for him to talk because his grammar is so poor. Says he always ends up with a headache trying to choose the words he needs in order to say what he wants to say."

"Really! Did you feel that way while he was preaching today?"

"Not at all. I thought he spoke clearly and made his points well."

Wonderful! She wanted to sing it out, but did nothing more than slip her arm through his. "Me neither. I was impressed with how well he knows the scriptures. And did you notice? He didn't have a single page of notes."

"I did," came the quick reply, and he seemed impressed. The pastor at Carl's church, which was really Carl's father's church, always brought in a large sheaf of meticulously written text, then read from it word for word. They were polished and wonderful sermons, but somehow Brigham's simple, straightforward presentation seemed a welcome change to him.

"I'm going to miss Derek and Matthew," she said. "It's been so good to have them here."

"I like Derek," came the response. "He'll be a good missionary."

"He will, especially among his own people."

They walked on. The evening was coming on quickly and the air was turning cold. Their breath hung in little clouds in the last of the daylight. Melissa laid her head against his shoulder as they walked. "Thank you, Carl."

"For what?"

"For going with me today."

He shrugged. "I told you. I did it because I wanted to hear Brigham as a preacher."

"I know, but thank you anyway."

He nodded. After a moment, he looked down at her. "If you want to go to your services from time to time and take the children, I wouldn't mind, Melissa."

Her head came up with a start. He laughed. "I don't know if I'm just trying to be nice to you, or if I just want to pick a fight with Pa. But I've been thinking. I don't think God really cares very much about which church a man goes to. I think what's more important is how you live. How you treat people. Whether you try to be a good Christian. I've known some pretty good men that don't go to any particular church at all, and they seem particularly happy."

Melissa was almost dizzy with surprise at this unexpected turn. "Would you come with me to our services?" she asked, holding her breath.

Again his shoulders lifted and fell slightly. "Oh, perhaps. Actually, to be truthful, I'm getting tired of our services. I've even thought about going to the Campbellite congregation a couple of times, see what they're like. Maybe even visit the Congregational church. That would send Father in a spin, I'll tell you. Mormons and Congregationalists. They're not his favorite peoples."

Melissa's face fell and she had to turn away lest he see it. This wasn't so much a response to Brigham Young's teaching—though he seemed to have genuinely enjoyed it—as it was a general restlessness. Or maybe even more to the point, a way of showing his father that he was chafing under being told what to do, where to live, whom to accept and whom to reject. It was sharply disappointing, for she had momentarily hoped for much more than that. But then her mood brightened. Even if Carl never showed interest in the Church, if he would let her start attending services with the children, and maybe even come himself occasionally, that was miles from where they had been just two weeks ago. And because of that, she would be forever grateful that Derek and Matthew had swept into town and brought Brigham Young and Heber Kimball with them.

———◆———

The Apostles and their companions who had converged on Kirtland early in November left the city on the twenty-second, determined to travel together to New York City. But as usual, plans quickly changed. Heber dropped off to visit his family in western New York. Brigham Young and George A. Smith ran out of funds and stopped to work. At Brigham's insistence, John

Taylor went on with Derek and Matthew and Theodore Turley. They reached New York City two weeks before Christmas, exhausted, half-frozen, totally destitute. Gratefully, they found three of the Apostles already there and waiting for them—Parley and Orson Pratt and Wilford Woodruff. Had they delayed any further, they would have missed Wilford Woodruff, for he was planning to book passage on a packet ship scheduled to depart for Liverpool on December twentieth.

———•———

They were sitting around the small but comfortable parlor of the house Parley Pratt had procured in New York. Supper was done and they were enjoying a few minutes of each other's company before retiring. Derek sat between Theodore Turley and John Taylor. Like John and Derek, Turley was also an English immigrant, making three of them going back to their native land to proclaim the gospel. Matthew sat on a stool beside the sofa. Wilford and Parley were across from them. Orson Pratt was on the floor beside Parley's chair. As usual, the conversation turned immediately to the question of when to sail for England. And as usual, Wilford firmly rejected any suggestion for further delay.

"I already canceled plans to sail once. It could be weeks before Brigham and Heber arrive. The *Oxford* sails on the twentieth," he said bluntly. "I plan to be on it."

"I agree, Brother Wilford," Parley said. "Orson and I can wait for the others. There is still much to do here in New York. I would like to get A *Voice of Warning* and some other tracts published so we can use them in the work."

"Well spoken," Wilford said quickly. "I think you should stay." He turned to John Taylor. "But you could come with me, John. Book passage with me on the *Oxford* and we'll be gone from here in four days."

John Taylor nodded thoughtfully. "If you think it best that I go with you, Derek and I are willing, aren't we, Derek?"

"Absolutely." Like Wilford, Derek had been through enough delays.

"I should like to go too," Theodore Turley said.

Wilford turned to Matthew with a quizzical look. Matthew shook his head immediately. "I promised Brother Brigham I would wait for him here."

"And I think you should," John Taylor said. "Joseph called you to be a companion to him and Heber." He turned to Woodruff. "But I think the three of us can leave with you, Wilford."

"Wonderful!" He was greatly relieved.

"Book us passage, then," John said, "and we shall make our preparations."

Parley leaned forward. "What about the money for your tickets?"

Taylor smiled enigmatically. "There shall be no difficulty with that. Go ahead and book passage for the three of us."

Parley was ecstatic. "Then it's true? I have heard you say to several people that you have plenty of money."

"Aye, that I do," John responded easily.

Derek gaped at him. As far as he knew, it had taken every farthing they had to get to New York.

Parley clapped his hands. "Then could I borrow two or three hundred dollars from you to see to the printing of my tracts?"

"You are welcome to whatever I have," John answered gravely, reaching in his pocket. He withdrew a coin purse, stood, and walked over to Parley. Parley stretched out his hands as John tipped the purse upside down. One copper penny fell out. "There you are," John said with a smile.

Parley was dumbfounded. "But . . . but you said you had plenty of money."

"Aye, and that I do. I am well clothed, you are feeding us plenty of good food here, we have a warm roof over our heads, and I owe no man anything. With all of that, I have a penny extra. Is not that plenty?"

Wilford laughed heartily at the crestfallen expression on Parley's face. Then he turned to John. "So you have no money for the passage?"

"Book our passage," John Taylor said confidently, "and if it is the Lord's will that we accompany you, we shall have the funds."

———✦———

"Perhaps it might have been better if we had died in Germantown."

John Taylor rose up in the bunk across from Derek. In the faint light of the one lantern, which swayed and danced with the movement of the ship, his face looked as gray as chalk. "What was that you said?" he called.

The ship pitched sharply downward again, the timbers shrieking in protest at the punishment they were taking. Barrels and boxes, trunks and suitcases slammed about the compartment, making a horrendous din.

Derek was too weak to shout over the noise, and he simply waved it away and fell back. Theodore Turley, squeezed in beside him in the narrow berth, turned his head. His color was more green than gray, and he looked like he had aged twenty years in the ten days since they had set sail. "What happened in Germantown?"

"That's where Brother Taylor and I were so sick. I thought for sure one of us was going to die." He forced a weak grin. "Had I known this was coming, I might have been tempted to pray less vigorously for our recovery."

Turley nodded grimly. "Was it this bad when you came over?"

"No," Derek grunted. "Nothing like this."

When he and Peter had sailed from Liverpool to America two years before, there had been only two or three days of rough weather, but it was nothing compared to the violent storm that raged around them now. He thought he had been seasick then. Now he realized he had barely understood the word. Conditions were bad enough without the weather turning on them too. Steerage was the least expensive way to travel on the packet ships, and therefore offered the least amount of comfort and convenience. The steerage compartment—so named because this area of ships sometimes contained the steering apparatus—was below deck. It was overcrowded, offered no privacy, was poorly lit, and because it had virtually no ventilation it reeked with the stench of sweat, rotting food, vomit, and human waste.

All of that would have been bad enough, but it wasn't until the first night at sea that they discovered that the selling agents had severely overbooked the ship. Normally a ticket with a berth number was given to each passenger. The sellers had assured everyone there would be no more than two people per berth. In actuality, they had sold the same bunk to as many as five people, and several had no bed at all. Sixty-four people in a space meant to house little more than half that—it was a criminal disgrace. The crew rigged a few bunks in a storage compartment, but there were still some berths where four people slept in shifts, and some passengers had no choice but to sleep on the deck or on boxes.

"No," Derek said again, "it was nothing like this."

Wilford Woodruff must have heard him, for his head came up. He was wedged into the bunk beside John Taylor. "Brother Derek," he called.

Derek rose up as best he could. Wilford was sick, but was faring better than any of his three companions. He grinned and waved. "Do you know what day the day after tomorrow is?" he shouted.

Derek thought for a moment, then shook his head. He wasn't even sure what year it was anymore.

"It's New Year's Day."

Derek ducked as the ship took a particularly hard roll and a small barrel came hurtling past him. It crashed against the bulkhead and shattered. "Bully!" Derek said through gritted teeth. "Happy New Year."

Wilford was still looking at him. "It *will* be a new year for us. A glorious year, Brother Derek. Keep that in mind. This storm cannot last forever, and we shall soon be in England."

Chapter Notes

The idea, expressed in the novel by Josiah McBride, that Joseph Smith patterned the Book of Mormon after the Spalding manuscript was used by enemies of the Church to try and explain away a remarkable book translated by an unlearned young man. Because of his skills in speaking and writing, Sidney Rigdon was often credited by proponents of the "Spalding theory" as being the one who actually wrote the Book of Mormon, even though he did not meet Joseph for the first time until almost a year after the book was published. The manuscript for Spalding's book was lost for many years, so that it could not be compared to the Book of Mormon. But a copy was discovered in the 1880s and shows that it bears no resemblance to the Book of Mormon. (See CHFT, p. 59.)

The Twelve came into New York City on widely different dates. Wilford Woodruff arrived on 8 October, the first of the Twelve to do so. Parley arrived on 25 October with his wife and three children; his brother Orson came three weeks later. John Taylor and his companion came on 13 December. (See MWM, pp. 75–80.)

John Taylor's interchange with Parley over having "plenty of money" is told by John Taylor. Though he had no money at all at that time, within a day or two, contributions sufficient for him and Theodore Turley to pay for their passage came in from the Saints. (See B. H. Roberts, *Life of John Taylor*, Collector's Edition [Salt Lake City: Bookcraft, 1989], pp. 72–74.)

Wilford Woodruff, John Taylor, and Theodore Turley set sail on the *Oxford* five days before Christmas. Their decision not to wait for the others was a wise one, for Brigham, Heber, and George A. Smith did not arrive for another five or six weeks and did not embark for England until March. The miserable conditions of the passage—the storm, the overbooking of the ship—are accurately portrayed here as recorded in the missionaries' journals. (See MWM, pp. 78–80.)

Chapter Seventeen

30 Dec. 1839   Nauvoo, Illinois

Dearest Melissa,

Your letter dated 22 November reached us yesterday afternoon. I need not tell you what a welcome surprise that turned out to be. We gathered the whole family around the fire last evening and read it over and over. After receiving the letters from you and Derek and Matthew a short time before that, another letter came as a surprise. By now you should have received the letter I wrote back to you at that time containing all the news of the family, so I will not repeat any of that here except to say we received another letter from Will. He had not yet reached China when he wrote, but it took two months to get to us, so he may be there by now. Caroline still misses him terribly, but hearing from him on a regular basis now has done much to make it easier for her.

We are pleased to hear that Derek and Matthew have continued on their journey, though surely you will miss having them with you. We thank the Lord they were able to come by way of Kirtland and stay with you as long as they did. Jenny and Rebecca have written letters back to them. However, they wrote to New York, fearing they would be gone from Ohio before the letters got there. Your letter confirmed the wisdom of this choice.

Most gratifying was your report about Carl. His attendance at the worship services is a major step forward, considering how he has felt about Mormonism before. Joshua was a little disgusted with our response. He assumes we are happy only because we think Carl may be on the way to conversion—a thought that Joshua thinks is ridiculous. He doesn't understand that our joy lies in something else. It is not good when a man and a woman who share their lives together do not share at least a mutual understanding and tolerance for each other's faith. I speak from personal experience in this regard. Those days when your father was so bitterly opposed to Joseph and all that the Church meant still burn painfully in my mind. How different is our marriage now that we share like beliefs! So in that regard, we were most pleased with Carl's response. Even if he never joins the Church, the fact that he got to know Brigham Young and Heber Kimball and felt kindly disposed toward them will go a long way in helping you and him be more as one on the matter.

We were sorry to hear that his going to that meeting with you has further strained his relationship to his father. I remember well how Hezekiah Rogers opposed us when we were there, so your report did not come as a surprise, but it still saddened us. However, Joshua was elated at that. Not at our sadness, but that Carl and his father are fighting over this issue. He thinks Carl's father is the only thing stopping Carl from coming out here, so he's hoping the distance between them widens even more. It has been a bit of a surprise to all of us how strongly Joshua feels about getting Carl to come. Caroline told me this morning that he is even talking about writing to Carl directly. <u>Unheard of for Joshua</u>!

Well, I do not wish to go overly long on the matter, but we were most pleased with the news. Please give Carl our love and affection. His coming with you to Missouri and Illinois earlier this year to bring us food and supplies has deeply endeared him to all of us. He is a wonderful man and a good husband and father.

In closing, just a word or two of advice from your mother. Your last paragraphs were filled with discouragement, almost despair, about the chances of ever coming out west. You say that with the feelings now between Carl and his father, there is no way that can happen.

I would only say this. Nine years ago, your father was stubbornly opposed to the Church, bitterly antagonistic toward Joseph, and absolutely, unbendably, unmovably against our moving to Kirtland. You will remember that well, for you too despaired that we would ever be able to follow Nathan and Lydia to Ohio. I was deeply discouraged. Then one day, while your father was in town, I began reading in the Bible. I won't go into all the details, but I came across a passage where the Lord taught that some problems are of such size and difficulty that only prayer <u>and</u> fasting can bring the victory. I read it over and over. And on that day, I decided I would fast and pray about the matter. As you know, it wasn't long after that that Martin Harris was talking to your father about selling the farm, and in a matter of a few weeks we were in Kirtland.

Melissa, I don't know if the Lord wants you and Carl out here with us. We would love to see it happen, but what matters is what the Lord feels is best. But I do know this. Fasting and prayer can change circumstances and hearts and outcomes. Don't lose heart. Don't lose faith. Importune the Lord about this.

New Year wishes and love from all of us,
Your loving mother

Will Steed was agog. His eyes darted here and there and his head jerked back and forth so quickly, he was getting dizzy. He had heard men try to describe the scenes he was now seeing, but words completely paled beside the reality. He couldn't believe the number of people. It was like trying to ford a river after a cloudburst. He kept his arms up slightly to fend off the crowds swirling and eddying around them. Will had never imagined there could be so many people in one place at the same time. As they pushed through them, heads turned and people stared at the fair-skinned strangers who towered above them.

Will leaned forward and shouted at his companion. "Are there so many people because of the holiday?"

Timothy O'Malley, first mate on the *Bostonia*, gave him a puzzled look. "What holiday?"

"New Year's Day. This is New Year's Day."

O'Malley laughed, tossing his head. "Not in China, it's not, lad. They have what they call the Chinese New Year, and it's not the same as ours. No, no holiday. This is Canton. Just a regular day in the land of China."

"There are always this many people?" Will asked incredulously.

O'Malley laughed again. "Wait until just before dark when the factories let out. You can almost walk on their shoulders."

"Hey, Guailous! Wanna buy chop carving?"

Will turned. It was a boy, maybe ten or twelve. He was pushing his way through the people toward them.

"Chop carving. Veddy cheap. Veddy nice."

O'Malley slowed, turning to Will. "You want a chop carving?"

"What's that?"

He smiled. "You said you wanted to buy something for your family. I'd recommend this. It's something you'll never find in America." He turned to the boy and nodded.

Grinning widely, the Chinese lad pointed over the heads of the crowd to somewhere down the street. "You come. I show."

As they fell in behind him, Will moved up alongside the first mate. "What's a Gwai-loh?"

"Guailou? That's a foreigner. A white person."

The boy heard them. "You Englee?" he demanded.

"No," O'Malley said easily, "American."

"Ah, Mericee." He was obviously pleased, and Will understood why. China and Great Britain were at war. O'Malley had explained it to Will. They were calling it the Opium War. China had been ruled by the Manchu dynasty for almost two hundred years. During that same time, England had become a great colonial power. As Will had learned in Liverpool, a common saying among the English was, "The sun never sets on the English empire." The Manchus, like most other Chinese rulers, deeply distrusted foreigners and ruled that the only port open for trading with the outside world would be Canton. Britain, flush with her conquests over France during the Napoleonic wars and with her growing industrial might, chafed under those limitations and began to press for ways to bust the doors wide open. Seeking a way to balance their trade deficit with China, British merchants began shipping in opium grown on their vast estates in India. There was a great demand for the drug among the huge Chinese population, and the Chinese merchants paid in silver. Alarmed at the growing numbers of their people addicted to the drug and at the huge outflow of silver, the Manchus declared the drug illegal. That only drove the market higher and made smuggling opium a highly profitable enterprise. Furious at England's refusal to cooperate, earlier in the year the Manchus had raided dozens of British ships and seized millions of dollars' worth of opium. England promptly declared war.

"Would we be in danger if we were English?" Will asked in a low voice.

The officer shook his head. "Not during the day. But it's best not to be down one of the back streets at night. Not even if you're American."

"Why? We're not at war with them."

"You know that and I know that, but to the Chinese all Guailous look alike, and they don't much like the English right now."

They turned into a side street and the boy grabbed O'Malley's arm. "Here," he said, pointing to a tiny shop built into the wall of a larger building. "Chop carving. Good deal. Veddy cheap."

Inside, an old man, sixty or more from his looks, sat at a small table, carving on a round plug of stone shaped like a cylinder. His hands moved rapidly, wielding a stubby knife with a short but thick metal blade. Will was surprised to see the stone flaking off almost like wood chips. On the table in front of the man was a whole collection of similar pieces of stone, two to three inches long and about an inch and one-half in diameter. Will leaned forward, fascinated. The stones were capped with intricately carved figures—a fierce-looking creature that was half lion, half eagle; a Chinese man, fat and round; a crowing rooster; an Oriental dragon.

"Look at that," Will breathed, moving closer and bending down to see. He reached out and touched the dragon. Barely an inch high, it was complete in every detail—flaring nostrils, scales on its body, sinuous tail. The old man hardly looked up, just kept his hands moving over the stone. "You like?" the boy asked, moving up beside Will. "Veddy nice."

"Look," O'Malley said. He picked up one of the stones and turned it so Will could see the bottom of it. "This is why they call it a chop carving." A Chinese character was etched into the bottom side of the stone. O'Malley leaned over. There was a small tin with some kind of red paste in it. He touched the stone to the paste, turned it back and forth a little to distribute the paste on the carving, then pulled it out and pressed it to the paper that covered the table. Magically, the Chinese character was imprinted on the paper.

"Ah," Will cried.

The boy grabbed a small square of paper and thrust it at Will. "You write!"

Will took it, not sure what the boy wanted. "Write what?"

"He wants you to write your name," O'Malley explained. "Then his grandfather will carve it for you. Or put the name of your mother. They'll do whatever you want."

"How much?" Will asked.

"How much?" O'Malley asked the boy.

"One pound, one chop."

"No Englee," the officer said, shaking his head. "Dollars."

"Three dollah," came the instant reply. Will smiled. Since the English pound was worth about five American dollars, they had already brought the price down. But three dollars was still more than he could spend on one person. He had three people to buy for, and he made only ten dollars a month.

O'Malley touched two of the stones. "Three dollar, two carvings."

The boy looked like O'Malley had just asked him to sell his grandmother. He shook his head sharply. "No. Too much. Three dollah, one carving."

O'Malley took Will's arm and turned him toward the front of the little shop. "Thank you," he called over his shoulder.

"Wait!"

They stopped. The boy conferred quickly with his grandfather. The old man's face was inscrutable. The boy watched him closely, then turned back. "Five dollah, two carvings."

The first mate pushed Will toward the door again. "Thank you."

"I'll do it for that—," Will started, but O'Malley squeezed his arm sharply, cutting him off. They were almost back out into the street again.

"Wait!"

They stopped and the boy darted forward. "Three dollah, two carvings." He held out a pen and pointed at the paper Will still held. "You write!" he commanded.

Will was grateful to Captain Sperryman. He knew he had specifically asked O'Malley to shepherd Will on his first visit to Canton and make sure he didn't get into trouble. Surprisingly, the ship's officer didn't seem to mind. He had a wife and two children back in Salem, Massachusetts, and seemed happy to do some shopping of his own. So they shopped for almost an hour while they waited for the chop carvings.

The shops were incredible. One had hundreds of birds of every shape, size, and color, some in huge bamboo cages, others you could cup in both hands. There were spice shops and lantern shops and shops with jade, that precious stone that looked almost like glass. At a china shop, Will looked into buying his mother a set of the blue and white plates and saucers that were in such high demand in America now, but they wanted fifteen dollars and wouldn't go any lower.

They moved a few blocks down to the Pearl River and walked among the hundreds of little kiosks that lined the water. This proved to be absolutely fascinating to Will. O'Malley explained that the Chinese insisted that their seafood be fresh at the time of purchase, so the sellers simply kept everything alive until the moment of purchase. In jars and buckets, iron pans and tightly woven reed baskets, there was a bewildering variety of creatures from the sea. Like a proud father taking his son on a tour of some exotic zoo, O'Malley pointed out the various species—octopus, squid, crab, sea turtles, fish of every kind imaginable, eel, lobsters, shrimp.

They passed other restaurants with items that turned Will's stomach. Bird's nest soup, thousand-year-old eggs. When Will nearly gagged at the sight of one of the latter, O'Malley, laughing, explained that that was just what they called them. Actually they were planted in the ground and left there for a year or so, then served in their decayed and rotted state. In one window, a slithering collection of snakes made Will fall back a step. O'Malley poked him in the ribs. "You hungry, Steed? Want some cobra steak?"

As they moved back toward the carving shop, a sudden explosion of noise behind him jerked Will around. For a moment he thought a fire fight had erupted. It was like a hundred pistols all going off at once. "Those are called firecrackers," O'Malley said, noting Will's expression. "Come on, let me show you." They moved through the crowd to where two small boys sat on the sidewalk. They carried long strings with hundreds of brightly colored sticks or twigs tied to them, only each stick was perfectly round, like a tiny little tube. Taking a coin from his pocket, O'Malley gave it to the older boy, motioning for him to do something with the sticks.

The older boy carried a piece of a reed, from a marsh somewhere. It was smoldering, a wisp of smoke coming from its blackened end. As the younger boy undid about a third of the tiny tubes, making a separate collection of them, the older boy blew on the reed softly until it glowed. Then he touched the end of the string to the glowing tip. Will's eyes widened as the string caught fire, sputtering and sparking. The younger boy flung the collection of little sticks away from him and jumped back. When the string of firecrackers went off, Will jumped nearly a foot, and O'Malley and the boys roared in delight. Crackling, popping, spitting fire, the little sticks danced on the ground like something possessed.

When the last one had finally exploded, leaving clouds of blue smoke and an acrid smell hanging in the air, Will turned to O'Malley. "How much?" he asked.

Matthew sat back in his chair, listening to Parley Pratt, who had just returned to New York City from Philadelphia, and again marveled at how the hand of the Lord could orchestrate things. The day after Wilford, John, Theodore, and Derek had sailed for England, Orson Pratt left for Philadelphia. The missionaries had been preaching in New York, but Orson was restless and felt impressed to go farther out and chose Philadelphia, about a hundred miles south of New York. To his amazement, when he arrived he found Joseph Smith. Joseph, frustrated with the slow-moving wheels of government, had left Washington, D.C., and gone north to visit the Saints in Philadelphia.

Orson immediately sent a letter back to Parley telling him to come to Philadelphia. That had been just before Christmas. Now, three days into the New Year, Parley had returned. Matthew had taken a room next to the Pratts' apartment so he could help Mary Ann Pratt with the children while Parley was gone. Addison Everett, one of the earliest converts in the city, and his wife had heard Parley was back and came over to hear his report. Parley's three children were in bed, so Matthew was the youngest present.

The room fell quiet for a few moments after Parley reported what Joseph told them about his lack of success in Washington. It was depressing to know that in spite of the Constitution, no one cared enough for justice to act in behalf of the Mormons. But then Parley reached out and took his wife's hand. "Yet there is some wonderful news too."

Mary Ann Pratt looked up. "That would be nice to hear."

He leaned forward, peering into her eyes, his face infused with excitement. "While we were with Joseph, he spent many hours teaching us about God and the heavenly order of eternity. He said that—" He paused, almost breathless with excitement now. "Think about this. Joseph taught us that the family organization is eternal."

Her eyes widened. "Eternal?"

Addison Everett leaned forward. "Eternal?" he echoed.

"Yes," Parley cried, "eternal! Father, mother, husband, wife. These precious relationships, which we so deeply esteem here, are not to be broken by death. They are to continue in the next life. The eternal family is the organization of heaven. Joseph called it sealing," Parley went on. "It is part of the keys of the priesthood restored to earth by Elijah. And through these keys, a husband and a wife can be sealed together for all eternity. Parents and children can be sealed together into an eternal family unit. Think about that for a moment."

Matthew *was* thinking about it. The image of Jennifer Jo McIntire swam before his eyes and he felt them start to burn. And in that instant, he knew the doctrine was true. Of course! Would a loving God strip a man of that which meant more to him than any other living gift? Would he tear apart the one relationship that bound two people together and made them one? If so, then hollow indeed would be the victory over death. The grave would have its spoils.

Parley half turned, and now took both of his wife's hands in his. "Do you understand what this means, dear Mary Ann? This fountain of love which so endears you to me and me to you comes not just from the human breast, it springs from God! And God has prepared the way so we may be joined together for the eternities."

Her eyes were glistening as she kept nodding to each of his statements, responding without words. Now the Apostle pulled his wife toward him, bringing her hands up to rest against his chest. "It was as though I was on fire as he spoke. The Prophet lifted a corner of the veil and allowed us to peek beneath it. I have thought of nothing else since leaving Philadelphia."

Suddenly his voice went very soft. "My dearest Mary Ann, I had loved you before, but I knew not why. Now I love with a pureness, with an intensity I never believed possible. My love is elevated, exalted, lifted from the transitory things of this groveling sphere and expanded like the mighty ocean. You are the wife of my bosom, an eternal, immortal companion, a kind, ministering angel sent to me as a comfort and a crown, and we shall be together forever and ever."

He had to stop. She was weeping now. Sister Everett was weeping. Matthew and Addison were swallowing hard themselves as they listened to the impassioned words. Parley dropped his head and kissed his wife's hands. "That is what Joseph taught us, and that is why I rejoice with you on this day."

Nathan put the pen down and capped the inkwell, then shut the book and pushed it aside. He yawned, stretched, then leaned over and blew out the lamp. The store fell into darkness, with the shelves and racks and barrels and boxes transformed into nothing more than black masses. Coming out from behind the counter, he threaded his way without hesitation. Even if he had been totally blind, he could have found his way to the stairs. After four months of working in the McBride store, he didn't need light to find his way through it.

Wearily he climbed the steps that led to the residence area that filled the second floor of the building. He walked through the darkened living area and stepped inside the hallway which led to the bedrooms, then stopped for a minute. The first bedroom was dark and quiet. So Hannah, Lydia's mother, had gone to bed early with Josiah. That was happening more frequently now.

He shrugged and went to the next door. It was partially open and he stepped inside, tiptoeing now. Emily's bed was closest to the door, so she would get the most light from the hallway. She was lying on her back, one arm above her head, the other across her stomach. Her hair, as dark as her mother's, spread across the pillow, framing her face and making her look all the more angelic. Smiling, he reached down and pulled the blanket up around her chin, then tucked Susannah, the doll they had given her for Christmas, under one arm.

When he turned, he saw that young Joshua was still awake. His eyes were heavy and drooping, but they followed him as he came to the bed. Nathan bent down and kissed him on the forehead. "Good night, son."

"Good night, Papa." He mumbled something about tomorrow, then turned over on his side, pulling the covers up and over his shoulders. The eyes closed, and he was asleep.

Elizabeth Mary slept in the smallest bed, which stood closest to the flue from the downstairs fireplace. Nathan could feel the heat radiating from the bricks and nodded in satisfaction. He had banked the fire downstairs a few minutes before and was pleased that it was doing its job. Their youngest had turned eighteen months the first part of November. She was on her stomach, one knee cocked up and the opposite hand bent over her head. Against the white of the pillowcase, she could almost be missed completely in the semidarkness. As opposite in every way from Emily as one child could be from another, Elizabeth Mary was a towhead, her short hair as white as sunlit snow. She was fair of skin and had pale blue eyes. Where Emily was confident and aggressive, Elizabeth Mary was shy and often lost in her own thoughts. Where Emily loved people—adults, children, male, female—Elizabeth Mary felt comfortable only with her own family. Even with her grandparents it had taken her weeks to feel comfortable enough to lapse into those chattering conversations she held with herself when she was playing. But let anyone else come into the room, and nothing they did, said, or begged her to do would break through her inscrutable soberness and utter silence.

Nathan leaned clear over to get low enough to kiss her hair, and as he straightened, once again he offered the little prayer that he said every time he came in to kiss her good night. They had lost little Nathan to the fever. Days later they had come within inches of losing this one too. If Joseph hadn't come and blessed her . . . "Thank you, Lord," he murmured once again.

As he came out and started towards the end bedroom where he and Lydia slept, he stopped again. The door was open only an inch or two, and the light was on. This was no surprise, for she always waited up for him when he worked into the night doing the books. What surprised him was that he could hear her softly humming. Reaching down, he untied the laces of his boots, then removed them, taking care not to make any noise. Finally, he moved forward to stand just outside the door. His face softened as he recognized the melody. She was humming the lullaby his own mother had taught her, the lullaby that Mary Ann had used with each of her children and that was now being used in four additional households.

The angle of the door was such that he couldn't see clear into the room, so very slowly he pulled the door open another inch or two, hoping it would not creak and give him away. He still couldn't see the bed where she was, but he could see the mirror above the dresser, and in it he could see Lydia's reflection. She was propped up with both of their pillows. The Book of Mormon was in her lap, open but facedown. Her eyes seemed to be looking off at nothing. Her hair was undone and cascaded in dark waves across her shoulders, just as Emily's did. He shook his head, marveling again at her beauty.

The humming stopped, and for a minute he thought she was going to go back to her reading. But she only fluffed up the pillows a little, then settled in again. Then she laid her head back slightly, and, to his surprise, she began to sing.

> Thy mercy, my God, is the theme of my song,
> The joy of my heart, and the boast of my tongue;
> Thy free grace alone, from the first to the last,
> Hath won my affections and bound my soul fast.

Nathan recognized the song immediately. It was one of the songs Emma Smith chose for the hymnal published a few years before. It was not one of the most popular hymns, but it was sung frequently enough that Nathan knew part of the words. He was surprised that Lydia knew them all.

> Without thy sweet mercy I could not live here,
> Sin soon would reduce me to utter despair;
> But, through thy free goodness, my spirits revive,
> And he that first made me still keeps me alive.

He felt a lump forming in his throat as he suddenly realized something. It had been a long time since he had heard Lydia sing like this. She had always sung the lullaby to the children; but alone, singing to herself—that hadn't happened for a long, long time, and it made him want to weep.

Now she straightened and sat up fully. Her hands were folded in her lap and her face was filled with happiness.

> Thy mercy is more than a match for my heart,
> Which wonders to feel its own hardness depart;
> Dissolv'd by thy goodness I fall to the ground,
> And weep to the praise of the mercy I found.

Memories of a day in an apple orchard came flooding back to him now. He had gone to town looking for Joshua and been told that Lydia might know where he was. She was at her aunt's house south of town, so Nathan went there to ask her about Joshua. The aunt said he would find Lydia out in the orchard. It was spring, and the whole orchard was in bloom. And he had indeed found her there, dancing among the trees, singing the hauntingly sad and tragic love song "Barbara Allen." Only later had he come to realize that it was at that moment he had started to love her.

The singing stopped now for a moment, and Nathan leaned forward to see better. At first he thought she had forgotten the words. But she had only lifted the Book of Mormon and clasped it to her bosom. He could see her eyes in the mirror. They were shining, but not tearful. It was not sadness that filled her face, but a quiet, inner joy.

> Great Father of mercies, thy goodness I own,
> And the covenant love of thy crucified Son;
> All praise to the Spirit, whose whisper divine,
> Seals mercy, and pardon, and righteousness mine.

She stopped and the words hung in the air, not willing to die. As he watched her, he was struck again with an overwhelming feeling of love for this woman. Slowly, Nathan pushed the door open.

She started as she saw him in the mirror, and stood quickly. "Oh, Nathan. I didn't hear you." She saw the boots in his hand and her eyebrows arched in surprise. Then she understood. "I . . . How long were you there?"

"Long enough," he said softly.

She laughed, embarrassed and suddenly shy. "You did that to me once before, many years ago. Do you remember?"

"I do. And I remember that I had never heard anything so lovely or seen anything so beautiful as what I heard and saw that day in the orchard. And I have not again until this very moment."

The color in her cheeks deepened. "Why, thank you, Nathan."

He set the boots down and went to her. Taking her face in his hands, he looked deeply into her eyes. Then he leaned down and kissed her softly. "Thank you," he whispered. "Thank you for singing again."

Now the tears did come, but she was smiling through them. She reached up, her hands touching his. "No, thank *you*, Nathan, for making me *want* to sing again."

———

Wilford Woodruff was right, of course. The storm didn't last for the entire trip, though they had semirough seas a good part of the way. On January eleventh, under a slate gray sky, twenty-two days after leaving New York, the packet ship *Oxford* was towed slowly up the Mersey River and into Liverpool.

Derek had to resist the temptation to drop to his knees when he finally stepped off the gangplank and onto the solid planking of the wharf. He stopped, lifting his head and breathing deeply, savoring the sheer joy of being freed from the smell, from the confinement, and from the everlasting movement of the ship.

"Hey, mate!" someone snarled behind him. "Move it ohver, eh, what?"

Derek jumped as a dockworker rattled past with a cart full of hemp.

"Stupid colonials," the man muttered angrily as he went by. "Why don'tcha go back to America where ya come from?"

"Ah, put a button on it, mate," Derek called back without rancor, letting his best English accent roll out. The man gave him a startled look, then moved on, still muttering.

There was a movement beside him and Derek turned. John Taylor was standing there, smiling broadly. "Sounds good, doesn't it? To hear a good old Cockney accent again."

"I'll say."

"Welcome home, Derek," he said. "Welcome home."

Chapter Notes

While in Philadelphia with Joseph, Parley Pratt and others were taught the doctrine of eternal marriage and the eternal nature of the family. The personal feelings Parley expresses to his wife here in the novel come largely from his own words. (See *PPP Auto.*, pp. 259–60.)

The hymn sung by Lydia here is number 73 in the original hymnal that the Church published under the direction of Emma Smith.

As the train moved slowly out of Penwortham Station, Derek felt his heart begin to race a little. Preston was the next stop, just five or six miles away. He had once told Rebecca that his home was America now, and that he had no regrets about leaving England. So his excitement at returning was surprising to him. For all its harshness, for all the grim realities of their existence here, it was still home. Suddenly he desperately wished that Peter were here beside him to share the moment.

It had been a hasty three days since their arrival. They docked in Liverpool on Saturday afternoon and spent a miserable night in a most distasteful inn. The next morning, the Sabbath, they attended two different Anglican church services, then sought out the only contact they had in Liverpool. John Taylor's wife, Leonora, had a brother here. George Q. Cannon was completely bowled over to find his brother-in-law standing at the door. The missionaries were received warmly and fed a hearty supper, and the Cannons listened very favorably to the message of the Restoration.

Anxious to get to Preston, they had spent most of this day, Monday, getting their limited amount of luggage out of customs; then, leaving most of it at the Cannon home, they caught the six o'clock train for Preston. Now at five minutes of eight p.m., they had almost reached their destination.

It was full dark, and outside, the air was cold and filled with a touch of fog. But Derek didn't need light to know what lay just ahead of the train. In a moment they would come along the bluffs that marked the edge of the River Ribble Valley, with its sweeping curves and beautiful green vistas. Here the river was wide and deep, moving slowly, with barely a ripple. On the north side would be the city proper, with its endless rows of two- and three-story apartment buildings that overlooked the river. These were the nicer housing complexes. Behind them, between the river and the great textile factories, would be the housing for the poor—gray-black apartment houses, windows almost covered with black soot, the streets and alleys no more than a rabbit's warren where the laboring poor crammed eight and twelve deep into one-room flats.

Without thinking, Derek wrinkled his nose. He could almost smell the open sewage running down the streets and alleyways, the stench of half-rotten cabbage cooking in pots with very little meat. He could almost hear the clatter of the wooden shoes worn by the factory workers, the raucous shouts of the gaunt-eyed children playing some game with a stick and a rock, darting in and out among the great cotton wagons which thundered by, day and night.

Derek closed his eyes and lay back against the seat. No, he didn't need the light of day to know what lay waiting for them. But smells or no smells, filth or no filth, it was home, and he was excited to get off the train and be in the midst of it again.

———•———

As the train began to slow for the station, Wilford Woodruff lowered the window, letting the cold air pour into the coach.

No one seemed to mind, for several people had done the same. Men and women and a couple of children leaned way out, eyes half-closed against the freezing air as they tried to see who was waiting for them at the station.

"There's Willard Richards," Wilford cried.

John Taylor jumped up and thrust his body half out of the train. He was searching the crowd for his old friend Joseph Fielding, who had also come on the first mission and stayed behind to keep the work going. John Taylor and Joseph Fielding had emigrated from England to Canada together some years before and were longtime friends. It was in Canada that Parley Pratt and Nathan Steed had found both families and helped convert them to the Church. He sat back, disappointed to see that Joseph was not there.

Derek went up on the balls of his feet to see over their heads. The train was nearly stopped now, huffing and puffing, sending heavy black smoke and hot cinders over everything. But through the smoke and the light fog, he saw the heavy girth of Willard Richards, and a woman standing by him. There was a small group of Saints crowded around them, already starting to wave a welcome to the new arrivals.

"There's Sister Richards," Derek said.

"Is she the 'prophecy' girl?" Wilford asked Derek.

He nodded.

They pulled back inside the coach, shivering and red faced. "Prophecy girl?" John Taylor asked Derek.

"Yes, she's the one that Heber baptized, then wrote and told Willard that he had baptized his wife that day."

"Oh, yes, I remember Heber telling me that now."

"And did Heber tell you about Brother Willard's proposal to her?"

Taylor shook his head. "No, I don't recall that."

"Tell us," Brother Turley and Brother Taylor said simultaneously.

"Jennetta Richards—yes, that's right, Richards was her maiden name too—lived a short distance out of Preston. After Heber's declaration, Willard, of course, wanted to meet her. He did, and was quite taken with the lass, and determined right then and there to make Heber's prophecy come true."

Derek was grinning now, remembering well his delight when he first heard this story. "So, sometime on the day that they met, while he was walking to a meeting with Jennetta and a friend, Willard casually said something like this, 'I find the name Richards to be a fine name. I never want to change it. Do you, Jennetta?'"

Turley hooted right out loud. "You're joshing us."

"Nope," Derek said solemnly. "I swear, that's exactly what he said. And then Jennetta, properly demure, replied, 'No, I do not wish to change my name. And I think that I never will.'"

The train gave a hard lurch, throwing them forward as it ground to a halt. Derek reached down and grabbed his valise. "Let's go," he cried. "We're here."

It had been two and a half years since Willard had left Kirtland, and nearly three years since he and Wilford had last seen each other. Wilford was first off the train. Willard was waiting for him and practically engulfed him as he stepped onto the platform. They pounded each other on the back with blows that would have dropped lesser men. Then Willard looked over Wilford's shoulders. "Derek! Derek Ingalls!" he cried. "Are my eyes betraying me?"

"Hello, Brother Richards," Derek said, stepping forward and sticking out his hand. "How good to see you again."

The hand was ignored and, just as Wilford Woodruff had been, Derek was suddenly engulfed in a crushing bear hug. "Derek, I can't believe my eyes. You've come as a missionary."

"Brother Ingalls? I declare."

Extracting himself, Derek turned. "Sister Jennetta. I am delighted to see you again."

She curtsied slightly, smiling happily. "This is a most pleasant surprise. We had no idea that you would be returning."

John Taylor and Theodore Turley were next to be introduced. Neither of them had known Willard before. Then Willard introduced Jennetta, for Derek was the only one who knew her.

It was at that point that Derek heard a shriek of joy behind him. He turned. An older woman was waving wildly from the midst of a crowd. "Derek! Derek!" Pushing her way through to the front of the crowd, she broke free and dashed toward him. Derek stared for a minute. The lamps were behind her and her face was partially in shadow. Then suddenly he straightened. "Sister Pottsworth!" he shouted. He took three great steps and swept her up, swinging her around and around as she threw her arms around his neck.

"It *is* you!" she kept saying over and over. Abigail Pottsworth, a woman of about forty, lived just a few doors down the street from where Derek and Peter had lived. Peter and Jenny Pottsworth worked at the same textile factory and were best friends. The Pottsworths had gone with the Ingalls brothers to the first preaching meeting to hear the American missionaries. All four of them had been baptized on the same day. Leaving Jenny had been the only real pain for Peter when he and Derek emigrated to America.

He set her down, and looked around. "Where's Jenny?"

And then he saw her. She too had pushed her way through the crowd and was walking slowly toward them, smiling shyly. Derek's eyes widened in surprise. Jenny was about fifteen months younger than Peter and had just turned twelve a few weeks before Derek and Peter had left for America. He had to look twice to be sure it was her. The skinny, pug-nosed, freckle-faced, pig-tailed tomboy had turned into a lovely young woman. He calculated quickly. Her birthday was in August sometime, which meant she would be fifteen in the summer. Had he passed her on the street, he probably wouldn't have recognized her at all.

"Jenny?" he exclaimed. "Is that you?" The nose was still the same—as if she had leaned against a window with a trifle too much pressure—but it fit very nicely into her straight, even features. The freckles were totally gone. Her hair was long—well past her shoulders—and was the color of sunlit sand. Her eyes, very wide and a soft blue, were smiling at him, pleased with his reaction.

"Yes, Derek. It's me."

He looked at her mother. "I can't believe it. She's all grown up." Then he introduced them to John Taylor, Wilford Woodruff, and Theodore Turley. "The Pottsworths were baptized on the same day Peter and I were."

"How is Peter?" Jenny asked as soon as the introductions were made.

"Peter is fine. He said if I made it back to Preston, I was to be sure and look you and your mother up and say hello."

"Say hello, nothing!" Sister Pottsworth cried, feigning a hurt look. "Why, you're coming to stay with us. Me and Jenny are saving to go to America. We want you to tell us all about it."

———◆———

On January sixteenth, Joseph Fielding, president of the British Mission, returned to Preston to a warm and touching reunion with his longtime friend John Taylor. The next day, not yet a week since their arrival in England, the missionaries met at the home of Willard Richards in council with the British Mission presidency. Brother Fielding was president, Brother Richards his first counselor, and Brother William Clayton second counselor. Clayton was one of the first converts to be baptized when Heber C. Kimball and Orson Hyde had come in 1837. Though there were two Apostles present, they deferred to Joseph Fielding as mission president.

After considerable discussion, John Taylor was assigned to labor in Liverpool. With the Cannons already showing interest, this gave Taylor a base from which to work in that seaport town. Theodore Turley was originally from Birmingham and pressed vigorously for permission for him and Wilford Woodruff to go there where he still had many family and friends. Wilford finally agreed to go south, but only as far as the Staffordshire Potteries, and then they would decide from there. By assignment, Derek was asked to accompany Wilford rather than Brother Taylor, and it was decided that Willard Richards would stay in Preston and serve as the central communications point for all the missionaries. It was also determined that Willard should be free to go wherever the Spirit led him.

On the eighteenth, they met again at the Richards home for what Wilford described as a "season of fasting and prayer." They gave blessings to each other and then went to the railway station, where some of them left for their previously determined fields of labor. The mission to England had begun in earnest.

———————

It was snowing lightly in Palmyra, New York. The air was cold, and the humidity off Lake Ontario sent the chill creeping through even the heaviest of clothing. There were a few people on Main Street going about their business, but generally it was quiet. With the Erie Canal closed for the winter, much of the normal bustle of Palmyra came to a halt.

Inside the McBride store, they had a fire well stoked in the large black potbellied stove. The air around it shimmered as it sent its heat throughout the room. The store too was mostly quiet. Lydia was behind the counter, helping a farmer and his son. There were no other customers. Nathan was in the back room of the store, assembling a cast-iron stove for a family in nearby Vienna. Elizabeth Mary played beside him, content with a set of blocks Lydia's mother had bought her for Christmas. Young Joshua and Emily were in school and wouldn't be back for another couple of hours.

The McBrides' living quarters were behind and above the store, and now the door at the top of the stairs opened. Lydia looked up. Hannah McBride was standing at the doorway, looking down. Her face was white. She looked around, dazed and confused. Lydia dropped the pen, letting it clatter to the counter. "Mama?"

There was a strangled cry and her mother half stumbled, groping blindly for the rail.

"Mama!" Lydia screamed. She darted out from behind the counter and raced toward the stairs. Nathan was closer and took the steps three at a time, reaching his mother-in-law just as her knees started to buckle. She sagged against him.

Lydia had reached them now too. She grabbed her mother's hands and peered into her face.

"It's your father," her mother said, almost like a bewildered child. "I can't wake him."

Lydia fell back a step. A great sob welled up inside her. "Oh, Mama! No!"

One by one they came up to Lydia and her mother, standing beside the open grave. The coffin now filled the bottom of the hole, the first shovelful of dirt on top of it. The dark brown of the recently opened earth contrasted starkly with the snow around it. They shook hands, murmured their last condolences, then moved away. The pastor of the Presbyterian church where Josiah McBride had been one of the elders for many years was the last to come up. Lydia stepped forward to meet him. "Pastor Gordon, thank you so much. It was a lovely service. You have been most helpful."

"Your father and I have been friends for many, many years," the man responded soberly. "He was a good man. It was an honor for me to do this." He shook hands with Nathan, then stepped to Hannah McBride. She started to express her thanks, but immediately tears welled up, and she just shook her head. He patted her shoulder. "It's all right, Hannah. It's all right."

He turned back to Lydia. "Is there anything more I can do for you?"

Hesitating only for a moment, Lydia nodded. "Could you take my mother and my children back to the house? I would like to stay with Papa for just a few minutes more, if that's all right."

"Of course." He took her mother by the elbow and steered her toward the carriages. "Come children," he called to young Joshua and his sisters. "Your mother will be along in a while."

Nathan started to turn away too, but Lydia reached out and took his arm. "No, please stay with me."

They stood there in the cold, waiting until everyone had gone. The sexton of the cemetery, seeing them there, quietly backed away. He would complete the work when they were through. Nathan had his arm around Lydia, trying to help ward off the cold. Finally, she looked up at him. There were tears in her eyes. "Thank you, Nathan, for letting me be here for him."

He nodded, grateful to his own father for having the wisdom to insist that Nathan take Lydia home. "I know your father didn't change his mind about Joseph Smith," he said, "but he changed his mind about us. He changed his mind about what Mormonism has done for us. Three nights ago, while I was sitting up with him, he said that to me."

She looked up in surprise. "He did?"

"Yes. He said that he would never be able to understand why we believed in Joseph, but then he said that he had to admit that our religion made us better people. He went on and on about the children, how well we have raised them, how pleased he was that they are so confident and happy. And he said that he knew it was partly because of the gospel."

"Why didn't you tell me?" she whispered.

"I knew his time was short. I decided I would save it until now, so you would have something happy to think about."

She nodded, understanding and appreciating that. She reached out and took his hand. "Nathan, I think we need to stay long enough to help Mama find someone to run the store for her, and settle up any of Papa's affairs, then I'd like to go home."

That startled him. "Don't you want to wait until the weather turns?"

"No," she said firmly. "I want to go home."

He pulled her more tightly against him. "All right."

They stood there in silence for several minutes. Then she spoke again, her voice barely above a murmur. "Nathan, do you remember the night I got my patriarchal blessing from Father Smith?"

"Yes, very well."

"Do you remember what it said?"

"Some."

"He told me that I would yet have sons and daughters."

"Yes, I remember that very clearly."

Early this morning, while Nathan was still asleep, she had slipped out of bed and read her blessing over and over. She began to quote it softly. "'You are to devote your time and your talents and your energies to being a righteous mother in Zion. If you are faithful—'" She stopped, the words choking off. She took a quick breath and started again. "'If you are faithful in this calling, you shall be as a river of pure water which rushes down from the mountain, bringing life to all that is nearby.'"

He was nodding. "You are that, Lydia. You bring life to me and to our children. You bring life to my family. My mother loves you as dearly as her own daughters."

"And I her," she said, sniffing back the tears. She slipped her arm around his waist. "I'm ready to go home, Nathan."

"So am I," he murmured.

"I want to have another baby." She smiled at him as he stared at her. "I want to have me another little Nathan."

"I would like that very much," he said.

She pulled free from him, brushing at her eyes with the back of her hand. Then she bent over and scooped up a handful of dirt. She stepped to the edge of the grave and opened her hand, letting the dirt fall in upon the coffin. "Good-bye, Papa," she called softly. "I love you."

Then resolutely, she turned back to Nathan. "Let's go home."

———————•—•———————

Nathan lifted the last case and put it in the third seat of the sleigh. He shoved it down between the other cases, wedging it in tightly so it wouldn't bounce around too much. He checked the packages that contained the gifts for the family, and the box that held some dried food for the journey and a jar of quinine powder for treating the ague in the upcoming summer. Everything was where it needed to be. He pulled the tanned deer hide over it all and poked the ends beneath the seat. Now, even if it should snow while they were on the road, their luggage would remain dry.

He turned and looked to Lydia. "All right, we're ready."

The children were already in the sleigh. They had said their good-byes to their grandmother and were now bundled up beneath the heavy buffalo robes furnished by the driver. Emily and Elizabeth Mary were in the middle seat. They would ride with Lydia. Young Joshua sat in the front beside the driver. Nathan would be beside him. Lydia nodded, the tears already trickling down her cheeks. She turned and threw herself into her mother's outstretched arms. "Good-bye, Mama."

Hannah McBride was weeping too. "Good-bye, dear Lydia. How I will miss you and the children."

"It's not too late to change your mind, Mama," Lydia sniffed. "You could come with us."

Hannah shook her head. They had gone over this more than once. She had never lived anywhere but Palmyra. All her friends were here. The store was her means of livelihood. This was her life. There was no point in going through it all again, so she changed the subject. "I am so glad you came," she whispered. "It meant so much to your father."

Nathan had come up to stand beside them. Lydia stepped back, and Hannah reached out and took Nathan's hand. "Thank you, Nathan, for bringing my daughter back. And the children. My Josiah wasn't much at words, but it meant more to him than he could say."

"I know, Mother McBride." He kissed her quickly on the cheek, then took Lydia's elbow. "We'd best be going or we won't make it to Canandaigua by dark."

"Nathan?" Hannah was fumbling in the pocket of her dress. She pulled out a flat black pocketbook as he turned back to her. "I want you to have this." She thrust it out to him.

Puzzled, he took it. It was thick and heavy. "What is this?"

She inclined her head toward it. "Open it."

When he did so, his mouth opened slightly. Lydia stepped over to see better. She gasped. "Mother!"

Nathan couldn't tell how much there was, but the purse was stuffed with bills. There were at least a dozen five-dollar bills—Vs, as they were commonly called—and at least that many Xs (ten-dollar bills). There was easily three, maybe four hundred dollars in his hand. He was shocked into silence.

"But Mama—," Lydia started.

"Now," Hannah scolded, "don't you say a word. That's part of your inheritance from your father. Josiah has left me well situated. And you have a long way to travel. I don't want you letting my grandchildren go hungry because you don't have enough money."

"But it won't take nearly—," Nathan began.

"Besides," she went right on, ignoring him, "you've worked at the store now for almost six months. Let's just call it part of your wages."

"I . . ." He was stammering, feeling like a fool. Had she heard him and Lydia expressing to each other their worry about how they were going to make their forty dollars stretch across half a continent? He didn't think so.

Hannah suddenly went up on her toes and kissed Nathan on the cheek. "The money isn't for that," she said, "but if you could bring them back again in a year or two, Nathan, I would be forever grateful."

"I will," he said, feeling the wetness of her tears against his cheek. "I promise."

He helped Lydia into the sleigh and poked the buffalo robe in around her. Then in a moment he was up and beside young Joshua. "Good-bye, Grandma," the children called, waving.

"Good-bye, children." As the driver picked up the reins, Hannah looked at Nathan. "By the way, the driver has already been paid for taking you to Buffalo." As Nathan's head jerked around, she gave a little wave of her hand, motioning for the driver to be off. He flipped the reins and the horses began to move. Nathan turned, waving the purse. "No," he called, "not after this."

She laughed and waved. "Remember, you promised to come back."

The horses picked up speed and broke into a steady trot. The runners of the sleigh hissed over the snow-packed street. Nathan looked at Lydia, who was shrugging helplessly at him. He turned to the driver. The man nodded soberly. "It's true, Mr. Steed. I have already been well paid. So you just settle back and enjoy the ride."

The minute the door opened, Joshua shot to his feet. Rebecca came out first, but Mary Ann was right behind her. In three great steps he reached them. "Can I go in now?"

His mother nodded. "Yes. Congratulations, Papa."

He nodded and smiled, then pushed past them into the bedroom. Caroline was half propped up with pillows and had the baby cradled in one arm. She looked drained, but glowed with happiness. He moved quickly to her, pulling around the chair that sat at the edge of the bed. "Are you all right?" he asked anxiously.

"I'm fine," she answered, touched that he had inquired about her first. "Tired. But I'm fine. How are the girls?"

"Fine. Rebecca went to get them. They're dying to see the baby. Savannah says she gets him first." He looked at the bundle lying on her stomach. "So it's a boy."

She nodded and pulled the blanket back.

He leaned over, peering at the tiny round face, still partially flat and with red splotches from the birth. The eyes were screwed tightly shut, and there was the barest touch of dark black hair across the top of his head, no thicker than frost on a window. A great sense of wonder filled Joshua as he looked down into his son's face. "He's beautiful, Caroline."

"He's got a lusty set of lungs on him," she said. "Did you hear him?"

"I did," he said proudly. "In fact, he woke up some of the people across the river in Montrose."

She laughed, reaching down to run the side of her finger across the fuzz of his hair. "Do you want to hold him?"

"Of course." Carefully, he reached out and took the bundle into his arms. The baby gave one little whimper, then immediately settled down again. "Our little Charles Benjamin," Joshua said, pulling the blanket down farther enough to reveal the tiny hands with the perfectly formed little fingernails.

"Do you still want to call him that?"

He looked surprised that she would suggest otherwise. "I chose Savannah's name. Charles is fine with me."

"I don't want to call him Chuck. No one ever called my father Chuck. It was always Charles."

"Then Charles it shall be." He looked down at his son. "First one to call him Chuck gets a good pop from his father."

Caroline watched father and son, feeling contented. It hadn't been a particularly difficult labor, but she was almost thirty-four now and could tell it took more out of her than giving birth to Will and Olivia.

Joshua turned to her. "Know what I was thinking out there while I was waiting?"

"What?"

"He could easily live into the twentieth century."

Her eyes widened. "If he lives to be sixty or more, that's true."

"Oh, he's going to live to be ninety or more. I can sense it." As she laughed at his pride, he sobered, speaking now to his son. "Imagine that, Charles Benjamin Steed. The twentieth century. And you'll get to see it."

Chapter Notes

Two missionaries from Nauvoo arrived in England in December, but John Taylor and Wilford Woodruff were the first of the Apostles to come. They arrived in Liverpool on 11 January 1840 and journeyed to Preston on 13 January as described here. On 17 January, a council was held and the assignments were given for the missionaries' various fields of labor. (See MWM, pp. 106–9.)

By some quirk or twist of nature, Staffordshire, about thirty miles south of Manchester, had been blessed with rich deposits of pottery clay. For over a hundred years it had been a major center for the English pottery industry. A major factor in that happening came as the result of one man. In the latter half of the eighteenth century, a master potter in the area came to prominence. Brilliant, clever, and possessing a fine sense of art, the man began to experiment with different mixtures and firing temperatures. He developed a beautiful light blue porcelain, then found a way to lay white porcelain designs over the top of that. Expanding from the normal line of dinnerware, he developed decorative art pieces—vases, cameos, statuettes, pedestals, flowerpots, busts, and medallion portraits. In a very short time, the name of Josiah Wedgwood was world famous. Royalty around the world vied for his creations. People in Europe and America sought pieces of Wedgwood as visible proof of their own economic success. Eventually even the name for a particular color—Wedgwood blue—would honor the work of the crafts-man. As much as any other man, he had brought the Potteries into the industrial age.

Consisting of six adjacent towns, the Potteries employed thousands of people in the digging, mixing, molding, decorat-ing, and firing of the wonderful Staffordshire clay. Every town had its potbank yards, the factories where the clay was fired. Massive "bottle ovens" filled these yards, some three and four stories high. They spewed clouds of black smoke into the sky. The bottle ovens got their name because they were shaped like the top half of a whiskey jug. Fat at the bottom, they tapered off into rounded cones at the top, the chimney forming the mouth of the "bottle." Derek Ingalls had heard about the Potteries, of course. Who in England hadn't? But he never dreamed how ex-tensive the factories were, and even now, after being here for six weeks, he found himself staring in wonder at the great ovens.

Derek looked across the street to the shop where some of the area's finest Wedgwood was on display. He was tempted to cross over, but pushed it away. The small vase, not much bigger than a coffee cup but so exquisitely shaped, would still be there. It had been for six weeks and he didn't expect it to be gone now. The reason he didn't go look at it again was that it de-pressed him terribly. The floral design, laid in such delicate bas-relief over the powder blue surface, was so like Rebecca's own loveliness. But the ten-pound cost—somewhere around fifty American dollars—was so astronomically beyond his means, that it only made him feel the worse each time he looked at it. *Oh, my darling Rebecca. How I would love to bring it home to you.*

He walked on, not looking back, head down in dejection.

———•———

As Derek moved along, past the factories and into the resi-dential section of Hanley, back toward the home of William and Ann Benbow, his spirits fell even further. Would they be leaving this place? Would they be saying good-bye to the members and the new converts they had made in the past month and a half?

It had been a wonderful six weeks. The people were warm and generous, even in the midst of their own poverty. England was undergoing hard times at the moment, even more than when Derek had been here, and there was widespread unemployment. The Potteries drew thousands of people looking for work. Often men, women, and children worked around the clock in the potbank yards, nearly suffocating from the heavy smoke or fainting from working too close to the great ovens. They made barely a pittance for ten- and twelve- and fourteen-hour days, and yet they gladly shared their food and their homes with the missionaries from America. Derek had grown very close to many of the families.

They had already baptized forty people, and looked forward to further success as they continued their labors. Then all of that had changed three days before when Theodore Turley returned from Birmingham. He spoke in glowing terms of the richness of the harvest there and urged Wilford to go and labor in that place. To Derek's surprise, Wilford had been willing to entertain the idea. He would leave Derek and Turley to continue the work in the Potteries, while he went on to Birmingham by himself. Derek had been greatly relieved to hear that he could stay.

Then yesterday, during the worship services, Wilford had shocked everyone with an announcement as he got up to speak. "As we were singing the opening hymn," he said, "the Spirit whispered to me, 'Brother Wilford, this is the last meeting you will hold with these people for many days.'" That brought cries of dismay from all around. Wilford himself was saddened and shocked, but he was sure enough of the impression that he turned the sermon into his farewell address.

Last evening, as the missionaries sat around the table with William and Ann Benbow, discussing the implications of what all of this meant, there was no agreement. Turley saw the prompting as confirmation that the Apostle should go to Birmingham. The Benbows urged him to go even farther south than that. William had a brother, a well-to-do farmer in the Herefordshire area, southwest of Birmingham. John Benbow and his wife, Jane, were members of a group called the United Brethren. The people who belonged to this group were earnest seekers after the truth, and William and Ann were sure there would be a positive response from the group to the message of the restored gospel. So strongly did William feel about it that he offered to pay Wilford's way to Herefordshire. So, in typical fashion, Wilford decided to turn it over to the Lord.

He had left early this morning, saying that he would "go in secret before the Lord" and find out what he should do. Derek was returning from an errand for the Benbows, and hoped he hadn't missed Wilford's return. He wanted to be there when the answer was announced.

As he rounded the corner and started down the street toward the Benbow home, he saw Theodore Turley hurrying toward him. Turley looked up, then started waving. "Derek! Oh, good. Wilford is just back. He has his answer."

They were all a little breathless as they finally got settled in the parlor. Wilford waited until all were seated, then he rose slowly. "Brethren. Sister Benbow. As you know, I have sought to know God's will concerning this work. And he has given me the answer and showed me what it is I must do."

Every eye was on him now. William Benbow leaned forward, his hands clasped together. Turley was poised on the edge of his seat. Without thinking about it, Derek found himself clutching the arms of his chair.

"It is the Lord's will that I shall go immediately to the south of England."

Turley leaned forward eagerly. "So to Birmingham as you planned?"

Wilford shook his head slowly, then turned to William Benbow. "No, the Spirit whispers that we are to go on beyond that. On south to Herefordshire."

Benbow leaped up. "Wonderful!" he cried. He turned and

took his wife's hands. She was nodding happily. Then he turned back to Wilford. "I shall take you there myself and give you introduction to my brother."

"Thank you, Brother William." He turned to Turley. "Brother Theodore, I should like you to remain in Staffordshire so that the work here does not suffer."

"Of course," Turley said immediately.

Derek held his breath, waiting. Finally, Wilford turned to him and smiled. "Brother Derek, the Spirit whispers that you are to accompany me."

———◆———

Derek Ingalls had basically known two areas of England. His family had always lived in the heavily industrialized area of Lancashire, which was in the west-central part of England, bordering the Irish Sea. His father was a factory worker, his mother a laundress. Times had been very difficult. Their diet was poor and their living conditions barely marginal, so when a cholera epidemic swept through western England in 1829, it hit the Ingalls family very hard. When it was over, only Derek and Peter were still alive. Over the next few years, Derek had moved from town to town in Lancashire to avoid the social welfare people who wanted to take Peter away from him. Eventually they settled in Preston, with both Peter and Derek working the textile factories.

Then six weeks ago, Derek had moved to his second area, the area of Staffordshire, with Elder Woodruff. Like Lancashire, this area was also crowded and filled with factories, only here it wasn't textiles but pottery which drove the wheels of industry. Both enterprises left the air thickly polluted, the living conditions for the workers wretched and grossly overcrowded. In both cases the slightest downturn in the economy would throw thousands out of work and greatly add to the misery of the population.

So Herefordshire came as a wonderful surprise to Derek. As they walked along, enjoying a brief time of early spring sunshine, Derek was reminded of the beautiful farmland of Pennsylvania and upstate New York. Here the soil, where it had been recently plowed for spring planting, was rich and black. Many houses were large and well constructed, clearly testifying to the prosperity of their owners. Others, obviously the residences of the tenant farmers, were little more than one-room cottages, but they were clean and the yards well kept. Livestock dotted green sweeps of pastureland. Fields were divided off into a patchwork of squares and rectangles by rock or rail fences or thick hedgerows. A short distance to the east of them, the land rose gracefully to form the Malvern Hills. This was a small range of gentle peaks rising a few hundred feet higher than the surrounding countryside and covered here and there with trees.

He turned to William Benbow. "I can scarce believe my eyes," he said enthusiastically. "I've not ever dreamed there was such a place in my native land."

"Aye," Benbow replied. "This is a lovely place, and the people are just as fine as the land itself. Mark my words, Brother Wilford, you have made a wise choice."

True to his word, William Benbow had paid their passage down, bringing his eight-year-old son along for company on the return home. They had taken an omnibus—a covered coach with benches that seated up to twenty passengers—to Wolverhampton, then taken a coach to Worcester. From there they had started walking. The March air was cool, but the late-afternoon sun was out and Wilford had his coat off. Sweat beaded most of their foreheads and stained their shirts.

"How much farther, Brother William?" Wilford asked.

"Not far now at all," Benbow's son answered. "We just passed through the village of Castle Froome. Uncle John's house is just down the road a bit."

"Less than half a mile, I'd wager," Benbow agreed.

"How far have we come from Worcester?" Wilford asked.

"Nearly fourteen miles, I'd wager," William answered.

"It's Woos-ter, Brother Wilford," Derek teased, "not Wor-chest-er."

Wilford muttered something under his breath, and Benbow

laughed heartily. "You've got to get that American pronunciation out of your head," he said.

"Well, why don't they pronounce it like they spell it? What's with you English? Don't you know your own language?"

"It makes perfect sense," Derek retorted. "It's Woos-ter, not Wor-chest-er. Glahs-ter, not Glou-chest-er. Lehs-ter not Lay-chest-er. The term *shire*—what in America we call a county—is simply added to get the larger geographic designation. So Woostershur, Glahstershur, Lehstershur. It's as simple as that."

"Ha!" Wilford snorted. "*Simple* isn't the word. Black treacle, you say? Why not just call it molasses? And where do you get off calling your day's plan a shed-jule. Any one with half a brain knows it's a sked-yool."

Benbow put his hands over his ears, feigning pain. "Oh, please," he cried.

"Speaking of eating black treacle," Derek laughed, "please don't ask for a napkin at dinner tonight."

"Why not? Must I call it a nahp-kin?" Wilford rolled the "ah" sound with great exaggeration.

The Benbow boy squealed with delight. "A napkin, or a nappy, as we call it, is something you put on a baby's bottom. They shall think you daft if you ask for one at dinner."

"Ask for a serviette instead," Derek explained. "It is much more refined."

Wilford just shook his head, thoroughly disgusted. "And you say I'm daft. Well, here's one for you. You never say a person is in the hospital, like a normal man would. You drop the article and say he is *in hospital*." He pulled a face. "In hospital. It sounds like you're talking baby talk."

Derek had an answer to that one. "If someone is arrested, where do they put him?"

"In jail."

"Not in *the* jail. Does that sound like baby talk to you?"

Benbow rescued Wilford at that moment. He looked up, pointing down the road a short distance. "There! There it is. The large stucco house with the two chimneys. That's the home of my brother John. We're here."

"Where's the American preacher?"

Derek turned. Just behind him, a large man was shoving his way through the crowd of people at the doorway and coming into the room. John Benbow heard him too, for he broke loose from the group and started through the crowded room toward them. Derek didn't wait for him. "Here, sir," he said, raising a hand.

The man looked surprised. There was no mistaking Derek's accent. "Are you Mr. Woodruff?"

"No, I'm Derek Ingalls, most recently arrived from America."

The man frowned, suspecting he was being tricked. He was a burly man with thick black eyebrows and a heavy scowl. "Where's Woodruff?"

Before Derek could answer, John Benbow reached them. "Ah, Constable Pexton. Good evening to you, sir."

Derek's face remained expressionless, but inwardly he jumped a little. *Constable?* By the man's demeanor, this did not bode well.

"Mr. Benbow, good evening." They shook hands perfunctorily as the constable looked around the room. "Quite the crowd you have, and there's still more queued up outside."

"Yes, we've been most gratified by the response to our invitation."

"So it *is* a preaching meeting that you've called here?"

"Aye." Benbow smiled easily. "This room is licensed as a preaching room now, you know."

"Aye, I knew that before I came. But it takes more than a licensed room now, doesn't it? It takes a licensed preacher as well." Pexton reached in his pocket and pulled out a folded paper. "I'm looking for a Mr. Wilford Woodruff from America. Is he here?"

"Yes, I'm here." Wilford was pushing his way toward them. When he reached them, he stuck out his hand. "The name is Wilford Woodruff. And you are . . . ?"

"Constable Pexton. Richard Pexton."

"How do you do, sir?" Wilford said warmly. Now Jane Benbow came over to join her husband. "Is there a problem?" she asked.

"Is there, Constable?" Benbow asked.

He nodded curtly, waving the paper slightly. "I should think so. I have here a warrant for the arrest of Mr. Woodruff."

Shocked, John Benbow fell back a step. "On what charge?"

"Preaching without a license. The rector of the parish here has sworn out a complaint against you."

So that was it, Derek thought. Now it began to make sense. The four of them—Wilford and Derek, William Benbow and his son—had arrived in Herefordshire Wednesday night, where they were warmly welcomed by John and Jane Benbow. The Benbows were members of a religious group called the United Brethren, a group of about six hundred in this and nearby counties who were earnestly seeking for a restoration of the gospel as it was taught and practiced anciently. The day following the arrival of Wilford's party, the Benbows invited friends and neighbors into their home to hear the missionaries. A second meeting was held the next day, and John and Jane Benbow, along with four of their friends, were baptized. Sensing a rich harvest, and understanding now why the Lord had sent them here, Wilford and Derek spent most of Saturday—yesterday—clearing out a pond on the farm property. "We'll be needing a baptismal site," Wilford said simply.

Then today Wilford began preaching in earnest. The Benbows and their friends had lined up three different United Brethren congregations for Wilford to preach to throughout the day, the third being the one now gathered at the Benbows' home. People flocked to hear the missionaries from America. Derek estimated there were more than a thousand between the three meetings. And that was the rub. Someone reported that the Anglican parish church had no more than fifteen or twenty people in the afternoon services. No wonder the rector was upset.

Wilford Woodruff didn't seem at all perturbed by the news

that the warrant was for him. "Well, Constable Pexton, I admire a man faithful to his duty. There is only one slight problem."

"What is that?" the man asked, half suspiciously.

"I happen to have a license to preach, just like your rector does. I obtained one when we first arrived at Liverpool in January."

"You did?"

"I did." Wilford's smile would have melted the heart of the devil himself. "I'd be happy to get it for you, but as you can see, we have a group of people here who have come to listen to my sermon. The hour has arrived and it's time to begin. If you don't mind waiting until I'm finished, I'll then show you that I am in full compliance with the law."

The law officer seemed impressed by Wilford's open manner. "Fair enough, sir," he said. There was a quick, self-conscious grin. "To be perfectly honest, I've been a little curious myself after hearing everybody talking about you. I'd like to hear what you have to say."

"Then find yourself a chair," Wilford boomed, "and we'll get the meeting started."

This was the third sermon Wilford Woodruff had preached in the last eight hours, and Derek worried a little that his voice might give out on him. But he should have known better. They sang a hymn, and John Benbow called on his brother to give an opening prayer. Many of the people crowded into the room had been in one of the earlier worship services, so John took only a minute to introduce Wilford and Derek.

The moment the Apostle stood, it was evident that the power of God was upon him. Wilford Woodruff was thirty-two years old and the product of backcountry Connecticut. He was a miller by trade and a missionary by profession, as he liked to say. From the earliest days of his conversion to the Church, he had been an indefatigable emissary for the gospel. As they had walked the fourteen miles from Worcester to the Benbow farm, he had shared with his companions some of his missionary experiences in the southern United States. Though he had been only a priest at the time, he had had numerous experiences with the power of God, with angels, and with God's protective hand.

Now all of that collective experience came to bear. He began by talking about the Great Apostasy, how many of the powers and offices held in the Church that the Savior established on the earth had been lost. New doctrine was introduced. The ordinances were altered. The authority to act in God's name was lost. New churches were formed. Wilford understood his audience well. Heads began to nod all over the congregation in response to that.

Abruptly, Wilford turned to the story of the Restoration. Simply but powerfully he bore witness that God had called upon a young man to restore His church to the earth again. He told of how the angel Moroni had come to Joseph and had told him about the Book of Mormon. He told them about the return of John the Baptist and Peter, James, and John with priesthood keys.

Derek glanced up at the clock on the mantel at that point and was amazed to see that forty minutes had already passed. As he looked around he could not spot anyone, including the constable, who seemed either bored or offended.

Then Wilford simply described The Church of Jesus Christ of Latter-day Saints and asked his listeners to compare it with other Christian churches. He didn't rail against the current churches. He didn't criticize their ministers. He just simply asked the people to compare them with the original Church—in organization, in doctrine, in practice.

"Brother Derek?"

Derek jumped a little. Wilford was through. Now he was calling his name.

Derek stood slowly, his heart suddenly pounding. "Yes?"

"Would you care to bear your testimony to these good people?"

Wilford had done this once before and it had terrified

Derek. But this was why he had come. John Taylor used an expression shortly after their arrival in Liverpool which sprang now to Derek's mind. "I feel the word of the Lord like fire in my bones," he had said. Yes! That was it! Derek walked slowly to the front of the room to stand beside Wilford.

"This is Derek Ingalls. He's an Englishman, like yourselves. I'd like for you to hear his testimony." And then the Apostle turned and sat down beside John Benbow and his wife.

To Derek, it looked like there was a whole sea of faces before him. They were watching him closely, but there was nothing but interest and acceptance in their eyes, and that gave him heart. "As Brother Woodruff has said," he began tentatively, "I am an Englishman. My brother and I lived in Preston. Like many of you, we were laborers. I shoveled coal in one of the large textile factories there. My brother worked in the cutting room." He took a quick breath. "I didn't believe in God then. . . ."

Without his realizing it, the shaking in his hands ceased, and the trembling in his knees steadied. He told them how two Apostles of the Lord Jesus Christ, Heber Kimball and Orson Hyde, had come to Preston. He told of his initial skepticism and reluctance to go hear them. Heber and Orson, like Wilford tonight, had told them about the Book of Mormon, and Derek had suddenly been filled with a desire to get a copy and read it.

Now his voice rose with power. "I was a poor reader." He shook his head. "I had to have my little brother help me. But as we read, we prayed. For the first time in my life I prayed to Heavenly Father. 'Is this book true?' we asked. 'Is this book from thee?' And, my friends, I am here to testify to you that the Lord heard those prayers and he answered them. It was like . . ." He groped for the right words, and then smiled. "It was like fire in my bones. And I knew it was true."

Oblivious now to anything but those upturned faces, he told of going to America. He told of coming to Kirtland and then going to Missouri and meeting the Prophet Joseph Smith for the first time. He told of working with Joseph in the fields, of reading the revelations he had given. Fighting hard to control his emotions, he told them about the great day of healing along the banks of the Mississippi River. "Like the prophets of old," he concluded, "this man has the power of God."

He took a deep breath. "My brothers and sisters, I have a beautiful wife and a wonderful little boy back in Illinois. My son will be a year old in June. I'm sure he's crawling by now. Before long he will be walking." He stopped, blinking rapidly to stop the burning in his eyes. "And I won't be there to see that."

He shook his head. "I love them very much. There is nothing in the world that would take me from my family except to share this truth with you."

His voice cleared. "My friends, my fellow countrymen, I know the true church of God has been restored to the earth. I know Joseph Smith is a prophet of God. I have sat at his feet and had the Spirit bear witness to me that he is a prophet. I have read the Book of Mormon and testify to you that no mortal man could have written that book. It required the gift and power of God. Every fiber of my being is on fire with this knowledge." He straightened, pulling back his shoulders. "And that is why I have come back to England."

He stepped back. Instantly, Wilford was up and standing by his side. "Thank you, Brother Derek," he said softly. Then, as Derek made his way back to his seat, Wilford looked across the faces of the audience. "Friends and brethren, you have heard our message. We testify that we bring the priesthood of God and the authority to baptize. Your friends and neighbors the Benbows have chosen to be baptized. John has graciously allowed us to clear a pond here on his property so that we can baptize those who have the same mind as him. I make that invitation to you now, if the Spirit has witnessed to your soul that you should do so. Thank you all for coming."

He sat down, and instantly people were up and swarming around him. "I wish to be baptized," said one. "I accept what you have said," cried another. "I want to join this church."

John Benbow and his wife stood and came to Derek. "What

a wonderful testimony," Sister Benbow said, touching his arm. "You must have a wonderful wife and child."

"I do."

"Look," John said, grabbing his wife by the arm. Constable Pexton was waiting behind two men who were asking for baptism. As Wilford nodded and they moved away, Pexton stepped forward. He had the warrant in his hand. "Mr. Woodruff?"

"Yes, Constable?"

He tore the paper in half. "I would like to be baptized if I may."

Wilford reached out and gripped his hand. "Of course," he said, not seeming in the least surprised. "Of course."

Chapter Notes

Though some details have been added—including, obviously, Derek's presence and his bearing of his testimony—the meeting in the John Benbow home on the first Sabbath after Wilford Woodruff's arrival in Herefordshire is accurately portrayed in the novel. Seven people applied for baptism, including four preachers of the United Brethren and the constable who had come with the warrant for Wilford's arrest. The rector of the local parish, furious that his attempt to stop Woodruff had failed, sent two of his clerks to the next sermon to gather evidence against the Mormon preacher. Wilford laconically records that they too were "pricked in their hearts" and requested baptism. Not surprisingly, the rector sent no more people after that. (See MWM, pp. 124–25.)

Brigham Young and George A. Smith didn't arrive in New York until early February of 1840. They were so bereft of funds that they made the final leg of the journey only when the captain of the steamboat on which they had come down from New Haven, Connecticut, saw their plight and paid for their stagecoach fare.

Heber C. Kimball arrived in mid-February. Like his fellow Apostles, he too had exhausted his funds. When he reached Jersey City he didn't have the necessary twenty-five cents to purchase a ticket for the ferry ride across the river. Fortunately, a passenger overheard him discussing this with the ferry captain and simply gave him the fare.

The three brethren immediately set to work to get enough funds to buy passage across the Atlantic. They had been gone from home for six months and were now a full two months behind their fellow Apostles. Brigham's patience was at an end.

So it was that at last, shortly after eleven a.m. on the ninth day of March, a small boat set out from the dock of New York Harbor and rowed to where the *Patrick Henry*, a packet ship of the Black Ball Line, lay at anchor. In the boat were five of the Twelve—Brigham Young, Heber C. Kimball, the Pratt brothers, and George A. Smith—and two additional missionaries, Reuben Hedlock and Matthew Steed. The last of the missionaries were under way.

Matthew offered to row, but the crew members of the small shuttle boat just shook their heads and bent to the task. So Matthew sat in the very back of the boat. As they moved slowly away from the wharf and out into the choppy waters of New York Harbor, he wished he had something to do rather than just watch the shoreline fall away. That was America slowly moving away from him now. That was family and friends. That was Jennifer Jo. It was a thousand miles of rolling prairie, and days of walking barefoot along a hot dusty road. It was nights sitting around a crackling fire reading Bible or Book of Mormon stories to his nieces and nephews. The pain twisted in his chest, surprisingly sharp. How long would it be before the prow of a boat similar to this headed back in to shore? How long before they rounded that great bend of the Mississippi River and saw the city of Nauvoo again? And would there be a bonnie Irish lass waiting at the dock for him? Or would there be disappointment and—

"It leaves one with much to think about, doesn't it?"

Matthew swung around and saw that Brigham was watching him.

He nodded, not trusting himself to speak.

Brigham turned his head back and set his gaze on the packet ship before them. It was just a few rods off now and looming huge out of the water. "That's all right," he said, lifting his eyes to the towering masts. "Now there are other things to set our thoughts on."

Matthew took a deep breath, then moved away from the

322

stern of the boat and sat down beside Brigham, turning his back on his homeland. "Yes," he said firmly. "Yes, there are."

———— ◆ ————

"Mama!"

Caleb Rogers, who would be four in September, tugged hard on his mother's skirt. Melissa had just taken the chicken from the pot of boiling water and was working quickly before it cooled too much, plucking the feathers with quick, hard strokes. "Caleb, Mama's very busy right now. What is it?"

"There's people at the door, Mama."

She looked up in surprise. She hadn't heard anyone knock. "Who is it?"

His shoulders lifted and fell. "A man and a lady and some kids."

Melissa frowned. "You don't know them?"

"Nope."

"Well, tell them I'll be out in just a few—"

"You don't even have time to see your own brother?" Nathan asked from behind her.

She whirled. He was standing in the doorway, grinning at her. The chicken dropped to the counter with a loud plop. "Nathan!" she shrieked.

"Hello, sis."

She was across the room instantly and flung herself into his arms. "Nathan! Nathan!" Her wet hands were covered with the feathers, and as she grabbed him, some of them stuck to his jacket. She didn't even notice. She pushed him away, staring in disbelief. "What are you doing in Kirtland?"

Before he could answer, she stiffened. Over his shoulder, down the hallway, Lydia was standing with her three children, all of them smiling broadly.

———— ◆ ————

"What do you want to do, Carl?"

He sat back, frowning slightly. Melissa watched him closely.

She was surprised that the conversation had so quickly turned to this. They had barely gotten supper over with and the children bundled up and out to play when Lydia began to ask Carl about coming west. Equally surprising was the fact that it was Lydia who was pressing it. Even Nathan seemed a little uneasy with her directness.

"Well," Carl said slowly, "Melissa, of course, would love it if we were closer to your family."

"No," Lydia said with soft persistence, "what do *you* want to do?"

He looked at her for a long time, then finally shrugged. "I guess I'm ready for a change."

Now Nathan leaned forward. "But does the idea of going into business with Joshua appeal to you?"

"Oh, very much. I'm not even sure I want to stay in the livery business anymore. Something totally new sounds exciting to me."

"Then do it!" Lydia exclaimed. "Do it, Carl."

He blew out his breath in exasperation. "I can't."

Melissa came to his defense. "Carl's father is very strong on this. If Carl even tries to mention it, it becomes a major battle. And Carl's mother, of course, doesn't want to see us move so far away."

"Yes," Lydia said quietly, "I know. It was very hard for me and my parents for us to be so far apart."

Melissa said nothing. She was looking at the floor. Carl seemed to read her thoughts. "On the other hand, Melissa hasn't lived near her family for two and a half years now. So that's something else to consider."

"Carl," Lydia said with some firmness. "All of those things are things to consider. But what matters most is that you do what is best for you and for your family."

"But my family doesn't want me to—"

"No," Lydia cut in quickly, "*your* family. Melissa. You. Your children. What is best for *you*." Now she turned to Nathan and there was a mistiness in her eyes. "If I had done only what my father wanted, I would never have married Nathan. But even after that it went on. We went back for a visit in '34. Papa wanted Nathan to take over the store for him." She looked directly at Carl. "If he had, he would have hated every minute of it."

Carl nodded glumly at that.

"My mother wanted us to stay with her now," Lydia continued. "She needs us. But that's not where we belong." She leaned forward, as earnest as Nathan could remember ever seeing her. "I loved my father very much, Carl. Very much. I love my mother. But I'm a married woman now. I have my own life, my own family. And I can't live that life for my parents. That's why the Lord said, 'For this cause shall a man leave his father and his mother, and shall cleave unto his wife.'"

She sat back, calm and composed, but filled with determination. Nathan was watching her in wonder. Finally, he looked at his brother-in-law. "Carl, we're not trying to talk you into anything you don't want to do. But if you are seriously thinking about coming west, now is a good time. Lydia and I will wait here while you settle things up. Then we can all travel together."

"I don't know," Carl said, the discouragement heavy in his voice. "It's just not that simple."

"Of course it's not," Lydia answered. "But who said life was supposed to be simple?" She smiled, letting him know there was no criticism in that comment, then turned to Melissa and started talking about the children.

———◦———

Melissa didn't dare slip out of bed. Carl was asleep, but he wasn't breathing deeply and she was afraid he would awaken if she moved too much. Instead, she turned over onto her stomach, went up on her elbows, and clasped her hands together beneath her chin. She closed her eyes.

"Our Father in Heaven," she began, her lips barely moving, "hallowed be thy name. . . ."

Carl watched his two brothers. They were finishing hitching up a team of sorrel mares to their newest buggy. Isaiah Burton was taking his family to Cleveland, and as one of the wealthier families of Kirtland, he was going to travel in style. The Rogers and Sons livery stable had the finest buggies and carriages in town to help him do so.

"There," William said, tugging on one of the straps to make sure it was tightly cinched. "David, why don't you take this rig to Mr. Burton. Then he won't have to come down here to get it."

The youngest of the Rogers brothers nodded and climbed up in the carriage. Carl walked to the barn door and pushed it open. They waved as David drove it out and turned into the street.

William brushed off his hands on his pants and turned to go back into the office. Carl pulled the door shut again, then spoke. "William?"

His brother stopped.

"I'd like to talk with you for a minute."

William was just two years younger than Carl's thirty years, and they looked quite a bit alike. But in temperament, they were quite different. William was more outspoken, almost fiery at times, not in anger but in passion and intensity. Yet in spite of that, he and Carl were quite close. Now William was looking at his brother quizzically. "What about?"

Carl cleared his throat. "About leaving."

William's eyebrows rose a fraction and he leaned back against one of the stalls. But he didn't seem particularly surprised. The whole family knew about Carl's desire to go west, even though no one spoke of it openly. It didn't take much to know that the arrival of Nathan and Lydia three days before had only intensified whatever was going on in Carl's mind.

Carl rushed on. "You and David can run this place fine. You don't need me."

"That's not what Pa thinks."

"Well, Pa is wrong," Carl burst out.

There was a slow smile. "David and me think so too."

"It's time, William."

Now William grew as serious as Carl. "I know, big brother. You've been restless for almost a year now."

"How do I convince Pa?"

"You don't," William said flatly.

Carl's face fell. But then a smile stole across his brother's face. "But David and I have been working on Mama. She agrees. She starts to cry every time she thinks about you and Melissa leaving, but she agrees that it's best for you, and best for us."

Carl was dumbfounded. "Really?"

"Really. You thinking of going with Nathan?"

Carl nodded, still reeling a little.

"How soon?"

"Nathan says they'll wait however long it takes for us to get ready."

William straightened again. He began smoothing the dirt floor with the toe of his boot. "Tell you what. Come over tonight after supper. About eight. Just you. David and I will go over first and brace Pa for it before you get there." He pulled a face. "Might not do any good, but we'll see."

Carl was soaring. "That's great, William, thank you."

"For taking the business away from you?" He grinned. "Any time." Then he got a little bit of a wistful look in his eyes. "In a way, you know, I envy you."

Carl blinked. "You do?"

William nodded. "A new start. A real challenge. It does have its appeal."

"Look," Carl said eagerly, "let me get out there and get established. I keep telling Pa we can start a livery stable out there too. You could come out—"

"We'll see," William drawled lazily, "but right now, we've got some chickens that ain't hatched yet. We'd best not be counting them until they do."

Melissa was waiting for Carl at the gate. It was full dark, but she saw the dim figure coming down the road toward her and recognized his striding walk. Breathless now, she opened the gate and went out to meet him.

"Carl?" she called while he was still twenty feet away. "What happened?"

He didn't speak. He just came up to her, shaking his head, his face grave. She felt her heart drop. "Tell me," she whispered.

Then he couldn't hold it. He gave a little holler, swooped her off the ground, and twirled her around and around.

She grabbed onto his shoulders, trying to look into his face. "Does that mean . . . ?"

He set her down, laughing joyously. "Yes! He said yes!"

Now she was laughing and crying all at once. "Do you mean it?"

"I surely do," he crowed. "He didn't like it, but William and David finally convinced him." He reached down and kissed her soundly. "We're going, Melissa. We're going."

She couldn't believe it. "How soon?"

"A week. Maybe ten days. Soon as we can get things ready."

Now the woman in her took over. "Oh, my! A week." There were a thousand things to pack. The house to sell. Children to prepare. The reality of it settled in like mud in a sinkhole. They had a long trip to make. What would they need once they got there?

That brought her up with a jolt. They were going to need funds when they got to their new home. Quite a bit of funds. Reluctant to bring him down from his euphoria, she lifted her eyes slightly. "Did you talk about a settlement?" she asked.

"David wants to buy our house," Carl said, sobering now too. "For a thousand dollars. But Pa said I was to get nothing from the business."

That hit her hard and she felt sick. "After all you've done? That's not fair, Carl."

Now he grinned, delighted that he had taken her in. "That's exactly what Mama said. She got really angry. Papa finally agreed to give us another thousand dollars."

She slapped his arm. "You!" she scolded. "You're going to give me heart failure." It still wasn't fair. Carl had practically run the business by himself for the last five or six years now. But two thousand dollars! That would make all the difference in the world.

He was watching her face and he nodded quickly. "I know, Melissa," he said softly. "But it's enough. It's enough." Then he grabbed her hand. "Come on. Let's go tell Nathan and Lydia."

———◆———

Derek reached out and took the woman's hand and helped her out of the pond. She was smiling and crying all at once. The water poured from her hair and her clothing. "Thank you," she cried, clasping Derek's hand. She turned to Wilford, who was still waist deep in the water. "Thank you."

She moved away, and the next two came up, both women also. "You first, dear," the older one said, putting her hand on the younger one's back and helping her into the water. "I'll be right behind you."

Beaming with joy, the younger woman moved out to where Wilford waited. He took her by the hand, then turned her around. His right hand came up into the air. All who were on the bank bowed their heads. "Sister Elizabeth Bubb, having been commissioned of Jesus Christ, I baptize you in the name of the Father, and of the Son, and of the Holy Ghost. Amen."

Down she went, and then up she came.

"Eight," Derek said under his breath. That left three more. He watched Wilford with concern. He had been in the water now for almost a quarter of an hour. The sky was overcast and the air was cold. It was early April, but England could still show her harsher side from time to time and this was one of those times. The water was cold enough to shock when one first stepped into it, and Wilford was looking very cold and very tired.

Wilford Woodruff Baptizes in England

It had been a glorious month but an exhausting one. Each day was much like the other. They would rise and have breakfast, then set out for the next farmhouse or village. The people would be waiting for them. Wilford would preach. Derek or John Benbow or Jane Benbow or some of the others who had been baptized would bear their testimonies. And then they would look for a place to baptize, for invariably someone came up and asked to be baptized.

Wilford had a formal record in the journal he meticulously kept every night, but Derek also kept a mental count. With the eleven they were baptizing this afternoon, that would make one hundred twenty-nine people they had baptized since arriving in Herefordshire. It was a miracle. They were baptizing four and five people a day, sometimes more.

A major factor in that success was John Benbow, of course. He had opened the way. But of ever greater significance was the steady conversion of several United Brethren preachers, fifteen of whom had been baptized between the sixth and the twentieth of March. Then on March twenty-first, Wilford baptized Thomas Kington and his wife. Kington was the superintendent of all the United Brethren congregations. Kington gave the Apostle the "United Brethren Preachers' Plan," the schedule of meetings to be held in Herefordshire and the surrounding counties for the next three months. With few exceptions, the preachers on the list were now members of The Church of Jesus Christ of Latter-day Saints, so Kington suggested they just leave the list basically as it was and let the preachers go out and teach these congregations about the restored gospel. And thus the work rolled on at a breathtaking pace.

Finally, the last young woman came out of the water and into the arms of her fellow converts. "That's the last," Derek called out to Wilford.

Wilford sighed, then came slowly out of the pond. Jane Benbow was holding a towel for him and wrapped it tightly around him. Wilford raised his hands, and the group fell quiet. "Let's allow a half hour or so for changing our clothes," he called. "Then we'll assemble again for the confirmations."

They moved away, Jane Benbow and two other sisters leading them toward the nearest member's house. "You look tired, Brother Woodruff," John Benbow said with some concern.

"Aye," Wilford said, not conscious that he was starting to speak a bit like an Englishman. "That I am." He looked around. "There is so much to do. So many places. So many people wanting us to come and teach them. How can we possibly keep up?"

"Perhaps Brother Richards even now has help on the way," Derek suggested. Wilford had written to Willard in Preston and begged him for more missionaries.

"Perhaps." Then he looked up at the darkening sky. He shook his head slowly. "Where are the rest of the Twelve? That is what I want to know. It is the fourth of April. Why haven't they come from America?"

As the packet ship *Patrick Henry* approached the mouth of the Mersey River, it struck its sails. A steamer was waiting there which would take her under tow the rest of the way into Liverpool. As the ship moved up the crowded channel, the five Apostles and their two companions crowded around the railing, talking excitedly.

"Well, Matthew, what do you think?" Brigham Young asked.

Matthew was staring at block after block of ships and buildings and warehouses and crowded streets. "It's . . . it's . . ." There were no words to describe it. "It's so big," he finally said.

"Yes, over two hundred thousand people, according to the captain."

"Whew!" Matthew said, not even comprehending. New York City hadn't seemed this big.

"And they say London is ten times that many," Heber Kimball said. "Two million people."

"Two million?" George A. Smith exclaimed. "How can one

place hold them all?" At twenty-two, George A. still had a lot of Matthew's youth and wonder about him. In the past two months his eye affliction had improved considerably and he could now see pretty much near normal, which left him only the more excited, youthful, and exuberant again.

Brigham laughed. "The better question is, how can so few missionaries get to all these people?"

Parley Pratt spoke up now. "It truly is a boundless harvest for the next fifteen or twenty years."

"At least," his brother Orson agreed. "How shall we possibly get it all done in a year?"

"We cannot," Parley replied, with sudden determination. "I shall write to Mary Ann this very day and tell her to pack our things and come over from New York City. I shall stay four or five years and I shall need my family with me."

Reuben Hedlock, standing beside Parley, looked a little shocked. "That long?"

Brigham laid a hand on his shoulder. "We shall not all stay that long, but we must thrust in our sickles with our might so that we can do the work that is here to do." He looked around the circle. "Brethren, you know what day it is today?"

They all nodded solemnly.

"It is the sixth day of April. I do not think it accidental that we are arriving on the anniversary of the organization of the Church. Ten years ago today, the kingdom was set up on the earth for the last time. We have seen great things happen in this first decade. Now we begin the second on the shores of another land. Let it not be said of us that we did not do our best to make this next decade as significant as the first."

———— ◆ ————

It was incredible, and Matthew could barely drink it all in. He and Heber and George A. were together, waiting for Brigham and the others to return from the customs house with information on when they could clear their luggage. Heber, who had been here before, decided to take his two young charges in hand and expand their horizons a little. So he walked them a few blocks into the city, and there they came upon the market-place.

It was huge, covering almost two complete city blocks. There were stalls and carts and wagons containing fruits and vegetables and nuts and spices. Coming from all over the world, they presented a bewildering variety, and Matthew hadn't, in his wildest dreams, imagined there was such a thing anywhere under the sun. They pushed their way slowly along, gawking like kids at a carnival. Heber could identify several varieties, but even he was stumped on some things if there was no identifying sign. Many of them Matthew had never heard of. There were oranges, tangerines, lemons, limes, kumquats, papaya, pine-apples, bananas, avocados, figs, grapes, olives, currants, half a dozen kinds of berries. Down another row were the vegetables in the same incredible variety—potatoes, yams, carrots, beets, something that looked like huge parsnips, turnips, tomatoes, taro, artichokes, asparagus, broccoli, okra, Chinese cabbage, cu-cumbers. There was one whole corner where spices were sold. Another half a row of stalls sold nothing but nuts of every kind.

"I can't believe what I'm seeing," George A. said in wonder. "I would have called anyone an outright liar if they told me about this and I hadn't seen it for myself."

Heber laughed. "Tell you what. I'll buy each of you one thing of whatever you want. You choose." As they looked at him dubiously, he handed them a couple of shillings each. "Go on, pick whatever you want."

Matthew was in a jubilant mood anyway, having just ended their four-week-long voyage at sea, so he decided to be bold and go for something exotic. A man had some pineapples stacked up on a two-wheeled cart, with one sliced in thick pieces. Matthew handed him a shilling and picked the largest piece. He was startled, then delighted by its tart sweetness. He reached up and caught the juice dripping out of his mouth with his fingers, then licked them clean.

Curious now, he looked around for George A., wondering

what he had picked. He saw him and Heber in the vegetable area and walked over to join them.

"What did you have?" Heber asked.

"Pineapple. It was delicious. What did you have, George A.?" He stopped, staring at the young Apostle. Tears were streaming down George A.'s cheeks and he was blinking rapidly. "What's the matter?" Matthew asked in alarm.

Heber roared. "Nothing's the matter." He looked at George A. "Show Matthew what you chose."

George A., weeping like a desolate child, held up his hand. In it was a huge onion, easily as big as a man's fist. Three bites had been taken from it already, and even as Matthew watched, George A. took another big bite, just as though he were eating an apple.

Heber shook his head. "Which just goes to show, there's no explaining a man's tastes."

Chapter Notes

The last five of the Twelve—Brigham Young, Heber C. Kimball, Parley and Orson Pratt, and George A. Smith—arrived in Liverpool on 6 April 1840. Matthew, of course, is a fictional character, but the incident with George A. Smith and the onion is true (see MWM, p. 133).

The results of the Herefordshire mission were astounding. Eventually all but one of the six hundred members of the United Brethren joined the Church, as well as hundreds of others in the area (see CHFT, p. 230).

Chapter Twenty-One

W illard Richards strode steadily along in the April sunshine, his walking stick swinging back and forth as he covered the last mile or two to Preston. He was humming softly to himself, his mood as buoyant as it had been for several months. Two things were responsible for that. First, Jennetta seemed in much better health, something remarkable for someone as frail as she had been of recent months. It had been so poor recently that three weeks before, Willard sent her to live with her parents while he traveled for the Church. Second, just last evening her father had invited Willard to stay the night with them. Jennetta's father was a minister and bitterly opposed to the Mormons, so this was indeed something worth celebrating. It was the first time it had happened since their marriage.

As he rounded the corner of his street, he looked up. Jenny Pottsworth was coming out of the door to his home.

She reached the street and turned the other direction, walking swiftly. "Jenny?" he called.

She swung back around. Instantly she began to wave, and then broke into a trot toward him, her long hair bouncing on her shoulders. "Oh, Brother Richards! You're back."

"Hello, Jenny. What brings you out this way?"

To his utter amazement, she grabbed his hand and started dragging him toward his house. "Come on, Brother Richards, I have a surprise for you."

"What? What is it, child?"

"Just never you mind," she laughed. "You must see this for yourself." They had reached the front gate, and she pulled him through it and up to the front door. "All right," she commanded. "Close your eyes."

"What is it?" he asked again. He was weary and not in much of a mood for girlish games.

"Close your eyes."

Exasperated, he finally complied. He heard the door open and then Jenny had him by the elbow. "Don't open them. Not yet."

He felt for the step with his foot, then was inside.

"Now!" she said.

He opened his eyes and looked around, then he gasped. Heber C. Kimball and Brigham Young were standing by the small fireplace, grinning at him like bankers looking at a pot of gold. "Brother Richards, I presume," Heber said, stepping forward and holding out his hand.

———•———

About a hundred miles south, a very different kind of welcome was starting to transpire. As they approached the small pool that would be their baptismal site here in Hawcross, Derek felt the hair on the back of his neck start to rise. The men were waiting for them, and they were muttering angrily as they saw the Mormons coming. Derek looked around, hoping to see a constable, but conveniently, none was around. That was partly due to the lateness of the hour—it was near midnight—but Derek also suspected that the constable didn't want to know what was going on. It was easier that way. The rowdies could make trouble for a constable too.

The fantastic success Wilford Woodruff was having in Herefordshire and the surrounding areas was not without its attendant problems. Anglican ministers railed against the Mormon missionaries Sunday after Sunday. There was talk that one group of ministers were even thinking about writing the archbishop of Canterbury and asking him to go to Parliament and have laws passed making it illegal for the Mormons to preach in England.

All of that was to be expected, and Wilford and Derek went about their business, ignoring it as much as possible. But as it often had in America, the invective and bitterness being spewed from the pulpits stirred up a different kind of problem. Young toughs—"rowdies," as the locals called them—began appearing at the preaching meetings, and more especially the baptisms. The missionaries had come a week ago to Leigh, a small village a few miles out of the town of Gloucester, and had worked there and in the surrounding areas. As usual they had great success, and on Sunday they prepared to baptize ten people. One of the members offered the use of a pool on his property as the baptismal site. But as the preliminary services were drawing to a close, a mob of about a hundred people showed up. Hollering, jeering, threatening violence—they succeeded in frightening the member to the point that he withdrew permission to use the site.

As Derek and Wilford moved off, looking for another place to do the baptisms, the mob followed them, elated with their success. "Where you gonna wash your sheep now, Mormons?" they yelled.

Finally, the mob broke up, and the member, a little chagrined at his previous loss of courage, relented and offered his pool again. Before they were able to finish, the rowdies were back, pouring out a constant tirade of sneers, taunting gibes, and catcalls, but Wilford ignored them and went ahead and was able to baptize nine people, stopping only briefly when the mob threw a yelping dog into the pool.

After continuing their labors in Leigh and the neighboring areas for another three days, Wilford and Derek had moved on and arrived in the village of Hawcross earlier this evening. But the same spirit of opposition followed them. Only here, if anything, the mood was darker, uglier. At the preaching service where the missionaries had spoken upon their arrival, a mob had done what they could to break up the meeting, preventing the people who wanted to be baptized from receiving the ordinance. But among those who believed in Wilford's words, there were some who wanted baptism so badly that Wilford finally agreed to meet them just before midnight. There had been no general announcements. They came as quietly as they could. But somehow, as it always did, word got out, and the rowdies were waiting for them.

Derek counted quickly. They were only shadows against the light of the street lamps, but he estimated there were ten or more—enough to be a serious problem. He turned to Wilford, not wanting the candidates for baptism to see his concern. "What shall we do?" he asked softly.

The Apostle's face was grim but his jaw was set. "Why, we shall baptize them," he said.

They had reached the small pool now, and the jeers and catcalls began in earnest. Derek saw that some of the women were fearful.

"Sister Bundy," Wilford said calmly, reaching out his hand to the nearest one who had asked for baptism. "Shall we proceed?"

She looked around at the mean-spirited faces that half surrounded them; then her chin came up and she nodded. "Yes."

"Go home, Mormons!" "Get out of our town, Americans!" "Leave our people alone!" "Get outta that water!" The mob swore and they cursed as Sister Bundy and then Brother and Sister Rook and Elizabeth Collett were baptized. The rowdies shook their fists in the air. From the slurred speech of some of them, it was obvious most of them had come here straight from the only pub in Hawcross. Derek shook his head. He had seen that enough in Missouri. Take a natural tendency to hate, stir in a generous share of hard liquor, add some encouragement from the local preachers to make it a religious "mission," and you quickly had the recipe for anti-Mormon violence. It worked every time. The one fortunate thing was that courage was typically not a part of the mix. The group hung back, noting that Derek and the other brethren were not backing down.

But the mood of the rowdies was growing more threatening now. As Sister Collett came out of the pool and Wilford called for Benjamin Hill to join him, Derek saw one of the men in back raise his arm. It flashed against one of the street lamps in the distance, and there was a splash of water. "Take that, you blasted Mormons," someone shouted.

Suddenly, arms were swinging everywhere.

"They're throwing stones!" one of the women yelled, throwing up her arms to shield her head. They all turned their backs and held up their arms as rocks came pelting down. A few were larger rocks, but most of them were only about the size of the end of one's thumb. But even that size stung sharply when they hit exposed flesh. The splashes and ripples on the surface of the pool made it look like a rainstorm was going on as the mob targeted the two men in the water, determined to stop the baptism. Derek saw two or three stones bounce off Wilford's body and he flinched in pain. "Hey!" Derek shouted, holding up one arm to shield his head. He stepped forward, angry. This was more than just harassment now. But just then he saw a heavy black object flash against the light from a window. A rock about half the size of a man's fist was arcing overhead. "Wilford, watch out!" Derek called.

Wilford jerked, ducking away. But it was too late. The stone caught him on the back of his head, just above and behind his left ear. There was a solid thud, a cry of pain, and Wilford staggered forward, nearly going down into the water before Brother Hill grabbed him and steadied him. The water was splashing all around them now.

"Here comes the constable!" Derek shouted.

There was a momentary flurry of excitement. "He's lying!" "I don't see no one!" "Let's get out of here."

Behind him, he heard Wilford's voice. "Brother Benjamin Hill, having been commissioned of Jesus Christ. . . ." Stones still rained down into the water.

A rock thudded onto the ground next to Derek, and then the group of rowdies lost heart and fled. In moments, they were alone again.

———◆———

"It's a nasty bump," Derek said, "but the flesh isn't split."

Wilford winced sharply as Brother Kington pressed his finger gently against the lump on Wilford's head. "You'll be smarting for a time, but I think it will be all right," he agreed.

"I'll be fine.

After the baptisms at Hawcross, Wilford and Derek had immediately left to go to the village of Dymock, a distance of about nine miles. In Dymock they went to the residence of Brother Thomas Kington, the man who, until his baptism nearly three weeks before, had been the superintendent of all the United Brethren congregations. It was late, but the Kingtons didn't mind attending to the missionaries for whom they felt so much gratitude and affection.

Hannah Kington was watching anxiously from one corner. "Brother Woodruff, how can you go on with this kind of opposition?"

He turned slowly, then walked to where his coat hung on a chair. He reached and extracted a letter from the inside pocket. He looked at it for a moment, then smiled at their hostess. "This is how, Sister Kington."

Both she and her husband were surprised at that. "What is that?" Brother Kington asked.

Wilford grinned at Derek. Derek grinned back. The letter had come just as they left Leigh to come to Hawcross. "It's from Brother Taylor in Liverpool," Wilford said, "and it contains wonderful news."

"What?" Sister Kington asked.

Wilford was beaming. "They're here!" he exclaimed.

"Who's here?" the Kingtons asked as one.

"The rest of the Twelve. Brigham, Parley, Heber. They're all here." He looked upwards and his eyes closed for a moment. "They're here," he breathed. "They're finally here."

Sometime after midnight, in the early morning hours of April twenty-sixth 1839, seven members of the Quorum of the Twelve Apostles had quietly gathered in the public square of Far West, Missouri. They had come at great risk. Their purpose? To formally begin their mission to England. Now, just twelve days short of one full year after that meeting, once again seven members of the Quorum of the Twelve assembled together. This time it was far across the ocean in a small house in the town of Preston, Lancashire, England.

It was a happy time of reassembly. Friendships and bonds forged in times past were now renewed. News from America was greeted by Willard Richards and Joseph Fielding like water after a drought. In the case of Derek and Matthew, it was a happy family reunion. As part of the gathering, a conference of all members in the British Isles had been called for the fifteenth. Important business would be sustained there. But equally important were the items to be dealt with by the Quorum of the Twelve in private meetings. Brigham had come. It was time to get to the business of running a mission in a foreign land. Thus, in the next three days, between conference and council meetings, numerous items of business were decided on and approved.

The first thing that needed doing was to ordain Willard Richards to the Quorum. The Lord had designated him as an Apostle in a revelation in July of 1838, but at that time he was still in England. Until his fellow Apostles crossed the sea to reach him, he couldn't be ordained. Acting now with the majority of the Quorum present, they ordained Willard, officially giving them their eighth quorum member, a clear majority. As they finished, someone noted that there were more Apostles in England at the moment than there were in America.

Next, the brethren formally sustained Brigham Young as President of the Quorum.

It was unanimously decided to immediately write to America and ask Joseph to send twenty more missionaries.

Various priesthood ordinations were performed, including the calling and ordination of a patriarch "to perform patriarchal blessings on the fatherless."

Brigham Young proposed that arrangements begin immediately to print the Book of Mormon, a hymnbook, and a monthly publication in England, a concept that was greeted with great rejoicing by the Saints. Wilford Woodruff suggested the publication be given the name *The Latter-day Saints' Millennial Star.* Elder Parley P. Pratt was chosen as its editor.

All of that was well and good and important for the work of the kingdom, but something else was to have a far greater and more lasting impact on the Church. To this point, many of the Saints converted during the first mission and the continuing labors that followed wanted to emigrate to America. America was where the Prophet Joseph and the Church were. America was Zion. America was the land of opportunity. For people who suffered extreme poverty and widespread unemployment, America was like a paradise in their minds.

Joseph Fielding had strongly discouraged any emigration. Though he was president of the mission, and therefore the Church's presiding officer in England, he didn't feel that he could approve such a thing without the sanction of the Quorum of the Twelve. But now the Twelve were here. It was their decision.

From the beginning it was not a question of if, only when and how. The Lord had called his people to gather. Currently, they were gathering to Nauvoo. The only thing causing hesitation on the part of the Twelve was considering how to do it wisely. Fearing they might unleash a tide that could not be controlled, the brethren moved cautiously. Those who were ready to leave immediately could do so, they decided, but without making a lot of public announcement about it. No one with means should go without also assisting the poor to do the same. The Church would immediately begin raising funds and preparing the way for others, especially those too poor to get passage on their own.

They were cautious, but there was no mistaking the message. The center of the Church was in America, and if it was at all possible, the British Saints should go to America.

Never one to let grass grow under his feet, two days following the final day of council meetings, Parley Pratt preached to the members in Preston. This time, it wasn't the restored gospel that was the topic of his sermon. This time he spent one hour talking about the *country* in which the gospel had been restored. When he finished, he had one very excited congregation of Latter-day Saints on his hands.

Derek and Matthew walked out with Jenny Pottsworth and her mother. They had barely cleared the hall, when Jenny reached out and grabbed Derek's arm. "Is it really like he says it is?" she burst out.

"Aye," Derek said soberly, "and more. Words cannot fully describe America. Only the eye and the heart can experience it."

Matthew smiled at Derek's eloquence. "England is a pretty wonderful place too," he said nobly, "but America is so big. You can't imagine. For example, Nauvoo is only about a third of the way between the Atlantic and the Pacific Oceans, and yet it is a thousand miles from New York City."

Jenny's eyes grew large. England was an island nation. It was no more than four hundred miles from north to south, not counting Scotland, and there was a place not far north of Preston where the country was less than a hundred miles across. A thousand miles! It was almost impossible for her to imagine.

"But it's more than the land, Jenny," Sister Pottsworth was saying. "It's where the Church is."

"I know, I know." Jenny's eyes were dancing with excitement. She turned to Matthew. "How much did your passage cost?"

"It was eighteen dollars steerage."

"Eighteen dollars?" Sister Pottsworth mused. "How much is that in pounds?"

"Roughly four pounds."

Jenny's face fell as she looked at her mother. "How much do we have saved now, Mum?"

"Barely five."

"Oh." The excitement died in her. They had been saving whatever they could, the both of them, since the day Derek and Peter had left for America. With only five pounds, it would be another year at least, maybe more.

Matthew watched her and felt her disappointment. He liked this pugnacious English girl. Her spunk and zest for life reminded him of his Jennifer Jo in many ways. "Look," he said, "you can't give up hope. Brigham has asked Brother Taylor to go to the shipping lines when he gets back to Liverpool. He expects we'll be sending hundreds of passengers to America. He wants Elder Taylor to negotiate a better price."

"But remember," Derek said, always the realist, "eighteen dollars was just from New York to Liverpool. Then there's the getting on out to Nauvoo. You'll have to either sail around to New Orleans, then go by riverboat up the Mississippi, or get land passage from New York. Either way will take more money."

Matthew acknowledged that with a nod, but pressed on with his point. "But Brigham is asking that those with means help those without. If you have five pounds already, you're better off than many. You won't have to wait as long."

Jenny's eyes brightened again. "Do you really think so?"

Now Derek was nodding, feeling a little guilty for being a wet blanket. He and Peter hadn't waited until they had sufficient means. They had just gone and made it work. His mind was racing now, thinking about the possibilities. "There's a group who want to go immediately," he said. "They've been asking permission to go for some time now. They'll probably leave immediately, by June for sure. There may be others who could go sooner, but Brigham wants to be ready to send a large group by September, a hundred and fifty, maybe two hundred. He's instructed Matthew and me to begin the preparations. Part of our task will be to see if we can raise funds for those who can't pay their own way."

Now Jenny was fairly dancing. "So it's possible that we might be on our way as early as September?"

"Yes," Matthew said eagerly. "You continue to work hard and keep saving your money, and Derek and I will see what we can do to find someone who might help you."

With a squeal of joy, Jenny threw her arms around Matthew. "Oh, would you?" she cried. Then instantly she realized what she had done. Backing away, blushing furiously, she turned to her mother to try and cover her embarrassment. "Wouldn't that be wonderful, Mum? September! Can you imagine that?"

Sister Pottsworth's eyes were shining. She nodded slowly. "September. Yes, let's plan for September."

———— • ————

They had lined up along the railing of the *New Orleans Queen* while the big riverboat was still two miles south of Nauvoo. Now the dark mass of land jutting westward and making the great river detour around it was visible through the rain. There were eleven of them, all told—Nathan and Lydia and their three children, and Carl and Melissa and their four. No one else was out on the deck. The weather was too cold and wet, and no one else seemed to be headed for Nauvoo.

Emily looked up at her father, her cheeks rosy red from the stiff breeze blowing across the decks. "Papa?"

He leaned over so he could be heard over the constant roar of the great paddle wheel behind them. "Yes, dear?"

"Will Grandma and Grandpa Steed be there to meet us?"

"I don't think so, Emmy. They have no way of knowing which boat we'll be on or exactly which day we'll be arriving."

Young Joshua had gone through this same conversation the previous evening with his father. "They may not have even gotten Papa's letter yet," he explained patiently to his sister and the three Rogers boys beyond her. "So they may not know we're coming at all."

"But that's all right," Nathan added. "We don't live far from the boat landing. We'll be there in just a few minutes."

Lydia was peering through the rain. The shore was close enough now that details were beginning to be visible. "Look," she said, tugging on Melissa's arm, "there's the Old Homestead. That's where Joseph and Emma live."

Suddenly Nathan was leaning forward, squinting. "My heavens, Lydia, would you look at that. Look at all those new houses."

She was staring too. Where there had once been only the Old Homestead and a few scattered cabins, now there were a dozen or more homes. Most were log cabins, but here and there were some nicely built frame houses as well. And beyond that, where they couldn't see beyond the trees that lined the banks of the river, there were dozens of plumes of smoke.

Carl was staring out at the approaching city. "You said everyone was moving here as quickly as they could. I guess they need homes." He grinned suddenly, almost shyly. Carl was typically a quiet man and not much given to showing his feelings, but now he couldn't hide the excitement. "And if they need homes, they're gonna need someone to freight in lumber and stuff for them."

Melissa was holding little Sarah, but she reached out with her free arm and slipped it around his waist. "And food and clothing and a hundred other things," she said happily.

"Some of which they'll have to come to the store to buy," Lydia added smugly. "Our store." She laughed merrily, then reached down and scooped Elizabeth Mary into her arms and hugged her tightly. "Oh," she cried, "we're almost home. I think I am even more excited than you children."

An island came between them and the east shore, blocking

their view for a few minutes. Then as they passed it they could see the steamboat landing dead ahead. The roar of the great paddle wheel dropped off sharply, and the ship began to turn slowly to the right, toward the shore.

Then to their surprise, people began appearing. A series of lean-tos had been built at the land's end of the dock to provide some shelter from the weather. Now a dozen or more people were streaming out from behind them, waving and calling out.

Suddenly, Emily was hopping up and down and shouting. "It's Grandpa! It's Grandpa!"

"And there's Joshua and Caroline!" Lydia cried. She grabbed Elizabeth Mary's hand and started waving it wildly back and forth. "And there's Grandma! Do you see Grandma, Joshua?"

"Yes," he called back. He was searching the children's faces. "And there's Savannah."

"And Rebecca and Jessica," Nathan threw in. "Looks like the whole family has come out to see us. Somehow they must have known we were coming today."

Something in his voice made Lydia turn. He was grinning so broadly it looked like it might split his face wide open. "What?"

"That man you saw me talking to last evening when we docked at Warsaw?"

"Yes."

"He wasn't just a salesman come on board to find a buyer. He was one of Joshua's teamsters." He began to laugh, pleased with his surprise. "The family did get our letter. Joshua sent him down there and he's been meeting every boat for the past four days. And I'll bet he had a long, wet ride last night to beat us here and pass the word."

"Look," Lydia said, jerking on Melissa's coat. "There's Joseph."

Melissa leaned forward over the rail. Joseph had been in Liberty Jail when she and Carl had brought the wagonload of food out to the family a year ago last February. That meant she hadn't seen him since the Saints had left Kirtland, over two years before. But there was no mistaking the tall figure. He hung back behind the family, letting them surge forward. His hat was off and he waved it slowly back and forth. "There's Joseph Smith, Carl," she said, pointing. "There in the back."

———◆———

Joseph stayed at the rear of the crowd while the Steed family had their reunion. There were tears and smiles, children dancing around the dock and shouting excitedly, adults shaking hands or embracing warmly. Young Joshua, acting very mature, introduced the Kirtland cousins to their Nauvoo counterparts. Jenny and Kathryn McIntire joined Mary Ann, Jessica, Lydia, and Melissa to cluster around Caroline and the new baby. Joshua began giving Nathan and Carl a quick update on the store and the freighting business until Caroline shot him a dirty look and he said they would take it up after they got home. Mary Ann hugged Carl and gave each of his sons a piece of hard candy. Benjamin, holding Savannah, introduced her to Melissa and baby Sarah.

The riverboat was gone again and almost out of sight upriver before things on the dock finally began to settle down a little. Then Joseph stepped forward. Without a word he swept Nathan up in a hard embrace, pounding him on the back. "Welcome home, Nathan. Welcome home."

He turned to Lydia, taking both of her hands in his. "Sister Lydia, it is so good to have you home again. I was most sorry to hear about your father. He was always a fair and honest man."

Tears sprang to her eyes. How like Joseph not to hold bitterness toward one of his avowed enemies. "Thank you."

"And you?" he asked softly, peering deeply into her eyes. "How are you?"

She nodded quickly, smiling through the tears. "I'm fine, Joseph. I really am fine."

"That's wonderful! Emma wanted so much to come, but as you know the baby is due in a couple of months now and I advised her to stay home."

"How is she doing?" Lydia asked.

"Fine, fine. Don't know whether this one is a boy or a girl, but it's got the kick of an irritated mule," he said proudly.

Now he turned to Melissa. "Dear Melissa." He took her hands now too. "How good to see you again after so long."

"And you, Joseph. It is good to see you again."

"Welcome to Nauvoo." He looked at Mary Ann and smiled. "The whole city heard your mother's whoop when Nathan's letter came the other day saying you were moving out to join us. That was good news for all of us."

"Thank you."

Now he looked up. Carl was standing right behind his wife. "Carl Rogers." Joseph extended his hand. "It's been a long time."

"Yes it has. How do you do, sir?" Carl said, a bit awkwardly, taking Joseph's outstretched hand.

"You are the main reason I came down to meet the boat today, did you know that?"

Carl reared back a little. "I am?"

"Yes." Joseph was very solemn now. "I wasn't here when you and your wife came out from Kirtland last year. But I have heard much about it. I have been hoping that I would have the chance someday to thank you personally for what you did."

Carl was at a loss for words. It was so straightforward, and yet so genuinely meant. "It was . . ." He shrugged. "We wanted to help the family."

"You helped many more people than that. It is a pleasure to welcome a man of such integrity to our city."

"Why, thank you."

Joseph nodded, then turned around to face the group. "Well, I suspect you've got some celebrating to do, and I promised Emma I'd stop and get some bread from the bakery." He gave a cheery wave, then turned and strode off.

"Well, wasn't that nice?" Melissa said, deeply pleased.

"Yes," Carl replied, still watching the retreating figure. "That was very nice."

Chapter Notes

Wilford Woodruff received word of the arrival of the rest of the Twelve on 9 April, the same day as the rock-throwing incident. In Wilford's journal entry for that date, he briefly describes the shower of stones and being hit. He was struck more than once, but the blow to the head was the most serious. Referring to that hit, he writes, "But the Lord saved me from falling & I continued untill I had closed my Baptizing & my mind was stayed on God." (See MWM, pp. 128–29; also CHFT, p. 230.) Nearly all the names of those mentioned as being baptized by Wilford Woodruff in this and other chapters are the actual names for British converts baptized on the days described.

When Caroline walked into the bedroom, she stopped short. Joshua was standing at the full-length mirror. He had on a pair of best-dress trousers and a long-sleeved white shirt. He was adjusting the cravat that he liked to wear when he wanted to dress his best. He saw her face in the mirror and his fingers paused for a moment. "We did some business with Mr. Brunson," he said, noting her startled look, "so Carl thought maybe we should go too."

"Oh." She nodded slowly. When she left to take the children over to Jessica's, he had said nothing about going to the funeral services. She went over to the wardrobe and began unbuttoning her dress. "The children are settled. Kathryn and Peter are going to stay too, so Olivia will really only have to watch the baby. I feel better about that." Charles was six months old now. Caroline had considered taking him, but he did not do well in the humid heat, so she had taken him over to Jessica's and nursed him before leaving. He would be good for three or four hours now.

"The whole family is going?" he asked, finally stepping back and surveying himself. He seemed satisfied.

"Of course."

Seymour Brunson was a relatively young man, not yet forty-one years old, so his death a few days earlier had come as a shock to the community of Saints. Caroline knew him and his wife only through a few visits they had made to the store, but the rest of the Steeds had known him for several years. He had been one of the very early converts to the Church, a priesthood leader, and a longtime laborer in missionary work.

Caroline slipped off her housedress and took out the blue gingham dress that was the coolest thing she owned. It was the middle of August, and it would be midafternoon by the time the services actually started, so it was going to be hot. As she slipped into the dress, Joshua came over to help her since it buttoned up the back. She moved over to the mirror and began to brush her hair as he did so.

"This will be the first time Carl has heard Joseph preach," she ventured. *And the first time you've done so for a long time.*

He grunted, not looking at her.

Caroline and the children were attending worship services almost every Sabbath now, going with the rest of the family. Joshua wasn't particularly pleased by that, but he never said anything openly against it, and she didn't ask him directly in case he said no. Carl didn't go either, but he kept promising Melissa he would when things settled down a little. Since their arrival in Nauvoo four months before, he had been so busy building a house and getting established with Joshua at the freight office that generally he worked every Sunday.

So Melissa and Caroline took their children and went with the family while their husbands found other things to do. At first, Caroline's primary motivation had been to get her daughters attending church. She also liked the association with the family. But then, as the weeks went on, she found herself drawn by the services themselves. She had grown up in a religious home and had attended church regularly until the death of her first husband. She had always enjoyed a well-preached sermon. But she found the Mormon services markedly different. At first they seemed a little less polished, a little less controlled, but she quickly came to appreciate that. She found she liked it when people were spontaneously called upon to pray to open or close the services. Sometimes they stammered a little, sometimes they were frightened, but the prayers definitely came from the heart. Having them read from a prayer book or having the minister read a prepared invocation or benediction did not produce the same feeling for her. She liked having the men of the congregation pass the sacramental emblems rather than just the minister or the leaders of the church.

Most of all she loved to hear Joseph teach the people. And that, she thought, was the best way to put it. Rather than just giving sermons, he taught the people. There were the exhortations to better living, of course, but much more frequently he would pick up the scriptures, select a verse or a chapter or a principle, and begin to expound it. He was clear and yet often profound; he could be precise and yet practical. He did not launch into harangues and try to drive people to change their lives by frightening them with visions of hell or stoking up their guilt to the point that they felt compelled to repent. He would teach a principle, then show how the people could implement that principle in life and how it would bless them if they did.

Mary Ann kept saying that it was the Spirit that she liked, and Caroline didn't dispute that. When Caroline tried to put into words how she felt after Joseph taught, she came up with things like *lifted, inspired, enlightened,* or *joyful, peaceful, comforted.* Paul told the Galatians such things were the fruits of the Spirit, so she supposed that what Mary Ann said was true.

Her head came up as she realized Joshua had finished buttoning her dress and was watching her with a slight frown. "Thank you, Joshua," she said, putting the brush down. She turned, went up on her toes, and kissed his cheek. "I think it's nice that you and Carl would go to honor Mr. Brunson. Your father says he expects half the city will turn out for the memorial services."

Again he grunted, a response she had learned was his way of answering without having to commit to anything. "I'll go bring the buggy around front."

———•———

Benjamin was right. A large group of people turned out in honor of Seymour Brunson. With the summer's heat, Brother Brunson had been buried immediately, but today there would be the services so people could pay their last respects. They met at the grove, a stand of trees at the base of the bluffs which provided afternoon shade and almost a natural amphitheater. It was one of Joseph's favorite places for teaching the Saints.

The Steeds arrived early, and as the men moved over to visit with Joseph, the women took the opportunity to swarm around Emma Smith and the baby. It was her first time out with him in a public gathering.

"What are you going to call him?" Rebecca asked, as Mary Ann took the little boy from Emma and began to rock him in her arms.

"Don Carlos, after Joseph's brother."

"We're so happy for you," Lydia said. For Emma, never one of strong health, there had been enough tragedies in her life with childbirth, so every healthy baby was a blessing of special significance.

Emma reached out and touched Lydia's arm. "Thank you. Nathan told me about your news. That's wonderful."

Lydia blushed a little, but smiled happily. "Yes. We're hoping for a boy too. Right after the first of the year."

"My turn, Mother Steed," Caroline said, holding out her arms. Then, once she had him, she looked at Emma. "He's adorable, Emma. So much like Joseph with that nose and those wide eyes."

She laughed. "Yes, even Joseph says that, and with obvious pride." Then she half turned her head, looking over to where Joseph was standing with Benjamin, Joshua, Carl, Nathan, and several other men, talking quietly while they waited for the rest of the people to assemble. "I see Joshua is with you today, Caroline."

"And Carl too," Melissa broke in. "I was really pleased when Carl said he would like to come. He talked Joshua into it."

"That's wonderful."

"I'll tell you what's wonderful," Mary Ann mused, her eye also on the men. "And that's to have Joseph preach to us so often now."

"Oh, yes," Melissa agreed. "I wish he had done more of that in Kirtland."

Caroline looked a little surprised, and Emma saw it. "It's interesting," she explained, "Joseph has always taught the Saints from time to time, but he used to feel like he wasn't very good at sermons. He'd have Sidney Rigdon or Heber Kimball or Hyrum do the teaching. But since Liberty Jail, that all seems to have changed."

Jessica was nodding now too. "A lot of people have commented on it. It's like he wants to make up for all the times he missed before."

"Yes, exactly. He keeps saying that there is so much that he needs to teach the Saints, there is so much more they need to know."

Jenny didn't want to break in on the conversation, but she gave Caroline an imploring look and held out her hands. Caroline reluctantly handed little Don Carlos over to her. As she did so, Mary Ann spoke to Emma. "He is different since Missouri, isn't he?"

"Yes," she said simply, "he is. Very different."

Caroline chuckled a little. "He was in the store the other day and said he was driving you to distraction. Said you're not used to having him underfoot so much."

Emma's eyes were very soft now. "It has been wonderful. We've had Joseph with us more this past year, except for the trip to Washington, than almost all the rest of our married life. The children can't get enough of him."

"Along with everyone else," Mary Ann said with a rueful

smile. "I can't ever pass your house without seeing a horse and buggy there, or a lineup of people waiting to talk with him."

Emma shook her head, watching Joseph throw back his head and laugh at something Benjamin was saying. There was a touch of exasperation in her eyes, but much love as well. "Yes, that's just part of our life. And if he goes off to do an errand, I can never expect him back very soon, for he is always stopping here or there to talk, or going off to help this person or that."

"That's exactly why everyone loves him," Mary Ann said.

"I know. But it hasn't always been easy for his family. Every-one expects so much more of us. It's like we must be perfect."

Lydia, sensing the sudden downturn in her mood, stepped forward and hugged Emma quickly. Lydia had known Emma even before the Church was organized. They had been close friends now for over ten years. Being the Prophet's wife had not been an easy road, but Emma had borne it with grace and courage and faith. She was a model and a mentor for many of the sisters in the Church. And on more than one occasion, Emma had been the personal inspiration that carried Lydia through some difficult times.

"To me, Emma," Lydia whispered in her ear, "you are pretty near perfect right now."

<hr />

"And thus, brethren and sisters, we pay our last tribute to a good man." Joseph stopped and let his eyes run across the large crowd seated in front of him. "He was a man of faith. With his dying words he bore testimony of the gospel he had embraced." He looked down at the woman and children sitting on the front row. They were Seymour Brunson's family. "Such a man was Seymour Brunson."

People all across the congregation were nodding, and there were several soft murmurs of "Amen." Caroline looked around, a little surprised. She had expected Joseph to say more. It had been a warm tribute to the man, but barely ten minutes had passed since the service had begun. She had hoped for more than that. She looked at Melissa and saw her disappointment as well. She too was hoping for something that would let Carl see Joseph at his best.

And then, to her relief, Joseph turned and took a Bible from Emma's lap. "Now, my brothers and sisters, while we are on the topic of the resurrection, there is something more that I should like to unfold to you. I should like to begin by reading some of the words of the Apostle Paul."

Caroline felt a quick pang of regret. Normally she brought a Bible and a Book of Mormon to the services, but she hadn't thought about needing them for the funeral. Evidently not many others had either, for there were very few who reached for their scriptures.

Joseph opened the Bible, turning slowly until he found his place. "I shall read to you from the fifteenth chapter of the First Epistle to the Corinthians."

Feeling a movement beside her, Caroline turned. Jenny was scooting up beside her. She had a Bible open to First Corinthians, holding it out so they could both read from it. Caroline smiled gratefully at her and gave her a quick squeeze. How fortunate Matthew was, she thought. Jenny was a jewel of rare quality.

Surprisingly, Joseph read nearly the whole chapter to the congregation. This was Paul's great sermon on the resurrection, a chapter that Caroline had always loved. There was no pessimism here, no talk of hellfire, no pounding the sinner into the ground with threats of eternal retribution. Paul just bore powerful witness to the fact that not only had Christ risen from the grave but, through His power, all men would also rise.

What happened next would be talked about around the tables and over the fences and in front of the fireplaces of Nauvoo for some time to come. When he started in First Corinthians, everyone kind of assumed Joseph was going to give a sermon on the doctrine of the resurrection. But as he finished reading the chapter, he handed the Bible back to Emma, leaving it open at his place.

When he turned back, he let his eyes sweep slowly across the assembled body. Finally, his gaze stopped on a woman and three children. He raised one hand and pointed directly at her. "There sits a good widow woman, a woman who not only lost her husband but also had a child die before she joined the Church and could have that boy baptized. 'But, Brother Joseph,' says she, 'how shall my son do? For the Savior himself said that except a man be born of water and of the Spirit, he can in no-wise enter the kingdom of God. And, Brother Joseph, doesn't the word of God, every jot and tittle, have to be fulfilled? How, then, can my son be saved, seeing that he had not baptism?'"

Now, there was a question, Caroline thought. She hadn't thought of it in quite those terms before, but the Savior had been very specific on that point.

Joseph spun on the balls of his feet, turning to directly face the Steeds. "And there sits Lydia Steed. Her father passed away several months ago. He was not a member of the Church."

The family all turned to look at Lydia, but she was as surprised as they were at this sudden turn of direction.

"Suppose Josiah McBride gets on the other side of the veil and finds out that Brother Joseph was really not a false prophet after all, that the angel Moroni did in truth appear to him and give him the gold plates. Suppose Moroni himself meets him and tells him that the Book of Mormon is a true record of God. Would you say that is possible, Sister Lydia?"

She nodded quickly. "Of course."

"Then further suppose that Josiah McBride decides he was wrong in this life and wants to be a member of Christ's church—"

He stopped abruptly, looking around with challenge in his eyes. "Is this so far-fetched, brothers and sisters? Do you not remember what Peter tells us? During the three days that Christ's body lay in the tomb, where was his spirit? Peter says Jesus went to the spirit world and there preached to those that are dead. Why would he preach to people in the spirit world unless people might hear and believe and have a change of heart?"

He jabbed his finger in the direction of the audience. "It is only Seymour Brunson's body we buried a few days ago. Seymour Brunson himself is at this very moment living and walking and talking in the spirit world. And he rejoices in it. Seymour Brunson was a great missionary in this dispensation. How many of you here today are in the Church because Seymour Brunson came to you and preached the gospel to you?"

Caroline turned. A surprising number of hands were up around the assembly.

Joseph chuckled softly. "You who knew Seymour Brunson, what do you think he's doing at this very minute?"

"Preaching the gospel," someone called out. There was a ripple of laughter. If you knew Seymour Brunson, that was the only answer.

"That's right. Peter said that in the world of spirits the gospel is preached to the spirits. Read it for yourselves in the third and fourth chapters of Peter's first epistle. He says that the gospel is preached to them that are dead so they can be judged on the same basis as we who are in the flesh are judged."

Caroline had forgotten Lydia now. She wasn't thinking about how Carl was taking this or Joshua or anyone else. She was staring at Joseph, hanging on every word, the concepts stunning her like blows from someone's hand. Her father and mother were dead now many years. Donovan Mendenhall, her first husband, had succumbed to yellow fever about a year and a half before Joshua had come into her life. She had always believed they were still alive somewhere, in heaven. But she had not thought about that other sphere in such concrete terms before. And yet, it had to be. But if they were alive, then they were really alive—walking, talking, thinking, longing for happiness. The idea of sitting around on clouds for eternity had always been vaguely dissatisfying to her.

Joseph had risen to his full height now, and his voice was thunderous with power. "Can you not understand such simple doctrine! Life does not end with the grave, and if life does not end, then individuality does not end. And if the gospel is preached there, there will be some who hear it and believe it and want to be baptized for the remission of their sins. They know what the Savior taught. They know they cannot enter the kingdom of heaven unless they have been baptized. The Savior himself declared it. He said, 'Except a man be born of water and of the Spirit, he *cannot* enter into the kingdom of God.' So what shall we do?"

Joseph answered his own question by turning and taking the Bible from Emma again. "In Paul's great discourse on the resurrection, we have the answer. Let me read it to you again." He found his place quickly. "Verse twenty-nine. Here is what Paul says. 'Else what shall they do which are baptized for the dead, if the dead rise not at all? why are they then baptized for the dead?'"

He shut the book with a loud pop. "Did you hear that, brothers and sisters? In Paul's day, what were they doing? They were baptizing for the dead." There was a flickering smile and a touch of humor around his eyes. "Please. They were not baptizing dead people. We are not talking about baptism *of* the dead. We are talking about baptism *for* the dead. Yes, my friends and neighbors, those early Saints were being baptized in behalf of their dead ancestors.

"'But, Brother Joseph,' someone cries, 'must I not be baptized for myself? Can someone else do this work vicariously for me? Is acting as a proxy for someone else part of the gospel?'"

He shook his head, suggesting that such questions were very foolish. "Did not the Savior suffer for your sins? Was not that a vicarious work in your behalf? Then why not a vicarious work to perform the necessary ordinances for salvation?

"'But, Brother Joseph,' another cries, 'there is only one verse in First Corinthians that mentions this doctrine and that is but a passing reference. If that is true doctrine, why didn't Paul teach it more clearly?'"

He smiled patiently. "Brothers and sisters, Paul didn't teach that doctrine in its fulness to the Corinthians because he didn't need to. They already knew it. They were already doing it! And so Paul only made passing reference to the practice in order to make his point about the resurrection."

Joseph had to stop because the crowd was buzzing as people turned to their neighbors or family in reaction to Joseph's words. Joshua gave a little snort of disgust. Caroline shot him a withering look and then looked away. She wasn't in a mood for his skepticism at the moment. He just shook his head.

Caroline felt dazed. Now she was vividly remembering something she had not thought about for many years. When she was no more than six or seven years old, she had gone into Baltimore with her parents to hear a famous preacher from Philadelphia. He wasn't from their church but was well known, so they went to hear him preach. In his sermon he had used the very scripture Joseph cited a few moments before, where the Savior said all must be born again. The preacher's purpose was to get the congregation to make a decision to be baptized, and he kept hammering at the fact that the Savior said we must be baptized or we would be damned. To her utter embarrassment and her mother's total shock, after about the fourth time the man shouted that scripture at them, her father suddenly raised his hand. "May I ask a question, Pastor?" he said. Caught off guard, the minister had nodded. Her father then asked, "What about those people who are born into a country where they never have a chance to hear about Christ and therefore cannot choose to be baptized? Are they to be damned too?"

The man instantly bristled. "It is God's grace that chooses those who are blessed to hear the gospel," he snapped. "We do not question God's grace."

"Does God's grace save one man and condemn another based on a whim of chance?" her father asked. She could still remember how calm he was. And that calmness only made the preacher livid. "How dare you question the word of God?" he shouted.

Her father had stood up then, his head high. He had motioned for Caroline and her mother to get up with him. "I don't question the word of God," he said to the preacher. "It's your interpretation thereof that I find completely impossible to swallow." And with that, they had walked out.

For months, Caroline had been so humiliated she ducked down in the carriage every time they went back into Baltimore. Only much later had she come to realize what a profoundly courageous act it had been. When they had walked out of the hall, with people booing and hissing at them as they left, her father had said only one thing, and he said it to Caroline and not to her mother. "Don't you ever believe in a God that would send people to hell based on the accident of their birth."

"My dear brothers and sisters," Joseph went on now, obviously starting to move toward his conclusion. "In the ancient Church they practiced baptism for the dead. With the priesthood keys restored, that practice is also hereby restored. I tell you here and now on this day, you may be baptized for those who have died. The ordinance is exactly the same. You go down into the water. One with authority baptizes you. Only instead of being baptized for yourself, you act as the representative for someone who has died."

Now he turned to Lydia again, and his face was filled with kindness. "'But, Brother Joseph,' some may say, 'how will Lydia Steed know if Josiah McBride wants to be baptized in the spirit world? What if he hasn't heard the gospel, or what if, upon hearing it, he doesn't accept it? Then what?'"

His shoulders pulled back. "You don't worry yourselves about that," he said firmly. "If a person rejects an ordinance performed in his behalf, that is his agency. But since we cannot know who does and who does not, you may proceed where you feel it is best."

He stopped now for the last time. "This is good doctrine, my brothers and sisters. Listen to your hearts and you can tell. It tastes good because it is true."

As he stepped back, Caroline found herself nodding. She sensed that Joshua was glaring at her, but she didn't care. She nodded again. It *was* good doctrine, and she knew that because Joseph was exactly right—it tasted good.

"If you ask me, the whole thing is poppycock!"

Caroline felt a flash of irritation. "Why?"

"Baptizing someone whose body is rotting in the grave."

"Now, there's a nice way to put it," Nathan said dryly. They had all come from the memorial services to Benjamin's cabin and now sat in the shade of the front porch trying to beat the afternoon heat.

Joshua lowered his head stubbornly. "Nice or not, they're dead. This is absurd."

"Don't you just say it's absurd," Lydia said, smiling a little to take any sting out of her words. "Come on, Joshua, be fair. You can't just say it's absurd. You have to tell us why you think it is."

Caroline followed that up swiftly. "That's right. Otherwise, just admit that you don't believe it."

Joshua swung on her, angry that she would confront him in front of the family, angry at the moon-eyed look she had displayed while Joseph talked. "All right. Let's take Lydia's father that Joseph talked about. You never knew Josiah McBride, but we did, didn't we, Nathan? Didn't we, Lydia?"

"Joshua!" Mary Ann warned, watching Lydia closely.

Lydia was calm. "No, it's all right. I asked him to do this. Go on, Joshua."

"I'm not saying anything bad about Lydia's father. He was an honest, hardworking man." There was a momentary grin. "He didn't like me much, but that can't be all bad." Then he was sober again as he looked at Lydia. "Now, you answer honestly, Lydia. How much chance is there that your father is up there right now—wherever 'there' happens to be—saying, 'Glory, hallelujah, Joseph Smith is a prophet'?"

"I don't know."

"Come on, Lydia," he bored in. "How did he feel about Joseph right up to the day he died?"

She nodded slowly. "He thought he was a charlatan and a fake."

"There!" Joshua said, like a cat pouncing on a field mouse. "And you think that the minute he passes on to the next side, all that is going to change?" He spun around to Nathan. "You're the one always quoting that scripture from the Book of Mormon about whatever a person's like in this life goes with him into the next."

Nathan looked a little surprised. Then he laughed. "There's a switch. You're quoting me scripture to prove your point."

That broke the tension in the room a little and Joshua gave him a crooked grin. "Sorry, I don't know what came over me." Then he raised his hands. "Look, I know how you all feel about this. You believe in Joseph. And that's fine. I think Joseph's a fine man, but all this stuff about being baptized for someone who's been in the ground for a hundred years? Sorry."

He turned, looking for support from the only place he was likely to get it. "Does this make the slightest bit of sense to you, Carl?"

To everyone's utter amazement, Carl didn't answer right away. He had been sitting back, content to listen to the conversation, not saying anything either way. Finally, he pursed his lips. "What do you mean by 'make sense'?" When Joshua's jaw dropped a little, he went on slowly. "I guess that depends on another question. Do you believe in the Bible?"

"You know the answer to that," Joshua snapped, feeling betrayed.

"Well, then, no, the whole idea of being baptized for someone who has died is actually quite ridiculous. In fact, if you don't believe in the Bible, the idea of baptism even for a living person doesn't make much sense. I mean, going into the water and having your sins washed away."

"Aha!" Joshua said, mollified somewhat. Melissa was staring at her husband, but Carl seemed oblivious to both of them. "On the other hand," he said, "if you *do* believe in the Bible, as I do, it does kind of make sense in a different sort of way."

Melissa's worry turned to surprise. Joshua's triumph froze on his face. "How so?" he demanded.

"Well," Carl said, thinking it through even as he spoke, "Joseph quoted the Savior correctly. He did tell Nicodemus that unless a person is baptized he can in nowise enter the kingdom of heaven." But he frowned, and shook his head. "I don't know. I'm going to have to think about this one."

Caroline waited three days before she broached the subject. She waited until the baby was down and Livvy had taken Savannah over to their grandmother's and it was quiet in the house. She finished drying the last of the breakfast dishes, then came and sat down across the table from where Joshua was working.

He looked up at her, saw her face, and immediately pushed the ledger book aside.

Her shoulders lifted, then fell again. She tried to meet his gaze, but couldn't quite do it. "Joshua . . . ," she finally started.

He said nothing, just watched her steadily.

"I would like to be baptized."

There was not even a flicker of expression.

"I know how you feel about religion and the Mormons, but . . ." She stopped, groping for a way to make him understand.

If she had seen what was in his mind, she may have stopped altogether, for images from Independence rose up like specters before him. Mormonism had been a major factor—no, *the* major factor—in the disintegrating relationship between him and Jessica. That was one of the reasons he had fought the Mormons so bitterly in Jackson County. He knew that many things were different now. *He* was different now. But these were old wounds. And this was the primary reason why he had resisted moving to Nauvoo to be with his family.

"This isn't just because of the funeral services?" he said, watching her very closely now.

"No. I've been thinking about it for a long time."

"But Joseph's sermon helped you make up your mind?"

"Yes. After I am baptized I want to be baptized for my

mother. I would like Nathan to be baptized for my father and for Donovan."

He looked away and she wanted to cry.

"Joshua, this has nothing to do with my love for you. But I loved Donovan too, once. I don't know if he would ever hear and accept the gospel. Religion was pretty much a surface thing with him. But if he does accept it, I want him to have this chance. I owe him that much."

He started forward, the breath exploding out of him in total exasperation, but then he bit it back. On the day he had gone around with Joseph Smith and watched him heal the sick, Joshua Steed had come to a conclusion. He did not believe what Joseph believed. He wasn't even sure he believed what he had witnessed that day. But there was something there that changed his feelings about Mormonism. It wasn't for him, but now at least he understood to some degree the power it had over people.

He sighed. "And what about the children?"

"I won't tell Livvy what to do. We've talked about it. In some ways she'd like to be a Mormon just because a lot of her cousins and friends are. I told her that's not enough."

He nodded, accepting that. "Do what you want, Caroline," he finally said, more gruffly than he had intended.

Her eyes lowered. "I won't do it if it's going to come between us, Joshua."

He sighed again, fighting back the sick feeling in his stomach. "You know how I feel."

"Yes. And if you say no, I won't."

There was no mistaking the pain it cost her to say that. He watched her, his eyes hooded, his mind churning. "Caroline, you have been very good about not trying to make me act or believe in a certain way. I . . . I guess I'll not be trying to do the same thing to you."

It wasn't all that she hoped for, but more than what she feared it might be. Relief and gratitude filled her eyes. "Thank you, Joshua."

He nodded, then reached out and pulled the ledger book in front of him once more. He didn't look up again as she stood and went into the bedroom, but just as she was disappearing down the hallway, he spoke her name. She stopped. He still wasn't looking up.

"Carl and I have to go to St. Louis and meet with Samuelson on that new cotton crop he's got coming in. Will you at least wait until I get back?"

She felt a little stab of disappointment, but could think of no compelling reason why she shouldn't. "That's fine," she said.

"Thank you." His head was still down as he worked on his figures.

Savannah came through the open door first, running as fast as her little legs could pump. Olivia was right behind her. "Mama! Mama! Papa and Uncle Carl are back!"

Caroline dropped the sewing onto the floor and stood up swiftly. "They are? Where?"

Olivia was puffing. "They stopped at the store to see Lydia and Nathan."

Caroline brushed her apron down and unconsciously reached up to push her hair back. "Go tell Aunt Melissa. I'll get the baby, then we'll go on down to meet them."

Joshua waited for her in the parlor, but Caroline delayed getting the baby down and giving Savannah one last good-night kiss. She had seen it in his eyes the moment they met outside the store and she dreaded having him put it in words. But one could delay the inevitable for only so long. She closed the door to Charles's room quietly, then came down the hall and into the parlor where Joshua was waiting. She stopped just inside the room, watching him closely.

"Come sit down," he said, forcing cheerfulness.

She shook her head. "I'm all right."

He frowned slightly, then seemed to accept it. They were both silent for a moment. Small talk had been exhausted around the dinner table and afterwards.

"Samuelson inquired after you."

"That's nice. Did you give him my best?"

"I did." Again the silence. Then he patted the sofa beside him. "You sure you don't want to sit down?"

"I'm sure." She took a breath. "What is it, Joshua?"

He wasn't surprised. He couldn't hide much from her. "Caroline? I . . ."

She waited.

"I've been thinking a lot about this whole thing."

"What whole thing is that?" The hurt and the disappointment were too sharp inside her for her to want to make it any easier for him.

"Your becoming a Mormon."

"Oh?"

"I won't tell you that you can't," he said, his words suddenly taking an edge that he didn't intend. "I told you that. I won't be forbidding it."

"But?"

He took a quick breath. "But if you're wanting to know what I think, I would prefer that you not be baptized."

"Prefer?" she said, unaware that her fingers were digging into her palms. "Is that all? You would *prefer* that I don't. Not *strongly* prefer? Not command?"

He shook his head, knowing he had run into a full-scale blizzard here. "That's right. If you still want to, you can. But you asked me before how I felt about it. Well, I've thought about it, and I'd pre— I'd rather you didn't."

"Not ever?"

He started a little, then saw the danger. "Just for now," he said lamely.

She nodded, then turned and walked back into the hallway and down to their bedroom.

Chapter Notes

Joseph Smith first formally introduced the doctrine of baptism for the dead while preaching at the funeral service for Seymour Brunson on 15 August 1840. There is no known contemporary text for the discourse, so details had to be provided by the author. However, from Joseph's own comments about that day (see HC 4:231) and from the report of one man who was there, the following items are known: (1) Joseph did read most of 1 Corinthians 15, which contains the reference to baptism for the dead. (2) He pointed to a widow in the audience whose son had died before the family had joined the Church. He then cited the Savior's comments about the necessity of baptism (see John 3:5) and said the widow now had cause to rejoice for her son. (3) He noted that Paul was speaking to a people who understood the principle of baptism for the dead and practiced it. (4) He announced that the Saints could be baptized in behalf of those of their relatives and friends who they felt might receive the gospel in the spirit world. (5) He taught that the plan of salvation was calculated to save all who were willing to keep the requirements of God's law. The man who reported this also described it as "a very beautiful discourse." (See recollection of Simon Baker, in Joseph Smith, *The Words of Joseph Smith*, comp. and ed. Andrew F. Ehat and Lyndon W. Cook [Provo, Utah: Religious Studies Center, Brigham Young University, 1980], p. 49.)

Emma Smith gave birth to a baby boy, whom they named Don Carlos after Joseph's younger brother, on 13 June 1840. He was her seventh child, but only the fourth to live more than a few hours beyond birth.

Sunday, 30 August 1840—London, England

My dear Jennifer Jo,

As you will note from the heading of this letter, I am now in the great city of London, having arrived here a week ago Tuesday last. I am no longer in company with Brigham Young, but have come to England's capital by assignment with Heber C. Kimball, Wilford Woodruff, and George A. Smith. Derek remains behind in Manchester with Brother Brigham to help with the heavy load of running the Church here in England.

There is so much to tell you. I have waited until the Sabbath to write this letter so I have the time to say it all. First, I send my love to you and tell you how much I miss you. I often go to sleep with your face before me. Give my love to Mama and Papa. I will write to them next when there is time.

I shall tell you first about England in general, and London specifically. It is a wondrous place and has greatly expanded my views. It has also made me all the more thankful for America.

The people here are wonderful, in some ways even more warm and giving than those in our country. But conditions are very much worse, especially for the working classes.

We took some time to visit the sights the other day. We went to Buckingham Palace, the Tower of London, and Westminster Cathedral. As you know, Queen Victoria succeeded to the throne just three years ago when she was eighteen years of age. She was married in February of this year. She married her first cousin Prince Albert, who comes from one of the royal families on the continent. Derek says it was announced that she refused to wear anything at the ceremony that was not made in England. The people loved this, and she seems to be restoring a lot of pride among the people for their own country. We had not yet arrived in England by then, but Derek says the whole nation celebrated. She is very much revered by the people.

Anyway, I didn't get to actually see her, but we saw the palace and surroundings. She is surrounded by all the elegance and pageantry of a Roman Caesar. It is almost more than the mind can take in. We saw one of the queen's stables, and I swear, the places where the horses sleep are better than half the beds in London.

The difference in the classes here is shocking to me. The richest live in a manner that is almost impossible to imagine. They own about 80% of all the land in Great Britain and some have annual incomes of 5,000 pounds or more. That would be about 25,000 American dollars. I cannot conceive of such a fortune, but when I see their lavish houses I have to believe. Many own mansions in the city and in the country too.

But most of the people we see are called the "sunken sixth." They are the lowest classes and make up about one-sixth of the people. As we walk the streets of London the contrast between the upper and lower classes is stark and leaves one wondering when Christ will come and set things right again. It is not uncommon to see half-naked, half-starving children running along behind the most splendid chariots, with their liveried footmen and the beautifully matched teams of horses. Beggars are everywhere. You cannot believe the numbers. I have also seen women and children scouring the streets for manure and old cigar butts, which they scoop up and sell by the bucketful to the tanneries. It is a grim way to make a living, but survival drives them to it. Many turn to crime or other vices. Pickpockets are a constant worry in London, and many women—even young girls—are forced into selling themselves away to wicked men who have no morals.

There are taxes of every kind. Brigham says that smoke cannot go up the chimney or light come through the window without someone here trying to tax it. There are taxes for living and taxes for dying. Many of the poor have a difficult time even burying their loved ones when they die. Brigham, who gets quite exercised on this subject, says it would be cheaper for a man to emigrate to America and find a grave there than it is to be buried in Merry Olde England. There is a tax on nearly everything, except perhaps cats, mice, and fleas.

They tell me when winter comes and the weather turns cold, the air becomes almost unbearable. There is a thick black smoke from the factories, the locomotives, the coal-burning stoves, fireplaces, and open fires. Sometimes the air is so thick with smoke that candles are lit at noonday so one can read. A neighbor says on those days he feels like a horse with the heaves. I look not forward to those times.

Well, I shall dwell no longer on such dismal scenes. I mention them only to give you a feeling for this place. The people are bright and cheerful, even in their poverty. And London has many wonderful things that we could use to good purpose in America. I must tell you about something that has come forth since our arrival. We have now, since May, what they call the "Penny Black." It gets its name because it costs a penny and has a picture of Queen Victoria's head drawn over a black background. (This is what you see stuck up in the corner of this page. I thought you might like to see an actual one.) But here is what is most marvelous. The Penny Black is a postage stamp and it has glue on the back of it. Yes, glue. Instead of taking your letter to the postal station and having the postmaster stamp it with the amount, you can just buy a Penny Black. Then when you are ready to mail it, you just lick the back of the stamp with your tongue—it tastes awful!—then stick it on the letter. Then you can just post it by dropping it in a postal box. This is a wonderful convenience, and I hope America someday gets the same idea.

Let me now tell you briefly about the work here. It is a marvelous thing to see what is happening in so short a time. Last month we had a conference in Manchester, which is the Church's headquarters in England now. The Twelve are managing all the affairs here in Great Britain and it is helping immensely. At the conference, it was reported that in England there are now forty-one congregations or branches of the Church, with a total membership of 2,513. Almost 850 Saints have been added since the April conference in Preston, so you can see the work progresses with great success.

On the day of the conference, Parley Pratt received some bad news. He received a letter from his wife in New York City saying that she was ill and too sick to come to England to join him. This was a great blow to him, as he was expecting her arrival at any time. As I told you before, Parley plans to remain in England for several years and was anxious that Mary Ann and his children join him. He was so distraught at the news that the Quorum approved his returning to New York to get her. He left on the next available ship, and we hope to see him before winter sets in again.

Some good news especially for you. Just a few weeks ago, Brother John Taylor and two other brothers sailed for Ireland. They say that one out of every seven people in Liverpool is Irish, so it is not surprising that some of his converts were from your mother country. They persuaded him to go to the Emerald Isle and open the work there. They have already had baptisms. Oh, that your mother might have lived long enough to hear that news!

We spent three weeks in the Staffordshire Potteries and in

Herefordshire on the way down here to London. The work started in both those places by Wilford Woodruff continues forward in a miraculous way. In Herefordshire, on one Sunday we baptized forty people. Since we left Manchester in the middle of July, an additional 250 have joined themselves to the kingdom. What is most gratifying is to know that most of those converted by Wilford's earlier labors are still true and faithful. That is especially true of John and Jane Benbow. The Benbows lent Brigham 250 English pounds to help print the Book of Mormon. They are also paying for the passage to America of more than three dozen people. They are very generous in helping the work.

And that brings me to some other news which will be of special interest to Peter. On September 7th, about two hundred British Saints will be gathered in Liverpool and will board the ship *North America*, which will set sail the next day. Derek has been making all the arrangements, but Brigham has asked that I go to Liverpool to help with the final departure. I will leave in a few days. But here is what you must tell Peter. Among that group will be two people from Preston. I speak of Sister Abigail Pottsworth and her daughter, Jenny. Derek and Peter knew the Pottsworths well before they came to America. You will like them very much, I'm sure. Mrs. Pottsworth reminds me of your mother in many ways. However, you may wish to warn Kathryn about Jenny. I know that even though she is still too young to begin courting, Kathryn has always held fond feelings for Peter and hopes as she gets older that some mutual feelings might develop on his part as well. Jenny is only a year older than Kathryn but is very mature for her age. She and Peter were very close friends before Peter left, and I get a feeling that Jenny may have some hopes of her own when it comes to Peter.

One last thing, then I shall close. Brother George A. is with us here in London, which is a great pleasure to me. He is the youngest of the Twelve—he celebrated his twenty-third birthday in June—and has a wonderful sense of humor. He and I have become fast friends. I give you one example of his personality which should also be of comfort to you, since I, like him, am also a bachelor missionary.

Whilst (you'll notice from my use of that word that I am picking up some habits of speech from the British) on his way to his field of labor last April, he stopped in Manchester and took lodging at Alice Hardman's boardinghouse. He had no idea at that time that the Saints there, especially the young single ladies, took literally the admonition of Paul to "greet one another with a holy kiss." He had just seated himself on a sofa when several young ladies came in, obviously very excited to see the only Apostle who was not married. One of them, "decidedly a little beauty," as George A. describes her, boldly stepped forward and said, "Brother Smith, we want a kiss from you as Paul commands." George A. says that as she spoke thus, the eyes of the other young women "flashed like stars on a clear night."

Feeling very foolish, but determined to stand his ground, George A. firmly told them that kissing young women was no part of his mission to England. Vastly disappointed, they left, and George, with a twinkle in his eye, says they went out and ruined his reputation as a ladies' man in that area. The older brethren commended him for his wise course of action and have further commanded all the missionaries hereafter to follow the same course.

You will be pleased to know that I have never been caught in such a situation and will not be. I have room in my heart for only one "decidedly little beauty" whose eyes "flash like the stars on a clear night," and that is my Jennifer Jo. The journey to Liverpool will be a difficult one, for as we put those Saints on the ship and send them winging across the sea to join you, I will find it very difficult not to stow away with them. I shall not, of course, but it will be a sore temptation.

I will try to write another letter before their departure and send it with the Pottsworths. Till then, I am

Your devoted,
Matthew Steed

"Hey," Jiggers said, biting deep into an apple, "don't it feel good to be back where you can understand the language again and get something decent to eat?"

Will had his face buried in half a cantaloupe. He pulled back, wiping at the dripping juice with the back of his sleeve, then looked at the bosun of the *Bostonia*. They weren't back in America yet, but Jiggers was right. Being back in England was a welcome relief after a dozen ports of call where as many languages were spoken. But he only pulled a face at his shipmate. "I'd agree with the thought of something decent to eat. The language I'm not so sure of."

The woman who had sold them the fruit was watching the two sailors closely. She was an old crone and had been testy from the moment they had approached her stall. Now she shook her finger at them. "Ah, gawahn! Ya got a lot a cheek, you Americans. Yer not so easy to listen to yerselfs."

"Cheek?" Will whispered out of the corner of his mouth, trying not to smile.

"Yeah," Jiggers replied. "It means . . ." His face screwed up, trying to find an adequate word.

"It means impudent," she cawed. "Rude. Insolent. Now, be aff wit ya."

Will was chuckling as they moved away. It was good to be back even this far. It had been over a year since they left Liverpool and turned south for the long run around Cape Horn and on to China. And most important, after a few days here for replenishing stock and maybe filling up the last of the cargo bins, they'd be off for America. Another month or two and he'd be back in Savannah, seeing his mother.

Jiggers suddenly reached out and grabbed Will's arm. "Look, there's Mr. O'Malley."

Will looked up and spotted the first mate immediately. He was waving at them to come to him. "What gives?" Will growled. "We've just barely started our shore leave."

Jiggers just shook his head and they moved across the marketplace to where the officer was waiting.

"There's been a slight change of plans," O'Malley announced

without preamble. "The captain wants all crew members to meet at the shipping office." Seeing their disappointment, he laid a hand on Will's shoulder. "Shouldn't take long. Then you'll be free again."

The *Bostonia* carried a crew of twenty-eight. Five or six had scattered more quickly than Will and Jiggers, and so O'Malley had not been able to find them. But even with some missing, it was still too crowded in the office of the American shipping lines for all of them, so Captain Sperryman simply moved them outside and into an alleyway where it was somewhat quiet.

He waited until they were gathered in tightly around him, then began. "Men, I think Mr. O'Malley has already told you there's been a change of plans."

He had, but he hadn't said what, so a low rumble broke out among the group as they responded to the captain's words.

"I've been given a new ship, and a new cargo."

Now the murmur turned into cries of surprise and dismay.

"That's right," Sperryman said more loudly. "A new ship. It's the *North America*. It's just come across from New York and they've asked me to bring it back. I'll be giving the *Bostonia* to another captain. The *North America* is a larger and faster ship than ours, and I've been given permission to keep most of you as crew."

He let that sink in for a moment, then raised his hand. They quieted quickly. "The one good thing is, we'll be boarding the ship on the seventh, three days hence, then striking sail on the eighth. That's a week sooner than the *Bostonia* leaves. I don't know about you, but after eighteen months at sea, every day we save getting home is a blessing twice over."

"Amen!" someone grunted. "Glory be!" shouted another.

Will poked Jiggers. "I'd say every day saved is a blessing *ten* times over. I'm ready!"

Jiggers nodded, then turned back to the captain. "Question, Cap'n."

"Yes, Jiggers?"

"What's the cargo?"

The captain smiled. "Mormons."

Will stiffened as if he had been struck from behind by a loose spar.

"Mormons?" Jiggers drawled, looking puzzled. "What's that?"

"Not 'What's that?'" Sperryman laughed. "'What's them?' It's some kind of a religious group. We'll have two hundred passengers—all of them Mormons—and we'll be carrying them across to America. The whole lot of them are leaving England for good."

"But what's a Mormon?" someone else called out.

Sperryman shook his head. "Don't ask me. Ask Steed. He knows what Mormons are all about, don't you, Steed?"

But Will wasn't there. Sperryman turned in surprise. Half running, half stumbling, Will was just reaching the end of the alley. He plunged into the street, not looking back.

———————◆———————

"I don't understand this, Steed. These are English Mormons. They've never been to America. They didn't have anything to do with the death of your father."

Will stood at attention and stared at the bulkhead over the head of the captain. "Sir," he said again, "I would like to request permission to stay on as crew for the *Bostonia*."

The captain sighed in frustration. "Even though it means staying here a week longer? Maybe more?"

"Sir, I would like to request permission to—"

Sperryman slammed his fist down against the desk in his cabin. The inkwell jumped half an inch. So did Will. "Confound it, man! I want to know why."

"Sir, I have deep feelings about this religion and the people who are foolish enough to join it. I want nothing to do with them."

"And you feel so strongly about it that you are willing to leave this crew?"

"Yes, sir, I do. I'm sorry, sir."

Tipping back in his chair, Sperryman shook his head. "Well, let me tell you something, mister. The captain who's taking over our ship is fairly new. The company's worried about me taking all the experienced crewmen away from him, and so—"

"A good reason for me to stay on with him, sir," Will cut in.

"And so," Sperryman said again, his eyes hardening in warning, "I have agreed to send O'Malley as first mate with the new captain."

"You have?" That would be a disappointment for Will if he ended up not getting permission to stay on the *Bostonia* as well. Will liked O'Malley very much.

"Yes. That means I'll be making Jiggers first mate on the *North America*."

"Oh, good." And then the implications of that hit Will.

"That's right," Sperryman said, almost smiling now. "I'll be needing a bosun. And you're it."

Will started, gaping at the man. Sperryman had promised him he'd do that someday, but Will hadn't dreamed it would come this quickly.

"That's right, mister. I know people are going to think I'm crazy." He looked at the ceiling. "A sixteen-year-old as bosun." He looked back at Will. "But I have no choice. Permission to stay with the *Bostonia* is denied. Dismissed."

Dazed, thrilled, bitterly disappointed, Will turned away. As he reached the door, Sperryman spoke again. "Will?"

He turned back. "Yes, sir?"

"These Mormons have booked passage all the way to New Orleans, then they'll go upriver to wherever the Mormons are. That means we'll be stopping at Savannah. You won't have to find your own way down there from New York."

"I can find my own way, sir," he said stubbornly.

"Will," Sperryman said, shaking his head, "your mother is waiting for you, son. She's been waiting nearly two years now. Don't make me throw you in that storage locker again to get you back to her."

Will let his breath come out in a long, slow exhalation.

"No, sir," he finally said. He spun around and reached for the door, but again he stopped, this time not turning around. "Sir?"

"Yes?"

"With your permission, sir, I know the crew is not allowed to mingle with the passengers except for the officers."

"That is correct."

"Am I considered an officer?"

"You are, yes." He smiled. "Younger than most, but yes."

"I'll not be taking that privilege, sir, if it's all right with you."

Sperryman grunted, his face expressionless. "That's your affair, Steed."

"Thank you, sir."

<hr/>

Abigail Pottsworth began to cry as she threw her arms around Derek's neck and kissed him on the cheek. "Good-bye, Derek. We shall count the minutes until we can see you again."

"Good-bye, Sister Pottsworth. Remember now, the moment you step off that boat at Nauvoo, you give Peter a great big hug from me."

"I will. I will."

Matthew turned to Jenny and started to stick out his hand. He stopped, dumbfounded. Jenny Pottsworth was crying too. Jenny Pottsworth, who was so sure of herself, so controlled. Not sure how to deal with that, he fumbled awkwardly for his handkerchief, then thrust it toward her. She took it with an angry little jerk. "I'm sorry," she snapped. "I don't know what's the matter with me. I never cry."

Matthew smiled. "It's all right, Jenny. You're leaving your home. You're leaving your country, probably for the last time. It's all right to cry."

She wiped her eyes, then shoved the handkerchief back at him. "I never cry," she said again, sniffing away the last of her emotions. Now she stuck out her hand.

Matthew took it and shook it firmly. "Have a safe voyage."

She didn't let go. The tears were swimming along the bottom of her eyes again. "I know what Brother Brigham says about the practice of kissing the missionaries, but I think one farewell kiss on the cheek would be all right, don't you?"

The answer came, but not from Matthew. Brigham Young and Willard Richards were just passing behind them, walking with John and Jane Benbow. Brigham paused, smiling. "The answer is yes, Sister Pottsworth, *if* the kiss is only on the cheek and of considerable brevity."

"Thank you, Brother Brigham," she murmured. She went up on her toes and brushed Matthew's cheek with her lips. "Good-bye, Matthew."

"Good-bye, Jenny," Matthew said awkwardly. This had really caught him off guard. He was five years her senior. He raised a hand, blushing somewhat. "Godspeed."

"Better get aboard," Brigham called out, looking down the line of people moving slowly toward the gangplank. "They want all passengers aboard so they can assign them berths."

Derek gave Jenny a quick hug. "Good-bye, Jenny. Promise that you'll give our love to all the family."

She picked up her case. "We will," she cried, getting into line behind her mother and moving off. "We will."

Brigham came back down toward them, then stopped. "Derek?"

"Yes, Brother Brigham?"

"Willard and I have decided we shall stay on board the ship tonight with our members and then ride out with the steamer tomorrow. We shall be back when the steamer returns."

Derek nodded. "Would you like us to wait for you, or go on back to Manchester?"

"Oh, I think go on back. We won't be back until late tomorrow afternoon or early evening."

"We'll do it."

———•———

Will Steed deliberately stayed on the starboard side of the ship, as far away from the dock area and the gangplank as he could. When the first of the passengers came up the gangplank and looked around in bewilderment, he curtly showed them the way to the steerage compartment, then turned his back on them. They were queued up, as the English would say, and would follow each other down to the berths without someone nursemaiding them the whole way. He saw the men in suits—obviously some kind of leaders—come aboard and go directly to talk with the captain. One seemed vaguely familiar to him, but he shrugged that off. He had been to Far West enough times, but he knew no Mormons here in England. Backing away, he found something to keep himself occupied.

As the emigrants streamed aboard, he listened to their mindless chatter with growing irritation. They were so filled with excitement. He heard the word *Zion* two or three times. A husband and a wife were going on about what they would do when they first saw Joseph Smith. The awe in their voices sent shivers of horror up and down his spine. They were like sheep lined up for the shearer, and rejoicing in being taken.

Down deep, Will knew he was being irrational and unfair. After all, he had found out in that St. Louis warehouse that it wasn't the Mormon Danites who had killed his father and burned their house down. But once seeds of hatred got planted in the soul, they easily flourished, and rooting them out wasn't all that simple. And it was the whole Mormon situation which had led his father to his death. It didn't much matter who actually pulled the trigger.

"Hey there, missy, look lively now. Watch your step there."

Will half turned. He needn't have. That honeyed voice could belong to only one person. John Wolsey, barely twenty and one of the younger deckhands, fancied himself to be quite the ladies' man. He was always off the ship and looking for the nearest brothel before the anchor had fairly settled in whatever harbor they were in. Will didn't like him and he didn't like Will. But now Will was the bosun, and directly over John Wolsey in authority.

He started to turn away again, then stopped. Wolsey had singled out a young woman carrying a small trunk that was obviously heavily loaded. She was staggering slightly with the weight. Wolsey had come to stand beside her. At that moment, she turned to look at her would-be helper. Will couldn't help himself. He simply stared at her. She was about his own age, maybe a little younger, and very lovely. Long flaxen hair that now, in the sunlight, looked like spun gold. Wide blue eyes that surveyed the ship with open curiosity. A slim waist. Very pleasant features. She smiled and her whole face was transformed into something totally enchanting. With an effort, Will pulled himself away, his brow lowering. She was also a Mormon.

"Here." Wolsey was positively oozing now. "Let me help you with that case. What's your name, missy? John Wolsey at your service, ma'am."

Will spun around, the anger exploding inside him. He strode across the deck. Wolsey's back was to Will as he reached out and took the trunk from the girl's hand. Coming up right behind him, ignoring the startled look on the girl's face, Will leaned over until his mouth was right next to the deckhand's ear. "Drop that trunk, mister!" he snarled.

Wolsey jumped, and the trunk fell to the deck with a heavy crash.

"Ow!" The girl fell back, hopping about and holding her leg. The case had caught her a glancing blow, and Will saw that there was a small tear in her dress. He felt a momentary stab of guilt, but bored in on Wolsey. "You've got work to do, Mr. Wolsey. Now, hop to it, or take the midnight watch for the next three weeks."

Wolsey was backing away, head down in the face of Will's fury. "Yes, sir. Aye, sir." He turned and fled.

Will turned back, and picked up the trunk. He thrust it toward the girl, whose face was twisting with the pain. "Sorry," he said curtly. Then he couldn't help but add, "Passengers handle their own baggage on this ship."

He saw the shock in her eyes, then the anger. She dropped her hands to her side, refusing to take the case back from him.

Her mouth set into a tight line and the blue eyes darkened. An older woman right behind her came up beside her. "Jenny, what's the matter?"

Will wasn't about to play games with her. He set the trunk down heavily and spun on his heel. He got only about four steps away. "I *was* handling my own baggage," she snapped. "Thank you very much for getting my trunk back from *your* crew."

He didn't stop or turn around, just stalked away. Two other members of the crew had watched the whole thing and were staring at him in amazement. He shot them one blistering look and they hurriedly turned back to their work as he walked by.

——•——

The sun was well up in the eastern sky as they finally approached the mouth of the river and the steamer started out into the open sea. The passengers, still bubbling with excitement, were mostly on deck now, lining the rails and pointing things out to one another. With little to do until they got under way on their own power, Will stayed aft, near the back of the ship, trying to keep busy. Now he was re-coiling rope into neat stacks. *Let them have their excitement*, he thought grimly. The first of the Atlantic swells were already starting the boat slowly rocking. *Get out to sea and we'll see how excited they are.*

His hands stopped moving over the ropes as he saw a figure break away from the railing. It was the girl. She was looking around, as if searching for something. He ducked his head quickly as she saw him. He kept his head down and concentrated on the task, but out of the corner of his eye he saw that she was coming straight for him. He nearly dropped the rope and walked off, but he was already feeling guilty. He had treated her very badly, and he knew it was simply his way of taking out his frustrations. So he straightened slowly and waited.

She walked right up to him without hesitation. He winced inwardly as he saw that she limped slightly. "May I speak with you, sir?"

He glanced around, looking in the direction of the captain.

"It's all right," she said dryly, "I've already spoken with the first mate and have his permission." The blue eyes were crackling with a touch of fire now.

His eyes widened perceptibly. "You have?"

She nodded, quickly and curtly. "I have."

"I . . . I'm sorry about what happened. I didn't mean to make him drop that case on you."

Somewhat mollified by that, her mouth softened. "I see," she said. Her accent was rich and totally British. "And just what *did* you mean to do?"

"Wolsey knows better than to bother the passengers. He was out of line."

"And that was all?"

"Of course. What else would there be?" Will watched her closely, even while his mind was racing to keep up with her, thinking again how absolutely enchanting she was.

One hand came up and rested on her hip, and she cocked her head slightly. "It had nothing to do with the fact that I am a Mormon?"

He rocked back.

Now she went on the attack. "That's right. I've already been told by three different crew members that you're a Mormon-hater."

He swore under his breath. Wolsey probably led the pack on that one.

"Do I know you?" she asked, very cold now.

"No, I—"

"Have we ever even so much as seen each other before?"

He smiled lamely. "No, I would have remembered that for sure." It was an attempt at reconciliation, but it was like pouring water on a hot rock.

"Then I'd suggest you withhold judgment on me until you get to know who and what I am. I don't like blind prejudice."

She turned and stalked away. Irritated by her imperious

manner, Will struck back. "I don't have to know you to know what the Mormons are. And I don't care much for what you believe in or what you stand for."

She whirled around, her eyes blazing. "Oh, really? Well, you know what I think? I think you don't care much for anything. I think you are a rude young man who acts like his whole world is this sailing ship and doesn't know the least thing about anything else. I pity anyone who lives in so small and so blind a world."

Her skirts twirled around her as she spun and started away again.

"Steed!"

Will turned. Behind them, up near the wheelhouse, Jiggers was leaning on the rail watching them. He was grinning wickedly, which told Will he had heard every word.

"Yes, sir," Will barked, not amused. It was Jiggers who had told the girl she could seek him out.

"Cap'n says we'll be cutting loose from our escort in about half an hour. I want you to have the men ready to take in the lines and see that they are secure."

"Aye, sir."

Will turned back, burning inside, then stopped short. The girl hadn't left. She was staring at him, her mouth slightly open.

"What!" he snapped, in no mood for more of her lashing tongue.

"He called you Steed?" she said slowly.

"Yes, that's my name."

She started to say something else, then shook her head, as if dismissing something from her mind.

"What?" he said, more curious now.

"What's your first name?"

Puzzled by her sudden interest, he shrugged. "Will. Will Steed."

Her eyes widened, then again she seemed to shake it off. "You wouldn't ever happen to be related to a Matthew Steed?"

Now his mouth dropped open. "Matthew Steed?"

"Yes, from America. From Illinois?"

He started to shake his head, surprised at the sudden lurch he had felt. "No, I have an uncle named Matthew Steed, but he is from the state of Missouri."

Her hand flew to her mouth. "No! It couldn't be!"

He took two steps toward her. "What? What is it? Do you know Matthew?"

"Were you sold as a sailor and sent to China?"

His eyes registered his shock. "Yes, but . . . we've just returned from Canton. But how did you know?"

"Oh, my," she breathed, her eyes wide.

He stepped closer and stood directly in front of her now. He almost reached out and took her by the shoulders. "What? Do you know me?"

Her hand came down from her mouth, and any trace of anger and animosity was gone. "Derek and Peter Ingalls? Do those names mean anything to you?"

"You know Derek and Peter! How is that possible?"

She was shaking her head, as stunned as Will. "You're *that* Will Steed."

"How do you know Derek and Peter and Matthew?" he cried, wanting to shake her.

"But I was just with them," she breathed. "Last night. On the dock. They were helping us board. I can't believe you didn't see them."

"On the dock? You mean in Liverpool?" He was talking like a drunken man, staggering under the shock of her revelations.

Then suddenly her eyes grew very wide. "Then it's your father . . . ," she said, barely audible. "Oh, my heavens!"

"My father?" Will croaked. "What about my father?"

"You still think he's dead."

His face went ashen. "What . . . what do you mean?" he stammered.

Tears filled her eyes but she was laughing through the tears.

She reached out and grabbed his hand. "Will Steed, I want you to come and meet my mother. She knows the whole story better than me."

He hung back as she pulled on his hand. "What story?"

"Your father is alive, Will. Your father is alive."

———◆———

Captain Sperryman tipped way back in his chair, pulling at his lip. "Well, we could send you back with the steamer. That way you'd get to see your uncles and learn the whole story. On the other hand, I'd be out a bosun and you would have to wait another week before you sail. I'm sure O'Malley would be pleased to have you crew with him on the *Bostonia*, but. . . ."

Will let him muse. His thoughts had been running down many of those same paths.

"I'd be hard put to do without you, Will," the captain was continuing, "but I know what this must mean to you. If you want to go back to Liverpool and find your relatives, I won't stop you."

Will kicked himself mentally for the hundredth time. If he hadn't been so stubborn and deliberately stayed on the starboard side of the ship, away from the boarding Mormons, he might have seen them. "I—"

"On the other hand," the captain went right on, "if you stay with us, you could go with the group all the way to New Orleans, then upriver to where your parents are."

Will had thought of that too. He lifted his head, then pulled his shoulders back. "My father and mother are waiting for me. I'd best get there as quickly as possible."

"I agree," Sperryman said, obviously pleased.

"Thank you, sir, for even considering it."

"You're welcome, Steed. I'm very happy for you."

"Thank you, sir." He stood.

"Steed?" The captain was grinning now. "That Pottsworth girl is quite the girl."

Will didn't smile. "I'm afraid I've not made much of an impression on her."

Sperryman only grunted, then his voice went gruff. "Just see to it that you keep your mind on your work, Steed. Understood?"

Now it was Will who grinned. "Aye, aye, sir."

Chapter Notes

The details about England and London and the economic conditions of the time as mentioned by Matthew in his letter are authentic and come from contemporary sources (see MWM, pp. 12–16, 161–62, 181–90). Other details mentioned in the letter and elsewhere in this chapter—such as Parley's return to America, John Benbow's generosity in giving money, Brigham and Willard's boarding the ship to pass the night with the departing group of Saints, and George Albert Smith's "kissing" experience—are also historically correct (see MWM, pp. 159, 169, 172, 181).

John Benbow and his wife, Jane, sailed on the *North America* with the group of two hundred mentioned in this chapter. Brigham was greatly concerned that before the Benbows left for America, he had not been able to repay them the 250 English pounds that they had lent the mission for publishing the Book of Mormon. Prior to leaving, John Benbow signed a note relinquishing his claims on the debt. (See MWM, pp. 172–73.)

The first adhesive postage stamp in the world was introduced in England in May 1840 while the missionaries were there. Ironically, it was invented by an American who printed bank notes for the Crown. (See James Trager, *The People's Chronology: A Year-by-Year Record of Human Events from Prehistory to the Present*, rev. ed. [New York: Henry Holt and Co., 1992], p. 428.)

They were four days out before Will saw the girl's mother alone. He was off duty and dawdling around at the bow of the ship where he could see the passengers come out on deck. The girl and her mother came out every morning and afternoon except when the weather turned rough. Sometimes the girl came out alone, but then Will stayed out of sight. It would be a long voyage, and if there was anything Will had learned in the past two years, it was patience.

Now it paid off. The woman was alone. He moved swiftly aft, then cut across at midship and came up behind her at the railing. "Mrs. Pottsworth?"

She turned in surprise. "Oh, good morning, Mr. Steed."

"Good morning."

"You're not on duty this morning?"

"Not till third watch."

"Aye." She turned and looked forward, watching the prow of the ship nose into the waves, then shoulder them aside with a spray of salt water. "It's a glorious day, eh?"

Will nodded, and took a quick breath. "Ma'am, may I speak with you for a moment?"

"Of course." She turned to him and gave him her full attention.

"You know that shipboard rules forbid fraternizing with the passengers?"

"No, I didn't know that."

"On pain of five lashes."

"Oh, dear. Are you going to get in trouble?"

"No. Officers have more latitude, and I've also spoken with my captain and got permission. But I wanted you to know that I'll not be speaking much with you on the voyage, and I didn't want you"—he looked around quickly—"or your daughter to think I am ungrateful for what happened and what you told me."

"We don't." She smiled warmly at him. "Jenny didn't sleep well last night, so she's napping at the moment."

"I know, but . . . well, she tried to speak with me the other day, and I suppose I was a little abrupt with her, not wanting the crew to think I was taking liberties and all that. I think I offended her." Then, irritated that he was even trying to explain, he changed tacks. "Are you sure my family is in Illinois? I left my mother in Savannah. That's a long way from Illinois."

Mrs. Pottsworth was a plump lady with kind gray eyes and with wrinkles around the corners of her mouth from a ready smile. Now she looked a little distressed. "I wish I had paid closer attention to all what Derek was telling us, but at the time I had no idea . . ." She shrugged at him helplessly.

"I know, I know."

"But the part about Nauvoo, of that I am perfectly sure. Derek and Matthew told us all about the family so we could look them up when we arrive. I have a letter to Matthew's mum and dad to introduce us. It was while he was telling us about the family that Derek told us the story about a nephew who thought his father was dead and how he was shanghaied away to sea."

"And my father and mother are in this place called Nauvoo too? Not just my grandfather and grandmother? You're sure he said that?"

"Yes, positive."

"Good." He looked around, getting nervous now. "I'll be staying on as crew with whatever ship you take from New York to New Orleans, but once we get there, I'll be quitting the sailing business and going north with you if that's all right."

"That would be wonderful."

"Do you think your daughter would mind?"

She laughed. "Don't let Jenny get your goat, now. She was a little miffed at your unwillingness to speak with her, but that's just Jenny."

"Well, thank you."

The corners of her mouth pulled down a little. "Derek says if we're too late, we may have to winter over in New Orleans or go by land. He says the river gets choked with ice."

Will calculated quickly. "We'll be in New York in a little over two more weeks. It will take a day or two there to replenish our stores, then say another two weeks to New Orleans. That would make it about mid-October. That's too early for river ice, so we should be—"

"Hello, Mum, what's this?"

Will spun around. Jenny was walking toward them. She was frowning heavily, looking at her mother and ignoring Will completely.

"Mr. Steed here, he was just telling me about our river trip."

"I suppose he's an expert on riverboats too, just like he is on Mormons," Jenny said saucily.

Will winced. "Begging your pardon, ma'am," he said to Mrs. Pottsworth, "but I'd best get back. Thank you for the information."

"You're welcome. We're glad you'll be going all the way with us."

"Oh, yes," Jenny sniffed, "I don't know how we'd make it without you."

But Will had already spun on his heel and was heading aft, putting as much of the ship between him and her as possible.

Though it was now mid-September, the morning sun was already getting hot and the air was humid and heavy. Mary Ann Steed was openly worried as she and Benjamin hurried along. Word had come just a few minutes before that Father Smith was critically ill. "It's this thing with the Missourians," she muttered angrily. "It's those Missourians coming after Joseph and Hyrum again. That's what's done it. It was Joseph and Hyrum's arrest in the first place that sent Father Smith to his bed. Remember? He's never fully recovered."

Benjamin nodded grimly as they turned eastward onto Water Street. They had thought Missouri was behind them, but then a few weeks before, four brethren had been unexpectedly captured and ferried across the river by several Missourians. They bound the men, stripped them naked, beat one, hanged another until he was nearly strangled, and in all ways treated them shamefully. Two of the brethren finally escaped a few days later, but two were still in a Missouri jail.

Next, rumors started flying that Governor Boggs had issued a warrant for the arrest of Joseph and Hyrum. He was under tremendous pressure for letting his famous prisoners escape, and rumor said he was going to extradite them back to Missouri for trial. A few days before, the possibility became real enough that Joseph and Hyrum went into hiding and Father Smith went to his bed again, his aged system unable to withstand another such threat to his sons.

Benjamin fingered the bottle of quinine in his pocket. He was pretty sure Father Smith's problems were not caused by ague, but as Mary Ann said, they had to do something to help.

"Why can't they just leave us alone?" Mary Ann burst out. "They drove us from the state—isn't that enough?"

Benjamin reached out and took her hand. "They're not going to get them, Mary Ann. We're in Illinois now. Joseph has already appealed to Governor Carlin, and he'll not tolerate this criminality for one moment."

She sighed, hoping it was true, but feeling a great sense of dread. If Joseph and Hyrum had come out of hiding, which was what the boy who brought the news to them had said, then the danger was only increased. And Father Smith must be very bad indeed. "He's sixty-nine, you know," she said, the worry twisting her voice. "He can't keep taking this time after time."

"I know," Benjamin replied glumly. "That is a great concern."

The moment Emma opened the door, Mary Ann knew that it was worse than they feared. Emma's eyes were red and her cheeks tearstained. Mary Fielding Smith, Hyrum's wife, was crying quietly in one corner. Lucy, Joseph's youngest sister and just recently married, was sobbing uncontrollably. Mother Smith looked terrible. Her normally boundless energy was drained. Her face showed the depths of her exhaustion. Joseph came out of the bedroom and thanked them profusely. Through the door they could see Samuel and Don Carlos and the others gathered.

Benjamin took the bottle from his pocket and held it out to Joseph. "We don't know if this will help, but we wanted to do something."

Joseph took it, then laid a hand on Benjamin's shoulders. "Thank you," he said. "How wonderful to have friends such as you in times like this."

"If you need anything else," Mary Ann said, "just send word. You know where we are."

"Thank you," he said again, the weariness showing in his eyes.

Mary Ann gave Mother Smith a quick hug. "We'll be praying for him," she whispered.

Mother Smith nodded, numb. "I'm afraid that's all there is to do now."

Father Smith was on the bed, lying nearly motionless. His face was pale and gray. His hands, lying on his breast, trembled noticeably. Hyrum sat on a chair next to him, holding his hand. They were talking quietly. All of the children and their spouses and children were there except for Catherine and her family, who lived in Plymouth, about forty miles southeast of Nauvoo, and one of the sons-in-law, Arthur Millikin. Catherine was detained because her husband was sick, but circumstances being what they were, Arthur had been sent after her and her children.

Father Smith turned. Though his face was gaunt and ashen, his eyes burned like two coals of fire in his face. They were alert and filled with intelligence. "Mother," he called.

Lucy Mack walked swiftly to his side. "Yes, Father Smith." She reached down and took his other hand.

He rose up slightly, looking around the room, then at her. "Mother, do you not know that you are the mother of as great a family as ever lived upon the earth? The world loves its own, but it does not love us." He had to stop for a moment to catch his breath. "It hates us because we are not of the world. When I look upon my children, and realize that although they were raised up to do the Lord's work, yet they must pass through scenes of trouble and affliction as long as they live upon the earth. I dread to leave them surrounded by their enemies."

Hyrum leaned forward, grasping his father's hand to his breast. "Father," he cried, "if you are taken from us, will you not intercede for us at the throne of grace, that our enemies may not have so much power over us?"

His father fell back, his chest rising and falling. Finally he nodded slowly. "Come closer, son. I should like to leave a blessing with each of my children."

Scooting the chair even closer, Hyrum inclined his head. The long hands and slender fingers came up and rested on the head of Father Smith's oldest living son. "My son, Hyrum," he began, his voice slow but firm, "I now seal upon your head your patriarchal blessing, which I placed upon your head before, for that shall be verified. In addition to this, I now give you my dying blessing. You shall have a season of peace, so that you shall have sufficient rest to accomplish the work which God has given you to do. You shall be as firm as the pillars of heaven unto the end of your days. I now seal upon your head the patriarchal power, and you shall bless the people. This is my dying blessing upon your head, in the name of Jesus Christ, amen."

The hands came down and Hyrum straightened. "Thank you, Papa," he cried in a choked voice.

Father Smith turned until his eyes found Joseph. Hyrum stood and stepped back, and Joseph took his place. Again the aged hands came up, then rested on Joseph's head.

"Joseph, my son, you are called to a high and holy calling. You are even called to do the work of the Lord. Hold out faithful and you shall be blest, and your children after you. You shall even live to finish your work."

Joseph stiffened. "Oh! My father!" he cried with a great sob of relief and joy. "Shall I? Shall I truly?"

Emma had buried her face in her hands and was weeping quietly now.

"Yes, Joseph," Father Smith declared, "you shall live to lay out the plan of all the work which God has given you to do. This is my dying blessing upon your head, in the name of Jesus."

Joseph leaned forward, bending over his father. His shoulders shook as they embraced. Now there wasn't anyone in the room who wasn't crying. He continued one by one—Samuel, William, Don Carlos, and Sophronia and Lucy—until each of the children was blessed. Like the patriarchs of old, this first Patriarch of the dispensation of the fulness of times was leaving his family their richest legacy.

Exhausted and drained, after he finished with Lucy he had to rest for a time, but finally he reached out and took his wife's hand again. "Mother, do you not know that you are one of the most singular women in the world?"

She looked startled, but every head in the room began to nod. "No, I do not," she said.

"Well, I do. You have brought up my children for me by the fireside, and when I was gone from home, you comforted them. You have brought up all my children, and could always comfort them when I could not."

She dropped to her knees beside the bed. "Oh, Father, don't leave me."

He smiled and laid a hand upon her head with great gentleness. "We have often wished that we might both die at the same time, but you must not desire to die when I do, for you must stay to comfort the children when I am gone. So do not mourn. Try to be comforted."

She laid her head down on his breast, weeping as though her very heart was broken.

"Your last days shall be your best days, as to being driven, for you shall have more power over your enemies than you have had. Again I say, be comforted."

He fell back, and Joseph and Hyrum both took an anxious step forward. But his eyes were still open and his breathing deep but steady. The room grew very quiet now, for the blessings were over and everyone sensed he had fulfilled his purpose in gathering the family around him.

Suddenly he straightened noticeably. With great surprise and wonder, he looked around. "I can see and hear as well as I ever could," he exclaimed. Again there was a long pause. Then he cried out a second time, this time with great joy. "I can see Alvin."

Those present felt chills shoot through their bodies. Alvin was the older brother of Joseph and Hyrum. He had died nearly seventeen years earlier, about two months after Joseph had first been visited by the angel Moroni and learned about the gold plates. Just prior to the dedication of the Kirtland Temple, Joseph had seen Alvin in vision in the celestial kingdom.

Again Father Smith fell silent, this time for even longer than before. No one moved. Every eye was fixed on their father and grandfather. He turned his head, as though searching, then saw his wife kneeling beside him. "I shall live seven or eight minutes," he said, his voice now soft as a whisper.

He turned back, straightening out his body to its full length. He folded his hands upon his chest and closed his eyes. In moments, his breathing began to increase in rapidity and became shorter. It wasn't labored, but the deep rhythm was gone now.

Joseph glanced at the small clock on the table. It ticked softly, as though providing the tempo for his father's breathing. Then almost exactly eight minutes later, without a struggle or a sigh, the breathing stopped, and the spirit of Joseph Smith, Sr., took flight, leaving the tired old body behind.

For a long time there was no sound in the room but the soft crying of the family members. Then finally, Joseph straightened. He moved close to his mother, who was standing now, and put his arm around her waist. She put her head against his shoulder, still crying softly.

"It is right to mourn," Joseph said, "for we shall greatly miss this noble and great man. How blessed each of us is by having had him as our father and grandfather."

Every eye was upon Joseph now, and the crying began to lessen. "But let us remember, even as we mourn, that he now enters a world of peace and rest. He is with Alvin. He is with his own father and mother, who went on before. What rejoicing there must be, even as we weep, for a great and righteous man has entered into the paradise of God. And how grateful we must be for the knowledge that, thanks to the grace of Christ, we shall rise with our father again in the glorious resurrection and be reunited in our love and companionship forever."

While the Smith children were still gathered around their dying father, being blessed individually by him, Benjamin and Mary Ann Steed were walking along Water Street, much more slowly now, both of them lost in their thoughts. As they turned back onto Granger Street and started toward their own home, Benjamin finally spoke. "Mary Ann?"

"Yes?"

"I should consider it a great privilege if when I am ready to die, you would gather our family around me too."

Her first reaction was to be angry. Benjamin was fifty-five now. Many men never lived to be fifty-five, let alone sixty-nine, and part of her sadness lay in knowing that someday she, like

Lucy Mack, might have to stand beside this man and watch him die. But she also knew why he was making this request. "Yes," she said simply. "I understand."

———— •◆• ————

Joshua watched her out of the corner of his eye. She was near the lamp, doing needlepoint, her fingers moving quickly and smoothly. The lamplight, just behind her head, turned her hair to a flaming red, and with her head in profile she was achingly beautiful. She hadn't looked at him for nearly five minutes.

"Is this thing going to stand between us forever?"

"It's no longer standing between us, Joshua. I've accepted your decision."

He suppressed a groan. *Oh, really!*

She lowered the sewing. "I have. I am not going to be baptized."

"And you're not going to speak to me for the rest of your life?"

"That's not fair, Joshua, and you know it."

He raised one hand in surrender. "I was making a joke."

"Oh?" It was not a statement but a question, said archly, and it spoke her feelings more eloquently than a hundred angry words.

"Look, Caroline, are we ever going to talk about it?"

She carefully stuck the needle in the material, wrapped the thread into a neat circle, picked up the scissors, and then put them all away into the small sewing basket with great deliberateness. She picked small pieces of thread from the skirt of her dress, then finally looked up at him. "All right, Joshua, let's talk about it. I know you think I'm just trying to punish you, that this is my way of trying to make you give in and say yes."

He waited, just watching her.

"But you need to understand something. I won't be baptized, Joshua. Not knowing how deeply you would resent it. But you can't expect me not to be hurt and disappointed."

"Then be baptized!" he exploded. "Anything is better than this."

"No."

"Why?"

There were instant tears. "Because you don't want me to. Oh, you want everything to be happy, but down deep, you don't want me to. And so I won't." She looked away. "I can't."

He looked stricken. "You're asking something I can't give."

"I know."

He stood, unable to remain seated any longer. "I gave up St. Louis. I came to Nauvoo. I didn't want to. It's not like I haven't given in to you, Caroline."

"You don't even see it, do you, Joshua?" she asked softly.

"I guess I don't. What?"

"That's why I can't be baptized. I know what you've done, and I know why you've done it. You did it for me. Because you didn't want to see me unhappy." Her shoulders sagged as she looked down at her hands. "And that's why if my not being baptized is that important to you, then I will not be baptized."

"Good morning, Father Steed."

"Good morning, Lydia." Benjamin stepped inside the store and shut the door behind him. "Morning, Caroline."

"Good morning, Father Steed. You're up and about bright and early."

"Been looking at that new plat of building lots up by the grove. The surveyor is coming tomorrow to stake it out."

Lydia shook her head. "It just keeps growing and growing, doesn't it? It's really quite amazing."

"Yes, it is, especially when you think that it's not even been eighteen months since this was nothing but swamp and river."

"And mosquitoes," Rebecca piped in. She was in the far corner straightening up the shelves. Christopher was playing happily at her feet.

"Oh," Benjamin said, "I didn't see you. Morning, Rebecca." He walked over and gave her a quick kiss on the cheek.

Lydia turned to Caroline. "You see that?" she said, pretending hurt. "Daughters get a kiss, daughters-in-law get only a wave and a good morning."

Benjamin ignored that and reached down and picked up Christopher. He grunted as he straightened again. Christopher was fifteen months old now and built like a miniature draft horse. "Hello, Mr. Christopher."

Christopher said something that sounded vaguely like "Grandpa" and threw his arms around Benjamin's neck. Benjamin nuzzled at his neck and Christopher started to giggle.

For a minute or two they played like that, then Benjamin set him down again and swatted him affectionately on the bottom. He turned and walked to Lydia, leaned over the counter, and gave her a quick kiss on the cheek. "How are you feeling?" he asked.

"Like I'm going to be carrying this baby forever," she moaned.

He touched her arm. "At least it's getting cooler again."

"Yes, that does help. I may just survive after all."

He moved a few feet down the counter and reached across to take Caroline's hand. He squeezed it quickly and smiled. "And where's my other grandson?"

"Olivia is home with him."

"And what about that darling little redhead who thinks I'm the most wonderful man alive?"

Caroline laughed. "She's over with Lydia's children. You know Savannah. If there's not someone around, she is not happy."

Benjamin nodded absently, then looked directly at Caroline. "It's a beautiful morning out there. I was wondering if there might be someone who'd like to take a walk with me."

"I'm almost done here, Papa," Rebecca said. "Me and Christopher will go with you."

Benjamin smiled at her, then turned right back to Caroline. "It's a beautiful morning out there. I was wondering if there might be someone who'd like to take a walk with me."

"Oh!" Caroline said, as Rebecca laughed.

Then Rebecca's face grew serious. "I'm pretty busy right now, Papa," she said. "Why don't you go, Caroline?"

"Yes," Lydia said with equal gravity. "I don't think I could get away right now either. Why don't you go, Caroline?"

Caroline looked at them, then threw up her hands, laughing in surrender. "Why don't I go with you, Father Steed? It looks like the others are busy."

"I'd like that," he said.

———————•———————

They walked westward, down to the river, not speaking much, but enjoying the early-fall sunshine. When they reached the water, Benjamin found a grassy spot and motioned toward it. "Let's sit for a while."

Caroline did, spreading out her skirts around her. Benjamin sat beside her and began absently plucking at the blades of grass. She folded her arms across her knees and rested her chin on them, watching the muddy water swirl slowly past them.

"How are things?" Benjamin finally asked, not looking at her.

Her shoulders lifted and fell. She didn't have to ask what things he referred to. "We're in a truce of sorts, I guess."

He nodded.

"We just don't talk about it anymore. It's too painful."

"For you or for Joshua?"

She looked at him sharply; then, a little chagrined that she had been thinking only of herself, she answered. "For us both, I suppose."

"Hmm."

She smiled at him, loving him not only for his directness in getting her to leave the store with him but also for his reticence now about saying what he wanted to say. "Are you going to take Melissa for a walk too?" she teased.

He chuckled deep in his chest. "No. She and Carl have the problem without the pain."

Caroline frowned. "I know. Why is that? Carl is not a lot closer to accepting Mormonism than Joshua. He's not hostile about it, but I don't think he's got much interest."

"I agree."

"So why aren't they battling over it?"

"Why do redheads get freckles?"

She blinked in surprise at that totally unexpected response. "What?"

There was a layer of amusement behind the sobriety in his eyes. "Why do some men lose their hair? Why do women have soft voices and pretty eyes? I don't know. Some things just are."

"Oh." It was an answer, but it wasn't much comfort.

"You married Joshua, not Carl. Or Nathan. Or Derek."

"I know, but . . ." *But what?* Even if she had been able to see this far into the future, would she have backed away from marrying Joshua? As much as she liked her brothers-in-law, she suspected that if it had been Carl or Nathan or Derek who came to Savannah back then, she probably wouldn't have given them a second thought. This wasn't a question of love, she reminded herself again. Even here in Nauvoo she had seen men and women where both were Mormon who didn't have what she and Joshua had. But . . . And there she was again. *But what?*

Benjamin stopped picking at the grass and stared out across the river. "You know one of the things that brought me into the Church?"

She looked up. "No, what?" He had never talked about this, at least not in her presence.

"Joseph never made me feel like I didn't matter to him because I wasn't a Mormon. I never felt like I was some kind of project to him and that if I failed to make acceptable progress I would be dropped from his list of friends."

Her head had come up. "Do you think that's how . . . ?" She shook her head. Was this his way of rebuking her?

It was as if she weren't there. "I was pretty hardheaded at times. I said some things about Joseph that should have cut pretty deep. Found out later, people had told him about it too. Didn't make any difference. Mormon or non-Mormon, saint or sinner, somehow I knew that he cared about me."

"I care about Joshua!" she cried. "I love him very much. That's why this hurts so much."

He reached out and took her hand. "I think it's something we Mormons have to be careful about. We are so pleased to have the truth, we are on fire with the excitement and joy of the gospel, so it's only natural that we want others to have what we have. We want them to see clearly what is so clear to us. We want them to share in what is so important and so precious to us."

"Yes, I agree. But that's not *our* problem. Oh, there's no question, I would be thrilled if Joshua decided to accept Mormonism and we were baptized together. But I'm not asking that. I'm not saying that he has to believe like I do as a condition for us working out this problem."

He nodded, still bemused. "I know that. I'm talking about our people in general. We love the idea of being an instrument in bringing about another person's conversion. But if someone rejects the gospel, it's like we feel this loss of interest and break off the relationship. Can't we still accept a person who believes differently than we do? Shouldn't we respect their right to choose, just as we hope they'll respect our right to choose?"

"Of course."

"Well, that's easier said than done. It isn't always comfortable to be around people who think and act and believe differently than we do."

"But I do respect his right to choose, Father Steed. Why won't he respect mine?"

He gave her a small, twisted grin. "Why do redheads have freckles?"

"That doesn't make it any easier!" she cried.

He sighed, feeling her pain. "Caroline, let me tell you about Mother Steed and me. And if you were to ask her, she would probably give you a completely different answer than I would. She'd talk about prayer and fasting and the Lord taking a hand with a stubborn and ornery old man. And there's some truth to all that. But if you were to ask me what it was Mary Ann did that finally changed my heart . . ." He left it hanging.

She turned to him, wanting him to finish. "Yes?"

"If you were to ask me . . . ," he started again.

She laughed, unable to help herself. How she loved this gentle, wonderful man. He had that same quiet depth she had seen in her own father and that she had missed so terribly when he died. "Tell me, Father Steed, what was it that Mary Ann did that finally changed your heart?"

He leaned back. "She loved me all the more."

For almost a minute, Caroline searched his face, then she looked away. "I don't know if I can. Oh, I love him. You know that. But love him more? How can I when I feel so hurt? So betrayed? I can't just make those feelings go away. I've tried. That's what is so frustrating! What right does he have to stop me from doing something that means everything to me, when it doesn't hurt him at all?"

"Is that what he said?" he prodded gently. "That it doesn't hurt him at all?" He didn't wait for her answer. One hand came up and he began to rub his chin thoughtfully. "How far are you in the Book of Mormon now?"

"I finished two weeks ago."

"So you've read the chapter on charity? It's right close to the end."

"Yes."

"Do you remember how Mormon defined charity?"

"He said charity is the pure love of Christ."

"That's right. It means to love as Christ would love."

"I do love Joshua!" she exploded, highly frustrated. And yet, strangely, she was pierced with a deep sense of regret, for she knew she was still filled with bitterness over it all and that it had put a barrier between her and Joshua.

Benjamin didn't seem to hear her. "And do you know what I've learned as I've gotten a little older and wiser?" he asked.

"What?"

"Loving as Christ loves isn't something you talk yourself into. It's not a mental state, Caroline. It's not a set of steps you walk through and then everything is wonderful."

"Then how do you get it?"

"I wish I had the Book of Mormon so I could read it to you. But it says something like this. After talking about the qualities of charity, what it is like, and how important it is, it says, 'Wherefore, my beloved brethren, pray unto the Father with your whole heart and all the energy of your whole soul, that you may be filled with this love which *he* hath given to all those who are the true followers of Christ.'"

Now he turned his body so he was directly facing her. "Don't you see? Charity isn't a state of mind, it's a state of heart. It's a gift of the Spirit. It's not just a matter of wanting it. God has to bestow that kind of love on a person."

"So—" She stopped, her mind racing. "So you're saying I should pray to have this kind of love for Joshua?" She had never considered such an option.

"Yes."

"I've been praying that he would change his mind."

"That's fine. Just pray for the other too. That's what I meant when I said that Mary Ann loved me all the more. Somehow, she has that gift. Somehow Joseph Smith has that gift. I knew that their caring was not dependent on my Church membership. And eventually that's what brought me into the Church."

Now it was Caroline who leaned forward, and took his hands. "Yes," she said very slowly. "I see. I see where I have been wrong."

"Not wrong," he said. Then that slow smile came. "Just not as right as you could be, maybe."

She took a deep breath, feeling a great sense of release. "And do you think Joshua might ever join the Church, Father Steed?"

Their eyes locked for several seconds; then he squeezed her hands. "There is no one else besides Mary Ann and me who knows how deeply you long for that," he said, the pain making his voice heavy. Then he shook his head slowly. "I don't know. Perhaps not."

She slowly let go of his hands and straightened. "I don't know either."

"And if he doesn't?" Benjamin asked softly.

Caroline dropped her eyes to stare at her hands. Without looking up, she spoke in a whisper. "Tell me where that scripture is."

"In the book of Moroni, right near the end."

She repeated it softly. Then she looked up at him. "Thank you, Father Steed. I really needed a walk this morning."

Chapter Notes

Joseph Smith, Sr., died on 14 September 1840 after a long illness. The final moments with his family, including the blessings given to his children and his last three dying statements, are recorded by his wife in her history. Joseph's final comments presented in the novel are not part of Lucy's account. Immediately following the burial, Joseph and Hyrum again fled the city to escape the possibility of being arrested by Missourians. (See *Mack Hist.*, pp. 307–14.)

Chapter Twenty-Five

A general conference of the Church convened in Nauvoo on Saturday, October third, and continued through Monday, October fifth, 1840. Numerous items of business were proposed and approved. Two would have lasting significance for the Saints.

Joseph spoke at some length about the necessity of building a house of the Lord. When he was finished, it was unanimously approved that work commence no later than ten days from that date, and a committee was appointed. Among others, Brother Benjamin Steed was asked to serve on the building committee. It was also proposed and sustained that every able-bodied brother would give a "tithe" of his time, working one day in ten on the temple.

The second important item of business had to do with a charter for the city of Nauvoo. Joseph Smith, Robert Thompson, and John C. Bennett were sustained as the committee to draft a proposal for a charter. The conference also sustained Bennett as the delegate to Springfield who would lobby the legislature for its passage.

Joseph brought John C. Bennett over to where the Steeds were eating during the afternoon recess. In his mid-thirties, Bennett was strikingly handsome and had a smile that quickly put one at ease. He was a physician, a part-time preacher, a founder of a university in Ohio and another in Indiana. Prominent in Illinois politics, he was also a brigadier general in the dragoons of the state militia, and Governor Carlin had made him state quartermaster general, a position with considerable prestige and influence.

Earlier Bennett had written to Joseph from Springfield, volunteering to help with the settling of the Saints and also expressing an interest in becoming a Mormon. That such a man of learning and culture and political prominence should become a Latter-day Saint sent a ripple of excitement through the Mormon community. That such a handsome, suave man was still a bachelor sent tidal waves through the feminine population of Nauvoo. After some correspondence with the Prophet, in the summer of 1840 Bennett came to Nauvoo and was eventually baptized.

"Benjamin," Joseph said, after introductions were made, "since I have asked you to help with the planning and platting of the city, I wanted Brother John here to meet you."

"Joseph speaks most highly of you, sir," Bennett said grandly as they shook hands.

"And of you," Benjamin responded. "I was pleased that you were sustained to be on the committee to help us get our city charter."

Bennett nodded in satisfaction. "Thank you. We have a preliminary outline of what we think we should ask for. Brother Joseph will be proposing that this afternoon, right?"

Joseph nodded. "Yes, in the next meeting."

"I think the Saints will find it satisfactory," Bennett continued. "But Joseph has so much regard for your opinion, Brother Benjamin, we thought we'd let you know what we are thinking."

Flattered, Benjamin nodded. The rest of the family moved in a little closer, a little awed at the presence of the man and the fact that he was coming to their father and grandfather for advice.

"It is my firm belief," Bennett began, "that if the Saints are ever to have freedom from the depredations of Missouri, we must have the protection of the law. And a well-written city charter is how to get that protection."

"That sounds wonderful," Lydia spoke up. Several of the others were nodding.

"If the outline we are proposing is approved," Bennett said, "we shall ask for sweeping powers, powers that will protect us."

"Like what?" Jessica asked.

"Our own militia. Courts with the power to issue writs of habeas corpus."

Olivia, at nearly thirteen, and clearly dazzled by his presence, was hanging on his every word. She wrinkled her nose. "What's that?"

Joseph laughed. "It's a paper meaning that a person has to be taken before a judge or a court to be charged with a crime. It protects one against illegal imprisonment."

"It's what we tried to get over and over in Missouri but couldn't," Benjamin explained to his granddaughter. "That's why Joseph and the others spent so long in jail."

Bennett went on. "I've patterned it after the charters granted to Chicago and other cities in the state. We can form our own university."

Benjamin was impressed. *Sweeping* was a good word to describe those kinds of powers. "And do you think we have a chance of getting the legislature to accept such a charter?"

"Absolutely," Bennett said with complete confidence.

Joseph clapped Bennett on the shoulder. "And if there is a man in the state who can see to it that it gets done, that man is standing right here."

When the train from London pulled into the station at Manchester, Matthew was the first passenger off. He spied Derek in the waiting crowd immediately and started swinging his arm. "Derek! Derek! I'm over here."

Though it had been only three weeks since they had been together in Liverpool, they greeted each other as if it had been much longer than that. They shook hands warmly, and then Derek looked around. "What about your brethren? Didn't they come with you?"

"Yes and no. Brother Woodruff wanted to stop in Staffordshire on the way up and revisit the branches. Heber and George A. are with him. They should be here tomorrow."

"Well, then," Derek said, taking him by the elbow, "we're off. It's not far, no more than a mile or two. You'll be staying in our flat with me."

"Good. How many of the others are here?"

"Brother Taylor is still in Ireland. He's having a series of debates with a local minister which are creating a lot of interest, so he felt like he couldn't break away. Orson Pratt hasn't yet arrived from Scotland, but he is coming. When your three from London arrive, that will be it."

As they began to make their way through the crowded railway station, Matthew suddenly turned. "Have you gotten any letters?" he asked.

"I got one from Rebecca. One came for both of us from Mama and Papa yesterday."

"And that's all?" Matthew asked, disappointment pulling down the corners of his mouth.

Derek got an impish little grin. "Let's see. There was one other one, but I couldn't quite make out the handwriting. Looked like it might be written in Irish or some such thing."

"Really?" Matthew crowed. "I haven't gotten a letter since we went to London." He grabbed Derek's arm and pulled him into a trot. "Come on, let's get going."

———•———

Half an hour later, Matthew was going over Jennifer Jo's letter for the fourth time when there was a brisk knock on the door. It pushed open even as Derek called out, "Come in."

Brigham Young was into the room in three strides and swept Matthew up in a bear hug. "Matthew, you rascal. How are you?"

"Fine, Brother Brigham. And you?"

"Busier than a carpenter with four hammers and no hands." He frowned. "Can you imagine that? Me, who can barely spell good enough for a man to read, and I'm in charge of things here—publishing a hymnbook, getting the Book of Mormon printed."

"Yes, I can imagine it," Matthew said soberly.

"I try to have Willard write most of the letters, but when I do write one now and then, you can hear groans all over the British Isles."

Matthew laughed. Oh, it was good to see Brother Brigham again!

Brigham put his arm around his young friend. "What we need to do is open up a little carpenter and mill shop here. We could leave all this publishing and Church leadership to someone better qualified to do it."

"I'm with you," Matthew agreed. "It sounds great to get my hands on a good piece of wood again."

"How are the conference plans coming?" Derek asked.

Brigham brightened immediately. For all his protestations to the contrary, he loved being in the midst of the work. "It is going to be a grand conference. Did Derek tell you, Matthew? Since July, total Church membership here has jumped another eleven hundred members. That's an increase of almost fifty percent in just three months' time!"

Matthew felt a surge of exultation and a burst of discouragement at the same instant. Not many of those numbers had come out of London. Since their arrival there in late August, they had had very little success. Unlike the people in the central part of England, the people in England's capital were generally indifferent to religion or so crushed by their poverty that they had no time for spiritual matters.

Brigham saw his reaction and laid a hand on his shoulder. "Brethren," he said soberly, "I don't know how much longer the Lord plans for us to be here, but I think the general consensus of the Twelve is that we shall leave next spring. We shall have to intensify our efforts. There is so much to do. So much to do."

———————

When Mary Ann opened the door, Carl and Melissa were on the porch. None of the children were with them. Carl swept off his hat immediately. "Hello, Mother Steed."

"Well, hello." She was a little surprised. They lived just across the street and one house up, and usually Melissa didn't knock. "Come in."

As they did so, Carl looked around. "Is Father Steed at home?"

"Yes," came the reply from the back room. "Just a moment."

"Sit down," Mary Ann said, giving her daughter a quizzical look. But Melissa was evidently going to let Carl take the lead on this and just shrugged.

They sat down as Benjamin came out, drying his hands. "Well, hello, you two," he said.

"Hello, Father Steed," Carl responded. "Sorry to come this late in the evening, but we're wondering if we could speak with you for a few minutes."

"Of course." He came over and sat down beside Mary Ann.

Carl glanced at his father-in-law, then to Mary Ann, and then finally to Melissa. She nodded her encouragement. "I'd like to ask your advice on a business matter."

Benjamin raised one hand and laughed. "You and Joshua have five times the business sense I've got," he said. "How could I possibly advise you?"

"This is also a family matter, Papa."

He looked at Melissa. "Oh, all right."

Carl was not a man of many words, and he usually chose them carefully. It also meant he liked to skip any small talk and get right to the heart of the matter. He took a breath and plunged. "We'd like to leave the partnership with Joshua."

That stunned them both and he hurried on. "It's not that we are having problems. It's not that at all. Things are going very well there. It's just that . . ."

"Has Joshua said something?" Mary Ann asked, completely flabbergasted by this announcement.

"No, not at all."

Melissa jumped in. "Please understand, Papa, Joshua has been wonderful to us. In fact, that's part of the problem. Carl is worried that he might take it wrong."

"Then what is it?" Benjamin asked.

Carl looked at his wife, and when she nodded her encouragement he went on, excitement making him speak more quickly. "Actually, I've been thinking a lot about what's going on here in Nauvoo. There's so much building and growth going on. And . . . well, you know how expensive lumber is, having to bring it in from the East and all that?"

"I certainly do," Benjamin agreed. That was a major issue that the temple building committee was wrestling with at this very time. Illinois was part of the Great Plains and had few natural stands of timber. There were a few trees along the river and the numerous streams, but these were limited and were not ideal for sawing into long planks. So to this point, most of the homes built in Nauvoo were log cabins or mud-and-board shanties, with only a few frame homes here and there. Eastern lumber was coming down the Ohio and then up the Mississippi, but it was very expensive. With cash money scarce and barter the major means of commerce in Nauvoo, purchase of sufficient lumber to build a home was very difficult.

"So what if we make a brick kiln?" Carl said.

It took a moment for that to register with both Mary Ann and Benjamin. "A brick kiln?" Benjamin finally said.

"Yes. One of those British people that came in a month or

so ago was in the stable the other day. He used to work the big pottery kilns in England. He says making bricks shouldn't be a whole lot different. He's been along the bluffs and down by the riverbanks. He says there's plenty of good clay in the area."

Benjamin leaned back. "A brick kiln? Well, well. What an interesting idea."

Carl nodded. "Anyway, the more I've thought about it, the more intrigued I am with the idea. This is something that is really needed here. I'm enjoying the work with Joshua, but he doesn't need me. I'm just there to keep the books." Now he frowned. "But will Joshua be hurt after all he's done for us?"

Benjamin leaned back, pulling thoughtfully on one ear. "Well, there's one way to find out. Let's get Joshua over here."

Carl flinched a little. "You mean right now?"

"I do," Benjamin chuckled. "I think it's time for another family council. I think we ought to bring Nathan and Lydia too."

"Of course I'm not going to be upset," Joshua said, shaking his head at the notion that Carl would even think such a thing. "It sounds like a great idea to me."

"You really think so?" Carl asked.

"Yes, I do. In fact, I've been wrestling with exactly the same problem in my own mind."

"What problem?" Nathan asked.

"The problem of the shortage of lumber and the cost of bringing it in from the East."

"Can't you bring in lumber more cheaply than others are doing it?" Lydia asked. "You've already got the freight business set up to do that sort of thing."

Joshua shrugged. "Maybe a little. But that isn't the answer. Every mile you carry something, whether it's by wagon, boat, or mule, costs you money. We're just too far from the eastern lumber mills."

"So brick is one answer?" Melissa asked hopefully.

"It certainly is," Joshua replied. "And I feel like a fool for not having thought of it before. It is a brilliant idea, Carl."

The relief on Carl's face was openly visible. It was going to be all right. "Thank you. I think we can make a go of it."

"Make a go of it?" Joshua exclaimed. "With you being the first one in, I think you're going to find yourself with more demand than you can supply."

"I agree," Benjamin said, "but that doesn't solve the lumber problem. You can't build a temple with nothing but bricks."

Joshua looked smug. "That's why you and me and Nathan are going to take a little trip upriver to Wisconsin Territory." He laughed aloud at the expression on their faces. Even Caroline was dumbfounded.

"Wisconsin?" Nathan finally managed.

"They say up there, there are pine forests that stretch from horizon to horizon, as far as the eye can see. Millions of trees and straight as a nail."

"But that's six hundred miles from here," Carl said, "with not a lot of good roads between here and there. How's that going to help keep the price down?"

Now Joshua looked pleased. "Are you forgetting the greatest wagon of them all?"

Carl looked puzzled. Lydia and Melissa were watching Joshua closely, not understanding. But Nathan saw it instantly. "The Mississippi."

"You mean by boat?" Mary Ann asked.

"No, by raft," said Joshua. "Lumber rafts. Just get that lumber to the river during the winter when the ground is hard enough to carry sleds and wagons. Then when the ice breaks up, you just tie them logs together with a lot of rope and float them right on down to Nauvoo. No horses to feed, no teamsters to worry about. Just a hundred thousand board feet of lumber coming downriver like a great raft from heaven itself."

Nathan was nodding. It was brilliant. The brickyard was brilliant, but it was only part of the solution. Reasonably priced lumber was the other half of the answer. He looked at Lydia.

She was still trying to digest it. He reached out and took her hand, but he was looking at Joshua. "So when do we leave?"

———•———

Will hurried along the wharf, moving around the people who walked at a more leisurely pace than him. It had been nearly eighteen months since he had last been on the New Orleans docks, but he still felt right at home. He smiled. He felt more at home right now than he had felt in a long time. This was the last major stopping place. A week upriver and it would be over.

As he rounded the corner of one of the big cotton warehouses, he saw the Mormons, clustered on the dock not far from the customshouse. Theodore Turley and John Benbow were back and immediately broke off from the group when they saw him. On board, Turley and Benbow had jointly shared leadership, but since disembarking this morning and moving through customs, it was clear that Turley had taken the lead. Though English, he had lived in America for several years before returning with the Twelve. On board, he had seemed a bit stern to Will, particularly compared to John Benbow's warm openness, but when Will approached him and offered to help find a riverboat and book passage, he proved to be pleasant and congenial.

Will saw the crowd edging closer to their leaders so they could hear about their fate. He also saw that Jenny Pottsworth and her mother were near the front. "Did you have any luck?" he asked of Turley.

Both men nodded. "The shipping company says they have two boats leaving tomorrow," Turley explained. "The one is too small for our group, but the other, the *Blue Bay*, has plenty of room."

John Benbow leaned forward. "And the customshouse has promised to have our large trunks cleared by morning. So what do you think?"

Out of the corner of his eye, Will saw that Jenny was watching him closely, and there was a little bit of mockery in her eyes.

He could almost hear her saying it: Look at Mr. Big, playing the expert with these dumb Mormons.

He turned away from her. "I think it looks all right."

"You think we should give them the money, then?" Turley asked.

"When does it leave?" Will asked.

"Noon."

"Tell them you want to take boarding immediately. That way you won't have to try and find a place to stay tonight."

"Is that allowed?" Benbow asked in surprise.

Both Turley and Will nodded together. "If they don't have all the quarters ready, some of us can sleep on deck," Will explained. "It might be a little chilly, but it shouldn't be that bad."

"Thank you, young man," Turley said, extending his hand. As Will shook it, the missionary leader went on. "I have never met your father personally, but I heard about what he did for your family during the siege of Far West. You have every reason to be proud. I do know your uncle Nathan and your grandfather and grandmother very well. It will be a pleasure to have you travel with us."

"Thank you," Will responded, feeling a little guilty that he had thought the man to be stern. Then he had an idea. "Would you like me to take the people to the boat while you go and purchase the tickets?"

"Good idea." He turned. "Folks, we have passage. We leave tomorrow at noon."

A cheer went up and several clapped their hands together. They were glad to be off the ship and on land, but they were also as ready as Will to get the journey done with. They had set sail from Liverpool on September eighth. Today was October twenty-fourth. That meant six weeks at sea with only brief stops at New York, Savannah, and Tallahassee. The weariness showed in their bodies and in their faces, but so did their excitement to know they were about to begin the last leg.

"Mr. Steed here will be traveling with us," Turley went on. "He has family in Nauvoo too. So if you'll follow him, he'll show you the way to go. Brother Benbow and I will go purchase our tickets. We shall sleep on the boat tonight."

As the people sprang into action, grabbing suitcases and valises, trunks, baskets, fabric sacks, or whatever else they carried their things in, Will saw Jenny reach down and pick up the same heavy trunk she had brought aboard. It wasn't a full-size sailing trunk, but it was larger than most valises or cases and she lifted it with some effort.

Will stepped forward. "May I help you with that?" he offered.

She swung around, surprised. Then her face darkened. "I thought crew members weren't allowed to help with the luggage."

"I'm not crew anymore," he said evenly, trying to hold his temper.

"You are to me," she snapped.

"Jenny Pottsworth, you stop that this instant." Abigail Pottsworth was onto her daughter angrily and yanking the case from her hand. "This young man has apologized to us, and we'll not be treating him so flippantly if you don't mind." She handed the case to Will. "We'd be most appreciative of your help, thank you."

Jenny picked up a smaller case and stepped around them, her head held high. Will watched her flounce away, amused and intrigued and irritated all at the same time. He let her reach the street and start to turn the corner, then called out, softly laughing to himself. "Not that way, Miss Pottsworth. That's the way to the sailing docks. Unless you want to return to England, you'd better go the other way. The riverboat docks are to the left, up the street."

She spun around without a word and went the opposite direction.

———————•———————

The sky was clear, the stars so brilliant and so numerous as to make the mind hurt with the contemplating of their numbers. The moon was little more than a sliver just coming up in the eastern sky, but the lights on the far shore gave definition to the wide expanse of river that moved slowly past him.

Will watched the moon, lost in thought. Some six or seven hundred miles north of where he now stood, this same moon would be coming up over the place they called Nauvoo. Was his father even now standing on the porch and looking up at it? Was his mother there too, holding the baby brother he had never seen? Were Olivia and Savannah there with them, counting the same stars that filled the sky over his head? Probably not, he decided. The night air here was cool and pleasant, but that far north it would likely be putting frost on the ground about now. His family would be inside, but still under the same moon and stars and sky.

For six weeks now he had lived with the news that his father wasn't dead. He could scarcely believe it. There had been too many months of numbing pain, too many months of wishing there had been even a chance for one last farewell to his father. There was also the pain of living with his own stupidity, knowing that his bravado attempt to track down his father's killers had cost him two years away from his family. Now that was all the more bitter. It wasn't just his mother's company he had lost for two years.

A sound behind him brought him around. It was Mrs. Pottsworth and Jenny, walking slowly along the deck toward him. He straightened, unconsciously tensing in preparation for another verbal jousting match.

"Good evening, Mr. Steed."

Will inclined his head slightly. "Mrs. Pottsworth. Miss Jenny."

"Good evening," Jenny said, her voice bland and unreadable.

"We've come out to enjoy the evening. I had heard there were such places on the earth, where even in the dead of winter one could walk about in one's shirtsleeves, but I never thought I'd live to see it."

Will turned and looked out across the river. "And there are

places south of here, in the Caribbean, that would make this seem like a very cold night."

"And I suppose you've seen them all," Jenny said.

There wasn't anything definite in her voice but Will sensed the challenge. So did her mother, for she shot her a dirty look. But Will's previous mood was still on him and he was not willing to launch into another round of contention. "Only a few," he said.

"Like where?" Mrs. Pottsworth asked, genuinely interested.

He half turned, so he didn't have to watch Jenny's face. "Mexico. Cuba. Jamaica."

"What about China?" Jenny asked. "I thought you'd been to China."

He turned his head, but this time was surprised to see that she was watching him openly, without any rancor. "Yes, Canton was very warm too. We were there in January and saw many of the coolies working without their shirts."

"Coolies?" she asked.

"Yes, that's what they call their laborers over there."

"Well, I declare," Mrs. Pottsworth said. "No shirts in January."

Jenny was looking at him narrowly. "You're not just funning with us, are you?"

He laughed. "No, I swear."

"You've seen so much for a young man," her mother said.

"Not by any choice of mine," he muttered softly.

Just then Mrs. Pottsworth spied someone going inside the main cabin. She leaned forward, peering. "Oh, there's Brother Benbow. I have a question for him." She started away.

Jenny, watching Will steadily, called after her. "I'll be along shortly, Mum."

Mrs. Pottsworth waved airily. "All right."

Caught by surprise, Will watched Jenny for a moment, then blushed when she caught him at it. He turned back to lean against the rail. In a moment, she did the same, a few feet away from him. They stood there for almost a minute before she spoke again. "It's so big," she breathed softly.

"The river? Yes, it is."

"I thought the River Ribble in Preston was one of the grandest in the world. Then I saw the Mersey River in Liverpool and thought that had to be the biggest ever."

"Some of the men I sailed with, they claim there's a river in South America that is so big at its mouth you can't see from one shore to another."

"I can't imagine such a thing. This is big enough for me."

"*Mississippi* is an Indian word meaning 'big river.' They also call it the Father of Waters."

She turned now to look at him. "Have you seen a real Indian?"

He was tempted to laugh. It was such a childlike question. But then he remembered he had asked Joshua Steed exactly the same question that day in Savannah when he had told Will he was from Missouri. "Independence—that's in Jackson County, Missouri—that's where I lived. It's only about twelve miles from Indian Territory. We saw Indians all the time. There's thousands of them out there from a dozen or more tribes."

"Jackson County," she said in sudden awe. "You actually lived in Jackson County?"

Puzzled, he bobbed his head. "Yes, why is that so surprising?"

"That's where Zion is. That's where the New Jerusalem is going to be built."

"Oh," he said, feeling suddenly deflated. Mormon talk. He had heard it from the settlers in Jackson County. It was partly what had brought on the war.

"Why do you hate the Mormons so?" she asked abruptly.

Startled, he turned to look at her. "I don't hate the Mormons. I . . . I just used to. I thought they were the ones who killed my father."

"But they weren't."

"I know. So I don't hate them anymore."

"But you're having a hard time getting rid of it."

"Look," he said, enjoying this too much to let it end. "I said I was sorry. And I meant it."

"And I'm sorry too," she said with sudden contriteness. "I guess I've just seen so much of it back home. Ever since Mum and me joined the Church, people laugh at us, jeer at us. We've even had rocks thrown at us from time to time."

He stared at her.

She looked up at him from beneath lowered lashes. "I guess that's why your comments about not liking Mormons kind of set me off."

He gave her a rueful grin. "Kind of?"

She laughed, then totally surprised him by sticking out her hand. "What say we're friends, then," she said. "I'd like someone to tell me all about America."

He took her hand and shook it once, then withdrew it quickly. "Well, I don't know everything. But I'll be happy to tell you what I do know."

"Tell you what," she said, giving him a full smile, the first one he had seen from her that was directed at him. It completely dazzled him. "Let's meet out here on deck. Right at the front of the boat. Eight o'clock every morning. Then you can tell me about everything we are seeing."

He hesitated only for an instant, and then he remembered he wasn't crew anymore. He was a passenger, just like her. Just like all the rest. "I'd like that," he said.

"Good." She started away, after her mother, then abruptly turned back. "Will?"

He looked up, half-startled.

She blushed slightly. "Do you mind if I call you Will?"

"Of course not."

"Good. And I'm Jenny. No more of this Miss Pottsworth." She hesitated, growing very serious now. "It won't be anything more than just friendship."

"What?"

"It can never be anything more than friendship, you know. Because you're not a Mormon. I'm saving myself for a Mormon boy. Like Peter." Her color darkened even more. "Or Matthew."

He just stared at her, his lips parted in amazement. He

couldn't believe what she was saying. Was she always like this, just blurting out whatever was going through her mind?

"I just wanted you to know that," she said, then turned and was gone.

Chapter Notes

The proposal to build a temple was approved by the Saints in the October 1840 conference. Excavation for the basement began shortly thereafter, and a stone quarry was opened on the outskirts of the city (see *CHFT*, p. 242). John C. Bennett, who would figure so prominently and so disastrously in later history, joined the Church in the late summer of 1840. He was the one primarily responsible for drafting the Nauvoo Charter and getting it passed through the Illinois legislature in December 1840. (See *CHFT*, pp. 222–23.)

Brigham was sensitive about his poor writing abililty and his phonetic way of spelling. Some lines from a letter to Willard Richards show his willingness to poke fun at himself: "Be careful not to lay this letter with the new testment wrightings. If you doe som body will take it for a text after the Malineum a[nd] contend about it." (Quoted in *MWM*, p. 158.)

The first Mormon emigrant ship to leave England in the summer of 1840 sailed to New York, and then the Saints traveled by steamboat and train to Nauvoo, a journey which, with a winter layover in Pennsylvania, took them a total of nine or ten months. Later ships sailed on from New York around Florida to New Orleans and up the Mississippi to Nauvoo, an all-water route that was both less expensive and considerably shorter in time. (See *CHFT*, p. 234.) The author has taken the liberty to have the second official group of emigrants, who sailed on the *North America*, go by way of New Orleans. In actuality, the third group, who left five weeks later on the *Isaac Newton*, was the first to take this route.

A re we crazy to even think about it, Nathan?"

Nathan looked around, eyeing the exposed rock. It was a high-quality limestone, ranging from light gray to almost pure white. In his mind, he tried to picture how deep it went below where they were standing and what it would take to quarry enough out of the site to build a temple. Then he grinned. "Probably."

Joseph laughed softly. "You were supposed to say, 'Not at all, Brother Joseph. I think it is a wonderful idea.'"

"I do think it is a wonderful idea! But that doesn't make the task any easier."

"I know, I know. It's just that I keep thinking of the sacrifice it took to build the Kirtland Temple. And it took so long."

Down below them, closer to the river, Benjamin, Alpheus Cutler, and the others of the building committee came out of the trees. They were walking slowly, heads down as they examined the quarry site. There were four different quarries in the Nauvoo area, but this was the temple quarry, which had opened not quite three weeks before. The first of the large blocks had already been cut and moved to the temple site. Nathan watched his father and the others as he considered Joseph's words. "That's true. But look at what happened because we did what the Lord asked."

"Oh, yes," Joseph said instantly. "When I think of that great season of spiritual power we enjoyed, it made every sacrifice worth it."

"There are many more of us now," Nathan added. "That will help a great deal."

"Yes." Joseph laid a hand on his shoulder. "And Nathan, it is of great significance that we do it. God has important things to reveal to us, and they have to do with the temple."

"Like before?" Nathan asked, thinking of the stunning series of revelatory experiences that had come during the dedication of the Kirtland Temple.

"Even more. And we must have a place for our baptisms for the dead. The Lord has given us permission now to perform those ordinances in the river, but it will not always be so. The Lord wants them performed in his house."

Nathan was nodding. Benjamin had come home one night all excited and told the family about Joseph's plan to have a baptismal font in the basement of the temple. It was to rest on the back of twelve oxen, just like the great laver in Solomon's temple.

Joseph turned, looking toward the city now. "Ah, Nathan, it is a wonderful time. A wonderful time."

"It is, Joseph."

"I feel such an urgency about this," he said, half to himself. "The Lord has so much to give us and there is so little time."

That startled Nathan. "So little time?"

That brought Joseph out of his thoughts. "Yes. You know what I've said before. Our destiny does not lie here, but in the Rocky Mountains."

Nathan was shaken by that thought. Yes, he had heard Joseph say that very thing on more than one occasion, but that was before Nauvoo. That was before they had found themselves a new home. "Are we to leave this place, then?" he asked forlornly, suddenly feeling quite dejected.

Joseph laughed heartily. "Someday, Nathan. But for now, this is our home, and we are to do all we can to build it up. This is the task the Lord has given us to do."

He turned back toward the quarry and the river, watching the committee below them examining the walls of exposed limestone. Then he sat down and patted the ground beside him. "I can see the brethren are taking their assignment seriously. Let's sit for a spell."

Nathan did so. The day was overcast and right on the edge of being cold, but they had their coats on and it was not entirely unpleasant. Joseph pulled out a dried piece of grass and began to chew on it, his eyes thoughtful and far away again.

"Joseph?"

"Yes?"

"You're very different since Liberty Jail, did you know that?"

He chuckled. "That's what Emma keeps saying too. She says she can't believe I'm home so much now."

"No, it's more than that."

He looked at Nathan squarely now. "Like what?"

Nathan shrugged. "I don't know. It's like you're so . . ." He groped for a good word. "So seasoned now. So much more mature."

"Oh," Joseph said with a straight face, "so I was immature before?"

Instantly Nathan's face flushed. "No, I . . . I was only trying to say—" He stopped, knowing that Joseph was only having some fun at his expense. "I mean it. There is so much more depth to what you're teaching us now. That discourse on priesthood that you gave at conference, I'm still trying to digest it all. Baptism for the dead. Some of the things you've said about the second coming of the Savior. I mean, it's almost like every time I listen to you, I go away reeling."

"So not only was I immature, now I make you dizzy."

Nathan laughed sheepishly. "I'm not saying it very well, but . . . well, I'm not the only one who's commented on this."

Now Joseph sobered. "I know, Nathan. I'm just funning with you." He pulled the piece of grass out and flicked it away. "Do you know what day today is, Nathan?"

He thought for a moment, then shook his head.

"It was exactly two years ago today that the attack at Haun's Mill took place."

"Oh."

"We have been through the refiner's fire, Nathan. I have. The Church as a whole has."

"That I can agree with."

"You say I've changed. Well, you're right. And Liberty Jail was an important factor in that. I learned things there, and had things happen to me there that couldn't—or at least wouldn't—have happened in any other way."

"Like what?"

"Like understanding that until a man is tested even as Abraham, the Lord cannot bless him with greater blessings."

He saw Nathan's puzzlement and went on quickly. "Do you remember in the School of the Prophets how we studied the 'Lectures on Faith'?"

"I do."

"Do you remember that in one of the lectures I said that unless a man is willing to offer his all in sacrifice to the Lord, not holding back anything, he cannot know with a certainty that his life is pleasing to God?"

"Yes, I remember."

"Well, that is what has happened to Hyrum and me. By the time we had endured over four months in that filthy, unbearable hole that wasn't fit for animals, without losing hope, without losing faith, then we knew with unshakable certainty that our lives were acceptable to him. And so what has that done for my faith?"

Nathan was excited now. "It has deepened it."

"Yes. And the same holds true for the Church. Our people

went through those horrible depredations, endured persecution, mobs, looting, killing, loss of property, and still did not waver. In view of that, is there any doubt in your mind that our sacrifice is acceptable to God?"

"No." He said it slowly and in wonder.

"Faith is power, Nathan. When you see men and women of faith, they always have great power—the power to part the Red Sea, the power to heal the sick, the power to raise the dead." He leaned forward, his voice filled with great intensity. "Last July, during the sickness? Do you think that day of great power and healing would have happened if we had not been through the purifying fires of Missouri?"

"No," Nathan breathed softly. "I hadn't seen it in that light, but no, I don't think it would have happened."

"And that is what you are feeling now. The Lord is making us into a pure people, and the purer and more refined we become, the more he can give us, the more he can reveal to us."

"Whew!" Nathan exclaimed. "That's a lot to chew on."

Joseph laughed and slapped him playfully on the arm. "Well, you're the one who called me immature." He lay back, stretching out to his full length. "As you know, Nathan, I've been working on a journal history. I feel a great urgency to write a record of the Restoration. There are already things which are lost—specific dates, who was involved in certain events—because I didn't write them down at the time. Anyway, I was going through the Jackson County period the other day, reading again what has been written."

"Yes?"

"I ran across something I had nearly forgotten. And you were there, so this will have meaning for you too."

"What is that?"

"Remember that summer day in '31, not long after we arrived in Missouri? We were out in Kaw Township with the Colesville Branch—Newel Knight, Joseph Knight, and the other Saints. We laid the first log for the first house in Zion."

"Yes, I remember that very well."

"Well, speaking of that day, I wrote something like this. After noting that we had laid the log, I said, 'At the same time, through prayer, we consecrated the land of Zion and Sidney Rigdon dedicated it for the gathering of the Saints.'" He stopped, turning his head to look at Nathan. "And then I said, 'It was a season of joy to those present and afforded a glimpse of the future, which time will yet unfold to the satisfaction of the faithful.'"

Nathan was watching him intently, but said nothing, not wanting to interrupt his mood.

"Well," he continued, "I don't know if right now is that future time we glimpsed back then or not. And if it is, I'm not sure how long it will last. But it certainly is a time of rest and recovery for us—for me, for the Church. I'm not going to worry a lot about the future right now, Nathan. We have our season of joy. Let's make the most of it."

The boat's whistle, throaty and deep, rolled across the flatland, then reverberated off the bluffs to the east. Rebecca grabbed at her father's sleeve. "Oh, Papa," she cried, "let's hurry. We're going to miss it."

Benjamin took her by the hand, smiling at her impatience. "It will take it another ten minutes to reach the dock and we'll be there in five."

A little sheepish, Rebecca nodded. "It sounded more like it was over there," she said, pointing directly to where they were headed.

Jennifer Jo McIntire moved over and put an arm through Rebecca's. "I'm really excited too," she whispered. "Do you really think there might be somebody on the boat that knew Derek or Matthew?"

Lydia's Emily, with all the confidence of an eight-year-old, put one hand on her hip in open disgust. "If they are from England, they have to know them."

Nathan laughed and ruffled her hair. "Not quite, Emmy. There are lots of people in England."

"But not all of them are Mormons, Papa," young Joshua said. "And in Matthew's letter he said that he and Derek were going to take the people to the ship. Couldn't this be the same people?"

Caroline's Joshua hooted softly, then put a hand on his name-sake's shoulder. "Yeah, Papa," he teased, "how about that for logic? This son of yours has got a good head on his shoulders."

Peter listened to the banter with some concern. He was the one who had been down to the steamboat landing and heard the rumor that a boatload of English immigrants was due to arrive in Nauvoo about two o'clock this afternoon. If that rumor proved to be false, there were going to be some very disappointed people, especially Rebecca and Jennifer Jo.

———————

There was a large crowd at the landing. Peter's news had spread quickly through the city. All of Nauvoo knew of the great success going on in England and were anxious to meet their brothers and sisters from across the Atlantic.

As the steamboat began to turn slowly toward the shore, the captain saw the waiting mass of people and let off three great blasts of the horn. The dock erupted. People were jumping up, trying to see over the heads of the crowd. They pointed, called out to one another, talked with great animation. Joshua reached out and touched his mother's sleeve. "I think Peter just may be right," he said. "Look at those people. The whole boatload is waiting to get off."

She nodded. The people on board were lined up five and six deep along the railing. And they were close enough now that she could see bags and cases and boxes in their arms. They were waiting to disembark, and that was a good sign. Generally, there were no more than a dozen or so who got off the boats in Nauvoo.

As the boat came to within about fifty yards of the dock, someone suddenly shouted. "There's Theodore Turley!"

"Where? Where?"

"There! Right on the front. See him? It is him! It is!"

Benjamin leaned forward, straining to see, feeling his heart start to race. If it was Theodore Turley, that meant it was the very group of Saints they were looking for. Then Mary Ann had him by the arm. "It is him!" she cried. "I see him."

Benjamin turned to Rebecca, smiling happily. "Then you will have news of your husband for sure."

Suddenly Peter was hopping up and down and waving wildly. "Sister Pottsworth! Sister Pottsworth!" He swung around and grabbed Jessica. "It's our neighbor from Preston." Back around he went, jumping up and down and calling out. "And there's Jenny! Jenny's with her! Oh, I can't believe it. The Pottsworths have come, just like Derek and Matthew said they would."

The Pottsworths were well back in the crowd and didn't make it off the boat for several minutes. By that time, Peter could hardly contain himself. As they finally came down the gangplank, he was there waiting for them. The family pressed forward too as Sister Pottsworth dropped her valise and threw her arms open wide. Peter ran to her and let her sweep him into her embrace. Laughing and crying, they hugged each other like mother and son. Jenny was next, more demure, but unable to totally restrain herself. Peter took her hands and held her back away from him, saying over and over, "Jenny, is that really you?"

Finally, they turned and Peter led them to the family. "Don't tell me," Sister Pottsworth said to Peter. "Let me guess." She went right to Benjamin and Mary Ann. "You have to be Mother and Father Steed." She gave Mary Ann a quick kiss on the cheek. "That is from your son."

"Matthew?" Mary Ann cried, her voice suddenly breaking with emotion.

"Yes. Dear Matthew, how proud you must be of him. He and Derek were the last two people we set eyes on before we set sail. I have letters from the both of them in our cases."

"You have a letter from Derek?" Rebecca said, stepping forward.

Mrs. Pottsworth's smile broadened all the more. "And surely you are Rebecca," she said, reaching out to touch her arm. "Derek has described you perfectly. I bring you his love." She looked around. "And where is little Christopher? Oh, I must give Christopher a hug or Derek will never forgive me."

Jessica stepped forward. She had been holding Christopher so Rebecca could move in among the new arrivals. "This is Christopher."

"Oh, my," Sister Pottsworth said, stepping back. "What a handsome young fellow you are." She turned back to Rebecca. "And he's now almost what? Seventeen months, right?"

Rebecca laughed, highly pleased. "Derek must have told you everything about him."

She pulled a face, feigning pain. "You have no idea."

Almost instantly she sobered, turning now to Nathan and Lydia. "And you are Joshua and Caroline?"

Nathan shook his head. "No, I'm Nathan and this is Lydia."

"Of course," she said instantly. "Joshua is much darker than you, right?"

Nathan laughed. This woman had been thoroughly briefed on the family. He turned and motioned to Joshua and Caroline. Not having any direct stake in these newcomers from England, they had stayed behind the rest of the family. "Come up here, you two," Nathan called. Then, as they did, Nathan introduced them. "This is Caroline and this is Joshua."

Then to their complete surprise, Sister Pottsworth was suddenly crying. Jenny had tears streaming down her face. Completely taken aback by the unexpected reaction, Caroline and Joshua didn't know what to say.

Abigail Pottsworth reached in a pocket and pulled out a handkerchief. She wiped her eyes, then blew her nose. "I'm sorry," she mumbled, "you must forgive me for letting my emotions get away from me."

"That's all right," Caroline said, though she wasn't exactly sure what had caused the sudden change.

Then, unable to hold it back any longer, Sister Pottsworth broke into a radiant smile. "Jenny and me," she said, sniffing back the tears, "as we were boarding the ship in Liverpool, we met someone who thought he might know you two."

"Liverpool?" Joshua responded in bewilderment. "I don't think we know anyone from Liverpool."

Jenny started to laugh through the midst of her tears. "Oh, I think you do." She turned and pointed toward the boat. "We brought him with us just to be sure."

The whole family turned to look at the riverboat. The bow of the boat was empty now except for one figure. He stood alone in the sunshine, watching the group onshore. Then a huge grin split his face and he lifted one hand in greeting.

A collective gasp went up. Joshua gaped. Caroline's hand flew to her mouth and she staggered, her knees nearly buckling. Sister Pottsworth grabbed her arm and steadied her, now laughing and crying all at the same time. "You recognize that boy?"

Will shouldered a canvas bag he was carrying and ran lightly down the gangplank.

"Will?" Caroline cried with one strangled sob.

Joshua took her from Mrs. Pottsworth, putting an arm around her waist. Tears streaked his cheeks now as well. "It's our son," he said hoarsely. "Caroline. It's Will!"

***

Will stood across the room from them, his canvas bag at his feet. His family watched him expectantly. Savannah was wiggling with excitement. Olivia, trying to be more mature, was not much better. Will looked at his mother, who held Charles on her lap. Will shook his head. "I'm sorry, Mama. If I had known while I was in China that you were going to have a baby, I would have gotten something for him too."

Caroline just shook her head. "If there was any way we could have known where to write you about the baby, we would have."

"I know." Suddenly he had to look away. He blinked rapidly,

Reunion in Nauvoo

trying to stop the burning in his eyes. "And, of course, I thought Pa was dead, so I . . ." He just shook his head, his eyes shining.

Joshua leaned forward, barely able to keep his own emotions under control. "Will, you have brought me the only gift I wanted, and that's you."

Will blew out his breath, fighting to keep his face from crumpling. "Well," he said, finally reaching into the bag, "I did get Savannah something. Come here, Savannah."

Savannah had been about a year and a half old when Will had run away from the Montague plantation. Now she was almost four. The red hair was long, to her shoulders; the eyes, even more blue and arresting than Will remembered. Now those eyes watched him gravely. At first Savannah had been wary of this stranger who was causing such a fuss, but Will had quickly teased that out of her, and now with the promise of a present, all reticence was gone. As he pulled out the long, narrow package wrapped in paper, she walked straight over to him without hesitation.

"Close your eyes."

Her little hands came up and covered her eyes, but she kept her fingers spread apart, and behind them her eyes were wide open. Will laughed aloud. "You little imp. Here."

He took the paper off, revealing a child's parasol. Carefully, he opened it up. It was made of silk and had a beautifully carved bamboo handle. The fabric was a pale green and was covered with four exquisite landscape scenes. Savannah's hands dropped to her sides, her eyes grew very large, and her mouth opened in a long, silent *Oh!* Pleased, Will carefully placed it into her hands.

"Oh, Will!" Caroline cried. "That's beautiful. It's the perfect color with her hair." Then she motioned to her daughter. "Come here, Savannah. Let Mama and Papa see it."

Twirling the parasol like a grown woman on a Sunday walk in the park, Savannah came to her parents, willing to let them look, but not about to let it out of her possession.

"Savannah," Joshua said, chucking her under the chin, "you're going to have the most beautiful parasol in all of Nauvoo."

"I know," she said matter-of-factly.

"And what do you say to Will, young lady?" Caroline asked.

Savannah started to turn, then realized that hugging her brother with a parasol presented a challenge. Reluctantly she handed it to her mother, then ran to Will and threw her arms around him. She planted a kiss on his cheek. "Thank you, Will. It's beautiful!"

"You're welcome, Savannah." As she let him go and returned quickly for her gift, Will looked at Olivia. "Livvy, I had no idea that I would be arriving home on your birthday, or that you would be so grown up. When I left, you were still a girl. Now you're a young woman."

Olivia blushed with pleasure. To others, Will's description would have seemed like a bit of an exaggeration. Now thirteen, she was just starting to mature. But for Olivia, it was the perfect compliment.

"I wasn't sure what to get for you," he said. "I looked and looked." He pulled something out, but kept it low, behind his leg.

Olivia couldn't bear it. She edged closer. Smiling, Will brought it around, holding it out for her to see. Olivia leaned forward tentatively, not sure exactly what it was, and then she moved closer and took it from him. "Oh, Will!" she said, her voice filled with awe. "It's beautiful."

"Let's see, Livvy," Savannah cried. Olivia turned around and walked slowly toward them, peering at her gift. When she reached them, she held it out and they all began to ooh and aah. It was an ebony case with glass panels, about the size of a small loaf of bread in roundness, but only two or three inches thick. Inside the glass, carved out of a soft corkwood, was an intricate three-dimensional Chinese temple and garden. Every detail was perfect. The temple walls were delicately carved latticework. A bridge spanned the pond. Two storks, each no bigger than the fingernail on Olivia's little finger, stood together in the water.

Caroline looked up at her son. "Where did you ever find such a thing?"

"These are all over in China," he said, pleased with their reaction. "They are called cork carvings."

Joshua took it from Olivia to examine it more closely. "I can't believe the detail."

"What do you do with it?" Savannah demanded, eyeing it suspiciously.

"You set it on a table or on a dresser and look at it," Livvy said. And then, realizing another value of the treasure, she added, "And you let other people see what a beautiful thing you have." She swung around. "Oh, thank you, Will. It's beautiful. I love it."

Joshua was still examining it carefully. He looked at Caroline. "I'll bet you could import these and make a fortune selling them. They are absolutely enchanting."

Will was fumbling in the bag again. "Now, Mother. I want you and Papa to close your eyes."

"Will, you didn't have to bring us anything but *you*," Caroline said, but she put her hand over her eyes. Joshua simply closed his.

Putting a finger to his lips, Will motioned Savannah and Olivia over to help him. From out of the bag he drew two small identical boxes. He opened them and took out the two chop carvings, one with a lion carved into the top of the stone cylinder, the other with a dragon. Then he fumbled in the bottom of the bag until he found a piece of paper. The piece of paper had two red circles stamped onto it. Both had a Chinese symbol in the middle, and both had block English letters around the inside of the circle. The one had the letters C-A-R-O-L-I-N-E, the other J-O-S-H-U-A. Will moved to the table near his mother and laid the paper down. Then he placed each chop carving beside its appropriate circle.

"Almost ready," he said. He stepped back. "Now, Pa, you need to know something. I did get you something."

"But . . ."

"I didn't know I was buying it for you. I just wanted Mama to have another one like hers, a set." He paused. "All right, open your eyes."

They opened them and looked, then leaned forward, peering more closely. "Oh, they are beautiful, Will," Caroline said. "What are they?"

"They're called chop carvings. They are like a stamp or a seal," he said proudly, "only made of stone. See?" He picked one up and turned it so they could see how the Chinese character and the name had been carved in the bottom of the stone.

Joshua's eyes were suddenly blurring until he could no longer read his name. "And you bought one for me?" he whispered.

Will took one look at his father and started to cry too. "Yes, Papa. I don't know what came over me. I guess I couldn't bear to think of Mama ever forgetting you."

Joshua stood and walked to his son. Without a word, he took him in his arms, and for a long time they stood there, holding each other.

"Joshua?"

He turned his head on the pillow.

"I've been praying night and morning for almost two years now for Will."

"I know."

"Your whole family has been praying too. That he would be safe. That God would watch over him."

"Yes."

She was silent for several moments; then, very softly, so softly that he had to raise his head to catch her words, she continued. "Do you really think it's just a coincidence that Will ended up on the very ship that had a group of Mormons headed for Nauvoo?"

"I . . ." He too had been struck by that wonderful stroke of fortune. "I don't know. Liverpool was a stopping place for them coming and going. So that was fortunate. And the timing, to get changed to the very boat . . ." He shook his head. It did strain the imagination to think of that as mere coincidence.

She didn't answer him. She didn't have to.

After several moments of silence, he spoke again. "Caroline, I don't know what to call it. God. Providence. Good fortune. But whatever it was, I *am* grateful that our son has returned."

She nodded and reached out and found his hand. "I know." Then, "Joshua?"

"What?"

"I would like to thank God. Would it be all right if I did it out loud?"

There was a moment's hesitation, and then he squeezed her hand. "Yes."

She took his other hand too, then closed her eyes. "Our Father who art in heaven, hallowed be thy name." Her voice caught, and he felt the quick, angry shake of her head. She did not want to lose control. She wanted to say this. Finally, she took a quick breath and went on, her voice thick and labored. "Oh, Heavenly Father, how we thank thee this night for the gift of our son. How we thank thee for hearing and answering our prayers. We know that it was thy hand that kept him safe. We know that it was thy goodness that led him to that ship in England which brought him home swiftly to our side. We know how much thou didst love thy own Son, and we thank thee that thou hast cared for our son as well, and held him in thy safe keeping. And we offer this prayer to thee in the name of thy Son, Jesus Christ, amen."

For several moments, Joshua lay there, his own emotions swirling. Then finally, he spoke one word, softly but with great feeling. "Amen," he said.

Chapter Notes

The concepts of faith and sacrifice discussed by Joseph here are found in the "Lectures on Faith," lectures 1 and 6. The laying of the first log in Kaw Township happened on 2 August 1831. The "season of joy" quote is found in Joseph's history under that date. (See HC 1:196.)

Will watched with amusement as his Uncle Nathan took off his coat and scarf and hung them carefully over a dead tree limb next to the tent. Then Nathan started unbuttoning his shirt, first the sleeves, and then the front.

"You really are going to do it?" Will asked.

Nathan looked up in surprise. "Of course. Ten days without a bath? I get up in the morning thinking I've been sleeping with a bear, then I realize it's just me I'm smelling."

Will turned and looked at his father and Carl, who were sitting by the fire drinking coffee out of tin cups. Joshua took one last sip, then tossed the remaining liquid into the fire. "Now, don't you be getting any ideas, Will. I don't care what I smell like, I'm waiting till we get back to La Crosse, then I'm paying for a bath and a shave. A man's gotta be crazy to wash off in a creek when there's snow on the ground and frost in the air."

Nathan ignored the gibes and finished taking off his shirt.

"Mind the ice along the creekbank," Carl said soberly. "Wouldn't want you to be cutting yourself."

Nathan hooted in derision. By morning there would be a skim of ice across the places where the current was slower, but it hadn't been that cold today. "Couple of hothouse plants," he muttered to himself, unbuttoning his long johns now. He looked at Will. "Must be a real disappointment for you, Will," he said with a trace of sorrow.

"What's that?" Will asked.

"To come home and find your father's gone as soft as a Boston preacher. Body turning to mush. No backbone anymore. Whimpers at the first sign of discomfort. Tragic how some men let themselves go to seed."

Joshua grunted, picked up a rock, and lobbed it at his brother. It wasn't anywhere close and Nathan didn't even flinch. Will nodded soberly. "I hadn't wanted to say anything, but I was a little shocked."

Carl chortled as Joshua howled in dismay. Joshua grabbed a stick and took a swing at Will across the fire from him. "From my own son?" he cried. "I don't have to take that kind of talk."

"Careful, Will," Nathan called as Will rolled away from the swinging stick. "As the Book of Mormon says, 'The guilty taketh the truth to be hard, for it cutteth them to the very center.'"

Joshua was not about to be nonplussed. "And the Bible says, 'Only a fool taketh a bath in November in Wisconsin.'"

They all laughed at that. "I think you need to read the Bible a little more, Pa," Will said.

Nathan pulled his long johns down to his waist, stripped bare now except for his pants and boots. He moved to the creek, carrying a bar of soap and a pan. He knelt at the water's edge and bent over. Joshua began to laugh. "Hey, little brother, don't forget your cap."

Nathan looked startled, then reached up and removed the stocking cap Lydia had knit especially for this trip. He looked sheepish. "Oh yeah, thanks!"

Tossing the cap aside, he scooped a pan of water out of the creek and dumped it over his head. "Oh! Ooh! Oh my!" The cries came in swift succession as he began to scrub at his hair.

"That's better," Joshua laughed.

They watched in amusement as Nathan bent over and stuck his head clear under the water to rinse out the soap. Then he started on his arms and face and chest, howling and gasping at every new plunge into the water. Chuckling, Will looked at his father. "I'm with you, Pa. I think I'll wait for La Crosse. We should be back there in a couple of days, shouldn't we?"

"I'd say more like tomorrow night. I think we've found what we're looking for. I say we break camp and leave in the morning."

Will was a little surprised at that. His father hadn't said any-thing about being finished. They had been tramping these forests for the past four days, his father leading them like a man possessed. They scouted the Black River from where it joined the Mississippi above La Crosse all the way up several miles past the Black River Falls, a distance of some thirty miles or so. They found at least five good possibilities for a mill site—three on the Black River itself, and two more on Roaring Creek, a major tributary. They retraced their steps on several occasions, calcu-lating how a raft of lumber would fare in the various stretches of rapids. Joshua drew rough sketches of landmarks closest to the best stands of timber. It hadn't taken long for Carl and Nathan and Will to be infected with Joshua's enthusiasm. And the vast-ness of the virgin forests of western Wisconsin did nothing to discourage it either.

Though Carl and his Englishman partner were well into the construction of their brick kiln in Nauvoo, Joshua had per-suaded Carl to come north with them anyway. Carl would not be directly involved in the new partnership Joshua was contem-plating, but Joshua valued his quiet, solid business sense. Joshua's plan—mostly developed as they trekked through the woods—was for him and Walter Samuelson, his St. Louis busi-ness partner, to furnish the capital, and Nathan and Will and maybe Matthew, when he got back from England, to manage the day-to-day operations. Nathan had not committed to this as yet but seemed intrigued. Will hadn't dared say a word to either of his parents, but he was missing the sea and was still not ready to dismiss the idea of making a run for a sea captainship.

"Do you think Grandpa's group will be back in La Crosse when we get there?" Will asked his father.

"Could be. Either way we'll wait for one another."

Will nodded. Joseph Smith also saw the potential of the Wisconsin timber belt as a solution to the Church's building problems. So when he heard that Joshua and Nathan were headed north on an exploratory trip, he asked Benjamin and other members from the building committee to join them and see what the prospects for Church sawmills might be.

"Hey, Will," Nathan called, still bent over and soaked now to his waist. "I forgot the towel. Can you get it for me?"

Will went to the tent and retrieved the towel. Nathan stood as he came near, so Will opened it up as he approached Nathan. "Turn around. I'll get your back."

Obediently, Nathan turned, facing the creek, putting his back to Will and the fire. Will stepped forward, then went rigid. There was an audible gasp.

Nathan jumped and spun around, thinking Will had seen a snake or something. There was another sharp intake of breath as Will saw the bare chest. "Uncle Nathan! What happened to you?"

Nathan didn't comprehend for a moment. He never thought much about the scars anymore. Then as he realized what Will had seen, he reached out and snatched the towel from Will's hand and wrapped it around the upper part of his body. "It's nothing, Will."

"Nothing!" Will cried, barely aware that his father and Carl had come to their feet behind him. "You forget I've been on board a ship for the last two years. I know the mark of the lash when I see it."

Nathan finished drying himself, then pulled up his long johns and started buttoning them. "Really, Will," he said, smiling easily. "It's nothing to be concerned about. It happened a long time ago. I never think about it anymore."

Will turned to his father, wondering if his father had seen what he had just seen. To his surprise, Joshua was pale and visibly shaken. Carl also had a strange look on his face. "What?" Will asked, sensing that the scars were not a surprise to these two. "What is it?"

Joshua finally lowered his head and turned to stare into the fire. "Tell him, Nathan."

"No!" It came out softly and without emotion, but there was no question about the finality in Nathan's voice. "It's done with, Joshua. Let it lie."

"He has a right to know. It's part of his father's life."

"No!"

Will was totally bewildered. "Part of your life?" he echoed.

Joshua straightened slowly. He looked to Carl for help. Carl finally nodded. "I think you're right. Now that he's seen it, he has a right to know."

Nathan came up and laid an arm across Will's shoulder. "Let's sit down. There's more to the story than your pa's going to tell you."

———◆———

When it was finished, when Joshua and Nathan had told him everything, they arose and, with Carl, went to their bedrolls, leaving him sitting by the fire. For almost half an hour Will sat motionless, staring into the glowing embers. Strangely enough, his thoughts did not stay for long on what had happened between these two previously estranged brothers. Though it shook him deeply to think that this man who had become his father was capable of such a thing, the reconciliation between Nathan and Joshua was complete. The scars were not the only things that had healed.

Instead, his thoughts turned to Nathan's final words. "You know," he had said, half musing, not speaking to anyone in particular, "sometimes things happen that give a man cause to hate someone else. It may even be a good reason. So he takes hate to his bosom and holds it close, like he's afraid it will slip away from him if he lets go. But it's like putting a prairie rattlesnake inside your shirt. No matter how good a reason you may have for doing so, you're going to be the one who gets bit."

It was only now that it hit Will that Nathan had meant those comments for him. And now his thoughts turned to Jenny. When Hugh Watson and Riley Overson came to Independence and spun the web of lies about Joshua being killed by the Mormons, Will had swelled with hate. Even after he learned it wasn't the Mormons who had shot his father after all, he found that the bitterness didn't go away. As Nathan said. He had nurtured those feelings for too long. You didn't just root them out in one yank and have it be as it was before.

Jenny had sensed that hostility in him almost from the first instant they met, and it had nearly cost him any chance of becoming friends with her. Even now sometimes, when some aspect of the Mormons was mentioned, he felt himself turning away, bristling all over again. It was stupid. It was totally irrational. But it was there. And Jenny seemed to know that too.

There was the snap of a twig and Will looked up in surprise. Joshua was standing across from him, on the other side of what was left of the fire. "May I join you?"

"Of course."

Joshua came around and sat beside him. Like Will, he leaned forward to stare into the embers. After a long time, he turned his head. "I'm sorry, Will. I should have told you before. It's not something I can speak of very easily. I consider it to be one of the darkest days of my life."

"I understand. Thank you for telling me now, Pa."

"You would have seen Nathan's back sooner or later. I'm just glad I was here to be the one to tell you about it."

"Me too." Will pulled his legs closer and hugged himself. With the fire down, the cold was edging in on them. "Pa?"

"Yes, son?"

"I just realized that what Nathan said—about hate? Well, he was talking to me, wasn't he?"

Joshua stiffened. "You?"

"Yes. All those months of thinking you were dead and that the Mormons had done it to you. He knows how much I hated—"

Joshua was shaking his head doggedly back and forth.

"What?"

"Don't you understand, son? Nathan knows full well what's happening between your mother and me over this Mormon thing." There was discouragement in his voice now. "No, Will, Nathan wasn't talking to you. He was talking directly to me."

———•◆•———

In addition to his assignment as a member of the building committee for the temple, Benjamin was also doing considerable work with and for the acting city council. John C. Bennett had been in Springfield since October conference, vigorously lobbying the state legislature for the passage of the Nauvoo City Charter. In his latest letter to Joseph he reported that he was getting a surprisingly warm response to the proposal. Much of that was the result of the political parties' courting the growing bloc of Mormon voters, but be that as it may, Bennett predicted passage of the charter before the end of the year. So Joseph called together a committee and asked them to begin working out plans for implementation if the charter passed. Benjamin was one of those called.

All of that had happened just before Benjamin left for Wisconsin. Now, back only two days, he found that his desk in the room where the building committee had taken up temporary offices was still piled deep with papers. Most were related to the temple, but several were papers relating to the city's government. He was determined to get through the work and told Mary Ann not to wait supper on him. So when there was a knock on the door just after six p.m. and Caroline and Mary Ann walked in, it came as a surprise.

"I'm sorry to bother you, Benjamin," Mary Ann said without preamble, "but we have a question, or rather a proposal."

"All right."

"If you agree, we need to get started on it immediately, like even tonight."

He laid the pen down and pushed the papers aside.

"Go ahead, Caroline," Mary Ann said.

Caroline stepped up beside her. "Sister Charity Blackmun was in the store this afternoon. She's from Massachusetts originally, and somehow we got talking about Thanksgiving. She said what a disappointment it has been to her that Thanksgiving isn't celebrated here."

"Thanksgiving? You mean like the Pilgrims' Thanksgiving?"

"Yes. It's widely observed in New England. Several of the states back there have even made it a state holiday. But it's not here in Illinois."

He shrugged. He hadn't even thought about it.

"Well," Caroline went on, "Charity says she and her family are going to start it here. She's going to have a big dinner on Monday for the whole family, with all the things the Pilgrims ate—wild turkey, pumpkin pie, sweet potatoes."

Benjamin smiled. "She'll have to pass on the cranberries. Not a lot of cranberry bogs in Nauvoo that I know about. That's for sure." He paused for a moment. "Why Monday?"

"That's the last day of November," Caroline answered. "That's when they always celebrated it back home."

Now he saw what was coming. "And you think it might be a good idea if the Steeds did the same thing?"

Mary Ann was eager now. "Yes. We have so much to be thankful for, especially this year with Will home and Carl and Melissa here. Let's get our family together and thank the Lord."

That was not a difficult decision to make. "I like it," he said. "Let's do it."

———————◆———————

It was a sumptuous feast by any standard. Nathan and Carl and Will had rowed across the river and spent a full day hunting along the streams west of Montrose. Mary Ann had specifically ordered the things she wanted them to get, but that was easier said than done. Twice they heard the gobble of wild turkeys, but they never even got to see them. But they did bag three quail, two Canadian geese, and a yearling buck deer. Joshua had his drivers round up two bushels of apples, a large sack of potatoes, a whole wagonload of pumpkins—most of which Joshua then gave away to neighbors and friends—and enough flour, sugar, and honey to make a dozen pies. The children scoured the river bottoms for currants and other edible roots and berries, while the wives scrubbed the house until it shone.

On the thirtieth, Jessica took a rare holiday and dismissed school, mostly so that Peter and the McIntire girls could watch the store and tend the children, which would free the women to spend the day cooking. Joshua and Caroline had the biggest house, so they decided to have the gathering there, but even then, with the Pottsworths, there were thirty-one people coming to dinner, counting the babies. So out went the furniture and in came sawhorses and long planks. Two long tables were set up and tablecloths spread over them. Each family contributed their finest dinnerware to provide the place settings. When everything was in readiness, they all trooped back to their individual homes to wash and change. Promptly at six p.m., the banquet began.

———◆———

Benjamin stood at the head of the table and surveyed the faces around him. The room grew very quiet. "I think it is appropriate if we say a word or two before we begin. Mama tells me that we have a few minutes before the meat is done."

Mary Ann nodded beside him.

"As you know, this is Thanksgiving Day. I don't know why we haven't paid much attention to it before, but I, for one, am glad that your grandmother and Caroline proposed that this year we do so."

"Hear! Hear!" Nathan called out.

"Rather than hearing some long, boring talk from me, Mama and I would like to propose something else. We would like each person to think of one thing that they are particularly thankful for on this day and then tell us about it. It doesn't have to be the most important thing in your life. It doesn't have to be important to anyone else but you. Just tell us the one thing for which you are most thankful. That includes the children. When the last is finished, we'll ask Nathan to return thanks on the food and then we'll eat."

Murmurs of assent rippled through the family and heads were nodding. He looked down at Mary Ann and took her hand. "I would like to begin." Every eye turned to him now, and he straightened noticeably. "This was hard for me, because so many things came to mind. But . . . A year ago in July, I was lying on my bed, too weak to move, thinking I was going to die. But I didn't. So I am thankful for the gift of another year of life, another year to be with all of you"—he looked down at Mary Ann—"and another year to be with this woman. She still has much to teach me and I'm trying to learn."

He sat down amid murmurs of affection and approval. Then, as it quieted, everyone looked around. He hadn't designated any order and they weren't sure who was next. Benjamin noted the momentary confusion, but said nothing. After a moment, Joshua slowly stood. "I would like to be the first after Pa." He looked at his father and smiled apologetically. "I'm sorry, Pa. You said we could say only one thing, but I have two things that I am grateful for. First . . ." He looked around at the family. "First, like Pa, I am glad that I am sitting here tonight at this table with my family. I nearly died too, but it's more than that. I spent many years away from this table and away from you, and it is good to be back."

He took a deep breath and looked at Will. "Second . . ." Now his voice betrayed him, and he looked down. His hands gripped the back of his chair until the knuckles were white. Finally, he looked up. His gaze was still on Will. His eyes were filled with tears. "I'm sorry," he whispered. "I think you know what the second thing is." And he sat down. Two seats away from him, Will was blinking rapidly, trying to hold in his own emotions.

Joshua was barely down before Caroline was up. She had Charles in one arm, but she reached out with her other hand

and laid it on Joshua's shoulder. Her lower lip was trembling, but when she spoke her voice was clear and steady. "I am thankful for a God who hears and answers our prayers and who has brought our son home again." She sat down.

Olivia and Will both started to get up, but Jessica beat them to it. Her head was up and her eyes were dry, but the effect of her words was even more powerful than if she had been weeping. "I am thankful for John Griffith. Though he is not with us now, he was a blessing to my life that will last into the eternities. He gave me three wonderful sons." She looked down at Rachel. "And he was a good father to my daughter. And . . ." A wonderful joy filled her eyes. "And he taught me the meaning of love."

And so it went. It was not just a catalog of thanks, but a litany of remembrance and a listing of blessings. Lydia spoke of peace found and purpose renewed. Nathan said he was thankful they had followed Benjamin's advice and gone back to Palmyra because of what it had meant to Lydia's parents and to him and Lydia. Their Emmy, every bit the miniature replica of her mother, brought smiles all around when she gave thanks for her new little sister. Lydia wasn't due yet for another month, but Emmy wanted a sister, and so a sister it had to be.

Olivia also spoke of Will. Then, a little chagrined, she admitted that the piano her father had bought for her was also a treasure for which she was especially grateful. Abigail Pottsworth gave thanks for newness—a new country, a new start, a new "family," and a new life among the community of Saints. Jenny expressed joy in being able to hear the Prophet Joseph Smith in person. Peter said he was grateful that Derek had found the Pottsworths and helped them come to America.

Like his father, Will stood but couldn't finish. He didn't have to. When he finally sat down, shrugging helplessly, there were tears enough around the table to say it all. Young Joshua and Rachel both said they were thankful for the gospel. Red-headed Savannah was thankful for Will and her grandpa. Jennifer Jo McIntire (with two Jennys now, everyone had followed

Matthew's lead and taken to calling her by her full name) expressed gratitude for two people, both of whom were gone from her life—her mother, dead now for over a year, and Matthew, gone to England.

Kathryn echoed those sentiments regarding their mother, then thanked God for the new "mother" he had given them as a replacement. With that comment, everyone looked at Jessica and smiled. Now she couldn't stop the tears from rising up. Jennifer and Kathryn McIntire were far more now than just her boarders, and everyone knew it. Carl surprised everyone by talking mostly about how happy he was that he and Melissa had come west. Melissa almost duplicated Caroline in thanking God for answering prayers.

When it had gone all the way around, Benjamin turned to Mary Ann. "Mother?" he said gently. "I think you're the last."

She rose to her feet and let her eyes move slowly across the whole group. They were shining with happiness and contentment. "There is only one thing I ever really wanted, and that was to have all of my family together with me. I knew it was not possible. I knew it was only the dream of a sentimental old grandma. And yet, here it is. Here you all are." She smiled down at the Pottsworths. "And how happy we are that our family keeps growing."

"But what about Matthew and Derek, Grandma?" Emily asked with concern. "They're not here right now."

"Oh yes they are, Emmy," she exclaimed, putting a hand to her heart. "Oh, yes they are."

"And that about says it all," Benjamin said as she sat down. "Nathan, would you offer grace on the food, please?"

⸻ ⋅ ⸻

Jennifer Jo tiptoed into the bedroom and shut the door quietly behind her. Moving carefully so as not to bump anything and awaken Kathryn, she crept to the bed and started to get into it. Then she heard the soft sound of crying. "Kathryn?"

Her sister rolled over, and in the faint moonlight coming

through the window Jennifer Jo could see the wet streaks on her cheeks. "Kathryn, what is it? What's the matter?"

There was a quick shake of her head, and another convulsive shudder ran through her body.

"Kathryn," Jennifer Jo said, lying down beside her and putting an arm around her. "Peter didn't do it to hurt you."

"I know." It came out in a strangled little whisper.

Jennifer Jo sighed. This was not the first time Kathryn had gone to bed with tears because of Peter, and normally Jennifer just tried not to smile as she gave Kathryn the comfort she needed. Kathryn was still only fourteen years old, and her feelings for Peter hovered between juvenile infatuation and adoring adulation. Two years her senior, Peter was, for the most part, blithely unaware of the torture he was putting her through. They were good friends, but Kathryn read so much more into it than he did. And thus the constant seesaw between ecstasy and despair. On one day, Peter would share a poem with her that he had written or slap her playfully on the shoulder, as he would any other friend, and she would come home dreamy eyed and keep her sister up for hours talking about it. Then he would turn right around and go days on end acting as though he barely knew her. Those were the nights for the tears.

Jennifer Jo talked to Jessica about it once, but Jessica had just smiled and said that that was part of growing up for girls. Let Peter and Kathryn mature some more, she counseled. One day, and perhaps soon, he will open his eyes and see that Kathryn has become a lovely young woman. He will start to notice how comfortable she makes him feel, and how much they have in common. And then everything will be fine. In the meantime, they just had to help Kathryn learn to be patient.

This had proven to be wise counsel, until Jenny Pottsworth arrived, and then for Kathryn, the world seemed to collapse.

Jenny was fifteen, only a year older than Kathryn, but in many ways Jenny was leagues ahead of Kathryn. Not only was she more physically mature—much more a woman—than Kathryn, but she was emotionally and intellectually two or three years ahead of most fifteen-year-olds. And that was no surprise. Jenny had started working in the textile mills at age nine. The Steed family had been horrified one night a few days after the Pottsworths' arrival when Sister Pottsworth told them about the shameless exploitation of children in industrial England. Even with the law Parliament finally passed in 1834, children under the age of eighteen were still working sixty-nine hours per week! That was five twelve-hour shifts and a nine-hour shift on Saturdays. In essence, Jenny had been catapulted from childhood to womanhood, missing adolescence completely.

And Peter had done the same. Orphans battling together for survival, he and Derek had lived a lifetime by the time Peter was twelve. So this bond between Jenny and Peter was more than the usual friendship. They were products of the same bleak growing-up years.

"Kathryn," Jennifer Jo finally said, not knowing how else to comfort her. "You have to remember that Jenny and Peter were good friends in England."

"I know."

"*Good* friends!" she said again. "That's all they are now. Just good friends."

Kathryn's head came around and there was challenge in her eyes. "Did you watch Will tonight at dinner? Do you think he thinks they are only friends?"

Jennifer Jo didn't answer because there was only one answer. She had seen it too. All through the Thanksgiving dinner, she had watched the pain in Will's eyes too. Like Kathryn, he would wince when Jenny, in that totally natural way she had, would lay her hand across Peter's and they would throw back their heads and laugh together. Like Kathryn, he would look away quickly when Peter would whisper something to Jenny and she would smile and nod in delight.

"She sat by him at dinner," Kathryn began, her voice a mixture of sadness and anger. "She sat with him afterwards. She ended up as his partner when we played the games."

"Sometimes that was just by accident."

"Sometimes," Kathryn conceded darkly. "And what about the singing? Was that by accident?"

Jennifer Jo looked away. That had proven to be the worst disaster of the night. After the games, Nathan suggested they gather around the piano and sing songs. With Olivia playing for some and Caroline accompanying others, they went through their old favorites: first the more spirited ones—"Yankee Doodle," "Comin' Through the Rye," and "Ol' Zip Coon"—then the slower ones, the ones with more feeling and emotion—"'Tis the Last Rose of Summer," "Shenandoah," "Flow Gently, Sweet Afton." As they sang together, a wonderful, sweet mood descended on the whole family. And that is when it happened.

Jennifer Jo sighed. "I'm so sorry, Kathryn. When I suggested that Peter sing, I just assumed he would ask you to sing it with him."

"So did I."

Frowning, Jennifer Jo felt her own anger rising now. Lydia had sung one verse of "Amazing Grace." It was beautiful, and all were touched. Then on impulse she asked Jessica to sing with her. The results had been a deeply moving experience for all. That was when Jennifer Jo got the idea to have Peter and Kathryn sing together and maybe salvage something from the night. Kathryn had a favorite song, and Peter liked it too. The name of it was "Believe Me, If All Those Endearing Young Charms." Kathryn and Peter had sung it once as a duet in school, and so when Jennifer Jo made the suggestion she didn't feel that she had to suggest both their names. She wanted the request for Kathryn to come from Peter, and not from her. And that was when disaster struck. Peter had not turned to Kathryn. He had turned to Jenny and asked her if she knew the song. She did, and that was that.

"It was so beautiful," cried Kathryn. The anguish was heavy now. "I could never sing it that beautifully."

"You do sing it beautifully," Jennifer Jo said loyally. But it was true. If Lydia and Jessica's song had deeply stirred the family, then Jenny and Peter's stunned them. Both of their voices were so pure, so perfectly on pitch, that when they sang in unison, one had to listen closely to make sure there were two voices. And when they had sung harmony, Jenny's rich alto blending into Peter's clear-toned tenor, even Jennifer Jo had felt chills go up and down her back.

"It's my song," Kathryn suddenly burst out. "I taught it to him."

Jennifer Jo's eyebrows rose. "You did?"

"Yes. Margaret Naylor taught it to me." Suddenly the tears were overflowing. "And she's the one who told me the story behind it."

"The story? What story?" Kathryn had never said anything about this before.

Kathryn sniffed back the tears. "It's a true story, too," she said mournfully. "There was once a man and a woman who were very happily married. The woman was considered to be one of the most beautiful women in all the country. She had long hair, and skin as fair as the clouds. They were very much in love. Then one day she was struck down with smallpox. She nearly died, and her husband was not allowed to see her, lest he catch the disease too. When she finally recovered, she looked in the mirror and saw that she was horribly scarred. Her beautiful hair was mostly gone. She was so devastated that she locked herself in her room and swore she would never again see the light of day."

"So what happened?" Jennifer Jo asked, caught up totally in the story.

"Her husband pled with her to come out. He told her that he didn't care what the disease had done to her, that he loved her anyway. But nothing he said changed her mind. Desperate, he went downstairs and got a pen and paper. And then . . ." She looked away.

Now Jennifer Jo was nodding. "And he wrote those wonderful words."

"Yes." Kathryn began to recite very softly.

Believe me, if all those endearing young charms,
    Which I gaze on so fondly today,
Were to change by tomorrow, and fleet in my arms,
    Like fairy-gifts fading away,
Thou wouldst still be adored, as this moment thou art,
    Let thy loveliness fade as it will,
And around the dear ruin each wish of my heart
    Would entwine itself verdantly still.

The room was quiet now, and Kathryn was staring at her hands. "He walked up the stairs and sang that song to her through the door. For a moment there was no sound, and then the door opened, and with tears in her eyes, the woman threw herself into her husband's arms."

Now Jennifer Jo fully understood what Peter and Jenny had done to Kathryn on this night. This was Kathryn's dream. No matter that she was not as lovely as Jenny. No matter that she was not as mature and witty and composed and assured. Her Peter would someday see beyond those surface things and love her in spite of them. Singing that duet together in school had been their compact, their covenant to that fact. But tonight, the compact was shattered, the covenant was broken.

Jennifer Jo's lips set into a tight line. It was not just Peter that she resented now. Maybe it was innocently done, but Jenny had caused deep pain this night. And Jennifer Jo could not simply brush that aside. She put her arms around Kathryn and pulled her close. "I'm so sorry, Kathryn. If only I had known, I would never have asked him."

Chapter Notes

The Church was very much interested in the Wisconsin pineries, as they were called, as a source of lumber. For four winter seasons, commencing in the fall of 1841 and finishing in the spring of 1845, the Church ran sawmills along Roaring Creek and the Black River. With the influx of immigrants from England, these mills provided not only much-needed building materials but also employment for many brethren. Over those four years, the Church harvested an estimated one and one-half million board feet of milled lumber, over two hundred thousand shingles, and an unknown amount of loose logs, barn boards, and hewed timbers. (See Dennis Rowley, "The Mormon Experience in the Wisconsin Pineries, 1841–1845," *BYU Studies* 32 [Winter and Spring 1992]: 119–48.)

For some reason, the traditional Thanksgiving Day feast so popular in New England lost its place out west. Indications are that even the Saints were not observing the holiday. Eventually, some Nauvoo Saints apparently did take up the observance of Thanksgiving, though it may not have been as early as depicted here in the novel. We do know that Martha Hall Haven, a convert from Massachusetts who was determined to renew her own family traditions, held a Thanksgiving dinner in Nauvoo in 1843, the first that is recorded there. (See *Women*, pp. 64–65.) Gradually, various states made Thanksgiving a legal holiday until finally, in 1863, President Abraham Lincoln issued a general proclamation that the last Thursday in November would be a national day of thanksgiving. It was not until the beginning of World War II that, in an effort to stimulate business by providing a longer Christmas shopping season, Thanksgiving was moved up a week to the fourth Thursday and was designated as a federal holiday.

Ⅰt was a cold night. Snowflakes floated gently down from the sky, covering everything with a soft new layer of white. They met at Lydia's house so that Lydia, now only a couple of weeks away from delivery, didn't have to go out, but they came at the behest of Mary Ann. All of the women of the Steed clan were invited, including the McIntire sisters and the Pottsworths. Olivia, now thirteen, was, for this purpose, considered to be a woman too. They chose a Sabbath evening so the men could watch the children. In order that the two homes where there was no man would also be covered, Nathan took his and Lydia's children over to Jessica's house, and Rebecca brought Christopher there as well.

Jessica and Rebecca went to Lydia's early to help Mother Steed bake apple dumplings, so Jennifer Jo and Kathryn stayed behind to tend the children until Nathan came. Because of that, the McIntire sisters were the last to arrive. As Rebecca helped them off with their coats, Jennifer Jo saw that the only open seating left was between Caroline and Olivia on one side and Jenny Pottsworth and her mother on the other. Kathryn saw it too and shook her head quickly at her sister. But there was no other choice. Determined to make the best of it, Jennifer Jo led the way to the two seats.

"Oh, good evening, Jennifer Jo," Jenny said, looking up. "Good evening, Kathryn." It was said warmly and with genuine pleasure.

Jennifer Jo nodded and forced a smile. "Good evening." Kathryn murmured something that was not distinguishable.

"Hello, Jenny," Olivia said with a cheerful smile. She was the only one who still insisted on calling Jennifer Jo "Jenny." She didn't care about trying to keep the two Jennys separate.

"Hello, Livvy," Jennifer Jo said, taking the seat closest to Jenny so that Kathryn wouldn't have to sit right beside her. "What a lovely dress. Is that new?"

Olivia beamed with pleasure and held out the skirt so they could see more of it. "Papa bought it for me. He got Savannah one too."

Caroline was listening and shook her head ruefully. "Joshua spoils these two girls shamelessly. You'll have to come see Savannah's. It's green velvet with white ribbons. She is so proud of it, I can barely get it off her so she can go to bed."

Jennifer Jo laughed, as did the others. That was Savannah, all right.

Sister Pottsworth leaned forward. "Have you heard from Matthew of late, Jennifer Jo?"

She frowned and shook her head. "Not for about two weeks now. Since he's gone to London, it seems like it takes even longer for his letters to get here."

Jenny reached out and touched Jennifer Jo's arm. "Olivia was just telling us how she used to think she was going to marry Matthew."

As Olivia blushed, Kathryn smiled for the first time. "Yes.

For a time there, after Matthew announced that he and Jennifer Jo were promised, we didn't know if Livvy was ever going to speak to us again."

"But that's all behind them now," Caroline said. "Isn't it, Livvy?"

Olivia cocked her head, and the wide green eyes got a little impish look in them as she looked up at Kathryn. "Yes. Now I've decided I'm going to marry Peter."

At school, Olivia and Kathryn sat next to each other. Though there was a year-and-a-half difference in their ages, they had become very close friends. Olivia knew full well how Kathryn felt about Peter, and her comment was only meant to tease. Instead, Kathryn visibly flinched, and then she blushed deeply. She looked down, her hands twisting around each other.

Caroline saw instantly what had happened and decided to change the subject rather than try to smooth things over. "We were talking about Matthew," she said to Jennifer Jo. "Abigail was saying what a fine young man he is."

"Aye," the Englishwoman said, puzzled by Kathryn's reaction, but sensing this was a way to turn attention away from her and save her further embarrassment. "A finer lad I've not met. You've got good reason to be proud, Jennifer Jo."

"I know," she said, still half watching Kathryn out of the corner of her eye.

Jenny seemed oblivious to the undercurrents around her. She had a dreamy look in her eye as she turned to Olivia. "I don't blame you for setting your cap for Matthew," she said. "He would make anyone a fine husband." Then to Jennifer Jo she added, "You are very, very lucky."

Jennifer Jo involuntarily stiffened. "Thank you," she finally managed, forcing a smile only with some effort. Ever since the disastrous night of the Thanksgiving dinner, Jennifer Jo had been struggling with her feelings about Jenny Pottsworth. At that time, those feelings had sprung only from her natural defensiveness for her sister. But a few days later, Matthew's next letter came. In his first letter from London, he had told the family about the Pottsworths' coming to America, but had said little about Jenny, other than that Peter would be very thrilled to know she was coming to Nauvoo. But in the next letter, with his characteristic honesty, Matthew told Jennifer Jo about the farewell kiss on the docks of Liverpool. He made light of it, and mentioned that Brigham had given permission only if it were on the cheek and very brief. She knew that Matthew had not been influenced by it—she could tell that from the innocent manner in which he spoke of it—but since then, not all of Jennifer Jo's growing resentment toward Jenny Pottsworth stemmed from her sisterly concern for Kathryn. Now came this comment, wide-eyed and innocent, about Matthew's potential as a husband. Jennifer Jo looked away, feeling herself starting a slow burn.

Thankfully, Mary Ann stood up at that point, and the conversations stopped. She looked around, smiling at them with great affection. "Thank you all for coming. I think this is a first for us. We've had family councils before, but I think this is the first one exclusively for the women."

"I like it," Rebecca spoke up. "I say we do it every month."

There was general laughter and assent to that comment. "How about every week?" Lydia quipped. "I like having a night to ourselves."

"Well, actually," Mary Ann said, "what I am going to propose tonight will require that we meet together often, and I like that idea too." Now she grew more serious. "Let me jump right in. For the last two weeks, I've not been able to get Thanksgiving out of my mind. What happened before dinner, when we all expressed thanks for our blessings, was a special thing to me."

"Yes, that was a wonderful experience," Melissa murmured.

"But it is one thing to be thankful in our words. I think it's something else to show that thankfulness by our actions." She stopped, thinking how to best express what she was feeling. "We have had so many blessings from the Lord. I can't begin to count them. And thanks in large measure to the wonderful help we got from Joshua and Caroline and Carl and Melissa as we were driven from Far West, we are much better off than many of our brothers and sisters."

"Amen!" Sister Pottsworth said fervently. She and Jenny had not been in Missouri, but they too were recipients of Joshua's generosity. Shortly after their arrival in Nauvoo, Joshua offered them a small one-room cabin behind Joshua's freight office. Ashamed that it was so cramped and tiny, and also that it was close enough to the corral that one always knew which way the wind was blowing, Joshua charged them no rent. Abigail wouldn't accept that, so they finally settled on Abigail's doing laundry service for Caroline in exchange for their housing. Abigail and Jenny were ecstatic with the arrangement. Not only was the cabin larger than the flat they had occupied back in Preston, but here they didn't have to share it with anyone else. And the smell was no worse than that of the raw sewage that ran down the alleyways of Preston.

Mary Ann waved her arm at the room around them. "Look at us. We each have a comfortable home. We have the store. We have Carl's brickyard. We have Joshua's freight business. We are about to get into the lumber business. We are truly prospering, and I mean in the temporal sense as well as in our spiritual lives."

Caroline was looking at Olivia's new dress and nodding slowly. Joshua wouldn't tell her what he had paid for the two dresses he bought for his daughters, but she knew it was more than many families had to spend on food for a month, or clothing for a year. The cost of Livvy's piano would have built some families a home.

"If we are truly grateful," Mary Ann went on, "then we must show it to the Lord. And since we cannot give anything directly back to him, we must do it by helping others." She turned and walked to the big cedar chest by the fireplace. The large family Bible she and Benjamin had received as a wedding gift was sitting there. She picked it up and the others saw that she had marked a place with a piece of paper. She opened it to that place, then looked back at her family. "You all know what the Book of Mormon says about service."

Olivia's hand shot up. Jessica had made them memorize this in school.

Mary Ann nodded at her. "Yes, Livvy. Do you know that scripture?"

Olivia stood, as though it were a classroom, and recited quickly. "'When you are in the service of your fellow beings you are only in the service of your God.'"

"That's right, Livvy. Very good."

Turning, Olivia saw Jessica's smile and complimentary nod. She sat back down as her mother patted her shoulder.

"Well, besides King Benjamin's comment, which Livvy has quoted perfectly, I would like to read you something from the Bible. From the book of James." She looked down and began. "'Pure religion and undefiled before God and the Father is this, To visit the fatherless and widows in their affliction, and to keep himself unspotted from the world.'"

She shut the book, set it down, and returned to her place. She waited for a moment, letting the implications of the scripture sink in, and then she began again. "The fatherless and the widows. As I think about that, I think of Sister Mary Beth Bingham. Her husband abandoned her over a year ago, leaving her with three children and nothing more than a filthy shanty to live in. I think of the Leavitt children, both parents struck down with cholera, and cared for now by the oldest son, who is barely fifteen. I think of the Seegmillers, who came on the ship with Jenny and Abigail. They have four children and he cannot find work. They're living in Brother Brewster's wagon out back of his house."

She stopped. Caroline raised her head. "The Bartons, who live behind us—she has consumption."

Lydia was nodding now too. "And what about Sister Kohler? Nine children. Her husband is a hard worker, but they are still very poor. They don't even have enough shoes to bring all of the children to church at the same time."

Pleased, Mary Ann leaned forward. "That is exactly what I am talking about. We can't do everything. There is far too much need. But we can do something! I suggest we take the next few minutes to talk about who is in need and what we could do to help."

• • •

The meeting was breaking up. The pan of apple dumplings was almost gone. The bottle of cream, which Mary Ann left outside until it was so thick it had to be put on with a spoon, was empty. The warmth of the meeting still lingered in the air.

Abigail Pottsworth stopped by Lydia's chair to say good night. Lydia was too tired and too awkward to get up and bid everyone good-bye. "Thank you, Lydia, for having us. It's been a wonderful night."

"It has," Lydia said. "We're so glad you and Jenny would come. We think of you as part of our family, you know."

"I know, and that has been a great blessing to us." She straightened and turned to Mary Ann. "And that reminds me. I was so pleased with your idea for helping others. I have a proposal too."

"What?" Mary Ann asked. Jessica and Rebecca were at the door, their coats and scarves on, and were ready to walk out. Caroline and Olivia were just putting their coats on. Melissa, Kathryn, and Jennifer Jo were clearing the last of the dishes. At Sister Pottsworth's comments, they all turned to listen. Abigail walked over to stand by Mary Ann.

"One of the sisters I do laundry for was telling me that for Christmas you hardly do anything here. That there is no holiday celebration. Is that correct?"

"Well, yes," Mary Ann said, not sure what the question was getting at. "We do talk about Jesus somewhat on that day, but we know that he wasn't actually born in December. He was born in the spring."

"Yes, I know. But do you mark his birthday in the spring?"

Mary Ann shook her head. "No."

"Then why not use Christmas to celebrate his birth? We do in England. It's an important holiday there. I mean, this is our Savior, the most important person who ever lived on the earth.

Derek told me you have a big celebration on the Fourth of July, the birthday of your country. Don't you think we should honor the birth of the Master too, then?"

From her chair Lydia spoke. "I'd never thought of it like that. I think it sounds like a good idea. Tell us what kinds of things you do."

"Ah," Abigail said, shaking her head with a warm smile. "In the Old Country, Christmas is a wonderful holiday. We have a big feast. People go out caroling."

"Singing?" Olivia said. "What do they sing?"

Jenny couldn't believe it. "Christmas carols," she burst out in exasperation. "'Silent Night,' 'Good Christian Men Rejoice,' 'While Shepherds Watched Their Flocks by Night,' 'Adeste Fideles,' 'Joy to the World,' a dozen others." She had to stop to catch her breath. "We go out on Christmas Eve and carol from house to house, and then the people invite the carolers in and give them a drink of wassail."

"Wassail?" Rebecca repeated tentatively.

"Oh, yes. It's a hot drink with all kinds of good things in it—roasted apples, eggs, sugar, and wonderful spices." Suddenly one hand came up to her mouth. She looked to her mother. "And ale. I had forgotten that, Mum. We couldn't do that, then. Not with the Word of Wisdom."

"I've already thought about that," her mother said. "We'll use apple cider."

"I think it sounds wonderful," Caroline said.

Jenny turned back to Olivia. "And we hang our stockings by the fireplace at night so Father Christmas can come and put candy and gifts into them."

"Who is Father Christmas?" Olivia asked with a puzzled look.

Jenny threw up her hands. "You don't know who Father Christmas is? Santa Claus? Old Saint Nicholas? Don't any of those names mean anything to you?"

Olivia shook her head.

"He has many names, depending on which country you are in, but Father Christmas is the best part of the celebration. Each child hangs a stocking from the fireplace. Then, if they have been very good children, Father Christmas will come down the chimney after they are asleep and fill their stockings with candy and presents."

"Really?" Olivia asked with widening eyes.

"Really," Abigail said, giving the adults a knowing smile. "Father Christmas is the symbol of giving, of doing good things for others."

She looked around the circle now. "I could scarce believe my ears when Sister Colfax told me that you do practically nothing here to celebrate Christmas. She said you don't even close school. Is that right, Jessica?"

Jessica seemed a little startled by the question. "Well, no, I hadn't planned on it."

"Then I have a proposal. Jenny and I are going to give you Americans a good old-fashioned English Christmas. Just like we decided to start a family tradition and have Thanksgiving, I suggest we start another family tradition and celebrate Christmas."

Suddenly a look of concern crossed Jenny's face. "Do you suppose it's contrary to the gospel to do such a thing? Is that why you don't do anything here?"

Lydia shook her head immediately. "I wouldn't think so. Joseph is always telling us that a religion should be something that makes people happy. And those sound like very happy things."

"They are," Abigail agreed warmly. "Especially for the children." She brightened as a thought came to her. "I know. I'll find Joseph first thing tomorrow and ask him if that would be displeasing to the Lord."

Will stomped his feet and pulled his coat tighter around him. He reached up and cupped his hands over his face, letting the warmth of his breath thaw the flesh a little. It was well below freezing, and trying to hold back the cold was getting more and more difficult.

He turned his head at the sound of the door opening, and stepped back farther into the shadows. With the opening of the door came the noise of women's chatter and a flood of light. Then two figures stepped out onto the porch. He leaned forward a little, peering at them. It was Jessica and Rebecca. They called out their farewells, waved to someone standing at the door, then walked down the steps. The door shut again, but he was encouraged at least. The meeting was ending.

Two minutes later, the door opened again. Now his patience paid off. Jenny stepped out first, and her mother came right behind her. Calling her good-byes, Jenny came down off the porch and started toward the gate. She stopped. Her mother was still on the porch talking to Grandma Steed. Will smiled. Abigail Pottsworth was a talker, and this was the very chance he had hoped for. Lowering his head, he stepped out and started toward his parents' house, across the street from Lydia's, striding as though he were anxious to be home.

Jenny was waiting just inside the fence that surrounded Nathan's home. She turned at the sound of the footsteps on the snow, then took a step closer. "Will," she called. "Is that you?"

He looked up and slowed his step. "Oh, Jenny. Hello."

She seemed pleased to see him. "What are you doing out on a night like this?"

"I had to get something from the freight office. I'm just headed home."

"Oh."

"Evenin', Will," Mary Ann called from the doorway.

Mrs. Pottsworth waved. "Good evening, Will."

"Evenin'." He looked at Jenny. "Was it a good meeting?"

"It was a wonderful meeting. Mother Steed is such a good woman."

"Yes, she is." He hesitated for a minute. "Well," he said, half turning, "it was nice to see you." Then he stopped, as though an idea had just occurred to him. "Say, I could walk you home if you like."

There was an instant smile. "That would be nice." She

looked back at her mother, but it was obvious it was going to take some time if they waited for her. "Mum? Will's going to walk me home. We'll go on ahead."

"All right, dear."

Pleased, and feeling a little smug that his plan had worked out so neatly, he held the gate open and she came out to join him. The freight office, behind which Jenny and her mother lived, was about nine or ten blocks from the Steed homes, but Will still kept the pace slow so they'd have time to be together and talk. Still filled with excitement, Jenny told him all about what had happened in the meeting and of the plans they had made.

"I think that's a good idea," Will said when she finished. And he meant it. He was impressed that they would be concerned for those who were less fortunate.

"Yes," she said, hugging herself. "Sometimes I have to pinch myself. I can't believe we're here in America, living with the Saints. It's just too good to be true."

He decided to be bold. "Well, I'm certainly glad you decided to come."

To his complete surprise, she slipped her arm through his. "Really?"

The gesture was so unexpected, and yet so totally natural, that he had to catch his breath for a moment. This was Jenny. What she felt like doing, she did. It was enchanting, and it was maddening.

She had her head cocked to one side and was looking up at him, waiting. He started a little. "Oh, yes. Really."

"Why?"

He laughed. "Why?"

"Yes. Why are you glad *we* came to America?" She stressed the plural softly, teasing him.

He decided to tease right back. "Because your mother is a wonderful woman. I like her a lot."

Her lips formed into a tiny pout. "Oh." Then immediately she was smiling again. "Did you really have to get something from the office? It's the Sabbath, you know."

He had anticipated such a question and had covered himself. He reached inside his coat and withdrew one of the ledger books. He waved it at her as mute evidence. She only smiled the more brightly. "And it couldn't wait until morning?"

She had him and she knew it. And Will knew it. And then he didn't care. "Well," he grinned, "I had to have some reason for walking by at just the right moment."

Deeply pleased, she nodded. "And how long did you have to wait?"

He laughed. There was no avoiding her inquisitiveness. "Half an hour."

"Good," she said, with a matter-of-fact bob of her head. And she held his arm just a shade more tightly.

"Good?" he echoed. "I nearly froze to death. I thought you were never coming out."

"Yes, good. It shows you care."

"I do care," he said, instantly sober. "I care for you a lot, Jenny. You know that, don't you?"

Her head dropped and the smile faded. "I know."

And I care for you a lot too, Will. That's what you say now.

But she didn't say it, and they walked on in silence for almost a block, his frustration growing with every step. His honesty had abruptly changed her entire mood. Finally she looked up at him. "Is it true that your mother wants to be baptized into the Church?"

He stopped, surprised by that. "Yes," he finally said.

She pulled him into motion again. "And your father won't let her?"

He stopped again and pulled away from her so he could face her directly. "My father has said she can be baptized any time she wants." The words came out more clipped and sharp than he wanted. And he was a little puzzled. In actuality, he took his mother's side on this issue. Will understood very well his father's feelings about the Mormons. Very well! But to stop his mother when she felt so strongly about it—he didn't agree with that at all. But the bluntness of Jenny's question made him instantly defensive for his father.

She was watching him steadily.

"It's just that . . ." He wanted her to understand. "Pa means it when he says she can be baptized if she wants, but Mama knows Pa has strong feelings against it, and so she won't be until those feelings change."

Jenny nodded, seeming to accept that. Then her next question caught him off guard again. "And what about you, Will? If your mother joined the Church, how would that make you feel?"

"Me?" He shrugged. "I think that's her decision. I wouldn't care at all."

"But you wouldn't be particularly pleased?"

He gave a little grunt of exasperation. "I think she can do what she wants. It doesn't matter to me, either way."

"Oh." She turned and started again, this time not waiting for him to follow. He fell into step beside her, but she didn't speak again until they reached the small cabin by the corrals. They stood there for a moment, the silence awkward and heavy. Then she smiled again. "Thank you for being patient, Will. I'm glad you had something you had to get from the freight office."

But Will was still trying to cope with his frustration. "This is about me not being a Mormon, isn't it?"

She looked away.

"Do you know how that makes me feel?" he exploded. "I'm the same person whether I'm a Mormon or not. Why should that make a difference whether or not you care for me? I don't think—"

"I do care for you, Will," she said softly.

He stopped in midsentence. "You do?"

She nodded.

"Then why does this thing about religion always end up being such a big thing to you? I don't care if you're a Mormon. If that's what you want, I think it's wonderful."

She just looked at him, then shook her head. To his surprise, there was a touch of tears at the corners of her eyes. "What?" he said. "What did I say?"

She shook her head again. "Thank you for walking me home, Will." She started to turn away.

"Jenny?" It was a pleading call. "Why won't you answer my question?"

She stopped, without turning. But still she said nothing.

He threw up his hands. "I know," he said angrily. "You want someone like Peter. Or Matthew. Well, I'm sorry, but Matthew is already taken, or doesn't that matter?"

She whirled back. "I never said I wanted to marry Matthew, I said I wanted to marry someone like Matthew."

He knew he was only making it worse, but he couldn't help himself. "Or Peter? Is it someone *like* Peter, or just Peter?"

There was a quick toss of her head, and he could see he had struck home with that one. "Peter is a wonderful person."

"And I'm not, right? I'm not a Mormon, so that makes me some kind of outcast."

"You know that's not how I feel."

"Then why? Why is it that you can't accept me if I don't join the Church?"

Her head came up slowly, and there was a deep sadness in her eyes. "Because I don't want what your father and mother have, Will. I'm sorry." And with that, she turned and ran into the house, leaving him there in the cold to stare at the closed door.

Nathan looked around the main room of the store. "Any more questions before I leave, Jenny?"

"No, I don't think so."

"Good. Carl needs my help on getting another set of drying racks finished, so I'll be down at the brickyard if you need me."

"All right."

He grabbed his coat and started to pull it on. As Jenny watched him, she felt a great wave of gratitude. "Nathan?"

He looked up. "What, Jenny?"

"Thank you."

"For what?"

"For letting me work in the store."

Nathan smiled and nodded. Some of the British Saints came to Nauvoo with particular skills in manufacturing or in various crafts such as pottery making, metalworking, tanning, or shoe making. With the burgeoning growth of the Mormon city, these were skills that were greatly valued, and the immigrants who had them were quickly put to work. Many others, however, had been the poorer of the lower classes, and if they had been employed at all, it was in menial work or in manufacturing enterprises which did not exist in Nauvoo. These Saints found making the adjustment to American life much more difficult. Jenny and her mother were part of this latter class. The skills they had learned while working in the textile factories were not of much use to them now. Abigail took in laundry and sewing, but they were barely getting by. So in a family council held the day after their Thanksgiving dinner, it was decided to offer Jenny a job at the store. In exchange, she and her mother could draw goods from the store as needed.

But very quickly Jenny turned the Steeds' charity into a necessity. The plan for the store at first had been to have the Steed women do most of the clerking while Nathan handled the business end. But babies have a way of altering even the most careful plans. Rebecca had Christopher, who would be two in June. He had more energy than two sets of triplets, and with Derek gone, he required his mother or someone in the family to watch him around the clock. Caroline had given birth to Charles in February. He was crawling now and pulled things off the shelves faster than she could replace them if she tried to keep him at the store. Lydia was just a week or two away from having her baby, and being on her feet for long periods of time was difficult for her. And Jessica's school was filled to capacity and was taking her time and the time of the McIntire sisters. So more and more, Jenny became the one who filled in.

She went to school for two hours in the morning, then spent the rest of the day in the store. Nathan was amazed at how quickly she mastered the inventory and pricing. She was consistently cheerful and charmed the customers with her ready smile and British accent. And Nathan noted, with some amusement, that in the two weeks since she had started, the number of single young men coming to the Steed store—some from the far side of Nauvoo—had sharply increased.

"We are grateful to you, Jenny," he said, pulling his stocking cap on. "I don't know what we'd do right now without you."

"Well, it's been a great blessing to me and me mum."

"Speaking of your mum, did she ask Joseph about your idea for the Christmas celebration?"

"She did. She went right over the next morning."

"And what did he say?"

She laughed merrily. "He said he thought that such a celebration would not be displeasing to the Lord, but to be absolutely sure, he and Emma would have to come over and witness it first-hand."

Nathan chuckled. "That's Joseph."

"They'll be bringing their children too. Mum is very excited. Imagine, having the Prophet himself with us."

"Caroline said she finally convinced your mother to have it at their house."

She nodded, suddenly glum. "Mum wanted it very much to be at our house. She wanted this to be our way of saying thank you to your family. But there just isn't room."

"Well, you and your mother are in charge of seeing that everything gets done right, since none of us know for sure how to do this. So it will still be your gift to us. And a wonderful one at that. Emily talks about it every day."

"Good."

He opened the door. "Well, if you need me, I'll be with Carl."

"I'll be fine, but thank you anyway."

———— ◆ ————

Nathan held the ladder firm as Carl hammered the last nail in place, then eyed the top shelf one last time. "How does it look?" Nathan asked.

"Looks good." Carl dropped the hammer to Nathan, then came down again. "It looks real good. Thank you, Nathan."

"You're welcome."

"Come on. Melissa will have something on the table about now."

Nathan didn't move. "Carl, can I ask you a question?"

"Sure."

"If you'd rather not answer, I'll understand."

"All right."

Nathan looked at him, debating whether this was wise or not, but wanting to know. "Does Joshua say much to you about the Church?"

To Nathan's surprise, Carl laughed easily. "Yeah."

"Oh."

Carl's laugh deepened. "Go ahead, ask your next question."

Now Nathan smiled. "I don't have to. Not if you already know what it is."

They were in the long shed used in wintertime for drying the brick molds before firing them in the kiln. There was no heat inside it, but it was considerably warmer here than outside. Carl slipped off his gloves and stuffed them in his pocket. "Well, first of all, you have to realize that Joshua and I don't spend nearly as much time together as we used to. The brickyard is taking about every minute I have, and he's busy trying to get Wisconsin set up."

"I know."

"You going to go into business with him on that?"

Nathan shook his head slowly. "I was thinking about it seriously, but it means being gone for most of the winter every year. And now with the baby almost here, that's not good. Also, Joseph has just called me to be in the presidency of the elders quorum of the Nauvoo Stake. That will take some time too. Besides, we have the store. That's plenty for us right now."

Carl nodded thoughtfully. "When a man has three good reasons for not doing something, he probably ought not to do it. And by the way, I don't think Will is much excited about the prospects either. Joshua doesn't like to hear that, but I don't think Will is very anxious to leave for the winter either."

"Not as long as Jenny Pottsworth is around."

Carl nodded. "Anyway, as I was saying, Joshua and I don't see each other as much as we used to, but yeah, he and I have talked quite a bit about it. And he's always making some off-hand comment about the Mormons or the Church."

"I think I've heard them all," Nathan put in dryly.

"Mostly he just asks me questions about how I feel. That's because he knows that Melissa and I have a situation similar to his and Caroline's."

"Only in some ways," Nathan inserted.

"That's true. I've told him that too. I used to get all upset about Melissa being Mormon, largely because Pa hated them so badly, but all it did was cause us problems. And she has a right to her way of thinking, just like I do."

"Suppose she weren't a member and wanted to be baptized. Would you let her?"

"Absolutely! I can see where being a Mormon, especially if you practice what the Church teaches, can make you a better person. Why would I want to stop her from doing that?"

Nathan looked at him strangely and that won him a laugh from Carl. "I didn't say anything about me being baptized, just Melissa."

"What about the children?"

There was a quick shrug. "When they get old enough to choose for themselves, why not, if that's what they want?"

"But not you?"

Carl grinned. From the first day Melissa had brought him to meet the family, Nathan had liked Carl Rogers. But since he and Melissa had moved to Nauvoo, the bond between them had deepened into something that Nathan truly treasured. He liked Carl's quiet ways and unflinching integrity a great deal.

"I'm not trying to push you into a baptismal font, Carl, you know that. I'd just like to know. Once you were more like Joshua. Now you two are so different in how you deal with it. I'm curious as to why."

Carl leaned back against the shelving, his face thoughtful. "I don't know if I'd ever join the Church. To be honest with you, I mostly went to our church back home because Pa expected it of us. I never really got any real satisfaction out of it. I think a man can believe in God and live a good life without having to be a member of this congregation or that."

"You're proof of that," Nathan agreed.

"But I know how you feel too. I know that all of you see the Church as offering you so much more than just believing."

"Yes, and in a way, we believe that the Church is one way God has of asking more of us too."

"Yeah, and in a way, that makes sense too. But when all is said and done, I think I'm satisfied pretty much with the way things are for me."

"And you know that I—we, all of us—respect your right to feel that way."

"I know you do," he responded right back, "and I appreciate that. Joseph is the same way. I have a lot of respect for him. He's a good and decent man, and what he is doing here with his people is incredible."

"It really is, isn't it?"

"That's what I say to Joshua when he gets going on about the Mormons. You don't have to believe like they do to respect them and live with them as friends."

"And what does he say to that?"

"Oh, for all the bluster and grumbling, he is coming around more to that viewpoint too."

"Except when it comes to Caroline being baptized."

Carl shook his head slowly. "I'm not sure that is ever going to change. I don't understand what it is that's knotting up down in his gut like that, but it sure isn't going away."

"You tell him that?"

The quick grin flashed again. "Yeah, but it didn't do any good." He straightened and moved to the door. "Come on. Let's go see what Melissa's got to eat."

Joshua stepped to the kitchen door and stuck his head in. "Nathan. Joseph. The tables are down and the furniture is back in. They're about ready to begin the stockings. How are you coming in here?"

Joseph Smith was up to his elbows in a large kettle filled

with soapy water, and Nathan had a towel, trying to keep up with drying the dishes as Joseph washed them. Caroline and Emma were scraping out the last food from two big pots in preparation for having them washed as well.

Joseph turned to answer and Joshua immediately broke out laughing.

"What?" Joseph said. Then he looked down at himself. His sleeves were rolled up, and he was wearing one of Caroline's aprons, which was soaked all the way down the front. One lock of hair was in his eyes, and his face was bathed with moisture—whether from perspiring or from the steamy dishwater, Joshua couldn't tell.

Nathan saw what Joshua was laughing at and pointed a fork at his brother. "This is Christmas Eve, Joshua. It's not Christian to make fun of a man on such a night."

Caroline shook a finger at Joshua. "If you've come to make fun of the workers in here, we'll leave these pots to you."

Carl stepped into the doorway beside Joshua. "Are you ready in here? We're all set."

"Almost," Emma said. "We just need to put away the dishes. We can let the pots soak for a while."

Joshua was still chuckling at Joseph's appearance. "So this is what Jesse Crosby meant."

Emma's head snapped around. Joseph looked a little surprised. "Jesse Crosby?"

Joshua nodded. "I was over to his place a few days ago to talk with him about hauling some freight for him. He said that you had brought back a sack of flour you had borrowed from him a few weeks back."

Emma set the pot down slowly, her eyebrows lowering darkly. "And just what did he tell you?" she demanded.

Joshua kept his face impassive. "He said he had been a little upset by the fact that Joseph was doing all kinds of things which were women's work—carrying out the ashes, bringing in water and firewood, tending the children, washing the dishes."

There was a soft explosion of air as Emma expressed her disgust. "Joseph told me what he said," she snapped. "And he had the nerve to tell Joseph that some of his home habits were not in keeping with his idea of a great man's self-respect." She shook her head, her dark eyes crackling now. "It was a good thing he didn't say that in my presence. With as many people as we have at our house all the time, if Joseph didn't help me, I couldn't do it all."

Joseph was smiling at Emma. "Now, dear," he said, "don't be getting all worked up again." He looked at Caroline and chuckled. "I shouldn't have told Emma what he said. She has been steamed ever since."

"Well, he made me angry, talking about his great man's *self-respect*." She tossed the last term out with great disdain. "No one needs to tell me that I'm married to a great man. I know that. But since when is a great man's self-respect lessened by his washing a dish or sweeping a floor?"

Joseph looked at Carl and Joshua. "See what I mean?" Then he turned back to Emma. "Emma, I talked to him later. And that's exactly what I told him."

"You did?"

"Yes." Now he was speaking to Caroline. "He took me aside and told me that his wife worked a lot harder than Emma did."

"Oh, that man!" Emma cried.

"So what did you say to him?" Carl asked, genuinely curious now.

"Well, I reproved him a little. I told him that if a man does not properly love and cherish his wife in this life and take care of her, he will not be privileged to have her in the next."

Joshua had started to toss off another quip, but Joseph's words stopped him flat. Carl seemed impressed. Caroline and Nathan were both looking at him in surprise.

"Really?" Emma said. "Is that what you really told him?"

"I did." Joseph was completely serious now. "And I meant it."

"Say it again, Joseph," Carl urged. "How did you say that?"

"I said that if a man does not properly love and cherish his wife while he's living with her here, God will not give him the privilege of having her there."

Carl nodded, repeating it in his mind and considering the implications of the statement. "Very good. I like that."

Joshua turned back to Joseph. "Well, then that explains Crosby's comments."

"Oh? What did he say?"

"He said that after speaking with you, it had given him great cause to think and that he had had a change of heart and was trying to do better by his wife."

Emma's one eyebrow rose. "Is that true? Did he actually say it that way?"

"Yes, he did," Joshua answered. "And Mrs. Crosby supported him in it. In fact, she said she was going to come over sometime and thank Joseph because Jesse has been a much better husband since your talk."

"Good," Joseph exclaimed with satisfaction.

Emma was likewise pleased. "Well, maybe I can forgive him, then."

Just then Melissa came to the door. "My goodness, what is going on in here? We're all ready out here and the children are just dying to get started on their stockings."

"We're coming," Caroline said. And with that, they all left the kitchen and went into the parlor.

———————— ◆ ————————

For the first half hour, they made the stockings for the children. Abigail and Jenny had persuaded Nathan to bring a dozen pair of socks from the store. And these were not just any stockings. These were the long woolen ones that a man could pull up to his knees to keep warm and dry in the winter.

For purposes of getting ready for the visit of Father Christmas the next day, *children* were defined as anyone who had not been married. To everyone's delight, Will and Jenny, Peter and Kathryn, Jennifer Jo and Olivia, and Julia Smith, Joseph's oldest, were almost as excited as the young ones. They sprawled out on the floor and carefully wrote their names on the stockings with pieces of charcoal from the fireplace. The older ones finished quickly, so they helped the younger ones, including Joseph and Emma's, and then volunteered to make ones for the babies as well.

When everyone was finished, Abigail raised her hands. Parents shushed their children, who were finding it very difficult to contain their excitement. "Now, you know that each of you must hang the stocking by your own fireplaces so Father Christmas can find them when he comes tonight. Just take a rock or a brick or something heavy and use that to hold the stocking in place." She turned to Mary Ann. "Are you ready?"

Mary Ann nodded and stepped forward. "Now we have another special treat."

Instantly the children were bouncing up and down. "What is it?" they cried.

"Who knows why we have Christmas?" she asked.

Every hand shot up, some so eager they jumped to their feet.

"Mark? Can you tell us?"

Mark was the younger of Jessica's two stepsons. He rose slowly, suddenly not so sure of himself. He turned and looked at his mother. Jessica smiled encouragement at him. "It's all right, Mark. We talked about this, didn't we? Why do we celebrate Christmas?"

"Because of baby Jesus."

Joseph was watching closely. "That's right, Mark," he said. "That's exactly right."

"And so," Mary Ann said, "we have a special surprise. We are going to ask Grandpa if he will read us the Christmas story from the Bible."

"Hooray!" Luke Griffith shouted. Then he sat back, blushing as everyone laughed at his exuberance.

"But—" Mary Ann stopped for effect, and it got exactly what she hoped for. They went instantly quiet. Their eyes widened, and they leaned forward, holding their breath.

"But we are going to let you children act out the story as Grandpa reads it for us. Jenny and Sister Pottsworth and I have some things in the kitchen to help us. We'll need a Mary and a Joseph." Again hands started shooting up. "And some Wise Men. And shepherds and donkeys."

She laughed as they were all on their feet now, dancing and begging to be selected. "Come on," she said, waving her arm toward the kitchen. "Everyone in there. And you mothers, we'll probably need your help with costumes."

Joseph had their baby, Don Carlos, now just six months old, bundled up for the cold and tucked in one arm, but he reached out with his other hand and laid it on Abigail Pottsworth's arm. "Sister Abigail," he said, "that was a wonderful evening. Thank you."

"Oh, it was," Emma said, shepherding the rest of her family forward. "What do you say to Sister Pottsworth, children?"

It came out in an enthusiastic chorus. "Thank you, Sister Pottsworth."

"You're very welcome, children. Be sure you hang up your stockings tonight."

Young Joseph looked up at his father with concern. "Do you have Don Carlos's stocking, Papa?"

"I do," he answered. "In my pocket."

Benjamin and Mary Ann came over. "We hope you have a merry and joyous Christmas tomorrow," Mary Ann said. "We're so glad you came."

Joseph responded with a quick shake of his head. "No, we are the ones who are glad we came. It was just delightful."

"Oh," Emma said, "that thing with the Christmas story was so precious. I think we shall do that next year too."

Joseph turned to Joshua. "I don't know if the real Mary had red hair or not, but your Savannah was the perfect one to play that part."

Joshua laughed. "And how about that donkey?" He poked

Will with his elbow. "You can tell he's spent a lot of time down at the stable. He was a natural, don't you think?"

Will took that good-naturedly, then looked at Joseph. "What you missed was when we were in the kitchen. Mama had gotten 'Mary' into her robes and she was seated on my back. Mark was standing beside her, staff in hand, waiting to lead her to Bethlehem."

Mary Ann was laughing softly now. "And then Emily had the effrontery to ask Savannah who she was."

"What did she say?" Emma asked.

Will smiled. "She turned and gave her a disgusted look, quite offended that Emily didn't know who she was. Then she put one hand on her hip and said, 'Don't you know? This is Joseph and I am Married.'"

"Married?" Joseph hooted. "Oh, that's a good one."

"That's my Savannah, all right," Joshua said proudly.

Joseph turned to raise a hand to all the rest. "Well, good night, one and all. Thank you. Have a good Christmas."

A chorus of thanks and good wishes rushed back at him. Abigail walked with him and Emma to the door. "So you don't think it is displeasing to the Lord that we celebrate his birth with feasting and rejoicing?" she teased.

He tipped back his head and laughed heartily. "No, Sister Pottsworth, but I am surely glad you asked us to come see for ourselves so we could make a wise judgment on the matter."

Chapter Notes

Though it may not have happened at this particular time, the story of Jesse Crosby's interchange with Joseph and his concern that Joseph's home habits "were not in accord" with Jesse's "idea of a great man's self-respect" is true, including Joseph's answer (see recollection of Jesse W. Crosby, in Hyrum L. Andrus and Helen Mae Andrus, comps., *They Knew the Prophet* [Salt Lake City: Bookcraft, 1974], p. 145).

Like Thanksgiving, Christmas seems to have been largely ignored—or at least not celebrated with any consistency—by the early Saints. This was partly due to the New England heritage of so many of the first converts. The Puritans felt that too much paganism had crept into Christmas celebration and symbolism, so they eschewed them altogether. In some of the colonies, stiff fines or even jail sentences were levied for feasting or being idle on Christmas Day. Though the Puritan strictness was eventually abandoned, the lack of any traditional celebrations carried on to future generations. There is virtually no mention of Christmas in Latter-day Saint journals and diaries throughout the New York, Ohio, and Missouri periods of the Church.

Then the English Saints began to arrive in large numbers in 1840. In England, Christmas was a festive occasion and included many of the traditions mentioned by Abigail and Jenny in the novel. Gradually, these British converts began to have an influence on the American Saints. In this chapter, the time is December 1840. While there is no mention of any Christmas celebration that year by the Prophet or in other known contemporary accounts, the 25 December entry for the year 1841 in Joseph's history states that some of the Twelve and their wives attended a Christmas dinner. Then, in 1843, Joseph posted a formal notice in the *Nauvoo Neighbor* that he and Emma would be hosting a Christmas Day dinner and party at the recently opened Nauvoo House. It is also noted in the 25 December 1843 entry in Joseph's history that he and his family were awakened at one in the morning by Christmas carolers outside their window, which music, the Prophet said, "caused a thrill of pleasure to run through my soul." (*HC* 6:134; for more details on the celebration of Christmas, see George W. Givens, *In Old Nauvoo: Everyday Life in the City of Joseph* [Salt Lake City: Deseret Book Co., 1990], pp. 162–63, and *Women*, p. 64.)

Having the children put their names on their own stockings and act out the Christmas story is not based on any specific account from that time.

Chapter Thirty

S ister Griffith?"

Jessica had her back to the class as she wrote on the small slate board. She turned. Jenny Pottsworth's hand was up. "Yes, Jenny?"

"I have something I should like to share with the class."

"All right, Jenny," she answered after a moment, "let me finish writing the arithmetic on the board, then I'll be with you." As she turned back with the chalk, she gave a little sigh. She wasn't sure what this might portend, but judging from previous experience it would probably only further complicate things in her classroom.

Jenny was as open and fresh a person as Jessica had ever met. There was not the slightest bit of guile about her. Unlike so many women with her natural, striking beauty, there was no posturing, no demure pretending, no petty flirtatiousness. She spoke what was on her mind, and she did so boldly and without hesitation. But such frankness, along with the tendency to flit from one topic to another like a swallow darting after insects, could be both disarming and admirable all at the same moment. She was direct but ingenuous, innocent but straightforward, frank without being critical. Will Steed and Peter Ingalls were both deeply affected by her presence, and this is what complicated things in class.

Jessica laid the chalk down and turned around to face her students. She had not married Joshua until a month after her twenty-fifth birthday, so in her mind all of this between Will and Peter and Kathryn and Jenny was like children playing house. And yet she knew her life was not the norm. Marriage at an early age was common enough that just in the past week there was talk of passing an ordinance setting minimum ages for marriage without the consent of the parents. It would be seventeen for boys, fourteen for girls.

She frowned a little. Will would be seventeen in March, as would Peter less than two months later. Jenny was fifteen now and would turn sixteen in August. Kathryn would be fifteen in April. She wanted to throw up her hands and shout out her concerns. Even Olivia would turn fourteen in November. That meant that by the end of the year all of these "children" would no longer need their parents' permission to pursue their romantic interests.

She brushed the chalk dust off her hands and looked at Jenny. "Thank you for waiting, Jenny. What is it you'd like to share?"

Jenny stood slowly. Jessica saw that there was a folded piece of paper on her desk, but she did not pick it up. "Day before yesterday, you taught us about poetry, Sister Griffith. About how to recognize a good poem."

Will was watching Jenny closely, but that was nothing new, he always did that. What caught Jessica's eye was Peter. His head came up slowly and he was staring at Jenny, a touch of panic in his eyes. "Yes, Jenny," Jessica said, feeling a little uneasy but not sure exactly why.

Jenny picked up the paper and unfolded it. "You asked us if we could find a poem and bring it to class so we could talk about it. Well, I have one."

Peter came half out of his chair, his face flaming red. "Jenny, no."

Jenny turned and gave him an encouraging smile. "It's all right, Peter. You don't have to be embarrassed." She turned back to Jessica. "Peter wrote me a poem and gave it to me for Christmas."

With a groan, Peter slid back down in his seat, his eyes fixed on the floor in front of him. Kathryn was staring at him, looking like a child that had just been slapped. Jennifer Jo, watching her sister closely, sat back, her lips tightening into a hard line. Will, near the back of the class, sat rigid in his chair. Then, when he saw Jessica look at him, he instantly found something outside the window that captured his attention.

Jenny seemed unaware of any of this except for Peter's embarrassment. Again Jessica was struck with this girl's unusual nature. This was not malicious. She wasn't trying to pit Peter against Will, or force Kathryn out of the game somehow. That was the effect she was having, but Jessica really believed it was not what Jenny either wanted or intended. Peter had written her a poem, and she simply wanted to share with the others her joy and pleasure over the gift.

Jessica saw no way out of it. She had asked the students to find poems and bring them back for discussion. Again she sighed. "All right, Jenny, you may read it if you'd like."

Jenny looked around, smiled, then lifted the paper. "It's called 'Friends.'" She looked at Peter, but there was nothing that could have pried his gaze away from the floor at that moment. She turned to Jessica and suddenly her voice went very soft. "I'm not a good reader, Sister Griffith. Will you read it for us?"

After a moment, Jessica nodded and stepped forward to take the sheet from her. She too looked at Peter. "Peter, would you rather I didn't read this out loud?"

He looked up, stricken, but then finally shook his head slowly.

"Does that mean no, you don't want me to read it, or no, it doesn't matter?"

"Please, Peter, let her read it," Jenny pleaded with him. "It's so beautiful."

Finally his head came up a fraction. Kathryn was directly in his line of sight, but he forced himself to look past her. "All right," he said in a low voice.

Jessica raised the paper, read through it quickly to herself, and then, touched again with wonder at the gift given to this boy who sat before her, she began to read out loud.

Friends

Friendship's treasured touch
    Is sometimes lost,
When wind and tide and circumstance
    Demand their cost.

Sails that billow wide,
    Saltwater spray,
A thousand miles of ocean now
    Divide friends' play.

Lonely, aching heart—
    But resolute;
No turning back to ease the pain—
    Life's bitter fruit.

Years spin on and on,
    And mem'ries fade,
But somewhere deep inside remains
    The loss, unpaid.

But seas that draw apart
    Can reunite,
And wind and tide and circumstance
    Undo the slight.

Floating treasure chest
Upon the tide;
I open up and to my joy,
The jewel's inside.

Friend returned again—
Who cares the cost?
More beautiful and dear to me
Than what was lost.

Jessica finished, and folded the paper again. The room was very still. Then, with a stifled sob, Kathryn rose and stumbled blindly toward the door. Instantly, Jennifer Jo was up and hurrying after her. As the door slammed shut again, Will, stiff-lipped and grim, stood and followed them out. A little dazed by this unexpected result, Jenny Pottsworth stared at the closed door.

————

Jessica was sitting up in bed with the lamp out but the door open. Jennifer Jo tiptoed by in her nightdress, carrying a candle in its holder. Kathryn was directly behind her. "I'm awake," Jessica called out. "Come in for a minute."

As they came in, Jessica moved over and patted the coverlet. "Come on, it's time for some girl talk."

Kathryn crawled up on one side of her; Jennifer Jo set the candle down on the dressing table and sprawled out across the foot of the bed where she could look at both of them at the same time.

"How are you doing?" Jessica asked.

Kathryn blushed a little. "I'm sorry, Jessie. I didn't mean to walk out of class today."

Jessica shushed her. "That's not what I want to talk about."

"What?"

"I want to talk about houses."

"Houses?" Kathryn echoed.

"Yes."

"What kind of houses?"

Jessica smiled faintly. "The houses that we live in."

Both girls looked a little perplexed. This was what she felt was so important? But Kathryn pulled the covers up around her shoulders and snuggled in on one side of Jessica. Jennifer Jo liked that idea and moved up to do the same on the other side. Finally settled, they looked up at her.

"All right," Jessica began, "now tell me about houses. Do they all look alike? Are they all the same?"

"Of course not," Kathryn replied. "There are all different kinds."

"There are about as many different houses as there are people," Jennifer Jo added.

"That's exactly right." That was the answer Jessica was hoping for. "Now, let me ask you another question. How do you think Heavenly Father would feel if we chose to like a person based only on the house in which the person lived?"

"That would be terrible," Kathryn blurted out instantly.

"Terrible," Jennifer Jo agreed.

"Yes, it would be. I think we all see that who lives in the house is much more important than the house itself, right?"

"Right!"

She reached across Jennifer Jo and took the Bible from the small night table beside her bed. "Let me read you something the Apostle Paul wrote to the Corinthians." She flipped the pages quickly to where she had a small paper as a bookmark. "It's in the sixth chapter of First Corinthians. Here is what he says: 'Know ye not that your body is the temple of the Holy Ghost which is in you?'"

She shut the book and set it on the table again. "Now," she said, looking down at Kathryn. "Tell me what that means."

"Well," Kathryn began, her face twisting as she thought, "I think it means that our bodies are like a temple, a place where the Holy Ghost dwells."

"Yes, that's good. Jennifer Jo?"

"Well, a temple is a holy and sacred place."

"Excellent. And what do we call the temple? Don't we also say it is a house?"

Jennifer Jo saw it immediately. "Yes. We call it the house of God."

"So if your body is a temple, and the temple is a house, then we could also say your body is . . ." She stopped, leaving it for them to finish.

"A house," Kathryn exclaimed.

"That's right. Our bodies are simply the houses in which our spirits live. Agreed?"

Jennifer Jo guessed where all this was leading now. "And all of our houses are different, aren't they?"

"They certainly are," Jessica answered. Now, very softly, she asked the crucial question. "But which is more important? The house we live in, or the person that lives in that house?"

"The person." It came out as one answer from the both of them.

Kathryn was looking at Jessica strangely, and it was to her that Jessica now addressed her next question. "Jenny Pottsworth's spirit was sent to a very lovely house, wasn't it?"

"It certainly was," Kathryn said woefully.

"And you feel more like you're living in a log cabin, right?" Jessica asked, gently smiling now.

Kathryn's nose wrinkled. "More like a sod shanty, I think."

"Kathryn!" Jennifer Jo exclaimed.

"Well, it's true! Jenny makes me feel like a dingy little hut."

Jessica broke in with another question. "Do you think the person who lives in Jenny's house is a nice person?"

There was a long silence. Finally, Kathryn began to nod slowly. "Yes. Jenny is nice. In fact, she's so nice, I hate her."

Jessica laughed aloud.

"Well, I do," Kathryn said mournfully. "I wish I could say she was awful and selfish and . . . but she's not. She's a good person. A lovely person."

"For many, many years," Jessica said quietly, "I believed I

lived in one of the plainest houses God had ever created. I would barely look people in the eye because I was sure I was so homely and plain."

"But you don't feel that way anymore?" Kathryn said, her eyes wide and searching.

"No," Jessica replied with simple frankness, "I don't. And here's a lesson for you. The house I live in is still the same, just getting a little fatter and picking up more wrinkles, but it's still the same old house I've always lived in. But how I feel about that house is very different now."

"Why?" Jennifer Jo asked, surprised that Jessica had ever had such feelings about herself.

"Because I was fortunate enough to marry a man named John Griffith." Her voice faltered for a moment; then she went on more slowly. "You see, Kathryn, John was a man who cared more about what kind of woman lived in this house of mine than he did about the house itself. Thank goodness." She straightened and there was a sudden intensity in her eyes. "And because of his feelings toward me—not my house, but me!—I came to feel beautiful."

"You are beautiful," Kathryn said loyally.

Jennifer Jo smiled, then slipped her arm through Jessica's and laid her head against her shoulder. "That's how Matthew makes me feel too, Jessie."

Jessica nodded, then turned fully now to Kathryn. "I want you to think about that, about your house. You are a lovely person outside and inside, Kathryn McIntire. I know you don't think you are as pretty as Jenny, but you have a special beauty all of your own. But that doesn't really matter. You just worry about the woman you've got living in your house. If you do that, sooner or later some man—maybe Peter, maybe someone you've not even met yet—will see that woman and fall in love with her. And when that happens, nothing else will matter."

———— • ————

A movement out the window caught Will's eye and he looked up. He came out of his chair with a jerk, winning himself a startled look from Jeb Parkinson, Joshua's office foreman. But Will didn't see that at all. All he saw was that Jenny Pottsworth was crossing the street, heading directly for the freight office.

Moving quickly, almost in a panic, he brushed his hair back out of his eyes and looked down at his clothes. He had spent most of the morning out in the stable helping two of the hands fix a broken wagon wheel. There was a streak of grease across one pant leg, and his shirt front was smudged in several places. He rubbed at it hard, cursing his luck. There was nothing he could do now.

His eye fell on the desk. It was a jumble of papers. He began pushing them together, trying to get them into some kind of order. He grabbed the pen and inkwell and moved them to the front. He shoved an empty coffee cup and the stained paper beneath it into a drawer.

Parkinson was staring at him. "You all right, Will?"

Will started to turn, but there was a knock at the door. He jumped forward, cracking one knee against the desk. "I'll get it."

When he opened the door, Jenny was standing there, all bundled up in her coat, a scarf wrapped around the lower part of her face so that all that showed were those large, soft blue eyes. "Oh," he said, feigning surprise. "Jenny, it's you."

She pulled the scarf down, away from her mouth. "Good morning, Will." She was smiling up at him, and her head was partly cocked to one side in that way she had which Will completely adored. "I was hoping you would be here. May I speak with you for a few moments?"

"Of course." Will started to step back inside, but then he heard Parkinson chuckling behind him. He changed his mind in a hurry and came out onto the boardwalk porch. "Uh . . . why don't we walk?"

There was a quick look of disappointment. "I have to go to the store. I was just on my way to work."

"I'll walk you there, then," he said. He grabbed his coat from the peg behind the door. "Jeb, I'll be back in a few minutes."

There was an outright laugh. "Take your time, Will."

He shut the door behind him and put on his coat, and they started back up the street. She glanced up at him, suddenly shy. "I didn't mean to take you away from work."

He brushed that aside. "It's fine." He glanced down and saw that both of her hands were stuffed into a woolen muff, and he felt a little stab of disappointment. Unless she brought them out, there was no way to hold her hand naturally.

"How come you haven't been in school?"

He slowed for a moment, then shrugged. "With Pa in Wisconsin, I thought I'd better spend more time here at the freight office." He was watching her closely out of the corner of his eye to see her response. His answer was partially true. Joshua had taken three men and headed north two days after Christmas, eager now to see if he could get something started during this winter season. Once spring came, logging operations would stop. With him gone, Will did spend more time at the freight yard, but he had still found time for school until that day, almost two weeks ago now, when Jenny had stood and asked Jessica to read Peter's poem.

But if Jenny noticed the discrepancy she let it pass. "Jessica asked if I would tell you that we're going to be talking about China next week."

"Really?"

She nodded. "She would like your help."

"Well," he started slowly, "Pa *is* supposed to be back any day now."

"Good, I'll tell her." There was a brief pause, and then she spoke again. "I'm sorry about what happened in school the other day."

He came out of his thoughts with a jerk, then shrugged. He didn't really care to discuss it. "It's no big problem."

She ducked her head again, and as he looked at her, he was surprised to see that her cheeks had colored a little. "Would you like to come to supper tomorrow night?"

He stopped. She looked up at his face and laughed delightedly. "Does that surprise you so?" she exclaimed. "I can cook, you know. Mother Steed and Caroline have been teaching me."

"It's not that, it's just . . ." He nodded emphatically. "Yes, I would like that very much."

"Good." She withdrew her hands out of her muff and pulled the scarf up over her mouth and nose again. "Well, I'm late. I'd better run. Tomorrow night at seven, all right?" She touched his arm briefly, then darted off.

He watched her go, a little dazed, very much pleased, and already starting to feel a swell of anticipation.

———— ◆ ————

By the standards of New York, Boston, or Philadelphia, the meal wasn't much. In Nauvoo's slowly growing prosperity it was fine—nothing spectacular, but fine. By the standards of the working-class poor in England, however, it was a rich feast, and Jenny reveled in the cooking of it. In a way, though it meant a great deal more work for her, she was glad that her mother would not be home from delivering laundry until just before supper time. A week before, the family had been talking about finding some maple trees to tap. Nathan promised to give a bucket or two to the Pottsworths so they could make some syrup. "Make syrup?" Jenny had asked in surprise. "You mean it doesn't come out as syrup?" Will had laughed right out loud at that. What girl didn't know enough to boil down maple sap into maple syrup? It had stung Jenny, and so tonight it would give her great satisfaction to let it casually slip that she had cooked the meal completely on her own.

The main course was a piece of venison haunch, bought from a farmer who shot deer and sold the meat. It hung from a chain within the fireplace, over the "spider," a three-legged metal pot in which the makings of a stew—water, sliced carrots, potatoes, and turnips—were already starting to bubble. When the drippings from the meat finally stopped, Jenny put the heavy black lid on the spider, then with tongs carefully packed it with coals from the fire.

While that cooked, she carefully swept off the hearth of the fireplace, then molded small patties from a wet, sticky cornmeal paste. Flour was expensive and still in limited supply among the

Saints, but the ubiquitous cornmeal was not only cheap but very forgiving when it came to cooking it. Laying the patties in a neat row along the hottest part of the hearth, she then covered them with hot wood ashes and left them to bake. When they were done, she would wash them off, and these "ash cakes" would serve as their biscuits for the meal.

That task done, Jenny took the rest of the cornmeal and mixed it in a bowl of water. The resulting gruel, when poured into a pan of boiling water, would make "hasty pudding," a legacy from New England that Mary Ann showed her how to do. The hasty pudding, sweetened with honey or some of last year's maple syrup, would be their dessert.

Done at last, she looked at the small clock above the fireplace. "Oh, dear," she said. It was nearly quarter of seven already.

———◆———

Will caught himself humming as he rounded the corner of his father's corral and started down the snowy path that led to the door of the Pottsworth cabin. He was in a jubilant mood. After weeks of being jerked back and forth like a two-man saw cutting through a log, he felt that things were finally looking up. Jenny Pottsworth liked him. He knew that. He sensed it as clearly as he sensed when a horse was skittish or when a wagonload was about to shift. And that left him feeling wonderful.

From the moment she had stood beside him on the railing of the riverboat and asked him to teach him about America, Will had been lost. The eight-day trip up the Mississippi was one long, wonderful experience. He loved to watch her as she eagerly drank in the landscape around her. He loved the way she dropped her *h*'s and trilled her *r*'s. He loved to hear her call her mother "Mum," and the way her brows furrowed when she talked about her life in the textile factory. When he spoke of China, or described what it was like to climb the mast in a driving gale, or talked about hitching six span of oxen to one of the big Conestoga wagons, she watched him with such open awe that it left him totally intoxicated.

And then they had come to Nauvoo. He went from ecstasy to ordeal in a matter of one day. For all of his experience, for all of his travels, for all the fact that in the last two years Will had matured significantly beyond his natural age, he felt totally outclassed by Peter. There was only six weeks' difference in their ages, with Will being the older. But Peter was gentle and refined. Peter could express himself so precisely and so artfully. Peter wrote poems!

He shook his head and snorted softly in disgust, his breath making a cloud around his head in the cold night air. But then immediately his mood lifted again. Jenny had invited him to supper. Her eyes had danced with anticipation when she asked him, and had been filled with pleasure when he accepted. So all in all, Will was in a mood for humming. In fact, were he not almost to the door now, he might have burst into a lusty song of rejoicing.

He stepped up onto the small porch and rapped sharply. There was a sound from inside, then Mrs. Pottsworth opened the door.

"Good evening, Mrs. Pottsworth," he said, taking off his hat.

"Hello, Will," she said, stepping back. "Come in."

"Thank you." Will followed her through the door, then stopped dead. He gaped in openmouthed shock. Peter Ingalls was sitting on a chair near the fully laid table. Peter looked up, then shot out of his chair, his astonishment as great as Will's. And then in one flash of perfect clarity, Will understood. In one blinding, bitter instant, he saw it all. The dinner wasn't for him. It was for them. Peter and Will. Poor, helpless competitors brought and laid at the altar of their adoration.

Jenny was at the fireplace, bent over and stirring something in the big black kettle. She turned and straightened. As if time were suspended, Will saw her beauty, saw the color in her cheeks from the heat of the flames, saw the firelight dancing in the gold of her hair. Her eyes lit up and she dropped the wooden spoon into the pot she was stirring. "Oh, Will, it's you," she said. She started toward him.

He backed up a step. His eyes darted once to Peter. Peter was still staring at Will, not comprehending yet the game that was being played. "I . . ." Will saw the bewilderment on Mrs. Pottsworth's face. He saw Jenny's smile freeze. But none of that was enough. "I'm sorry," he blurted, and turned and plunged out the door.

"Will!"

He strode out all the more quickly, rounding the corner of the corral.

"Will Steed, you stop this instant!"

His step slowed, though he still didn't stop. He could hear her footsteps crunching in the snow behind him. Finally he stopped and let her catch up with him, but he didn't turn around.

She came around him to face him. "Will, what is the matter?"

"What is the matter?" he cried. "You mean you don't know?"

She shook her head, and he saw that she really didn't. For some reason, that infuriated him all the more. She was like an innocent playing with fire in a barn full of straw. "I thought you invited *me* for dinner."

"I did," she started, and then it hit her. She half turned, looking back at the open door of the cabin where her mother and Peter stood framed in the light from within. Instantly her hand came out and grabbed his arm. "You mean Peter?"

"Yes, I mean Peter," he hissed. "Did you tell me Peter was going to be there? Did you tell Peter I was coming?"

"I . . ." She looked hurt. "I thought you knew."

Let her be hurt, he thought. He was feeling a little pain of his own. "How was I supposed to know?" He pulled his arm free of her. "Well, that's fine. You can invite whoever you want, but leave me out of it."

He started around her, but again she grabbed at his arm, pulling him back. "Will, I didn't realize. Mum and I wanted to have a supper for some of my friends. Margaret Naylor is coming. Betsy Blake—who was on the boat with us—she's coming too. Peter is my friend. You're my friend. I wasn't trying to hurt you."

"You didn't hurt me," he shot back. "I just remembered I have something else I have to do." He reached down and gently pushed her hand away. "I'm sorry, Jenny. I can't."

"But why?"

He just shook his head and started away.

"Don't do this, Will. Please."

He could hear the quavering in her voice and for a moment he hesitated. He knew he was making a fool of himself. If the others were coming, it wasn't as if it were just him and Peter. And maybe it wasn't deliberate. But then he knew it was too late. The hurt was too deep. His hopes had been too high. "I'm sorry, Jenny," he mumbled, and then he walked swiftly away.

Caroline didn't know what else to do. For the past three days she had stood by, watching her son bear the hurt and the shame by himself. Twice she had tried to talk with him, to see if that might help. It didn't.

When Joshua returned home from Wisconsin the previous night, she told him the whole story. He tried to talk with Will, and got nowhere. Then Will made the mistake of telling his father that part of the problem was that he wasn't a Mormon and Jenny was determined she would have only a Mormon. That proved to be disastrous. Joshua was furious with "this snippety little English tart," and swore he was going to go over and tell her a thing or two himself. Horrified, Will began shouting at his father to stay out of his business, and Joshua started yelling back at him about having had enough of these narrow-minded Mormons to last him a lifetime. Caroline had finally walked out on the both of them, and that had jerked them back to some semblance of reason.

After that, Will only withdrew deeper into himself.

And so they waited. Will would mope around the house for hours, then launch into a furious burst of activity. The first night he walked the wintry streets until well after midnight. Late the previous afternoon, before Joshua had returned, Jenny came to the house looking for Will. But Will saw her through the window and fled. When Caroline told her that Will wasn't home, she turned and left again without a word. Caroline wanted so badly to tell Jenny that it was shame as much as hurt that was eating at Will now, but she couldn't. He would not tolerate any parental interference on this one.

Caroline walked from the kitchen to the hallway to where it opened into the parlor. Will was still sitting on the sofa, his back turned to her, the curtain drawn back so he could stare out into the night. "Where's Olivia?" she asked.

Will turned around, half-surprised. For nearly an hour Olivia had sat beside her brother on the sofa, pretending to read a book but really there to comfort him. Olivia was certain that she was the only one who fully understood unrequited love. But as far as Caroline knew, Will had not spoken a word to her. He shrugged. "I guess she went to her room."

Joshua was in the next room writing a letter to Abner Montague about next year's cotton crop. Like Olivia, he had come into the parlor and tried to strike up a conversation. But it was like conversing with one of the oxen down at the stable, so he too gave up and went into the study. Caroline sighed and started back toward the kitchen.

"Mother?"

She turned back quickly. "Yes, Will?"

"I'd like to talk with you and Pa."

She felt a little lurch of hope. "All right." She started to raise her head to call, but Joshua, hearing, was already standing at the door. They both moved over to the two overstuffed chairs that faced the sofa, and sat down.

Will stared at his hands, then traced the pattern in the upholstery with a finger. They waited. Then he looked at his mother. "You said Joseph Smith wrote and told the missionaries in England to come home?"

That was the last thing she had expected the conversation would focus on. "Yes," she said tentatively. "That's what Mary Ann Young—Brigham's wife—told us."

"When are they leaving?"

"She said Joseph asked them to hold conference in April and then come home after that."

"When in April?"

Joshua was as puzzled as Caroline. "Why do you want to know that, son?"

"When?" was all the answer he got.

Caroline shrugged. "The conference here is held on April sixth, the day the Church was organized. I assume it will be the same over there." She watched as he calculated behind the mask of his eyes.

Finally, he nodded abruptly. "If I tell you something, I want you to hear me out before you say anything, all right?"

Caroline nodded.

"All right?" Will asked his father pointedly.

Joshua nodded as well. "Whatever you say."

"I'm going to go over to England and meet Derek and Matthew, then come home with them."

He may as well have dropped a cannon ball at their feet. "What?" they blurted simultaneously.

"Just listen. The shipping company told me I have a job any time I want to come back. If I leave now, I can be in New York by the first of March and—"

"No, Will!" Caroline cried, her voice tight with anguish. "You can't leave us again so soon."

Joshua reached across and laid a hand on her knee. "Let him finish, Mother."

That won him a grateful look from Will. "I'm not running away to sea or anything like that, Mama. I just need time to think. I need to be away from here for a while. If I'm in New York by the first of March, I can be to Liverpool by the first of

April. Then I can come back home with Derek and Matthew. I would love to see them again. We'd still be home by early summer, in time for me to help you during the busy season."

He stopped. He had planned to say more, to give all the reasons why this was a good idea, but suddenly he couldn't say it, because he knew they would know they weren't the real reasons at all. He couldn't bear to put the real reasons into words.

Joshua turned to Caroline. For a long moment they looked at each other. Nothing was said. No facial expressions changed, but something passed between them. Caroline slowly turned back to look at Will. "And this will really help? Or is it just postponing something that you will still have to face when you return?"

"I don't know," he answered honestly. "But I need some time to sort it out. That much I'm sure of."

She exhaled slowly, and Will saw that her lower lip had just the slightest tremor to it. But she spoke evenly. "All right."

"Thank you, Mama. Thank you, Pa."

"How soon?" Joshua asked.

Will had already thought about that. "There's a stage for Springfield day after tomorrow."

"What about Jenny?" Caroline asked. "Are you going to tell her?"

"No!" It came out sharp and hard. "And I want you to promise you won't tell her until after I'm gone."

"Will," Caroline started, shaking her head, "that's not right."

"Promise me, Mother!" He spoke in almost wild desperation.

After a moment, she dropped her head. "All right, I promise."

When Jenny opened the door to her cabin she was completely taken aback. Jennifer Jo McIntire was standing there, bundled up against the cold. "Hello, Jenny."

"Jennifer Jo, why . . . Hello."

"May I speak with you?"

"Of course. Come in."

Jennifer Jo looked over Jenny's shoulder to where her mother sat at the table watching curiously. "Could we walk? Would that be all right?"

Jenny's eyes widened slightly, but she immediately nodded. "All right. Let me get my coat and scarf."

———•———

There was actually about three and a half years' difference in age between the two Jennys. Jennifer Jo had turned nineteen on January third, the same day that Lydia had given birth to a dark-haired, dark-eyed baby boy. Jenny Pottsworth wouldn't be sixteen until August. But they were much closer than that in maturity, and Jennifer Jo didn't really think much about Jenny's being younger than she was.

"May I be perfectly frank with you, Jenny?"

Jenny slowed her step, giving Jennifer Jo a curious look. "Yes. I like people to be honest."

"I know you do. I didn't understand that at first, but I do now. And that is why the first thing I have to say to you is, I'm sorry."

"For what?"

"For holding bad feelings about you."

Jenny blinked, then instantly looked bewildered. She looked away. "I didn't know you did."

Jennifer Jo reached out and took her hand. "Jenny, there are important things to tell you, but I have to say this first. The Lord told Joseph that if someone offends us, we should take him or her aside and try to be reconciled."

"What have I done that offended you?"

"Nothing." She took a quick breath. "I know that now. I let myself be offended by you, but actually you did nothing."

"I don't understand."

"I know." She gave a nervous little laugh. "This isn't easy, but . . . well, I was offended primarily because of Kathryn."

"Your sister? But why?"

"Kathryn has very deep feelings for Peter. And . . ." She shook her head. Honesty wasn't nearly as easy as it was touted to be. "And since you came, Peter doesn't even know that Kathryn exists anymore."

To her surprise, Jenny nodded. "I know."

"You do?"

"Yes, and I feel bad about it. Peter and I were such good friends over in England. But Peter is hoping for more than friendship now." She hesitated, blushing slightly, and then added, "I guess I was too. At first."

"At first?"

"In the last while I've come to realize that Kathryn is a much better person for Peter than I am."

Jennifer Jo stopped, staring at this girl who was so utterly open and honest.

Jenny laughed softly. "Well, it's true. Peter will always be very dear to me. Our friendship runs very deep. But Kathryn is a wonderful girl. You both are. She's better for him."

In complete wonder, Jennifer Jo started walking slowly again. "May I tell her that?"

Jenny's smile broadened. "Actually, I was going to, but I think she'll take it better from you."

They walked on for several yards. Then Jenny asked, "Is that all?"

"Is what all?"

"You said you were offended *primarily* because of Kathryn. Is there something else?"

Jennifer Jo looked down at the ground, totally embarrassed now.

"Well?"

"Well, yes. I . . . I thought you had your eyes set for my Matthew."

There was a slow nod. "I did."

"You did?" Jennifer Jo was finding it hard to keep up with this girl.

"Yes. Matthew is exactly what I have in mind for myself."

In spite of herself, Jennifer Jo had to laugh. "You have it all thought out?"

Jenny seemed surprised by the question. "Oh, yes. Ever since Mum and I joined the Church, I have thought about what kind of man I have to marry. And then I got my patriarchal blessing from Brother Hyrum Smith. And in that blessing, the Lord told me it would be very important who I married, that it must be in the Church. So especially since then I've been looking at who might make a good husband."

"And Matthew was one possibility?"

"He was . . ." She blushed now. "Until I met you."

"Until you . . ." Jennifer Jo let it trail off. "I don't understand."

"Matthew is a wonderful man—handsome, full of faith, kind, and with a wonderful sense of humor. He told me about you, of course, but I decided I would wait until he came home, then see if I could win him away from you."

Jennifer Jo couldn't believe what she was hearing. So the farewell kiss was more than just "one of the Spirit," as Paul the Apostle might say.

"But when I met you, I knew I had to make other plans."

Jennifer Jo held herself tightly. The cold was starting to penetrate through her coat, but she was only marginally aware of it. She was awash with shame. She had harbored ill feelings toward this English girl for more than two months now, and all along there was no cause. On an impulse, she suddenly turned to Jenny and gave her a quick hug. "I'm sorry, Jenny," she whispered. "You are a wonderful person, and I've been shameful for harboring those feelings. I wish I were more like you."

"Then can we be friends?" Jenny asked. It came out so plaintively and so filled with longing, that Jennifer Jo was shocked. "I would like that very much," the older girl replied.

"For some reason, I can't seem to make friends with other young women," Jenny said. "They all either shun me or talk about me behind my back."

The shame in Jennifer Jo was all the more bitter now. "It's because they can't believe that someone so lovely and so totally genuine can be real."

Jenny's eyes were shining in the reflected light from the snow. "Thank you, Jennifer Jo."

Now Jennifer Jo stood back. This confession had been only a secondary reason for her visit tonight. "And what about Will Steed, Jenny?"

A look of pain and utter dejection crossed Jenny's face. She turned away, holding herself tightly now too. "I think I'm falling in love with him, Jennifer Jo."

"What?"

"I know. I've hurt him so badly, and it's all because I've been so foolish."

"He thinks you are in love with Peter."

"I know what he thinks."

"Have you told him how you feel?"

"I can't," she said forlornly.

"Why?"

"Because he isn't a Mormon, Jennifer Jo. He's handsome and clever and funny and wonderful. But since my blessing I have made a deep promise to myself and to the Lord that I will not marry someone who isn't a member of the Church. I want what you and Matthew are going to have. I watch Lydia and Nathan and their family, and that's what I want. I . . ." She hesitated for only a moment. "I watch Will's mother and father, and I think, I don't want that. I couldn't stand it. It would break my heart."

"Then tell him *that!*" Jennifer Jo exclaimed. "Tell him how you feel."

Jenny just shook her head.

"Why not?"

"Because it only complicates things. He doesn't hate the Mormons anymore, but in so many ways he's still much like his father."

Jennifer Jo couldn't disagree with that and decided to step around it. "Did you know he's going back to England?"

Jenny's head whipped around, her eyes shocked.

"That's right. He leaves tomorrow on the stage."

"No," Jenny gasped. "Why hasn't he told me?"

"He's going to try and meet up with Derek and Matthew and come home with them. He made his mother swear not to tell you until after he's gone." Jennifer Jo got a devious look on her face. "But fortunately, he didn't make her promise not to tell me."

"But why? After being away from his family for so long, why is he leaving?" But she didn't need Jennifer Jo to answer that for her. She knew why very well. She wrung her hands. "I only asked the others to come to supper because I didn't want to seem too forward toward him. And I didn't want to hurt Peter, either."

She suddenly swung around and took both of Jennifer Jo's hands. "Thank you, Jennifer Jo. I just know we are going to be the best of friends." She leaned forward and they touched cheeks briefly. "I have to hurry. There's something I must get from home first."

Jennifer Jo smiled broadly. "You go. I'm fine."

Will looked up when the knock sounded, but he heard his mother's footsteps and settled back down into his chair, keeping one ear cocked to listen to who it might be at this late hour. He heard the soft murmur of his mother's voice, but couldn't make out if there was an answer. Then the door shut again and his mother walked by.

"Who was that, Mama?"

She didn't answer, just went on and disappeared down the hallway.

A little puzzled, he nearly called out again, but then shrugged it off. He settled back, trying to force his mind to concentrate on what things he must be sure to take with him.

"Hello, Will."

He visibly jumped, then leaped to his feet. Jenny was standing in the entryway to the parlor.

"Jenny, I . . ."

There was a faint smile. "Your mother let me in."

It was nearly eleven when Will tiptoed down the main hall-way. He stopped when he saw that a lamp was lit in the kitchen, then immediately smiled. Of course. What mother could go to sleep before she had a full report? He changed directions and went in to join her. Caroline was at the table with a Book of Mormon. She looked up, feigning surprise. "Oh, are you still up?"

He walked over and kissed her on the cheek. "Right, Mother," he said sardonically.

She closed the book and leaned back. "Well?" she finally said when he didn't respond to that cue.

He took a book out from under his arm, a book that was identical to the one she had been reading. He dropped it on the table with a soft clunk.

Caroline looked at it for a moment, then raised her eyes to his, not trying to hide her surprise. "She gave you a Book of Mormon!"

He nodded.

She wanted to take him by the shoulders and scream at him. He was just like his father. One-word answers at best, a shrug or a grunt more likely. "And?"

"She wants me to find out for myself if the Church is true."

One eyebrow came up slowly. "And if you do?"

His eyes filled with wonder. "She'll be waiting for me when I get back."

Caroline slowly nodded, seeing that the turmoil had been banished, at least for a time. "She told you that? That she would be waiting?"

"Yes."

"And what about Peter?"

"Peter is just a dear friend."

"Oh," Caroline said sagely. If that was a quote from Jenny, that was significant indeed. "And what if you decide the Church is not true?"

He looked away. "She'll be here when I get back."

"But not waiting for you?"

"That's right." Now a bit of the uncertainty was back. "She is unbendable on this, Mama. She will not marry anyone who isn't a Mormon."

"You're too young to get married," Caroline said automatically, her mind spinning a little. She had been delighted to find Jenny standing at their door. She hadn't expected quite this much from it, however.

"I know that," he said. "We wouldn't get married for another year or two."

"You talked about that?" she exclaimed.

He was suddenly sheepish. "Well, not in that much detail."

"Did you kiss her?"

"Mother!"

She laughed softly. "Well, did you?"

There was a little-boy's grin. "No," he half whispered, "she kissed me."

"And she didn't try to talk you into staying?"

"No, after I explained everything, she agreed that it's a good idea if we have some time. And this will give me a chance to really study the Book of Mormon and decide for myself."

"And are you planning to do that?"

Now he was dubious all of a sudden. "Well, I plan to read, but . . ."

"But you still have strong feelings about Mormonism?"

He nodded, touching his head. "I know up here that all of those feelings I harbored for so long have no basis, but"—he touched his finger to his chest—"down here they are not so easy to get rid of."

"I know." She glanced at the doorway quickly, then back to him. "And your father has told you how he feels about the Mormons and Mormonism?"

He was surprised by her perceptiveness. "How did you know that?"

"I just knew."

He reached out and picked up the Book of Mormon, turning it over and rubbing its cover absently. "You feel it is true, don't you, Mama?"

"I *know* it's true," she answered softly.

"How?"

She imitated his gesture, touching her hand to her bosom. "I know it down here, Will." But then she began to shake her head at him. "But that isn't good enough for you. Neither are your father's feelings in the other direction. You must decide for yourself."

He thought about that for a time, then slowly nodded. "That's what Jenny said, too."

"I think Jenny is a wonderful young woman, Will."

"Pa doesn't like her."

"Yes, he does. He just doesn't like her making his son so unhappy."

"He doesn't like her feelings about not marrying Mormons."

Caroline's lips pressed together. "And I don't like his feelings about being married to a Mormon," she murmured. "I guess that kind of evens things out."

Suddenly she stood and gathered him up in her arms. "How can you leave me again so soon?" she cried.

"I won't go if you say, Mama."

There was a long moment of silence. "No," she finally whispered. "Jenny's right. I think it's best if you do go now." She pulled him to her more tightly. "Just hurry back. Promise?"

"Yes, Mama. I promise."

$\mathbf{M}$atthew stopped sorting through the papers and picked up a newspaper clipping. He held it up. "Remember this?"

Derek was at the small table, reports from various branches and conferences spread all around him. Brigham had asked if he would tally the numbers in preparation for tomorrow's general conference. He looked up. "What?"

"This article in the *Millennial Star*. Remember when that story appeared in the *London Dispatch* last November, about the 'Mormonite' missionaries?"

"Oh, yes," Derek said, turning back to the reports. "And Parley's reply."

"Yeah." Matthew remembered very clearly how incensed Wilford Woodruff was when he read the article. Work in London had been slow and laborious. They had had some success and had baptized some wonderful converts, but compared to the work up north in Herefordshire or the Potteries it was discouragingly slow. So to have an article sharply critical of the Church appear in one of the leading papers was a further blow. Wilford had spent the better part of a day drafting a letter to the editor, then sent it and the offending article to Parley Pratt, who was editor of the *Star*. In the November 1840 issue of the *Millennial Star*, Parley reprinted the full article from the *Dispatch*, followed by a lengthy response.

Matthew sat back, reading it over again, able to smile now but remembering his own anger. A new sect calling themselves "Mormonites" had "pitched their tents in Gloucestershire," according to the writer, "for the purpose of plundering the ignorant people in the neighbourhood."

He looked up. "Well, at least they got this part nearly right."

"What?" Derek murmured, not looking up.

Matthew read to him now. "'These Mormonites are twelve in number, like the Apostles. They have a new bible of their own, in which it is declared that they are the apostles and prophets of the Church of Latter-Days, the only true and living church on the face of the earth.'" He chuckled. "And I like this part. He says, 'They tell the flocks of the learned clergy of the diocese of Gloucester and Bristol, that God has not revealed in the bible all that is sufficient to salvation.'"

"What an affront to the 'learned clergy'!" Derek said with amusement.

Matthew finished, shaking his head again at the perfidy of men. The article gave the report of a "gentleman of the neighbourhood," who accused the missionaries of plundering three families in Herefordshire and leaving them totally destitute, having robbed them of some two hundred pounds and more. He skipped down, skimming Parley's reply, looking for the most blistering paragraph.

"Listen to this, Derek. I love Brother Parley's answer to the charge that the Twelve stole all that money. Here's what he said. 'But again to this plundering business. The Bishop with two or three palaces and 9000 pounds a year, is a humble shepherd of the true fold, is he not? His scores of non-resident clergy and others, all supported by a salary, are not plunderers, are they?'" He moved down a few lines. "'No,—no,—it is this two or three hundred pounds, divided to twelve penurious missionaries (and this a falsehood) that is the only plundering known in England, is it not?'"

Derek put his pen down and sat back. "Did you know that after the tremendous success Wilford had in Herefordshire, ministers in the area petitioned the archbishop of Canterbury? They wanted him to ask Parliament to pass a law prohibiting Mormons from preaching in England."

"No, I didn't know that."

"Well, thankfully, the archbishop and his council rejected that idea out of hand. According to Wilford, the archbishop wrote back and told them that if they had the worth of souls at heart as much as they did the land where the hares and foxes and hounds ran, they would not lose so many of their flock."

"Good for him."

Derek sighed. "Well, I've got to get this report done before the Twelve finish their meetings. And you have got to get our stuff packed."

"I know." Matthew tossed the newspaper clipping back in the box with the letters from Jennifer Jo and other memorabilia he had been collecting over the past year. But in a moment, he had found something else and sat back and started to read again.

Will squinted up, trying to see a number on the brownstone apartment building. "You sure this is it?"

The boy was eleven or twelve and tall and gangly. He struck a belligerent stance. "G'wan, mate," he growled, trying to sound older than he was. "What kind of bloke do you think I am? I said I would find the address for you, and here we are. You owe me tuppence."

Will had to smile as he dug into his pocket for the money. The boy reminded him of another young man, hustling strangers on the docks of Savannah, offering to show them around town and hoping for a generous tip for doing so. Cocky, brash, impudent—this lad had it all, just as Will Steed did at that same age.

"Here's your tuppence and that much again for good service." He dropped the four pence into the boy's hand.

The eyes grew round. "Thank ya kindly, mate. You're a square joe."

"Thank you. Good evening to you."

The boy moved off, headed back in the direction of the train station to find another soul in need of a reputable guide to Manchester.

Looking up once more at the apartment building, Will took a quick breath, then shouldered his bag and ran up the steps.

———•———

At the knock on the door, Matthew jumped up. "I'll get it."

Derek sat back, looking towards the door. He was a little surprised. Brigham and the Twelve were meeting in council prior to the conference and had told Derek they would probably not be returning before nine. But then, with hundreds and hundreds of Saints coming into Manchester for the conference, it could be almost anyone.

Matthew went across the room and opened the door. "Good evening—," he started to say. He stopped. His jaw went slack and his eyes widened in astonishment.

"Evenin', Matthew."

"You?" he gasped. "But how . . . ?"

Derek craned his neck. Matthew was blocking his view of the door. "Who is it, Matthew?"

But Matthew didn't hear him. With one great cry, he swept the person up in his arms and was pounding him furiously on the back. "It *is* you!" he shouted. "It *is* you!"

He swung around, lifting the person clear off his feet, crushing him to his body. Derek stood, thoroughly baffled now. With all the swinging and pounding, he still could not see clearly who it was. "Matthew!" he said sharply.

Matthew swung back around and let his captive go. Now it was Derek who gasped. "Would you look at this, Derek," Matthew cried. "Would you look who's here in Manchester."

———•———

By midnight, there were still no thoughts of bed or sleep. The three of them sat around the table, their heads leaning forward as though, if they weren't careful, they might miss a word. Brigham Young and Willard Richards had returned a little before nine to get the tallies of Church membership. Will was introduced to and warmly received by the two Apostles. Brigham pumped him eagerly for any news of home, then left after fifteen minutes. The moment the two men were gone, Matthew and Derek started in again, peppering Will with questions in such a rapid-fire manner he felt like his head was starting to spin. It was as if they had been on a forty-day fast, and Will had brought them bread.

First came all the news of the family, with a special emphasis on Rebecca and Jennifer Jo. They were surprised to learn that Lydia and Nathan had a new baby boy. Somehow the family had neglected to mention she was expecting again. They would call him Josiah, Will reported, after Lydia's father. They fired off questions, wanting to know about the store and the brickyard and the freight business and how Jessica's school was going. The reports were highly encouraging, but Will surprised them with news of the trip to Wisconsin and the family's entry into the lumber business. Mary Ann had written Matthew about that, Will said, but evidently her letter had never arrived.

Then, suddenly more reticent, Will reported on the Pottsworths. He didn't have to admit to anything. By the time he was two minutes into talking about Jenny, Matthew slapped him on the shoulder. "You and Jenny like each other, don't you?" he said.

Will could only nod in embarrassment, not yet wanting to talk about all that was going on between him and her. So he turned the conversation to his parents. They all sobered as Will reported that nothing had changed there. When they received the letter saying Joshua had retracted his permission for Caroline to be baptized, both Matthew and Derek had started praying that Joshua's heart would be softened. They were hoping for a better report, and Derek seemed especially glum when Will flatly said he didn't see any hope of his father changing.

Finally, after almost two hours of their firing questions at Will, Derek sat back. "Ah, Will. I can't believe you're really sitting here in Manchester with us. And look at you. As tall as Matthew now and tan and muscular. The sailor's life must agree with you."

"I would have passed him on the street and not even recognized him," Matthew said, eyeing him now from across the table.

Will shrugged. "Well, it's been—what? We last saw each other in Far West. That's been almost three years ago now."

"And what a three years for you," Derek said soberly.

Will just nodded. He had been a boy the last time they had been together. Now he was a man and with more experience than many men twice his age.

"So tell us about you now," Matthew said. "How in the world did you ever come to be here in England? Mother wrote us, of course, about you being on the ship with the Pottsworths and about us just missing you in Liverpool. But we had no idea you were coming back."

"Neither did I until just a day or two before I left." There was a fleeting smile tinged with sadness. "I just decided I wanted to come over and sail back with you. Not wait another three or four or five months to see you."

"So you are going back with us?" Matthew asked.

"Oh, yes." He told them briefly about his experience with Captain Sperryman and how he had eventually become bosun. "When we arrived in New York about the first of October last year, the captain talked to the shipping company about me. They promised me a job whenever I came back. So I came to New York from Nauvoo mostly by stage, and when I got to the city I went down to the shipping office. They put me on as crew on the first packet ship coming across, and here I am." He smiled again, but this time it was full and genuine. "It felt good to be back to sea again."

Matthew pulled a face. "Are you serious? I've been dreading getting back on a ship now for over a month, and we don't even leave until the seventeenth."

Will leaned forward eagerly. "Are you sailing on the *Rochester?*"

Surprised, Derek nodded. "Yes, we're taking another load of emigrants with us."

"Great. That's what I hoped. The *Rochester* is owned by the same line I work with. I talked to the man here. He told me there was another big group of Mormons going across then. I thought it might be you, so I have tentatively signed on as crew for the trip back."

Derek reached out and laid a hand on his arm. "That's wonderful, Will. So tell us all about China. I can scarcely believe you've been halfway round the world and back."

Will nodded slowly. "It took a long time, but it was a good experience."

"Tell us," Matthew prompted.

"In a minute. First I'd like to talk with you about something else if I could."

"All right."

He stood and went over to his bag. Opening it, he fumbled around for a moment, then came back to the table, holding down low whatever it was he had gotten from the bag, so they couldn't see it. When he sat down he put it in his lap out of their sight. Settled again, he smiled, first at Derek, then at Matthew. "I need to tell you a couple of things first about me and Jenny."

He started slowly, recounting it all, putting words to his feelings in many cases for the first time. He began right at the beginning with that first day on ship and finished with their last time together when she came to the house.

At that point he brought up his hands. In them was the Book of Mormon. He laid it on the table in front of him.

Matthew stared at it, then turned to Will in wonder. "She gave you a Book of Mormon?"

His head went up and down slowly, his expression grave.

"And you've been reading it?" Derek asked, equally amazed.

"Every night on the journey from Nauvoo to New York, then every moment I was off duty on the ship. I finished it midway across the Atlantic and have started again."

There was a quick exchange of glances between the two missionaries, and then Derek spoke. "And?" he asked gently.

Now a forlorn look crossed Will's face and his shoulders fell. "I don't know."

"You don't know?" Matthew cried. "What do you mean, you don't know?"

"I don't know if it's true or not."

Derek reached across and laid a hand on Matthew's arm to steady him, but he kept looking at Will. "Tell me how you do feel."

Picking up the book, Will turned it over, looking at it with some perplexity. "Well, it's strange. When I read it, I feel good. In some ways it is a wonderful book, very much like the Bible. I'm almost sure that Joseph Smith could not have written it."

Matthew pounced on that. "But that *is* a testimony of the book, Will. Those feelings are how you know it's true."

"Go on, Will," Derek said, ignoring Matthew's outburst.

"I really liked the part where the Savior visited the people. That's probably the time when I felt most strongly it was true. But then, the next day I wasn't sure again."

"Did you see Moroni's promise right near the end of the book?" Derek asked gently. "It talks about how to know if the book is true."

Will opened the book to the very back, turned a page or two, then held it up. Someone had bracketed with a pen the very passage Derek was referring to. "Jenny marked it for me before she gave it to me."

"And?" Derek asked again.

The shoulders lifted and fell. "I've prayed every night about it," he said dejectedly. "Maybe it's because I don't know how to pray right. It's been a long time since I prayed, you know."

"If you prayed with a sincere heart," Matthew said, his directness softening now, "then you prayed right."

"Then why don't I know?" Will cried. "I want to know."

Derek sat back, watching him steadily. Matthew started to speak but, seeing Derek's face, stopped and sat back to wait. "I don't know," Derek finally said. "I think the Spirit works with different people in different ways. Maybe it will just take a little longer with you."

"But I want to know. I want to know for Mama's sake, and for Jenny. And Pa doesn't even know I'm doing this. I guess in a way I want to know for him too."

"Maybe that's part of it, then," Matthew said.

"What?"

"Moroni says you must ask with a sincere heart and with real intent."

"But I really want to know. Isn't that real intent?"

Matthew spoke very gently now. "It's real intent, all right, but maybe your intent is for Jenny, or Caroline." He hesitated. "Or for Joshua. And maybe unless, and until, you want to know for yourself, you won't know for sure. I don't know. It's just a thought."

Will sat back. He wasn't at all offended at Matthew's directness. In fact, during the last days of the voyage, he came to realize that he was looking forward to being with Matthew and Derek partly because he was hoping he could ask them his questions and get an honest response.

Derek stood up and walked over to a small table near the door. He picked up a paper and then came back. "Let me show you something, Will. This is a copy of the report I gave to Brigham tonight. He'll be giving this in the conference tomorrow. It's a report on the Church membership here in Britain. We've organized the Church here into branches, and then groups of branches are called conferences. Tomorrow, Brigham will call

on the leaders of each conference to report on their member-
ships. Here is what they are going to say."

Not sure what this had to do with the Book of Mormon,
Will sat back.

"You have to remember, this total does not include about
eight hundred Saints who have already emigrated to America.
But"—he consulted his paper—"there are now 5,864 members
of the Church in the British Isles. I don't know how many total
members there are in America, but with almost six thousand
here, that means a big portion of the Church are now English."

Will was suitably impressed. Almost six thousand members.
Jenny had talked about the phenomenal success of the missionaries, but she had never talked numbers.

"Now, here's what's amazing. A year ago at this time—that
was when Matthew and Brigham Young and Heber C. Kimball
were just arriving—there were 1,541 members. So counting
those who have emigrated, there have been over five thousand
people baptized in just one year's time."

That was impressive. But Will was still puzzled by it all.
"That is really something," he said, "but what does that have to
do with me knowing whether or not the Book of Mormon is
true?"

Now Derek made his point. "A good many of those five
thousand people are going to be here tomorrow, Will. They're
coming to the conference. Orson Hyde, one of the Apostles of
the Church, just arrived here from America about a month ago.
He is on his way to Palestine. That means there are now nine
members of the Quorum of the Twelve here in England."

Now Matthew saw what Derek had in mind. "They'll be
speaking to us," he said. "You'll have a chance to listen to them
and feel of their spirit."

Derek was nodding. "Before the Savior ascended to heaven
for the last time, he gathered the Apostles together. Do you
know what he said to them at that time, Will?"

Will shook his head.

"He said that the Twelve should go forth into all the world, baptizing those who would believe on their words. And then he said something like this: 'And these signs shall follow them that believe; they shall cast out devils, they shall heal the sick, they shall take up deadly serpents or drink deadly things and it shall not harm them, they shall speak with new tongues.'"

Now he sat back, watching Will with a great sense of calm. "Tomorrow you are going to meet people who have been healed of their sicknesses. There will be people here who have spoken in tongues. I've heard them. There will be a woman here who was possessed of an evil spirit. I was there, Will. I was there with Wilford Woodruff. This woman was raging terribly. She screamed and shouted, trying to rip her clothes off. Wilford laid his hands on her and commanded the evil spirit to leave her. In moments she was entirely calm, and then she went to bed and slept for the first time in days. The next day in church she stood and bore testimony of the power of the priesthood."

"And you saw all that for yourself?"

Derek nodded. "Will, what I'm telling you is, tomorrow you'll be meeting those people, people who heard the message of the gospel and believed, people who read the Book of Mormon and believed. Talk to them. Ask them how they knew."

Yes, Will thought, feeling a great sense of relief. *I don't have to know right this moment.* He began to nod. "I like that idea, Derek."

"Matthew's right, you know. It is important that you know for your mother or for Jenny, or even for your father. But that's only secondary. It's most important that you know for yourself, Will."

———◆———

Matthew went up on the balls of his feet, searching the crowd of faces. Finally he spotted Will in one corner, surrounded by several young ladies. Laughing at that, Matthew made his way over. Will was holding court and the girls were hanging on his every word. When Will finally looked up and saw Matthew grinning at him, he got a little flustered and quickly excused himself.

"Well, well," Matthew teased, "I can see the handsome young American sailor has made quite an impression on the belles of England."

"Go on," Will said, flushing a little. "They were just asking about what the crossing will be like. A couple of them and their families will be with us."

"Maybe you'd better not ship on as crew. That would leave you time to"—he grinned at Will—"to answer all their questions."

Will slugged him lightly on the shoulder. "You know better than that."

Matthew sobered. "So," he said, keeping his voice light, "what do you think?"

"About the conference? I thought it was great. Very interesting."

Nodding slowly, Matthew thought about that. Will had sat with him and Derek during the two meetings. He had listened intently, especially when Brigham Young spoke and bore testimony, and he seemed to like what he was hearing. "Have you had a chance to talk to anyone about how they felt when they joined the Church?"

Will shook his head. "I was about to ask some of those young belles, as you call them, when this other young American came up and started laughing at me."

"Who, me?"

Will smiled at the feigned innocence. "It's all right, Matthew. Actually, it's a little awkward to walk up to total strangers and say, 'Hello, my name is Will Steed. I'm confused and wondered if you could tell me the innermost feelings of your heart about the Church.'"

"All right! All right!" Matthew chuckled, surrendering. "There will be plenty of chances on the ship to talk with people."

Now it was Will who grew serious. "If you want to know the truth, there is one thing."

"What?"

The dark eyes were very thoughtful now, and touched with just the slightest hint of regret. "For a long time, I've had some very bitter feelings about the Church, even after I learned that it wasn't Mormons who had 'killed' Pa. Those feelings softened quite a bit in Nauvoo. But even then, down deep, there was still this resentment, this . . . I don't know . . . this revulsion about Mormonism. And I'm sure some of that came from Pa even before all the trouble in Missouri."

"Probably so."

"Nathan once told me hate is like being poisoned by a rattlesnake. And I guess I still had some of that poison in my system."

"And now?"

Will's shoulders pulled back as he tried to find the proper words. "Well, since I've been reading and praying it's been slowly changing. And particularly today, as I listened to those men speak, I suddenly realized it was gone. All those feelings are gone. I . . ." He looked directly into Matthew's eyes now. "If I should learn that the Church is true, I will be very happy to be a Mormon."

"Good! Good!" Matthew said, genuinely pleased.

"And if I don't . . ." He stopped. The corners of his mouth pulled down as he thought what Jenny would say if she were hearing these words.

"Yes?" Matthew prodded.

He pushed his thoughts away. "And if I don't find out it's true, I will always be a strong friend to the Church."

For several moments, Matthew considered that. Will could tell he was a little disappointed that it wasn't more, but he also could tell that Matthew understood just how much that was for Will. Suddenly, Matthew reached out and laid a hand on Will's shoulder. "That's great, Will. I think that's just great."

———— ◆ ————

By half past eleven, most of Nauvoo and much of the surrounding area, including many places in Iowa Territory across the river, were nearly empty of their inhabitants. All morning long they had been converging on a spot on the bluffs east of the city proper. Now they were there by the thousands, and still coming.

The assembly site for this vast congregation was not accidental. For the last several weeks the word had been sent out among the branches and the settlements. April sixth marked the eleventh anniversary of the founding of the Church. It was time for another general conference.

But that was only partially what drew them. Up high on the bluffs, overlooking the great horseshoe bend in the Mississippi River, was the site for the latest temple of the Church. In the October conference, Joseph had announced that they would build another house of the Lord. Immediately thereafter, construction work began. Now six months later, the excavation—itself a massive undertaking—was done. The foundations were in place. And on this day, starting with the southeast corner, the point of greatest light, and beginning at noon, the time of greatest sunlight, the cornerstones for the Nauvoo Temple would be laid.

"I can't believe how big it is going to be," Melissa said, letting her eye run the length of the foundation walls. "It's much bigger than the Kirtland Temple, isn't it, Papa?"

Benjamin bobbed his head. "I should say."

"How much bigger, Grandpa?" young Joshua asked.

"Well," Benjamin said, pursing his lips as he tried to remember the exact figures the building committee had been given, "if my mind is correct, it's about thirty feet wider and more than twice as long. It's going to be one hundred twenty-eight feet long."

Carl Rogers eyed the foundation walls that ran east and west. It was going to be huge. Carl had already been asked to furnish some of the brick that would be used to pave the basement floor and had done some calculations. But to actually see it like this, it was impressive.

"Where will the oxen be, Mama?" Rachel asked.

Jessica looked around. "I'm not sure, honey. In the basement here, but I'm not sure exactly where."

"Joseph says right there," Benjamin said, pointing to the near center of the excavation. "That's a well you see there. That will furnish the water they need."

"They're gonna let cows in the temple?" six-year-old Mark Griffith asked, his mouth open in amazement.

Everyone laughed at that. "No, Mark," Benjamin said, chuckling. "They're not real oxen. They'll be carved from the same stone as the temple."

"Then why do they need water?" Emily asked, as puzzled as her cousin.

"Yeah," Luke Griffith piped in. "Why?"

Lydia knelt down in front of her daughter. "Remember last year when Papa baptized you, Emily?"

"Yes."

"Well, instead of being baptized in the river like you were, there's going to be a baptismal font—a font is like a huge bath-tub—in the temple. And it will sit on the backs of twelve oxen. Not real oxen, but carved oxen, like Grandpa said. That's what the water is for, to put in the font so people can be baptized."

Olivia had been listening closely. She looked up at her mother. "When we get baptized, Mama, can we be baptized in the temple?"

A sudden, embarrassed silence swept over the family. For a moment, Caroline was taken aback, but then she looked around. "You can all relax," she laughed. "It's only Joshua who doesn't like you talking about baptism. But I have made up my mind to be baptized someday, you know."

"And so have I," Olivia said with conviction.

Caroline looked down at her oldest daughter. "But to answer your question, Livvy. No, I think this font will be used only for those who want to be baptized for the dead. We'll be baptized in the river, probably."

Benjamin started to make an additional comment, when the

sharp crack of cannon shot was heard from the direction of the city.

"Oh," Mary Ann cried, "they're coming. Quick, let's go over by the road so we can see better."

Rachel looked up in alarm at Jennifer Jo. "What is it? What's happening?"

Jennifer Jo took her hand. "It's the Nauvoo Legion, Rachel. They're coming. The parade has started."

They joined the flow of the crowd as everyone moved to where they could see the sweep of Nauvoo below them. And then the Steeds, along with everyone else, stopped dead, dumbfounded at the sight that awaited them.

"Oh, my!" Mary Ann breathed.

"Would you look at that?" Carl exclaimed with open awe.

"Oh!" Caroline said, in a drawn-out exclamation of amazement.

Carl reached down and picked up his two younger boys and held them up as high as he could. Lydia had her baby and couldn't do anything for Emily as the crowd pushed in and cut off their view. Benjamin already had Savannah on his shoulders, and Jessica did the same with John, her youngest. Cries of excitement were exploding everywhere now. People were shouting and pointing. Children who couldn't see were squealing to be lifted up. People near the back of the crowd were calling out, asking what it was. Those near the front with the best view whistled and clapped their hands.

"I can't see, Papa," young Carl complained.

"Me neither," cried Olivia.

Just then two men came riding up on horses. "Make a path! Give way!"

The crowd began to fall back in both directions, opening up a broad avenue. The Steeds were right at the split point and ended up along the second or third row of spectators. And now they all could see what was coming.

Sixteen companies of the Nauvoo Legion were marching up the road toward the temple site. In the lead was the Legion band, playing a rousing military march. Next came the officers and their staffs on horseback. And following behind was square after square of soldiers, boots crunching in perfect rhythm to the music, forming a phalanx of men and weapons almost a quarter of a mile long.

It was a grand sight and one to stir the blood. As the band passed, the Steeds and everyone around them applauded wildly. A *band, no less*, Benjamin thought. In Far West, they had had a few who could play instruments, and they had formed a band of sorts. But this was a real band. Most of the men had uniforms on, and the drum major was marking the beat with long up-and-down sweeps of his staff. As he passed by, he raised the staff above his head and twirled it around two or three times with a grand flourish. There were cries of approval and the applause increased. The children's eyes were big as wagon wheel hubs.

"There's Brother Joseph," Kathryn McIntire cried, pointing. "And Sister Emma." Joseph, mounted on his horse, heard her and turned and waved.

"My," Mary Ann said to Benjamin, "don't they make a fine-looking couple?"

Joseph and Emma rode side by side. Emma was in a full dress and rode sidesaddle. Joseph was resplendent, dressed in full uniform. There was a dark blue coat with gold braid epaulets and brass buttons, white trousers, knee-length boots, a wonderful belt with a sword and scabbard, and a plumed helmet. The plumes, made of ostrich feathers, waved gaily in the breeze as his horse pranced, sensing the excitement of the crowd.

Under the Nauvoo Charter, the city council was allowed to appoint the commanding general of the militia. To no one's surprise, Joseph Smith was chosen and given the rank of lieutenant general. John C. Bennett was made a major general as a reward for his role in getting the charter passed. Wilson Law and Don Carlos Smith, Joseph's youngest brother, were given commissions as brigadier generals.

Behind Joseph and Emma came the other general officers and their wives and the younger officers who served them. They waved and called out as they rode past.

"Where's Papa, Mama?" Emily asked, searching the rows of faces as the first company of men approached them.

"He is in General Law's company," Lydia answered. "I'm not sure which one that is, but if—"

"There he is!" Peter said, pointing to the third company back. Nathan was the second man in on the fourth row.

"Papa! Papa!" Emily cried. It was lost in the shouts of a hundred other children doing exactly the same thing, but somehow he picked her voice out. His head turned just a fraction as he approached and he winked at them. Then he snapped back to the front and marched on by, his right arm up to hold his rifle, his left arm swinging back and forth in cadence with the others.

Benjamin watched them pass, rank after rank, row after row. As the final company passed by, he leaned over to Mary Ann. "We owe John C. Bennett a great debt of gratitude," he said loudly enough to carry over the noise.

She looked up and nodded. The Nauvoo Legion was authorized by the Nauvoo Charter, and John C. Bennett was the man primarily responsible for the Nauvoo Charter.

"If we had had this in Far West," Benjamin said grimly, "it would have been a far different story."

Chapter Notes

As stated in the novel, the article critical of the Church and Parley Pratt's reply to it were printed in the *Millennial Star* in November 1840 (see MWM, p. 215). The reply of the archbishop of Canterbury to the request of the ministers was reported by Wilford Woodruff (see MWM, pp. 125–26).

The growth statistics given by Derek do not include the incredible success Wilford Woodruff and John Taylor had prior to April 1840 when Brigham and the rest of the missionaries arrived. The best calculations would indicate that there were approximately six thousand converts to the Church as a result of the mission of the Twelve to England. (See MWM, pp. 301–2.) Total Church membership at the end of 1839, just before the missionaries started to arrive in England, was over sixteen thousand (see *Deseret News 1993–1994 Church Almanac* [Salt Lake City: Deseret News, 1992], p. 396), which means the British mission swelled the Church's population by more than a third.

Wilford Woodruff records the account of the woman possessed of an evil spirit. While in Manchester, he was asked to go and heal the woman. There were several nonmembers in the room, skeptics who had come to see if the Apostle could work a miracle. Reluctantly, Wilford blessed her, but with no results. Her raging only increased. He then cleared the room and administered to her again, with the immediate results here described. (See *MWM*, p. 92.)

The general conference of 6 April 1841 began with a grand march by the Nauvoo Legion. Hymns were sung and Sidney Rigdon gave an impassioned speech about the significance of the occasion. Then the cornerstones of the temple were laid. (See *HC* 4:326–31.) Largely through the lobbying efforts of John C. Bennett, the Illinois legislature approved the Nauvoo Charter on 16 December 1840. This not only legally incorporated the city of Nauvoo but also authorized the city council to form a militia, much as other cities of any size were allowed to do. At its height, the militia had as many as five thousand men. They were well equipped, with many of the men having arms and the Legion itself having some light artillery pieces. (See Philip M. Flammer, "Nauvoo Legion," in *Encyclopedia of Mormonism*, ed. Daniel H. Ludlow, 5 vols. [New York: Macmillan, 1992], 3:997–99.)

T here was a loud crash and a piercing scream.

Will came out of his bunk in one leap. The ship shuddered like a frightened animal as it plowed into a wave higher than its foredeck and tons of water crashed over its length. Then, fighting to get its head out of the sea, the prow rose sharply.

"Watch out!" Will shouted at a shadowy figure across the steerage compartment from him. The man jumped to the side as a heavy travel trunk went hurtling by, smashing through a barrel of beans like an ax chopping through birch bark, and slamming into the bulkhead hard enough to splinter the wood.

Will made a leaping dive for the trunk as the ship crested the wave and plunged downward again. He grabbed on to one of the lashing ropes tied to a support beam, shoved his hand through the handle of the trunk, and hung on. In a moment, the deck changed its pitch from a sharp upward angle to what seemed like almost straight down. The trunk wanted to follow, and Will's arm felt like it was being jerked from its socket.

He shook his head, trying to clear his mind. When the rough weather had started four days ago, the captain had given Will permission to sleep in steerage with the passengers for just this kind of contingency. They were sick and frightened and in-experienced in riding a ship in a storm. Will had come off a double watch just an hour before, exhausted beyond belief, and fallen into his bunk. He was almost instantly asleep in spite of the wild ride. That's when everything started to break loose.

He jerked his head to the left. A woman screamed as the braces of her bunk tore out of the bulkhead, dumping her and a little girl onto the deck with a crash. Fortunately, they were in the lowest bunk and it was a short drop to the deck, but they both shrieked in terror as the deck slanted upward again and mother and daughter began sliding across it.

Up ahead of him another bunk gave way and a man was dumped onto the man in the bunk below him. That bunk couldn't handle the extra weight and it too ripped free. The two men slammed down against the deck and cried out in pain. Will's fingers were numb as the leather dug into the flesh, but he clenched his teeth and hung on the harder. The two men writhing on the floor were right where the trunk would pass if he let it go. It would smash them as easily as it had the barrel.

As the ship leveled again for a moment, Will whipped the lashing rope through one handle, then shoved the trunk against the nearest bulkhead and frantically tied the rope down, secur-ing the trunk from slipping further. Suddenly he was aware of someone beside him. It was Brigham Young and Heber Kimball, both with faces as white as the foam on the sea, but teeth set and determined. "We've got to get things secured," Brigham shouted into Will's ear, "or someone is going to get killed."

Will nodded, grabbing for Brigham's arm as the ship rose again and he nearly lost his balance. "Get every man who can walk. You take the forward compartment. Tell them to hang on when she's going up or down, then work quickly while she's more level."

"Right." The ship leveled, creaking and groaning like a living thing, preparing to shoot downward again. They ran like deer for the next hold.

Will looked around. Derek was half out of his bunk. Wilford Woodruff was beside him, trying to help him. They clung grimly to the bunk and to each other as the deck tipped downward again. On the next break, they were staggering across to him. Both had been violently ill for several days now and could barely walk.

Will met them halfway. "We've got to get anything that's loose tied down," he shouted. "Work while the ship is level. Stay close to something to hang on to."

He darted away, moving from bunk to bunk, hollering instructions. Matthew, right below Derek's bunk, tried to get up, but instantly collapsed back down again. Of all the passengers, he had been one of the sickest. "Stay there!" Will commanded. "You'll just get hurt."

They worked frantically for half an hour, shadowy figures in the semidarkness. The heavier items were their first objective. Then they began grabbing at smaller loose objects rolling or flying about. They helped people back into their bunks, put women and children who had lost their beds in with others, jamming two and three into bunks where there was barely room for one.

Through it all, Will was grateful for two years of sea experience. This storm was as bad as any he had weathered, and even some of the crew were seasick. That was why he had been working double watches. But Will was fine. His body anticipated the rolls and pitches and adjusted accordingly without conscious thought anymore. And compared to some tasks, the problems in the passenger compartment were simple to deal with. The day before, he and the bosun had scrambled up thirty feet of mast when the top foresail snapped clean off and tangled in the rigging. That was like trying to hang on with one hand to some massive, fiendishly powerful bucking horse while keeping the other hand free to untangle the rigging.

From the very start, any hopes for a pleasant passage to

America had been dashed. They were barely out of Liverpool when they ran into contrary winds. That made for rough seas and slow progress. Then, three days out, the winds rose to gale force. For the next four days, the winds howled unabated, and life became a living nightmare for the passengers. On this night, it had worsened, turning even the most harmless of objects into lethal weapons.

Finally feeling like things were under control, the men began to straggle back to the main compartment. They held on to the beams or clung to tables. They were sick, and numbed by the misery around them and their own living hell. Brigham and Heber and John Taylor made their way over to the center beam, and then Brigham raised one hand. "Brethren," he shouted, "we cannot bear much more of this. Our people cannot bear much more of this."

There were only grim nods. No one was going to dispute that. "We must petition the Lord for help. I would like my brethren of the Twelve to gather around me as best they can, and then we shall unitedly pray."

———— • ————

Will awoke with a start. The first thing he was aware of was that it was quiet, with only the barest of creaking from the ship's timbers. Next he realized the ship was barely rolling. There was the gentle up-and-down motion that was part of ship life even on the calmest of seas, but that was all. Then, as he turned his head, he saw that the hatch was open and bright sunlight and fresh air were streaming into the hold. He breathed deeply, savoring the smell of the sea like it was medicine to the soul. He swung his legs over, careful not to disturb Matthew and Derek below him, and dropped to the deck. He pulled on his shirt and headed for the ladder.

It was an absolutely breathtaking day, the air clear as a crystal goblet, the sun bright and warm and welcome. He looked up, hardly believing his eyes. The sails were full, and pulling the ship through the water at a steady clip. He had to look twice at the sun and calculate the direction before he realized that the wind was blowing straight out of the east. The contrary winds were gone. He shook his head in wonder, remembering Brigham's prayer of the night before.

There was no one about except for crew. The passengers were all still down in their bunks, finally able to sleep and rest. Breathing deeply, Will started forward, reveling in the day. As he came around the mainmast, he stopped in surprise. There was a figure at the railing up ahead, right at the bow of the ship. Then Will smiled, not really surprised. It was Brigham Young.

"Good morning," Will said as he came up.

"Oh," Brigham said, turning around, "it's you. Good morning, Will."

Looking around at the calm seas, Will gave a little shake of his head. "Can you believe this day?"

Brigham laughed softly. His face looked tired and haggard and he hadn't shaved for several days, but his eyes were bright and alert and invigorated. "Actually, no I can't. That's why I came out. I had to see it for myself." There was a pause. "And to give thanks."

Will only nodded. He was wrestling with that himself. It was not common for a storm to blow itself out so quickly, but it wasn't totally unusual either. But to have it happen so quickly after the prayer? He would have to think about that.

"Thank you for your help last night, Will. I don't know what we would have done without you."

"It was nothing. I'm just glad we got it under control."

"Very glad," Brigham said fervently.

Turning and leaning on the rail, Will looked down to where the prow split the sea, turning it green and white as it shoved it aside. "The sea is not always such a difficult lady," he said. "Sometimes she can be quite decent to you."

"Maybe so," Brigham muttered, "but as for me, I'd be downright pleased if I never had to make her acquaintance again."

Will laughed. "Really, she's not that bad. You can come to love her."

"*You* can come to love her," he retorted. "I'll keep my affection for something a little more reliable."

That really didn't surprise Will. There were many who hated the sea. Some—including a few sailors he knew—merely tolerated and endured her. Only a few really loved her, and at this moment, Will realized again that he was one of them.

Brigham turned around and leaned back against the rail. "Will?"

He looked up. "Yes?"

"Matthew told me about your desire to know if the Church is true."

Will only nodded. Matthew had asked if Will minded if he told others, and Will had said no because it gave him the opportunity to ask some of the questions he wanted to ask.

"Do you mind if I ask you some questions?" said Brigham.

"Not if you don't mind if I ask you some back."

"Fair enough." Brigham tipped his head back, letting the wind ruffle the reddish hair, and letting the sun fall full onto his face. "How long have you been trying to find out if the Church is true?"

"Since I left Nauvoo. That was the last part of January."

"And?"

There was a quick shake of his head. "I don't know. I've learned a lot. My feelings have changed significantly. But . . ." He didn't finish. He just blew out his breath.

"Do you think the Lord answered our prayers this morning?" The Apostle's arm swept out, encompassing the sea and sky.

Will turned and looked out across the ocean's breadth. "It sure seems like it," he finally said.

"It sure does."

"And yet . . ."

Brigham smiled, understanding. "And yet it could just be a happy coincidence."

"Yes. So, how do you know? How can you tell if it's real or not?"

"Well, let me tell you about a man I once knew who had

some of those very questions." He turned to face forward again, gazing out without looking at Will. "This was years ago, in up-state New York. The young man I'm thinking of was a plain man, a simple man. He was religious in his heart, but frustrated by what he found around him."

Will was watching him closely, immediately guessing that he was talking about himself.

"He got disgusted with what he called the long-faced, pious worshippers who bowed their heads on Sunday and acted like heathens every other day. For example, he knew one man and woman, both good churchgoers, who asked their minister if there would be two different banquet tables set in heaven; they were afraid they might have to eat with their hired hands up there. This disillusioned man also knew ministers who would not help a hungry man in need. And then there were the Bible-pounding preachers who were as sour as pickles left too long in the brine."

Will was chuckling. "Yeah, I've known one or two like that."

"So eventually, this man just kind of withdrew, determined that he would try and live as the Savior asked, yet give up on regular religion."

"But?"

Brigham looked a little startled by the question. He had slipped away into his memories. "What?"

Will laughed. "Here you are, an Apostle of Christ. Something must have happened to you."

There was that slow grin again. "Yes, the young man was me, all right."

"So what happened?"

"Well, Samuel Smith, Joseph's younger brother, came around with some copies of the Book of Mormon. A brother and a sister of mine got hold of copies and started reading them. They got me to reading it too."

This was getting to the heart of what Will wanted to know. "So when you read it, did you know it was true?"

Brigham thought about that. "Yes and no."

Will frowned, and that made Brigham smile. "Well, that's really the best answer. Let me explain. From the very first I felt there was something to Mormonism and said as much to Phineas—that's my brother. He agreed. But at the same time, I wasn't willing to just accept it at face value. You've got to remember, I was this hardheaded New Englander. I had seen too much of sham religion. I had heard too many sermons that didn't satisfy."

"I see." Will did see, and it made him feel better. That wasn't a bad way to answer his own question. Will Steed, do you believe the Church is true? Yes and no.

"When I undertook to sound out the doctrine of Mormonism," Brigham continued, "I supposed I could handle it as I had the doctrines of the other churches. But instead, I found it completely different. I liked the way the Book of Mormon seemed like scripture, and answered some of the questions the Bible didn't. I liked the idea that here was a religion that could embrace truth wherever it was found. I liked the way it answered some of the vexing questions I had. But what really surprised me the most was that I found it impossible to take hold of either end of Mormonism. It went from eternity, passed through time, and went back into eternity again."

Will was suddenly impatient, not sure what all that meant. "But eventually you came to know it was true, right? How did that happen? I keep asking and I just can't seem to get an answer one way or another."

Now Brigham turned to face him fully. "Will, let me tell you something. Some people are natural believers. There's something down deep inside that's kind of like a lodestone. They just know and they never seem to doubt. Your Grandmother Steed is one of those. So is your Uncle Nathan."

"And Derek. He said he and Peter knew the Book of Mormon was true almost the first moment they started reading it."

"Yes, Derek is another one. What a great soul he has. But others aren't like that. Others are more stubborn or hardheaded or more inclined to want to study things out. Whatever the reason, it just doesn't come so easily to them. And I was one of those."

"You were?"

There was a firm nod. "Will, I was given my brother Phineas's copy of the Book of Mormon to read sometime in the late spring or early summer of 1830. Do you know when I finally decided that Mormonism was true?"

"No, when?"

"I was baptized on April fourteenth, 1832."

Will just stared at him.

"That's right—1832! Two full years later! That's what it took me. I studied, I pondered, I watched and waited. I wanted to see if the Mormons lived up to what they taught. Two full years, Will. You think about that."

He was reeling a little. "So if I don't know right away, it doesn't mean . . ." He let it trail off, feeling a great sense of relief.

There was a soft chuckle from Brigham now. "No, it doesn't mean it's not true. And if you still don't know by the time we get back to Nauvoo, you're just going to have to tell that sweet Jenny Pottsworth to be patient. With us hardheads, sometimes it just takes the Lord a little longer."

"And what if I decide it's not true?" Will asked slowly. "Pa says I'm more like him, that down deep we don't really need outward religion."

"Will, your pa is a good man. His generosity and goodness with the Saints is beyond what many of our own people would do. But take it from someone who once thought that same way. I had decided I would just go my own way and forget about trying to be happy in this church or that. But I wasn't happy, Will. Not truly happy." He laughed suddenly. "You know what they used to say about my father?"

"What?"

"They used to say that no one ever saw John Young smile until he was baptized, and then he laughed for six months to think that he had finally found the truth. Once I made up my mind, that's kind of how I felt too. That's something to think about, Will. You can go your own way and be happy, but you'll never know true joy without the gospel."

———◆———

The *Rochester*, one of the fastest ships plying the Atlantic, sailed from Liverpool on April twenty-first with seven Apostles aboard. Parley Pratt, his wife and children with him now, stayed on in England to supervise the work and continue to publish the *Millennial Star*. Orson Hyde continued on alone toward the land of Palestine. The rest headed home.

Due to the contrary winds and the terrible storm, it took a full month to make the crossing, and they did not arrive in New York until May twentieth. The following Sunday, the Apostles preached to a large congregation of Saints in the city, reporting on their missions, and then made plans for heading west. As they had when they came from Illinois to New York, they split and went their separate ways. Some stayed in the East for a time to visit family or preach. Others started back immediately.

On June fourth, Elders Brigham Young, Heber C. Kimball, and John Taylor, in company with Derek Ingalls and Will and Matthew Steed, set their faces westward. Traveling by canal boat, by steamer, by stage, and on foot, they covered the eight hundred miles in twenty-seven days.

———◆———

It was past five o'clock in the afternoon when six tired and dusty travelers stopped at that point on the road between Quincy and Nauvoo where the trees opened up and they could see upriver for some distance. About two miles north of them, the river took a long, sweeping turn to the west. They could see the dark mass of land that had once been the swamps of Commerce. It was July first, 1841. For Derek Ingalls and John Taylor it had been two years less a month and a week since they had stood on this spot for one last look at their homes. For Brigham, Heber, and Matthew it had been twenty-one and a half months since they had walked south past this spot. Only Will had been along this route within the year.

For several moments they stood there, no one speaking, each one lost in his own thoughts and swept up in anticipation of sweet reunion. Then Brigham straightened, adjusting the rope slung over his shoulder which held his traveling bag. He cleared his throat. "Brethren, let's go home."

———— • ————

Over the past several months, it had become customary, unless there was rain, for the Steeds to gather together after supper at Benjamin and Mary Ann's cabin two or three times each week. They had benches and chairs and the breadth of the porch. They would sit in the cool of the evening, visiting quietly while the children played around them. Often the women brought sewing with them to work on while they talked—their current project was sewing shirts and pants for two families who had recently come from the East with nothing but what they carried.

As dusk drew closer, Benjamin would take out the Bible or the Book of Mormon. The children would stop their games and gather in around while Benjamin read a chapter or two, stopping from time to time to ask questions or discuss what this or that gospel principle meant in actual living. When he was finished, someone was called upon to offer prayer and give thanks for another day of life and daily bread.

At first, it was awkward for Joshua. He would come to the first part, sitting around to talk, but then he would quietly leave when they reached the point of scripture reading. Or sometimes he just found some reason to stay later at the freight yard. But more recently he had begun to stay, standing back, never participating in the discussions, but not leaving, and seeming not to mind at all.

There were times when work at the brickyard kept Carl Rogers away too, but when he was there, he wasn't bothered at all by the scripture reading and often became an active participant in the discussions.

It was a favorite time of the day for everyone, and Benjamin and Mary Ann derived great satisfaction from having their family around them.

On the evening of July first, the family had just settled in once again at Father and Mother Steed's. Joshua, Carl, Nathan, Benjamin, and Peter were sitting on the porch discussing the construction on the temple. Carl had delivered another wagonload of bricks, probably the last needed in order to pave the floor around the baptismal font. For Nathan, Benjamin, and Peter, this had been their "tithe" day, the one day in ten that they spent laboring on the temple. They had worked in the quarry all day, standing back as the stonemasons blasted out the huge blocks with black powder, then grunting and sweating to get them onto the wagons with block and tackle. The stones currently being cut were to be the first course and therefore provided the base of the massive walls. They were three feet thick and weighed close to four thousand pounds each. In the whole day of backbreaking labor, they had moved only three stones.

Lydia had just finished nursing baby Josiah and he had fallen asleep in her arms. The other women sat around her, sewing steadily as they talked. On the far end of the porch, Olivia and Kathryn were reading a story to the little ones. Young Joshua, Emily, Rachel, the Rogers boys, and the Griffith boys were out in the street playing stickball. Rachel and Emily were right in the thick of it and holding their own.

It was young Joshua who saw them first. As he stood up to take the pitch from Luke, he saw three men turn onto the street about a block away and start toward them. It was not unusual to have people out and about at this time of day, and he barely glanced at them. But then, something about them caught his eye and he lowered the stick slowly, squinting to see them better. One of them, seeing that he was staring at them, raised his hand and waved.

Young Joshua's mouth dropped open and the stick fell from

his hands. "Matthew?" he cried softly. He spun on his heel. "Mama! Mama! It's Matthew! Matthew's home!"

Conversations were cut off in midsentence. Every head turned to stare at the boy as though he were daft.

"Look!" he hollered. He swung around and pointed. "It's Matthew and Derek and Will!"

Pandemonium broke out on every side. Mary Ann jumped up, the sewing falling to the ground. Benjamin was right beside her and they ran out to the street. Nathan and Joshua leaped to their feet, going up on their toes and craning their necks to see. Peter was off the porch and out the gate, hard on the heels of Benjamin.

Rebecca threw her sewing onto Mary Ann's vacated chair. "Christopher! Christopher! Come quick!"

Olivia had lowered the book from which she was reading and was staring out into the street, not fully comprehending. Christopher, two now and proud to be one of the children, jumped and ran for his mother, frightened by her panicked call.

"Jennifer Jo," Kathryn said under her breath. She jumped up and raced out of the yard in the opposite direction. Jennifer Jo had been finishing up the last of the dishes and hadn't come over to be with the family as yet.

Laughing, crying, hollering, shouting, waving—like a tidal wave of humanity the Steeds flowed out into the street and surrounded the three men who had by now broken into a run to meet them. Though she wasn't the first to reach her son, Mary Ann was near the front. The others fell back as she rushed to Matthew and he swept her up in his arms. He was a full head taller than she was now, and he lifted her off the ground as though she were a little girl.

Caroline was only seconds behind Mary Ann as she flew into Will's outstretched arms, crying, "You did it! You did it! You found them!"

Benjamin was next. A great lump swelled up in his throat as he stepped forward to face his youngest son. He stuck out his hand; then, as Matthew took it, he pulled him in against him and threw his arms around him. "Welcome home, Matthew," he said.

Matthew buried his face against his father's shoulder. "We're back, Papa!" he whispered. "We're back!"

Joshua came up behind Caroline and Will and laid a hand on Will's shoulder. "Welcome home, son," he said in a hoarse whisper. Will turned, and in moments they too were in a crushing embrace, not speaking, not needing to.

Suddenly the group turned. Rebecca was pushing her way forward, trying to carry Christopher through the crush of people. Nathan reached out and took his nephew from her. "I'll bring Christopher," he said, giving Rebecca a gentle shove. "Go!"

Peter had already reached Derek and they were pounding each other on the back as they embraced. Then Derek saw Rebecca over Peter's shoulder. He broke free and covered the last few feet between them in three great steps. He swept her up, crushing her to him, a great sob of joy wrenched from within him. He kissed her hard, lifting her clear off the ground, then set her down. "Hello, my darling Rebecca. Oh, how I've longed for this day."

She was brushing at the tears, laughing and touching his face and holding him all at once. Then she turned to Nathan and said to Derek, "Come see your son."

Nathan stepped forward and handed Christopher to his mother. At the sight of the stranger, Christopher immediately buried his head in his mother's neck. Derek was staring, his own eyes wet with tears now too. "No," he whispered. "This can't be my son." He reached out in wonder, touching his back. "He's so big."

"It's Papa, Christopher," Rebecca said, reaching up to pull his head around. He would have none of it, and burrowed in all the deeper. "I can't believe it," Derek said. He looked around at the family, weeping unashamedly. "Look at my son."

Matthew saw the baby in Lydia's arms and moved over to her. He peered down into the baby's face. "So this is little

Josiah?" He reached out and touched the fat little cheeks. "Will told us about this. We didn't know." He looked at Lydia. "He's beautiful."

Lydia reached out with her free arm and put it around Matthew's waist. "Oh, Matthew, it is so good to see you again. I can't believe you are all home again. What a wonderful surprise."

Matthew nodded, and then his head lifted, his eyes searching the group. Lydia laughed. "Kathryn went to get her."

As if on cue, there was a cry from behind them. They all turned. Jennifer Jo McIntire was running toward them, her hair streaming out behind her. The family fell back, making a path for her. "Matthew! Matthew! Matthew!" she cried, and hurled herself across the last few feet into his arms.

He caught her, swinging her around and around as he had his mother. Finally he set her down, the both of them laughing and crying together now. He buried his face into her hair. "Hello, my darling Jennifer Jo," he whispered. "I'm home."

"Oh, yes!" Tears streamed down her cheeks. "I can't believe it. I can't believe it."

Matthew kissed her quickly, then stepped back, holding up his hands. "Could I have it quiet, please?" he commanded.

Everyone turned to him and he smiled broadly. "I just want you all to hear this." He turned back and took her hands. "Jennifer Jo McIntire, will you marry me?"

Her eyes widened, then instantly were filled with delight. "Yes!" she cried.

"Immediately?" he demanded.

She was laughing now, wiping at the tears. "Yes! Yes!"

"Good!" He looked around as the family broke out in applause. "I've been waiting long enough," he said. "It's time to get this done."

———◆———

Will stopped for a moment on the path that led to the door of the small cabin behind his father's corrals. Then, taking a quick breath, he stepped to the door and knocked. There was the sound of footsteps inside, and the door opened. Will put a finger to his lips as the shock registered on Abigail Pottsworth's face. Recovering quickly, she nodded, then looked over her shoulder. "Jenny!"

"Yes, Mum?"

Will felt his heart skip a beat.

"I think it's for you."

"Oh?" There was the sound of a chair scraping back, and then Jenny stepped into view. "Who is—" Her mouth opened, her eyebrows shot up, and there was a sharp intake of breath.

"Hello, Jenny."

In three running steps she had crossed the room and reached him, nearly bowling him over as she threw herself at him. "You're back!" she squealed.

"Yes, Jenny, I'm back."

"Oh, Will, I can't believe it. You're home." Impulsively, she went up on her toes and kissed him on the cheek, then instantly stepped back, blushing furiously. "I . . . I'm sorry, Will," she stammered. "I . . . I wasn't thinking."

He reached out and grabbed her hands, pulling her back to him, grinning till he thought his face would split from ear to ear. "It's quite all right, Jenny," he drawled easily. "There's no need to be apologizing."

Chapter Notes

The details of the passage across the Atlantic on the *Rochester* are accurately portrayed here, including the loss of a sail, the chaos below decks, and the prayer by the Apostles. The good weather did not last for all the remainder of the trip, but the winds did blow in the right direction thereafter. (See *MWM*, p. 304.)

Brigham's memories of his early years, his feelings about religion, and his eventual conversion to Mormonism are described in detail by himself. Many of the words he uses here with Will come from his own recollections of that time in his life. (See *American Moses*, pp. 27–30.)

Brigham Young, Heber C. Kimball, and John Taylor were the first Apostles to return to Nauvoo, arriving on 1 July 1841. George A. Smith arrived on 14 July; Orson Pratt also sometime in mid-July. Willard and Jennetta Richards visited family in the East and did not arrive in Nauvoo until 16 August. Phoebe Woodruff had gone east to visit her family, and after meeting Wilford there, they spent a long time visiting family and preaching the gospel. They did not return to Illinois until 6 October 1841. Orson Hyde went on to Palestine, an incredible story in and of itself, where on 24 October 1841 he dedicated the Holy Land for the return of the Jews. He came home by way of Egypt and Europe, taking more than a year to make the trip. He returned to Nauvoo in December 1842. Parley Pratt remained in England until late October 1842; then he and his family, sailing with another group of emigrants, left for America. Parley arrived in Nauvoo during the first week of February 1843, making him the last of the Apostles to return home from the British Mission. (See *MWM*, pp. 304–8.)

Will hopped up on one of the larger blocks of stone that had been smoothed for placement the next day. Then he reached down and pulled Jenny up to stand beside him. With a little wave of his hand, he indicated where she was to sit down. "Madame," he said, gesturing toward her place with a flourish.

She laughed merrily. "Actually, it is mademoiselle. *Madame* means I'm married. But thank you anyway, monsieur." She did a little curtsy and sat down. He dropped down behind her and leaned back on his hands. Above them, high overhead, long strings of thin, wispy clouds contrasted sharply with the blue of the sky. They were taking on the first touch of orange, promising a spectacular sunset in half an hour or so. The temple workmen were gone now and the site was deserted. Which was exactly what Will had hoped for. He had spent his first full day back with his family while Jenny worked at the store. Several times he had resisted the temptation to go there to be with her. He knew they had to talk and he wanted it to be when they were alone.

"I love it up here," Jenny said, tipping her head back and letting the golden hair fall back across her shoulders. "I come up here quite often. I like to try and picture in my mind what the temple will look like when it's finished."

He nodded. When he came to get her at her house, she had suggested that this be the place for their walk. Now he was glad. He waited a moment, then reached inside his shirt pocket. He withdrew a small square of cloth folded over on itself several times. Almost shyly, he held it out. "I brought you something from your old homeland."

Her eyes widened as she looked down at what lay in his hand. "Will, you didn't need to do that."

"I know I didn't need to," he chided her playfully. "I wanted to. I was hoping I could get up to Preston, but we couldn't. So this is from Manchester."

She took it from his hand and unfolded the cloth carefully. When it was fully open, there was a soft "Oh!" A small heart-shaped locket with a gold chain lay inside. She picked it up and looked at it more closely. "Oh, Will," she said again, "it's beautiful."

"Here, let me put it on." He took it, worked for a moment to undo the tiny clasp, then got up and knelt behind her.

"I love it, Will. It is so delicate."

He nodded, satisfied. He had worried for the past two months about whether she would like it. She reached back and took his hand. "Thank you, Will."

"You're welcome." He started to sit back down, but she held his hand there, not letting him go, pulling him forward with just the tiniest bit of pressure. Will's heart was suddenly pounding. Now she half turned her upper body, so she was looking back at him. Her eyes seemed to fill her entire face. Her lips were parted slightly, and their softness drew his gaze to where he couldn't pull away. Then, fearful that he would lose his nerve, he leaned forward and brushed his lips against hers. He started to pull back, afraid he had been too forward, but she reached up with her other hand and laid it on his cheek, holding him there. Then she kissed him back very softly.

"I missed you, Will Steed."

"And I missed you, Jenny Pottsworth."

Now she let him sit back down, but closer to her so their shoulders touched. "All right," she said, eager now, "tell me. I'm dying to know. Tell me everything."

"Dying to know what?" he asked innocently.

She slapped at his arm. "You know what!" she scolded. "Tell me all about your trip. And about reading the Book of Mormon. Did you do it?"

He nodded slowly. "Almost twice. I'm nearly through it again."

She clapped her hands in delight. "Twice! That's wonderful, Will."

A shadow darkened his face for a moment, but then he took a breath and plunged in. "I don't know yet, Jenny," he said simply.

There was momentary bewilderment. "You don't know what yet?"

"I don't have an answer. I don't know if the Church is true."

Her face fell and there was sharp disappointment in her eyes. "Oh," she said in a tiny voice.

"Jenny, I have really been trying to find out." And so he tried to tell her. He told her of the nights on the road to New York City and reading by candlelight on the voyage over to England. He talked about saying awkward, funny-sounding prayers and feeling foolish, and then about how, on other nights, they became deep prayers of longing during which he felt himself closer to God. He shared with her the uncertainty and the deep worry that somehow he wasn't going about it right. He told her of the conference in Manchester and how he had felt as he listened to Brigham Young. He spoke of the nights when he and Derek and Matthew talked long after the lamps were extinguished. And as he spoke, he could feel the gloom settling in on her, like the fog over England.

Feeling a sense of panic now, he rushed on, saving the best for last. He told her about the terrible night at sea, and the prayer by the Twelve. He slowed, choosing his words more care-fully now, and recounted his conversation with Brigham the next morning. Finally, he stopped, just letting the words run down to nothing. She had pulled her legs up and had her arms wrapped around her knees. She stared past him out to the river, where the sun was half disappearing behind the western horizon.

He waited for several moments. She didn't speak. Finally, he reached out and touched her arm. "Jenny?"

Slowly her head came up and he saw that her eyes were glis-tening. She wasn't crying, but close to it. "That's wonderful, Will."

He just looked at her in disbelief. The discontinuity be-tween her words and her expression was too great.

"It is," she sniffed. "I mean it. You've done all that I hoped. More!"

"Then what?" he asked, his eyes fastened on the tiny locket at her throat. "What is the matter?"

"It's just that . . ." She had to look away.

"It's just that what?" he asked.

Now her head came back around and the tears had come. They were squeezing out of the corners of her eyes. "I was so sure that you would have your answer when you returned."

"Jenny," he said in dismay, "I've been trying. I've really been trying."

She jabbed at the tears angrily with the back of her hand. "I know you have, Will. I am so pleased that you did. It means everything to me. I mean it."

He nodded glumly. *So much for the joyous homecoming.*

She scooted around on the stone now so she directly faced him. With some effort, she managed a smile, then cocked her head to one side in that way she had which he loved so much. "I do mean it, Will. If you had come back and told me you hadn't read the Book of Mormon, I couldn't bear it."

He watched her, cheered slightly but still feeling the let-down. The last rays of the sun caught her hair as it fell back across her shoulders, and turned it into burnished metal, like the gold on a fine watch. He reached out in wonder and touched it. Her hand came up and took his hand and laid it against her cheek. "Let's not talk about it anymore right now. Let's just be happy that you're home, all right?"

He couldn't let it go, not quite yet. "For some of us, I guess, it just doesn't come as easy as for others. Brigham said it took him two years to know for sure."

It was the wrong thing to say. She looked away quickly. "Two years?" she whispered.

Frustrated, he blew out his breath. "I'm not saying it will be that long for me, I—"

She turned back, not able to hide the hurt in her eyes. "How long will it be, Will?"

"I don't know, Jenny." It was a plea now. "My feelings have changed a great deal. I understand it so much better. I see why you and Mother and the family think it's true. There are a lot of things I really like about the Church."

"But you're not ready to be baptized?"

He looked into her eyes, wanting to make the hurt there go away, wanting to lie or stall or dodge the question, anything to make the hurt go away. "No," he finally said. "I'm not ready to be baptized."

Abruptly she stood up. The sun was nearly down now, and the sky was turning a golden blue. "Come on, let's walk." She jumped down and then held up her hand for him, smiling happily now.

He took her hand and dropped down beside her. She looked so beautiful, so lovely, so enchanting that he couldn't help himself. He took her by both shoulders and kissed her again. She tipped her head back and kissed him back, going up on her toes to do so.

"I love you, Jenny," he said, a little breathlessly, when he finally pulled away.

"And I love you, Will."

"I'll get an answer, Jenny. Just be patient with me."

There was a momentary flicker of uncertainty, and then she nodded brightly. "I know. Come on, let's go down by the quarry. You won't believe what they've done since you left."

———◆———

Matthew stopped and surveyed the half-finished house ahead of him. He let his eyes run over the partially bricked walls, then the rafters, open except for one end that was boarded but not shingled. Three of the Twelve were back in Nauvoo, and now they were learning the cost the mission had extracted from their families.

Brigham Young had left his family in 1839 living in the deserted military barracks in Montrose, Iowa. He had six children. Two older daughters were from his first wife, who had died of tuberculosis back in New York State. The other four children were his and Mary Ann's. The youngest, little Emma, was born just ten days before Brigham left for England. Now she was almost two.

During his long absence, Mary Ann Young had moved the family across the river so she could be closer to Vilate Kimball and the rest of the Saints. A woman of strong determination, she obtained a swampy lot in the lower part of Nauvoo and started to have a house built. That was what Matthew was staring at now. She hadn't been able to have it finished. So now there were eight people living in an unfinished cabin on a lot that was so muddy that the first time Brigham tried to plow it, the oxen mired in deep enough he had to call for help to get them out.

Compared to Mary Ann Young and Vilate Kimball and Leonora Taylor, Jennifer Jo had been well off, living in Jessica's home and with a dozen or more Steeds to watch out for her. Matthew offered a quick prayer of thanks to the Lord for his goodness, and then he climbed over the rail fence and started across the field toward Brigham's home.

Brigham was out back, playing with his children. Mary Ann

was hanging clothes on the line. When Brigham saw him, his face lit up and he strode across the yard to take his hand. "Ah, Matthew. Thank you for coming over."

"Gladly," Matthew responded. He turned. "Good morning, Sister Young."

"Good morning, Matthew. It's so good to see you again."

"Thank you."

"Has your mother gotten used to having you back home again yet?"

He laughed. "I think not. She's been feeding me five or six times a day."

"From what Brigham says about England, you probably have a few meals to catch up on."

"Aye," he laughed. Then he turned to Brigham. "Pa said to tell you he's sending over some things this afternoon—a sack of flour, some honey. Nathan's getting a box together from the store."

Brigham nodded gratefully. "That doesn't surprise me. What a good family you belong to, Matthew."

Mary Ann hung a shirt over the line, then walked over to join them. "I'm not sure that bringing us more food is a wise thing," she said with a laugh.

"Why is that?" Matthew asked, a little surprised by such an odd statement.

"Tell Matthew what you told Joseph, Brigham."

Brigham stuck his hand through his suspenders. "Well, Joseph came over the day after our return to hear our report. When we were done, he asked me how I would live now that I was home again."

"And?" Matthew asked, hoping he was going to say something about their going into business together.

There was a mischievous twinkle in the Apostle's eye. "I told him I would go out and make a living, of course, but only later. At the moment, I had enough money to buy a barrel of flour. I told him my plan was to stay home, work on the cabin, improve the garden, and eat bread with my wife and children until our flour was gone. Then I would go out and find work."

Matthew nodded, smiling. "Sounds like a good plan to me."

Now Brigham was really serious. "We had some wonderful news yesterday."

"Oh, yes," Mary Ann said.

"What?" Matthew asked.

"Joseph came over yesterday," said Brigham. "While he was here he received a revelation from the Lord."

"Really! What did it say?"

Brigham reached in his pocket and extracted a piece of paper. "I just happen to have a copy of it right here."

Mary Ann was smiling at her husband with great love in her eyes. "You'd think this was important to him. He carries it with him all the time."

Brigham unfolded the sheet and smoothed it with his hand. Now his voice was suddenly husky. "It is a revelation given specifically to me." He cleared his throat and began to read. "'Dear and well-beloved brother, Brigham Young, verily thus saith the Lord unto you: My servant Brigham, it is no more required at your hand to leave your family as in times past, for your offering is acceptable to me. I have seen your labor and toil in journeyings for my name. I therefore command you to *send*'"—he emphasized that word with quiet satisfaction—"'that you *send* my word abroad, and take especial care of your family from this time, henceforth and forever. Amen.'"

He folded the paper slowly and put it back inside his pocket.

"That *is* wonderful, Brigham."

"Yes," said Mary Ann, "it truly is."

Brigham looked at his children, playing happily around him, and all he could do was nod. After a minute, he straightened and slapped Matthew on the shoulder. "But I didn't send for you to hear me read that. It's time we talk, Matthew."

"All right, what about?"

"I hear that you and Jennifer Jo have set a wedding date."

"Yes, it will be a week from Saturday next. The twenty-fourth."

"That's wonderful, Matthew," Mary Ann exclaimed. "I'm so happy for the both of you. Jennifer Jo is a wonderful young woman."

"I know," Matthew grinned. "That's why I don't want her running around unmarried any longer." Then he sobered, turning to Brigham. "We'd be most pleased if you and Sister Young could come."

"Wouldn't miss it for the world," said Brigham. "Is Joseph going to marry you?"

"Yes. I wasn't sure I should ask him, as busy as he is and all that, but I didn't have to. When he heard we were engaged, he came right over." Now Matthew imitated Joseph's booming cheerfulness. "'Matthew Steed,' he says, 'I married your older brother Nathan, and I married your older sister Rebecca. It's a good tradition which I'm of a mind to keep going, if you and Jennifer Jo are of a mind to let me.'" Matthew laughed. "Of course we were delighted."

Now Brigham put his arm around Matthew and drew him against his shoulder. "You know that this means you and I really have a problem."

"No, what's that?"

"Well, you're getting married, and my flour barrel is almost empty. I think it's time you and I talk about getting that carpenter shop started, don't you?"

Chapter Notes

The situation of Brigham's family upon his return is factual, and his comments about the barrel of flour are extrapolated from his recollections given in an 1854 discourse (see *MWM*, pp. 270–72, 307; *JD* 2:19). The revelation to Brigham is now D&C 126 and was given through Joseph on 9 July 1841, just over a week after Brigham's return from England.

Saturday, the twenty-fourth of July, 1841, dawned clear and bright. There had been afternoon thundershowers the previous two days, and probably would be again on this day. They left the air clean and fresh and cooler than normal.

Matthew stepped out onto the front porch of his parents' cabin and carefully shut the door behind him. For a moment he stood there, breathing in deeply the morning freshness, smelling the river and the prairie beyond it and the ripening crops and the smoke from the brickyards and just a touch of someone's baking bread all in the same moment. He tipped his head back, savoring it all. It was going to be a perfect day for a wedding.

Moving quietly, stepping over the one board that always creaked, he left the porch and moved across the yard. Out on Granger Street he turned north. The six Steed cabins lined both sides of the street along this block—Nathan's, Benjamin's, and then Jessica's on the west (moving from south to north), and Derek's, Joshua's, and Carl's across from them. As he moved toward Jessica's place, his step slowed and his mouth pulled down a little. Jennifer Jo and Kathryn slept in the back room of Jessica's cabin. It was used as the schoolroom during the fall and winter, so it had two windows, and Matthew had simply planned to tap on one of those to see if Jennifer Jo might be awake. But he hadn't been thinking about Kathryn. Surely he would wake her up too, and he didn't want that at all.

His worry was needless, for as he approached Jessica's cabin, a movement on the far side of it caught his eye. Just rounding the corner and starting down the street toward him, Jennifer Jo was approaching, walking slowly. Her hands were behind her back; her head was turned to look eastward toward the temple construction site on the bluff. Matthew stopped, completely enchanted. She wore a simple housedress and was barefoot, but he couldn't imagine that anything could be more lovely. Her hair was slightly tousled, but still fell down between her shoulder blades. As he listened, he could hear her humming something softly.

As if sensing his gaze, Jennifer Jo suddenly turned her head and saw him. There was a brief startled look, then an instant smile. She started walking swiftly toward him. Matthew didn't wait for her. Grinning happily, he strode out to meet her.

"Hi," she said shyly as they met and he took both of her hands in his.

"Good morning. So you couldn't sleep either?"

"Not a wink. And you?"

He got a mischievous look in his eye. "Actually, I was sleeping quite soundly, until I heard the voice."

Her eyebrows lifted in surprise. "The voice?"

He nodded gravely. "Yes. This voice spoke in my ear and said, 'Get up and go outside. Out on the street you'll find a vision as lovely as anything you've ever seen in God's creation.'"

She blushed prettily and ducked her head. "Oh, Matthew," she chided him softly, but deeply pleased.

He pulled her to him and kissed her. "Sure enough," he declared. "The voice was right."

She kissed him back, then leaned against him. "It's finally here, Matthew. Can you believe it?"

He shook his head slowly, reaching up to touch her hair. "Every night for the last twenty-two months I've thought about this day. There were times when I thought it would never come, when I thought I would never leave England."

"Me too," she murmured. "It seemed like forever." Then suddenly she pulled back, frowning. "This is supposed to be bad luck, you know."

"What?"

"Seeing the bride before the actual wedding."

"Hmm," he said, pulling her back to him and putting his arms around her. "I need all the bad luck I can get."

Laughing, she nodded. "That's good. I feel the same way."

He turned her around and started walking up the street, going back the way from which she had come, following her footprints in the damp earth of the roadway. After a moment, she laid her head against his shoulder. He looked down at her. "What were you thinking while you were walking?"

She slipped her arm through his and held it tightly. "I was thinking how strange life is."

"In what way?"

"Well, think about it. The Mormon War in Missouri was a great tragedy. People were killed. Thousands of people were driven from their homes. Most lost everything."

"Yes?" This turn of her thoughts surprised him a little.

"Joshua was shot and nearly killed."

Now he understood and nodded. "But if he hadn't been . . ."

"If he hadn't been, your family would never have needed a place to hide him while he recovered."

"And Derek would never have thought of asking your mother if she would offer her home as that place."

"Exactly." There was a quick shudder, as if she had taken a chill. "And you wouldn't have come up with them to care for Joshua, and I would never have even met you." She shook her head in wonder. "And because of that one simple turn of events, even though they were tragic at the time, here we are today. I could still be out there on the plains of northern Missouri, hoping someday to meet the right man, not knowing anything about the Church or Joseph Smith. Never knowing that I could have been your wife. I—" Tears sprang to her eyes and she had to bite her lip. "Never knowing I could be so totally happy that I feel like I'm just going to burst wide open."

Matthew pulled her in more tightly against him. "I'm happy too, Jennifer Jo. More happy than I thought it was possible for one person to be."

She looked up at him, her eyes large and filled with love. "I'm glad."

At that moment, the tip of the sun cleared the eastern bluffs and the first rays of sunlight lit her face. She turned slightly, squinting a bit against the brightness. Then suddenly she was all business. "Oh, Matthew, we've got to get back. It's time to start getting ready. I'll bet Jessica is already up and wondering what happened to me."

Turning to face her, he reached down, put a finger under her chin, and tipped her head back. "I love you, Jennifer Jo McIntire."

"And I love you, Matthew Steed. Oh, how I love you."

He kissed her, only reluctantly letting her go. They turned and walked back to Jessica's home. As they reached the front gate, she went up on her tiptoes and kissed him quickly. "Remember, you can't tell anyone we were out here. It's bad luck."

"Right." He squeezed her hand and gave her a gentle push toward the cabin. "See you in a little while."

As she ran up onto the porch, Matthew turned around and looked up and down the street. Then he cupped his hands and tipped his head back. "Hey!" he shouted loudly.

Jennifer Jo whirled around, completely startled. He paid her no mind. "Hey, you Steeds!" he roared. "Get yourselves out of those beds. Don't you know there's a marriage to be done here today?"

Her head tipped back as she laughed merrily at this crazy

man she was going to marry. He spun around on his heel and looked at her with great seriousness. One finger came up to his lips. "Remember," he whispered conspiratorially, "not a word to anyone."

———•———

At Jessica's house, they had made Jennifer Jo and Kathryn's bedroom into the bride's dressing room. Caroline had brought a full-length mirror over and now it stood against one wall. Jennifer Jo was standing before it in her petticoats and corset, watching as Lydia and Rebecca and Jessica pinned the hem of the petticoats all the way around. Mary Ann stood back, eyeing the space between the hem and the floor with a careful eye. Finally, as the others stood up, she nodded. "I think we're ready."

Kathryn turned to Caroline. "Can Livvy and I get it, Aunt Caroline? Oh please!"

"Yes, Mama," Olivia begged. "Please! We'll be careful."

Caroline laughed. "All right. It's on the table at our house."

As Olivia and Kathryn darted out of the room, Jessica stepped forward. Her eyes were soft and misty as she looked at Lydia, who was holding a long ribbon in her hand. "May I?" she asked.

Lydia nodded and handed it to her. "Of course."

The others stepped back as Jessica moved behind Jennifer Jo. Watching her foster mother in the mirror, Jennifer Jo smiled as Jessica reached up and carefully took her hair. She pulled it back over the crown of her head and tied it there with the ribbon, making a small bow and letting the streamers hang down over her back. Then Jessica went up on her toes and kissed Jennifer Jo on the top of her head. "Your mother would be so pleased to see you now," she whispered.

Jennifer Jo nodded quickly. "I was just thinking about Mama. How I wish she were here." But then she turned and laid one hand on Jessica's arm. "But you're my mother now," she said, her eyes filled with gratitude. "You've been all that a mother could ever be."

Jessica hugged her quickly. "And I couldn't be more proud if you were my own flesh and blood."

The door opened and Olivia and Kathryn trooped in with a long flat box held between them. They set it on the dressing table as everyone gathered in closer to see. Kathryn stepped behind her sister and put her hands over her eyes. "You can't see it until we get it out of the box."

"That's right," Caroline agreed. "Keep them covered." She removed the lid of the box and carefully lifted the dress out, holding it up at full length. There was a soft intake of breath. "Oh, Caroline," Lydia exclaimed. "It's beautiful."

"I can't stand it. I want to see," Jennifer Jo cried.

Caroline shook it once to let it fall completely out, then nodded at Kathryn. "All right."

Kathryn withdrew her hands and Jennifer Jo opened her eyes. Instantly they widened. "Oh, Caroline!"

Caroline smiled, pleased at the reaction. The dress was more of an ivory color than just white, and the color gave the material a lustrous, rich look, even in the limited light of the bedroom. It was made of lightweight taffeta, and the design was simple but elegant. Chantilly lace came down off the shoulders in front and back, forming a gently scooped neckline just below the throat. The sleeves were puffed to the elbow and tight at the wrist. The skirt was full, with two deep flounces edged with matching lace all around. Caroline and Lydia had scoured every store in Nauvoo and then in Quincy looking for material and a pattern that were suitable. Nothing was satisfactory. So Caroline had simply told Joshua to move up by two weeks his next trip to St. Louis and to take her with him. Picking a wedding dress was simply not something you left in the hands of a man.

In a moment they had the dress on Jennifer Jo and were buttoning it up the back. When they finished, Jessica turned her toward the mirror, and they all stepped back to admire it with her. There were oohs and aahs, but Mary Ann said it about as well as any of them. "Olivia," she said with a smile, "you'd better go warn Matthew. When he sees this young lady, he is going to be knocked right off his feet."

"Just hold still," Joshua growled. "You'd think you'd never had on a jacket before in your life."

"Not one like this," Matthew said, holding out his arms to get a better look.

"Well, it won't do to have you looking like some sodbuster on your wedding day."

"But this is way too much, Joshua," Matthew protested. "I can't believe what you must have paid for this."

Derek was walking around him, looking carefully up and down. "He did the same thing for me and Rebecca, if you remember. I tried to tell him no, too." He grinned. "Didn't do a bit of good."

"I feel like the Duke of Buckingham," Matthew said, turning around slowly.

"Then I assume the Duke of Buckingham is a proper dresser," Joshua retorted. He might not know anything about picking out a wedding dress, but when it came to choosing what clothes fit the man, Joshua was not one whit behind Caroline. He had chosen fawn-colored trousers and a deep blue double-breasted coat. On Matthew's long-legged frame they looked very trim and fashionable. There was a white waistcoat which had a high collar and a cravat to match the coat.

Nathan and Benjamin were sitting on chairs, watching. Now Nathan stood and stepped to Matthew. He laid an arm across Matthew's shoulder. "Little brother," he said with soberness, "Joshua and I couldn't be more proud of you. We're proud to be part of your family."

"Amen!" Joshua said softly.

Benjamin took out his watch and stood now too. "If we're going to make it to the grove by ten, we'd better get started."

Rebecca opened the door wide and stepped back. As she reached the doorway, Jennifer Jo stopped, looking around at the women who would very shortly officially become her family.

"Are you nervous?" Mary Ann asked.

"I don't think so," she said, giving her a crooked smile. "I can hardly get my breath and my hands are cold as ice, but no, I don't feel nervous."

They all laughed at that, and then Kathryn stepped forward. "We have one more little surprise for you."

"What?"

"Step outside." She took her by the hand and pulled her through the doorway.

As she stepped onto the porch, Jennifer Jo stopped immediately. Lined up before her were the five Steed family granddaughters. Each one had on a brand-new dress, which, like the wedding dress, had just a week before been residing in one of the finest dress shops in St. Louis. Each one carried a small bouquet of wildflowers in her hand. On their heads were circlets of wildflowers, interwoven with long streamers of ribbons that fell down their backs. They were trying to hold still, but the excitement was too much and so they were wiggling and squirming like little worms boring into an apple.

Kathryn and Olivia had set this whole thing up and trained them carefully. "What do you say, girls?" Kathryn asked.

They did a little curtsy, five cousins as different in personality and looks as any five could be, but in this one thing acting in perfect coordination. "Good morning, Jennifer Jo," they said in chorus. "Congratulations on your wedding day."

"Oh, thank you," Jennifer Jo responded, clapping her hands together in delight. "Don't you all look absolutely perfect?"

Caroline looked at them proudly, letting her eyes come to rest on her own daughter. "Savannah, do you have something for Jennifer Jo?"

Savannah nodded gravely. She stepped out of line and walked to the corner of the porch, moving more like a queen's escort than a four-year-old. Reaching down behind the chair there, she carefully picked up a large bouquet of fresh flowers whose stems were wrapped in a damp cloth. Turning, she came back to Jennifer Jo. The red hair bobbed softly up and down as she walked. The blue eyes were wide with excitement. She held the flowers out. "These are for you, Jennifer Jo."

Taking them carefully, Jennifer Jo lifted them to her face and breathed deeply of their fragrance. "Savannah, thank you. These are so beautiful. Did you pick these for me?"

"We all did," sang out Emily, Lydia's older daughter. "We went around last night and asked people if we could have some of their flowers."

Jennifer Jo looked up and down the line, touched by their eager innocence. "Well, thank you, every one of you. These are just perfect for today."

"Aunt Jennifer?" Savannah said.

"What, dear?"

"Wanna see my dress twirl?"

Jennifer Jo laughed softly. "I would like that very much, Savannah." She straightened and stepped back.

Savannah, very serious now, stepped forward. She held out her arms and then spun around on one foot. Her dress swirled outward, then settled back again.

Jennifer Jo looked down at these wonderful little girls who before the day was out would all become her nieces, and her face softened. "Do you want to see *me* twirl?"

"Yes!" came the instant chorus of replies.

Handing her bouquet to Kathryn, Jennifer Jo held out her arms, then spun around once, then twice, then a third time, smiling radiantly at the girls and the women, who applauded her as she finally came to rest again.

"Bravo! Bravo!"

Jennifer Jo turned in surprise. The men were just coming up the street from Benjamin's cabin and had witnessed the whole thing. It was Matthew who had cried out. Now he opened the gate and walked swiftly up the path. As he reached the women, he stopped. His eyes moved slowly up and down Jennifer Jo's figure. His mouth opened slightly as if he were going to speak, then shut again. He could only stare at her.

"Come on, Matthew," Lydia teased. "Aren't you going to say anything to your bride?"

"I can't," he finally answered softly, stepping up to take Jennifer Jo's hands. "There are no words that could possibly describe what I'm seeing right now."

Rebecca, who had always been closest to Matthew both in age and relationship, nodded in satisfaction. "That will do."

"Well," Benjamin said, "we'd better be going."

But Mary Ann didn't move. She was watching Matthew as he stood beside Jennifer Jo and looked down at her in pure joy. Suddenly, Mary Ann found herself blinking at the burning in her eyes. Matthew looked up, and when he saw her face he stepped across the porch to sweep her up into his arms. He bent down to whisper in her ear. "Thank you, Mama," he said. "Thank you for everything. I'm so happy."

She held him tightly for a moment, then pushed him back away from her. "Would you look at you," she breathed, "all tall and handsome in that coat." And then the tears spilled over and she had to look away.

Sarah Rogers, Melissa's three-year-old, left the line of cousins and came to stand beside her grandmother. She tugged on her dress, looking up with great concern. "Why you sad, Gramma?"

Mary Ann reached down and took her granddaughter's hand. Then she turned back to Matthew, smiling at him through her tears. "Because this is my boy," she whispered softly. "This is my little boy."

The sunlight filtered through the overhead canopy of leaves, dappling all beneath it with shimmering patterns of light and shadow. There were well over two hundred people gathered in the shelter of the grove to witness the marriage of Matthew Steed to Jennifer Jo McIntire. There were longtime friends and close neighbors, English converts who had known Matthew while he was laboring there, and the brethren with whom he had traveled and labored in the mission field. Joseph and Emma and Mother Smith were there. Hyrum and Mary Fielding came with them. There were people who did business with the store and those for whom Matthew had done carpentry work back in Far West. They came to honor the young man recently returned from across the sea. They came to honor his bride-to-be. And they came to honor this family that was loved and respected on both sides of the river.

The Steeds filled the first two rows of benches and chairs, with Benjamin and Mary Ann seated on the first row, directly in front of where Matthew and Jennifer Jo stood facing the congregation. The time had arrived and Joseph had asked the two of them to take their places. Kathryn stood beside Jennifer Jo. She had the ring and would step forward when required. On the opposite side, next to Matthew and a little behind him, the five little flower girls stood proudly, taking their part on the program—which was to look pretty and charm everyone—very seriously.

Joseph, who was standing directly in front of the two about-to-be newlyweds, turned and surveyed the audience. Seeing that everyone was in place now, he raised one arm as the signal that it was time to begin. Immediately the noise subsided and all in the congregation turned their eyes forward.

"Thank you, brothers and sisters. We are pleased to welcome you on this joyous occasion. As we begin, I should like to call on Brother Brigham Young, Matthew's business partner and missionary companion in England, if he would open these proceedings for us with prayer."

Brigham was seated four rows back. He rose and stepped forward quickly, stopping long enough to give a warm handshake to Matthew and to kiss Jennifer Jo quickly on the cheek. Then as heads were bowed and hats swept off he offered a short and simple prayer of thanks, asking the Lord's blessings to smile down upon the proceedings of the day.

"Dear friends," Joseph began again, once Brigham had returned to his seat, "we are here today to witness the joining of this fine young couple in marriage." He glanced over his shoulder at the two of them and smiled warmly. "If you can see what I can see, I think it's safe to say these two are in love."

Laughter rippled across the group, and both Jennifer Jo and Matthew blushed and ducked their heads.

"And that is as it should be," Joseph said, his voice rising a little. "God is pleased with the love between a man and a woman. He knows it is the source of our greatest happiness and our greatest fulfillment. There are some who would have us believe that marriage is a necessary evil, accepted by God only because there is no other way to perpetuate the human race. But we do not accept such doctrine; it is the doctrine of men, and not of God."

Now he turned around and faced Jennifer Jo and Matthew directly. "I have known Matthew Steed since he was a boy of six. I have pulled sticks with him and played ball. I have sat in his house on many occasions. We have broken bread together. We have labored side by side in the fields. This is a fine young man, a happy young man. But I wish to ask him this one question. Matthew, have you ever been happier than you are right now in the presence of this lovely young woman?"

"No!" he answered loudly and firmly. "I have not."

"And you, Jennifer Jo McIntire," Joseph said, his face softening. "Have you ever been happier than you are at this very moment?"

She slipped her arm through Matthew's. "No, Brother Joseph, I can truly say I have not."

"And that is as it should be, brothers and sisters," Joseph cried. "God wants us to be happy. He created man and woman so they could become as one and find a fulness of joy."

Now he swung around and his eyes found Emma. "There sits Emma Hale Smith," he said, his voice going softer now. "She is the love of my heart and the wife of my youth. Oh, how empty my life would have been without Emma. Oh, how bleak my days had she not been by my side through all these years." He smiled at her, and she smiled back, and now he was no longer speaking to Matthew and Jennifer Jo or to the crowd. "I love her as I love my own soul, and I thank my God for the gift he gave to me when he took me to Harmony, Pennsylvania, so I could find her there."

Emma's eyes were shining as he finally turned back again. "You have heard me speak of late about the eternal nature of the family. Here today, on the occasion of joining these two fine young people together in matrimony, I once again testify to you that the bonds forged here today are meant to last forever. The love that Matthew feels for this pure and wonderful young woman is not meant to end at death. Will the feelings that stir so deeply within Sister McIntire's heart on this day simply dissolve if Matthew should die before she does? Of course not. That is not the will of a Father who loves us and cares for us as his own children.

"Matthew, you embark on a great adventure this day. You will shortly take the hand of this young woman and swear to her eternal allegiance. You will swear to cherish and to love her, to make her happiness and joy more important to you than your own. I say to you, as I have said before, if a man cannot love his wife in such a manner and treat her in such a manner as to make her happy in this life, he will not be worthy to have her with him in the next."

He stopped for a moment, then reached out and took their hands in his. "Bless you, you two wonderful young people," he said, speaking only to them now. "This union is pleasing in the sight of God, and he will bless you forever as you honor and sustain it."

"We will, Joseph," Matthew said firmly. "We will."

He nodded, his face solemn now. He moved slightly so that he was directly in front of the two of them. "Matthew, would you take Jennifer Jo's right hand with your right hand please?"

Matthew did so, smiling down at her.

"As a minister of Jesus Christ and a holder of the holy Melchizedek Priesthood, I now act in my office and unite you in holy matrimony. Matthew Steed, as you hold her hand in yours, do you take this woman, Jennifer Jo McIntire, to be your wife and companion; to love her and to cherish her as you love and cherish your own flesh; to provide for her and to care for her in whatsoever circumstances may befall you; to nurture and sustain her whether that be in health or illness, poverty or riches, youth or old age; and do you do this in the sight of God and all of these people who have gathered here to witness these proceedings?"

He squeezed her hand. "Yes."

"And do you, Jennifer Jo McIntire, take the hand of Matthew Steed as a token that you do take him to be your husband; to love and to cherish him above all others throughout your life and into the eternities; to stand by his side as Eve did with Adam through whatever circumstances life shall place upon you, be they pleasant or ill, difficult or easy; and do you do this in God's sight and in front of those who are here with you this day?"

She squeezed Matthew's hand back and looked up into his face. "Yes."

Joseph smiled warmly now. "Then as an authorized representative of Jesus Christ, I pronounce you, Matthew Steed, and you, Jennifer Jo McIntire, to be husband and wife, legally wed in the sight of God and all men. Remember that you make this covenant with each other and with the Lord. If you keep that covenant, God will bless this union and bring you happiness and joy."

He turned to Kathryn and nodded. Almost shyly, Kathryn stepped forward and handed the ring to Matthew. "Now you're really my family," she whispered as she handed it to him.

Matthew took the simple silver band and slipped it onto Jennifer Jo's finger. Joseph was smiling broadly at them. "Matthew, you may now kiss this woman as your wife."

A cry went up and applause rang through the grove as Matthew turned to Jennifer Jo and took her in his arms. He gave her a lingering kiss before he let her straighten again. That sent the flower girls into a peal of giggles, which brought smiles all around.

"A Perfect Day for a Wedding"

Turning to Benjamin and Mary Ann, Joseph motioned for them to join him. "I think it's time for some congratulations, Mother and Father. You come up here and be the first."

Mary Ann got up quickly and went forward, her face shining with pride. She went to Jennifer Jo first and hugged her tightly. "Welcome to our family. We couldn't love you more, Jennifer."

"And I you," Jennifer Jo said, tears of happiness spilling over now. "You've been so good to me."

Benjamin had Matthew in a strong embrace. "We're proud of you, son. Very proud. You've got yourself a wonderful woman."

"I know, Papa. Thank you. Thank you and Mama for everything."

They switched places, and now Mary Ann couldn't bear it. The tears started all over again as she stretched up to kiss Matthew on the cheek. "Oh, my Matthew, my Matthew," she whispered.

"I love you, Mama."

"I know." She hugged him hard, then stepped back again. "You've made us very happy today, Matthew," she whispered.

The others swarmed in around them now. Mary Ann and Benjamin stepped back to make way. Family, friends, well-wishers—they all pressed in to give their congratulations to the smiling couple. Mary Ann took a handkerchief from her pocket and wiped at the tears. "This is it, Benjamin. This is our last one."

He nodded, not speaking.

They stood there together, off to one side, watching quietly. Finally, Benjamin put an arm around her waist. "That's your family," he said softly. "Look at them. Sons, daughters, husbands, wives, children, babies—this is quite the brood we've raised, Mrs. Steed. And every one of them here with us today."

She laid her head against his shoulder. "Isn't it wonderful? And they're still growing."

"There are not many finer things a man could ask for in life, are there?"

She shook her head, and her voice was suddenly a fierce whisper. "No, I can't think of anything I would trade for this. Not anything."